ESSAYS ✤ CONVERSATIONS ✤ RECIPES

FOOD FOR THE GODS

VEGETARIANISM & THE WORLD'S RELIGIONS

Books by Rynn Berry

The Vegetarians

The New Vegetarians

Famous Vegetarians and Their Favorite Recipes

Food for the Gods: Vegetarianism and the World's Religions

ESSAYS ✿ CONVERSATIONS ✿ RECIPES

FOOD FOR THE GODS

VEGETARIANISM & THE WORLD'S RELIGIONS

RYNN BERRY

PYTHAGOREAN PUBLISHERS

NEW YORK • LOS ANGELES

Food For The Gods: Vegetarianism and the World's Religions

Published in the United States by Pythagorean Publishers, New York

Copyright ©1998 Rynn Berry

This book is printed on durable acid-free paper.

Includes bibliographical references.
p.   cm.

ISBN 0-9626169-2-3
(pbk.: alk. paper)

1. Vegetarianism—Religious aspects. I. Title.

BL65.V44B47   97-29810
291.5'693—dc21   CIP

For information or correspondence please contact the author via the publisher:
PYTHAGOREAN PUBLISHERS
P.O. Box 8174
JAF Station
New York, NY 10116

Acknowledgements

······················

OUR YEARS AGO, I HAD THE idea of writing a book of interviews with vegetarian spiritual leaders from each of the world's religions; however, my friend Martin Rowe said that I would have done better to have written a book of essays on the subject, à la Huston Smith. This set me to thinking that I should do a book combining both essays and interviews. Moreover, since recipes had played such a big role in the success of my previous book, *Famous Vegetarians and Their Favorite Recipes*, I decided to add a recipe section incorporating the vegetarian dishes that were particular to each religious tradition. In the Asian religions of Jainism, Buddhism, Hinduism, and Taoism, food is often part of the religious service; therefore, finding tasty vegetarian recipes from these traditions was not an onerous task.

One of the joys of writing this book is that it has enabled me to travel the world to interview eminent vegetarian religious thinkers. To the people who provided food and lodging for me in my travels, I offer my heartfelt thanks. I am especially indebted to Shakuntala Jain, her sister Tara and their families for providing me with a place to stay while I was in Bombay, and for arranging for me to interview Muni Nandibhushan Vijayji at the Swantinath Jain temple; to Bernie Unti, former Executive Director of the American Anti-Vivisection Society, for introducing me to the Reverend Professor Dr. Andrew Linzey; to Andrew Linzey and his wife Jo for letting me stay with them in Oxford; to Steve Rosen for arranging for me to stay at the Krishna temple in London; to Arif Hamid, Patrick Andrews and the

ACKNOWLEDGEMENTS

M. R. Bawa Muhaiyaddeen Fellowship, for arranging my interview with Dr. Rehana Hamid; to my sister Ghislaine for putting me up (and for putting up with me) while I interviewed Kapleau Roshi in his Zendo in Hollywood, Florida; to Rebecca Hall and her husband Gordon Newman for arranging for me to interview Dr. Conrad Latto; to Mira Advani for putting me up while I interviewed Dr. Maoshing Ni; to the monks at the Po Lin Temple on Lantau Island in China for allowing me to stop for several nights at the monastery during my visit there; to the staff at the Ching Chung Koon Taoist temple in Hong Kong, China for their hospitality; to L. P. Gasparzinha and family for allowing me to complete the final stages of my book at their residence in São Paulo, Brazil.

In fairness to the people who have helped me and to the interviewees, I should like to make it clear that, unless otherwise indicated, the opinions that I've expressed in my essays on each of the world's religions are entirely my own. Therefore, they are exonerated from any responsibility for my more unorthodox views. I am particularly indebted to each of the interviewees for allowing me to interrupt their busy schedules and pepper them with questions. Of all the interviewees, Professor Robert Kole has probably had the greatest impact on my life. Thanks to him I've started incorporating more living vegetarian food into my diet. But in truth each interview has changed me in not imperceptible ways. In preparing for each interview, I was like a method actor who essays his role by inhabiting the person whom he intends to portray. So I tried to become a Muslim when I interviewed Dr. Rehana Hamid, I became a Jain when I interviewed Muni Nandibhushan, a Taoist when I interviewed Dr. Maoshing Ni, and so on.

Another of the pleasures of doing this book was that it allowed me to sample the distinctive cuisine associated with each religious tradition. To the people who furnished recipes for me to use in the culinary sections I am also beholden. I would particularly like to thank Brother Ron Pickarski for letting me reprint recipes from his two vegetarian cookbooks; to Dr. Maoshing Ni for allowing me to use recipes from his family's Taoist cookbooks; to Susan Rothman, "Wildman" Steve Brill, Ed Lieb and Dafne Mordechai for furnishing me with rawfood recipes for the Jewish section; to Yamuna Devi for generously allowing me to use recipes from her cookbook *Lord Krishna's Cuisine*; to Dr. Saurabh F. Dalal for providing me with the Jain recipes; to Kapleau Roshi, Bill Shurtleff and Hideko Abe for furnishing me with Buddhist recipes.

Special thanks are also due to two members of the Order of the Cross (American Branch): Alexander Guza for supplying me with the works of Todd Ferrier, and to my friend Marcia Pearson for providing me with the works of The Reverend Holmes-Gore and with out-of-print vegetarian esoterica.

For editorial suggestions and moral encouragement, I would like to thank Steve Rosen, and my friend Dr. Kristin Aronson. To Dr. Saurabh F. Dalal and Fakirchand Dalal, I am indebted for their helpful criticism of my essay on Jainism. I am grateful to Alison Riley and the staff of the New York Public Library and the staff of the Brooklyn Public Library for their help in my research. Space prohibits me from mentioning in detail the contributions of everyone who helped. So I must content myself with mentioning their names: Patty Breitman, The Authors Guild, Clay Lancaster, author of *The Incredible World's Parliament of Religions*, Rynn Berry, Sr., Max Friedman, Linda Orfield, Mark Braunstein, FM 2030, Anne M. Greene, Brian Graff, H. H. Moorhead and Jon Wynne-Tyson.

Dedicated to

....

BARBARA BERASI,
*the lady who designed this book:
for her patience, generosity
and superb design skills.*

In India, feeding the gods is a special route by which humans feed each other.

—C. Appadurai Breckenridge

Table of Contents

FOOD FOR THE GODS

Acknowledgements · *i*

Introduction · 1

ESSAYS & CONVERSATIONS

JAINISM

Essay · 11

Conversation / *Muni Nandibhushan Vijayji* · 23

BUDDHISM

Essay · 43

Conversation / *Roshi Philip Kapleau* · 57

HINDUISM:

Essay · 79

Conversation / *Steven Rosen (Satyaraj Das)* · 91

TAOISM

Essay · 117

Conversation / *Dr. Maoshing Ni* · 127

JUDAISM

Essay · 145

Conversation / *Professor Robert Kole* · 163

CHRISTIANITY (ROMAN CATHOLICISM)

Essay · 191

Conversation / *Brother Ron Pickarski, OFM* · 221

ISLAM

Essay • 241

Conversation / *Dr. Rehana Hamid* • 255

....

PROTESTANT CHRISTIANITY

Essay • 271

Conversation / *Reverend Professor Dr. Andrew Linzey* • 277

....

THE ORDER OF THE CROSS

Essay • 303

Conversation / *Dr. Conrad Latto, MD* • 315

RECIPES

....

JAINISM • 331

BUDDHISM • 336

HINDUISM • 342

TAOISM • 352

JUDAISM • 357

CHRISTIANITY • 363

ISLAM • 368

About the Author • 373

Introduction

·················

AMERICA USED TO BE A country of small towns and church steeples, the tallest building in the average American town belonging to a Christian church. Over the past 50 years, however, that skyline has changed: Christian towers continue to dominate the horizon, but the sacred canopies of Jain, Hindu, Buddhist, Islamic, and Taoist places of worship also thrust heavenwards. Most of the people in the United States are still Christian (81 percent of all Americans profess to be Protestant or Catholic, according to *The American Almanac*), but our culture is subtly influenced by other faiths, including four "vegetarian" Asian religions: Buddhism, Hinduism, Taoism, and Jainism.

These "vegetarian" religions — the quotation marks are necessary because these faiths encourage but they do not explicitly require their followers to practice vegetarianism — all have established branches in the West. California is a bastion of Taoism and Zen Buddhism; there are Hindu temples in many U.S. cities; there are more Buddhists practicing their faith in the U.S. than there are in India, the homeland of Buddhism; and even the tiny Jain sect has 20,000 members in America and 5,000 in New York City. In Europe, too, these religions are thriving. For example, the Hare Krishna movement is spreading throughout Eastern and Western Europe, and Zen centers are springing up from London to Moscow. These faiths do more than just throw up new religious edifices, they also bring in their train a whole set of common beliefs related to vegetarianism. And as their followers grow in numbers on this side of the hemisphere so does their influence on Western society. When the dinner bell rings and stomachs start to rumble, a growing number of people are reaching for tofu, tempeh and raw or stir-fried vegetables. According to Peter Golbitz, President of Soytech, 143.9 million dollars were spent on tofu in the U.S. last year, compared with 37.5 million dollars in 1980. Buddhists and Taoists have always made ample use of soyfoods, and it may well be that the current increase in the use of soyfoods—and the accompanying increase in the rise of Western vegetarianism—is at least partly due to the influence of these vegetarian religions.

Consultant to the soyfoods industry Bill Shurtleff certainly agrees. As a young American physicist, he traveled to Japan to study Zen. He returned home in the early 1970s with a Japanese bride, the tonsured pate of a Zen monk, skill in preparing tofu and the manuscript of a book that would change the eating habits of many Americans. Shurtleff's *The Book of Tofu*, has sold nearly a million copies. He went on to write the *Book of Miso* and *The Book of Tempeh*, which have also become bestsellers. As a result of these successes, Shurtleff and his wife Akiko were able to put bread and tofu on their table by serving as consultants to the fledgling soyfoods industry—an industry that his books helped to create.

Joining Bill Shurtleff in transforming the diet of many Westerners was another American student of Zen Buddhism, Philip Kapleau. While employed as a court reporter at the Far East War Crimes Trials in Japan, he gained an interest in Zen. The world's foremost authority on Zen, D.T. Suzuki, lived only a few miles away from the courthouse, so Kapleau arranged to meet with him. That meeting changed Kapleau's life. He returned to the U.S., sold his court reporting business and went back to Japan to train as a monk. Ten years later he returned to the U.S. and founded the first all-vegetarian monastery in America. He also helped start one of the first American tofu companies, Northern Soy. Two decades later, Kapleau wrote *To Cherish All Life: A Buddhist Case for Becoming A Vegetarian*, which did much to reinvigorate the Buddha's first precept—to refrain from killing all life forms.

Walk into any bookstore worthy of the name and you are likely to find an entire section devoted to the "New Age," which features a myriad of books on reincarnation and past-life regression. This trend reflects Westerners' growing infatuation with the belief that our souls have inhabited other bodies in the past.

The impact of the "vegetarian" religions can be measured in language, too, and the Eastern terms threaded into Western conversations reveal the extent to which the ethical strands of the four "vegetarian" religions are being woven into the fabric of Western culture. Because ideas like *karma* and reincarnation imply a retributive universe in which the killing and harming of animals can no longer be disconnected from human lives, ethical vegetarians in the West are encouraged by the extent to which certain concepts of the four "vegetarian" religions are now in common usage. The idea of *karma*, for instance, which holds that evil recoils upon the doer of evil, and which therefore makes non-violent eating a must, is no longer an esoteric one. People speak of their good *karma* and their bad *karma* so casually that it has become a commonplace in our language and in our thinking—as have many others of the once obscure terms of the Eastern religions. For example, the words *ahimsa, ch'i, dharma, satori, wu-wei* and yoga which would have sent a reader scurrying for an encyclopedia fifty years ago, are now part of every thinking person's vocabulary.

To get a better understanding of the "vegetarian religions," we ought to take a look at some of the other traits they share. In the course of writing this book, I've identified ten salient features. The first hallmark of these religions is their place of origin: India. (Even Taoism, which claims to be native to China, is heavily influenced by yoga philosophy, the *Bhagavad Gita*, and other Indian philosophical works that were probably carried from India to China by Chinese merchants as early as the middle of the first millennium BCE.)

The second hallmark of the "vegetarian" religions is a belief in the sanctity of all life. Whereas Judaism, Christianity and Islam tend to put the injunction against killing (which applies only to humans) pretty far down in their list of "thou shalt nots" (it's the sixth of the ten commandments)—the four *ahimsa*-based "vegetarian" religions make this prohibition their first commandment and include animals and even insects in their purview.

The vegetarian religions' third hallmark is their use of a substitute for animal flesh. The Asian Buddhist and Taoist religions substitute forms of soy foods for meat, while the Indian vegetarian religions use dahl or lentils. (Meat substitute does not imply that the original practitioners of Jainism, Buddhism, or Taoism may have been flesh-eaters at one time. There is every reason to believe, as they insist, that their ancestors were vegetarians ever since *Homo erectus* clambered down from the banyan trees.)

The belief in reincarnation is the fourth hallmark of the *ahimsa*-based "vegetarian" religions. Indeed, vegetarianism is a corollary of that belief, for if one believes that the soul of a departed relative (dear Aunt Agatha) or of a deceased friend may inhabit the body of an animal, it's hard to see how one could ever acquire a taste for animal flesh.

The fifth hallmark, which is directly related to the fourth, is a belief in the doctrine of *karma*: the idea that all our actions are morally fraught and that we will reap the fruits of our actions in this life or the next. Obviously, such a belief militates against eating animal flesh. If we kill an animal for flesh, we are committing an evil akin to murder, an evil for which it is almost impossible to atone. *Karma* makes it as unthinkable to eat a chicken's wing as it would our dear Aunt Agatha's left forearm.

Western religions view time as linear, as a progression from A to Z. People start with conception or birth, then end with death, which may encompass, heaven, hell, or some other state (or "un-state") of final being. On the other hand, the four "vegetarian" religions view time as unfolding in ever-recurring cycles. A sixth hallmark of the "vegetarian" religions, which is also related to the fourth and the fifth, is their cyclical view of time. This has implications for their attitude towards animals; for those who perceive time as a straight line, animals are too-often perceived as road-kills on the superhighway to heaven, mere episodes on life's upward journey; whereas, in religions that view time cyclically, animals are seen as being potential vehicles for the soul's reincarnation, fellow travelers on a circular highway that returns upon itself.

In the West, it was only recently that religious freedom expanded to allow, say, a Christian to practice Buddhism, or a Jew, Hinduism, without being shunned, excommunicated or worse. The increasing religious tolerance, albeit slow-paced, may or may not be a result of influence by the "vegetarian religions," but it is undeniable that followers of these *ahimsa*-based systems of belief have largely practiced inclusiveness and tolerance towards other faiths. (Their inclusiveness, and tolerance towards other faiths is the seventh hallmark of the four *ahimsa*-based "vegetarian" religions.) In China, Taoism, Buddhism and Confucianism have coexisted in relative harmony for more than fifteen hundred years. In Japan, Shintoism cohabits with Buddhism. In India and Nepal, Buddhist temples sit cheek-by-jowl with Jain and Hindu temples. In China, at one and the same time, one can be a Buddhist, a Taoist, and a Confucian without being excommunicated. Because the *ahimsa*-based religions practice such religious tolerance, it's easy to see why there have been far fewer fratricidal religious wars in Asia than there have been in the West — whose history is soaked in blood spilled because of fights over belief. Western religious intolerance may have hindered the speed at which some Eastern beliefs (e.g. *karma*) and practices (e.g. vegetarianism) have been integrated into Western culture. Consider, for example, the story of Franciscan monk, Brother Ron Pickarski. Less than ten years ago, he attended a series of lectures on vegetarian diets while working as a monastery chef. The lectures inspired him to learn how to prepare vegetarian food for the monastery, but when he tried to serve the meatless dishes to his fellow monks, his efforts to improve their physical and moral well-being were stoutly resisted. Brother Ron was eventually ostracized from the community — an ironic outcome considering that his order was founded by Saint Francis, well-known for his compassion toward animals. Forced to make his way outside the order, Pickarski has become one of this country's foremost vegetarian chefs. Still a staunch Catholic, Brother Ron recently said that although it may not happen in his lifetime, he believes that "someday, the Western Church will adopt many of the features of Asian religions such as karmic doctrine, reincarnation, vegetarianism and *ahimsa*."

Cobra, lion pose, *pranayama* and *mudras*. Anyone familiar with these terms for some of the physical and psychological techniques of yoga has probably taken yoga classes, and most likely remembers the feeling of peace and well-being that followed them. In India, the Jains, Buddhists and Hindus practice yoga, which is a set of practical exercises for attaining *samadhi,* or spiritual transcendence. The eighth hallmark of the *ahimsa*-based "vegetarian" religions is that they have attached to them a set of physical and psychological techniques for achieving ecstasy. In East Asia, the Taoists and Zen Buddhists have also evolved yogic techniques of meditation and diet (vegetarianism is a prerequisite) for achieving spiritual illumination. In the Western Church, however, only saints and mystics have been permitted to achieve these states of ecstatic illumination. There is no yoga — probably because in classical yoga, spiritual progress is predicated on eating a diet of plant-based foods, a diet that the Western Church has confounded with Gnostic and Manichean heresy — available to the laity. Instead people have had to import it from Asia, or else resort to the taking of narcotics and hallucinogens to stimulate their mystical faculties. Lacking a Christian yoga and the *sattvic* diet that goes with it, the Westerner is forced to use hashish or LSD, in Aldous Huxley's phrase, "to cleanse the doors of perception."

Ever wonder why Indian children don't keep pet gerbils or own dogs named Shiva? The *ahimsa*-based religions go beyond abstaining from killing and eating animals: They discourage turning them into pets. (This is the ninth hallmark of the *ahimsa*-based "vegetarian" religions.) Jainism, in fact, has a tacit prohibition against keeping pets because the Jains do not believe in interfering in the lives of other creatures, let alone turning them into domestic playthings. In the Jain view, no matter how pampered or well-cared for, pets are slaves. Buddhists, Taoists, and Hindus are also disinclined to keep companion animals. Thus, they avoid the Western dilemma of having annually to "euthanize" millions of abandoned and abused animals who were once household pets.

The tenth hallmark of the "vegetarian" religions is the manner in which the followers of these faiths convey their food to the mouth. Followers of *ahimsa*-based religions tend to use chopsticks and fingers; Westerners, on the other hand, use the barbaric instruments of the knife and the fork, which can easily be turned into weapons. In his book *To Cherish All Life*, Roshi Kapleau points out how the Chinese, when they first saw Westerners slashing and tearing at their flesh dinners with knives and forks, "fancied themselves in the presence of sword swallowers." It's interesting to note that the fork didn't enter Western culture until flesh consumption began to increase. (Prior to this, flesh had been the prerogative of the rich and well-born, who took it to their mouths with a knife.)

The impact of any religion can best be measured in the lives of its disciples. Many Westerners who were influenced by the vegetarian *ahimsa*-based religions have, in turn, been influential in advancing their teachings in the West. Steve Rosen, a brilliant, tough-minded young Jewish intellectual, who had been something of a religious skeptic, attended his first Hare Krishna service and was captivated by the preaching of its charismatic leader, Swami Prabhupada. After closely examining the sacred Vedic texts of India, especially those of Vaishnavism (the tradition from which the Hare Krishna Movement was born), Rosen embraced Vaishnava Hinduism and eventually became one of Swami Prabhupada's initiated disciples. Since then, Rosen (now Satyaraj Das) has become a widely recognized Vaishnava scholar and author, whose books, such as *East-West Dialogues* and *Om Shalom*, have done much to spread the *ahimsa*-based teachings of Vaishnava Hinduism in the West.

Dr. Rehana Hamid grew up in New York City, the daughter of a Muslim father and a Jewish mother. In her twenties, she gravitated to Sufism, the mystical branch of Islam. Sufism is believed by some scholars to be a syncretistic faith that was formed from elements of pre-Islamic Mediterranean religions, such as Ebionite Christianity, Pythagoreanism and Gnosticism, many of which advocated a vegetarian diet. Although Sufism does not require its members to become vegetarians and many of its *shaikhs* are in fact non-vegetarians, it was Dr. Hamid's contact with a singular vegetarian Sufi *shaikh* named M. R. Bawa Muhaiyaddeen that helped put her on the vegetarian path.

One optimistic sign for the continuing influence that Eastern *ahimsa*-based religions have on Western religions is the (relatively) new presence of an English church called the Order of the Cross. Founded in 1904 by the Reverend John Todd Ferrier, members of the Order hold that Jesus, or "the Master," was originally a vegetarian and that references to Jesus's having eaten fish in the gospels are largely symbolic. This sect has adopted many other ethical teachings of the four great Eastern religions, including reincarnation, *karma*, and compassion for animals. The Order of the Cross also requires that every would-be member take a vegetarian vow.

A ray of hope for the continuing influence of Eastern *ahimsa*-based religions on Western religions is Oxford University's recent appointment of the Reverend Professor Dr. Andrew Linzey, an Anglican priest and theologian, to the world's first academic post in the ethical and theological aspects of animal welfare. Professor Linzey, who has written or edited more than thirteen books on the moral status of animals has said, "From my perspective, it's not inconceivable that Jainism, in its care and respect for creation, has more understood the Christian doctrine of love than the Christians have themselves."

Simply observing how the Jains treat insects shines light upon the reason that Professor Linzey and many others, consider this religion to be the embodiment of compassion towards animals. Jain priests use a whisk broom, or *rajo haram* (a "*karma* remover"), while they are walking, just to push aside any tiny beings that would otherwise be stepped on, and they may even wear air masks to keep from inadvertently inhaling them. Jains are increasingly becoming involved in animal rights and vegetarian activist groups in the West, some of them even rising to the forefront of the vegetarian movement.

In the Order of the Cross, in the life of Brother Ron Pickarski and in the works of the Reverend Doctor Linzey we can, perhaps, glimpse the shape that Christianity might take if it were to become an ethical vegetarian religion. Were that day to come, mainstream Christian churches would recognize that animals have souls and that, instead of having dominion over them, we are their sisters and brothers into whose bodies we may reincarnate after death. Such a realization might inspire us to put a higher value on life and might also keep us from falling upon "our brothers and sisters the animals," as Saint Francis would have called them.

Essays & Conversations

Essay

. . . .

JAINISM

CONTRARY TO POPULAR belief, the wellsprings of *ahimsa* (non-violence to all life-forms) are to be found in the smallest, the wealthiest, the fussiest and the most durable of the Indian religious groups—the Jains. Many people unwittingly regard Jainism—the religion of ten million Indians and an increasing number of devotees worldwide —as an offshoot of Hinduism. The Jains, however, maintain, not without cogent archaeological evidence, that Jainism is the parent religion of India.

Ask any Jain maharaj or priest and he will tell you that Jainism is the oldest religion in the world; it is the ur-religion from which all other religions, including Hindu-

ism and Buddhism, have sprung. Now, at first blush, this might seem to be the sort of chest-thumping to which religious enthusiasts are often prone. But recent scholarship lends color to this Jain boast. In his recent book, *Nonviolence to Animals, Earth and Self in Asian Traditions,*[1] Professor Christopher Key Chapple traces the origins of the doctrines of *ahimsa* and even *karma* from the earliest times to the present. Chapple says that we are wrong to look for the beginning of *ahimsa* in the early sacred texts of Hinduism—the *Vedas* and the *Upanishads*. Their ethical view of animal life is at best rudimentary. The Vedic texts in particular, he feels, reflect the exploitative attitude towards ani-

. . . .

11

mals of the Aryan nomadic tribes that had invaded India in the middle of the second millennium BCE. It was these cattle-herding, warlike tribes that fathered India's patriarchal religion; *varna* (its caste system based on color prejudice); the institution of animal sacrifice; *sati* (the suicide of widows on the death of their husband); and other unedifying practices.

According to Chapple, the ethic of *ahimsa* goes back thousands of years before the *Vedas* were composed. *Ahimsa* was the cardinal principle of the native religion of India, which he calls *Sramanic*[2], or ascetic, renouncing and proto-yogic. This religion was practiced by the pre-Aryan inhabitants of such extinct cities as Mohenjo Daro, Harappa and Lothal that had the misfortune of lying almost directly in the path of the Aryan incursions. Before they fell to the invaders, these early Indian cities were teeming with people, who, from the archaeological evidence, appear to have been highly civilized and cultivated. Their buildings were solidly constructed of brick and mortar, and they were equipped with such amenities as indoor plumbing and bathrooms (clearly the mark of a high civilization). The stratigraphic levels, which date back more than a thousand years, have yielded some intriguing artifacts. Although the Harappan script has not yet been deciphered, the mute clay figurines and faience seals speak volumes. Some of the figures show humans in the advanced attitudes of yoga. Other, four-faced figurines bear a strong resemblance to the Jain Tirthankaras, who customarily carried their teachings to the four cardinal points.

Chapple confirms the work of previous scholars such as Heinrich Zimmer. Writing in the 1940s, Zimmer said that Jainism was more Dravidian, pre-Aryan, in structure than any other Indian religion and that "it was a non-Brahman, pre-Aryan vision of man's role in the cosmos native to the Indian subcontinent. The way of perfectibility taught was that of yogic asceticism and self-abnegation, while the image constantly held before the mind's eye was that of the human savior as the redeemer even of the gods."[3] And further, "Jainism retains the Dravidian structure more purely than the other major Indian traditions — and is consequently a relatively simple, unsophisticated, clean-cut, and direct manifestation of the pessimistic dualism that underlies not only Sankhya, Yoga, and early Buddhistic thought, but also much of the reasoning of the Upanishads, and even the so-called non-dualism of the Vedanta."[4] On the evidence, Chapple has concluded that the inhabitants of these pre-Vedic communities practiced an early form of Jainism that comprised elements of yoga and *ahimsa*. Despite the presence of animal bones in the rubbish heaps, Chapple believes that the inhabitants of these cities were strict vegetarians, possibly even vegans.[5]

As Chapple sees it, the parent religion of India must have been very much like Jainism as it is practiced today. Indeed, he points out that although Jainism has spawned a number of subsects, it has changed remarkably little since the *Acaranga Sutra*—the earliest surviving Jain text—which was composed in the sixth century BCE. Therefore, the much vaunted vegetarianism and concern for animal welfare on which the Brahmins pride themselves are in all probability the result of Jain influences. In this Chapple is supported by the great French Indologist, Louis Dumont, who observed that India's vegetarianism and veneration for life came not from upper-caste Hindus but sprang from the *Sramanic* pre-Vedic renouncer religions of Jainism and Buddhism; "Vegetarianism forced itself on Hindu society, having begun in the sects of the renouncers, among which are Jainism and Buddhism."[6]

Chapple points out that there is no mention of *ahimsa* in the *Vedas*. Moreover, in the *Rg Veda*, the high-caste Brahmins were depicted as being meat-eaters, but due to the reforming efforts of Mahavira and the Buddha—among other exponents of the *Sramanic* religion—by the time that the *Chandogya Upanishad* was committed to writing (circa 200 BCE), a vegetarian diet and the practice of *ahimsa* had become status symbols associated with upper-caste Hindus. Chapple also cites passages from the Hindu martial epic the *Mahabharata*, which he takes as evidence that the Jain reforms of Vedic animal cruelty and animal sacrifice were beginning to take hold: "The meat of other animals is like the flesh of one's son. That foolish person, stupefied by folly, who eats meat is regarded as the vilest of human beings." (*Mahabharata* XIII: 114:11); and *"Ahimsa* is the highest *dharma."*(*Mahabharata* XIII:125:25). Even the yoga school of Patanjali (founded in the first century BCE), which enforced a strict vegetarian diet on its adherents, was guided by the five moral precepts that are identical to those taught by Mahavira five centuries earlier. The five precepts are: 1) not to take life or commit violence, *ahimsa*; 2) to abstain from lying, *satya; 3*) not to take what is not given, *asteya;* 4) not to overindulge in sexual activity, *brahmacharya;* and 5) not to become excessively attached to anything, *aparigraha.* It is interesting to observe how the five precepts are interrelated. For instance, the third precept (against taking what is not given) is related to the first (against taking life). For all animals desperately cling to life—by killing them for food or for some frivolity, one is taking what has not been offered. Or, as Schopenhauer remarked, "Murder is the ultimate form of theft."

For a striking instance of a Jain evangelist in action, Chapple gives us the well-documented account of the Jain monk Hiravijaya, who was invited along with sixty other Jain monks to the court of the Mughal emperor Akbar at Fatehpur Sikri in the sixteenth century. Akbar, like all the Mughal emperors, was a ferocious old carnivore, who liked his quadrupeds spitted and grilled. However, so strong was the impression that Hiravijaya made on him that Akbar made him his spiritual adviser, giving him the title Jagat-Guru (World Teacher), and actually flirted with the idea of becoming a vegetarian. In the end, Akbar couldn't quite bring himself to give up Tandoori Chicken, Stuffed Goat and other Mughal gastronomic abominations, but he made a conscious effort to eat less meat, and he issued royal decrees that animals were not to be eaten during the first month of the lunar cycle; leather was to be avoided during the sixth lunar month. This may not seem like much, but it marked an ethical advance over his predecessors, and he did much to foster the Jain philosophy of *ahimsa*, even if he couldn't quite bring himself to put it into practice. The case of Hiravijaya and Akbar is a telling example of how the Jains quietly, but effectively, accomplished their ends. In fact, their devotion to spreading the doctrine of *ahimsa* throughout India was so self-effacing that their contribution to the growth of a moral consciousness in Indian civilization hadn't begun to be really appreciated by Western scholars until the late twentieth century.

The Jains were the first religious group, of which we have any record, to affirm the sanctity of animal life. It was the Jains who —sometime in remote antiquity—founded the world's first animal hospitals, called *pinjarpols*. In every Jain community, *pinjarpols* are still being operated by Jain monks and nuns who look after animals that have been rescued from the slaughterhouses and from the streets. Rooms in the *pinjarpols* are set aside for insects, birds and reptiles as well as for quadrupeds. (Jain compassion is not selective, but extends to all creatures, small and great.) The Jains assign senses even to objects we would consider too small to matter, such as water sprites, flame bodies, wind spirits, and *nigoda* (microorganisms).

As spiritual as they are pragmatic, Jains have used their wealth to build the most splendidly decorated temples in India. The Jain temples at Ahmedabad, Ellora, Ajmere, Mount Abu in West India, and the delicately wrought monolithic Jain temple in Kaligamalai are among the architectural marvels of the land. As a pragmatic inducement to visit these spiritual palaces, it is bruited that if a Jain makes a pilgrimage to any of these temples he can work off some of his karmic debt. As spiritual pragmatists, the Jains have resigned themselves to the reality that living on earth entails the destruction of other life forms. Recognizing that it is impossible to entirely eliminate the amount of harm that we do to other creatures, they believe we must try to mitigate the suffering of other life forms as much as possible—by eating as far down on the scale of pain as possible. This means eating as far down on the *food chain* as possible. For by consuming one-sensed creatures instead of five-sensed creatures, we are minimizing the amount of pain we might cause to other beings.

In the Jain scheme, animal souls and human souls are accorded equal weight. The Jain word for soul is *jiva* (sentient essence).

The highest number of senses, five senses, are assigned to animals that humans are wont to look down upon as inferior beings. For instance, fish are endowed with as much sentiency as are humans. Among the five-sensed beings are reckoned: monkeys, parrots, fish, birds, cattle, horses and octopuses. Insects fall into two classifications—those that have four and three senses. The higher insects are considered to have four senses: smell, taste, touch and hearing. They include the larger insects, such as bees, flies and grasshoppers. Insects with three senses are thought to lack the sense of sight and hearing; they include moths, ants, mosquitoes and bed bugs. Creatures with two senses are held to have only the senses of taste and touch; they include mollusks, crustaceans, worms, leeches, and so on. One sense is assigned to trees, plants, water bodies, fire bodies and wind bodies. Rocks and minerals are *pudgala* (inanimate matter), but within their interior spaces may live microscopic beings; therefore, we must treat even rocks and minerals with respect.

For the Jains, the material world is charged with vitality. Thus the ethical and ecological implications of the Jain world view are stunningly clear: if one is cruel and unfeeling towards other life forms, be they even so footling as a water sprite, a tree, or a worm, one runs the risk of attracting to one's own *jiva* the gluey, greasy, gummy residue of bad *karma* that sticks like tar to the spirit and that can turn one's next incarnation into an unhappy one—one's *jiva* might be imprisoned in a stone, or it might live for an instant in the flare of a fire body or the splash of a water body. On the other hand, if one is compassionate towards other life forms, one's soul becomes *sattvic* (light, spiritual); in such a case one may escape the wheel of rebirth and dwell in omniscience.

Non-interference is a key idea in Jainism, as it is in Taoism, and it may not be farfetched to suggest that the Taoist idea of *wu-wei* or "non-action," may derive from Jainism.[7] By meddling in the lives of other beings, particularly the lives of animals whom we manipulate and exploit for our own selfish ends—we attract bad *karma* to our *jiva;* to counteract the bad *karma*, we must practice quietness and abstention—what the Taoists call *wu-wei.*

Jains carry non-interference to the point of refusing to earn their living in agriculture (lest they tread on bugs), silk-weaving, the military services, food preparation and leather curing, or other trades where fellow beings could be injured or killed. Ironically enough, this has forced them to make their way as merchants, brokers and economic middlemen with the result that they have become one of the richest religious minorities in the world. Partially out of envy, partially out of contrariety, their detractors have accused them of having a "Let George do it!" theology in which they use their wealth to employ other people to raise their food and fight their wars for them; in this way they don't have to run the risk of incurring bad *karma*. But that criticism seems harsh and unfair. Non-interference, for the Jains, is a precept, not a quixotic ideal; in the cruelest of worlds, sometimes one must resort to cunning and expediency to carry it through. Furthermore, if more people followed the Jain first precept, which forbids killing and doing harm to all life forms, there would be fewer wars, less animal exploitation, and the Jain point of view would not seem so radical.

Surprisingly enough, Albert Schweitzer who was inspired by the Jains to coin his deathless phrase "reverence for life," says that the Jains' doctrine of *ahimsa* arose not out of compassion for other living creatures, but out of a fetish for purity.[8] According to Schweitzer, they practiced *a-himsa* (*ahimsa* is the negative substantive of the verb *hims* "to wish to kill and to damage") so as to avoid defiling themselves with bad *karma*. No doubt this was true of some Jains, but Schweitzer had never traveled to India, nor had he ever met a Jain in the flesh. If he had watched a Jain housewife carefully remove the insects from the food she was preparing, and gently place them in her garden, or watched a Jain monk rescue an animal and bring it to a *pinjarpol*, he would probably have formed a higher estimate of Jain compassion.

To sustain ourselves, the Jains would have us take our nourishment exclusively from the class of one-sensed beings (fruits and vegetables). Killing animals for food or self-gratification is considered an inexpiable *karmic* sin for which one will have to atone for countless lifetimes. *Karma* in the Jain scheme is no mere abstraction; rather, it's regarded as a viscous substance that sticks to the soul like tar; it "gums up the works" — much as plaque and cholesterol gum up the arteries of those who eat five-sensed beings.

Like the other Asian religions that espouse nonviolent eating, the Jains view time as being circular. Time returns upon itself with the inevitability of death and rebirth. The universe has no end and no beginning. It is an eternal return. Unfolding in two great cycles, each 600 million years in duration, the cycles are subdivided into six smaller parts. The two main cycles are divided into periods of ascent in which everything on earth aspires and improves, and into periods of descent in which everything on earth deteriorates and degenerates. Perhaps not surprisingly we are living through one of those abysmal periods of decline. In each of the main half-cycles there appear twenty-four Tirthankaras, or "world teachers," to guide us.

Tirthankaras are paragons of all the virtues and Jainism is the most high-minded of religions; however, we would be wrong to think that there is no trouble in Jain paradise. Like all religions, Jainism has been riven by factional strife. The first schism arose in 466 CE between Jains who insisted on going sky-clad like Mahavira and those who insisted on wearing cotton garments. The naked Jains were known as Digambara (naked) and the clothed Jains were known as Shvetambara (white-robed). The Digambaras claimed that they were more faithful to the original teachings of Jainism — for instance, that *sadhus* go sky-clad and eat their food from their cupped hands rather than from the wooden begging bowls favored by the Shvetambaras. In spite of their dedication to pacifism, at times Digambaras and Shvetambaras have come to blows over the ownership of shrines and holy places,[9] but today the acrimony has dissolved into a friendly rivalry between the two sects. Still the Digambaras in Bombay have their own temples in which the *acharya* (head monk) holds forth to audiences in cloud-clad splendor. It's important to emphasize that only the male Digambara *sadhus* go naked; the female *sadhus*, or *sadhvis*, are not permitted to go sky-clad. (Misogyny is also a feature of the Digambaras: they hold the misogynistic view that female Jains cannot attain *kevalajnana* in this life; rather, they must wait to be reincarnated as males before they can reach this exalted state.) The different attitude of the Shvetambaras and the Digambaras toward nakedness is reflected in their respective *pujas*. The Shvetambaras do *puja* to clothed statues of the Tirthankaras whereas, the Digambaras do *puja* to statues of sky-clad Tirthankaras.

The most renowned of the twenty-four Jain Tirthankaras is its historical founder, Mahavira, who was a contemporary of the Buddha. Among the Tirthankaras, Mahavira is *primus inter pares* because he was the last of these twenty-four world teachers, and he lived in historical times. Although Mahavira scorned the worship of sky gods and father gods like Indra, Yahweh and Zeus, who thunder, hurl lightning bolts, and snuff up the smoke of burning animal sacrifices—there is an ironic sense in which Mahavira, like the Mahayana Buddha, has been apotheosized into a god. In innumerable temples all over India, worshippers do *puja* to Mahavira and to the other Tirthankaras as if they were praying to a deity.

A brief biographical sketch of Mahavira is not out of place here because his life story stands as an exemplar for the Jains. Much as Muslims imitate the life of Muhammad, the Jains emulate Mahavira. The salient features of his life—renunciation of his princely privileges and his energetic propagation of the first precept (to cherish all life and to do no harm)—are watchwords among modern Jains. Like the Buddha, he was born into a princely *kshatriya* family, and in his twenties he renounced the prerogatives of his rank. To symbolize his break with his princely life of comfort and ease, he plucked out all his hair (a rite that Jain monks still practice); he stripped off all his clothes and stepped forth as a sky-clad *sadhu*. (Today, as we have noted, members of the Digambara sect, as they age, and their wisdom increases, emulate Mahavira by discarding their clothes and going sky-clad. Nakedness signifies maximum independence from material comforts, and eliminates the peril of inadvertently crushing insects in the folds of cloth.) Next, Mahavira slipped off his sandals; for then as now, the Jain *sadhu* is forbidden to wear sandals or shoes; they routinely walk vast distances barefooted. Heavily calloused through constant wear, their feet become as tough as old boots. Finally, Mahavira completed the transformation from prince to *sadhu* by removing his earrings and casting aside his chunky gold jewelry; he exchanged them for two other appurtenances of the Jain *sadhu*—the alms bowl and the *pincha*, which is the soft broom that Jains use to sweep the path whenever it might be covered with insects.

After joining the order of the sky-clad followers of Parshwa (the twenty-third Tirthankara), of which his parents had been lay members, Mahavira spent twelve years wandering the country as a *sadhu*, keeping body and soul together by cupping his hands and imploring householders to fill them with vegetarian food. Often, as he approached a village, he would be set upon by rustics who would pelt him with potsherds, rotten fruit and mud for having the effrontery to go about sky-clad. But he bore it all patiently. Finally, the ultimate experience that he had been seeking was not denied him. In the thirteenth year of his wanderings, in the fourth fortnight of summer, seated in a squatting position under a *sal* tree in the field of the householder, Samaga, he achieved *nirvana* and became a *Jina* ("Conqueror").

After achieving *nirvana,* he went out to preach *ahimsa.* Constantly on the move, he paused only to meditate, eat and sleep, which he limited to three hours per night—three hours of sleep is the quota for Jain monks today. In his travels, he met many other *sadhus* and *sannyasin,* and among them, he acquired a reputation as a teacher and as a religious reformer that rivaled that of his famous Brahmin contemporaries. In his sermons, he launched a vigorous attack against flesh-eating, animal sacrifice, the caste system, and the subjection of women. He taught his followers that they need not be born into the privileged priestly (Brahmin) caste in order to attain enlightenment. In fact, he insisted that every man or woman should be his or her own priest. To his followers, he stressed the importance of adhering to the first precept of Jainism. Many of the austerities that Mahavira practiced are still observed by members of the Jain religion today.

For instance, he would not eat food that had not been prepared the same day, lest it spoil and attract *nigoda* (microorganisms). Jains knew of the existence of germs and microbes thousands of years before they were "discovered" by Western science. He always ate his meals during daylight hours lest he inadvertently swallow flying insects. He always drank filtered water lest he consume submerged organisms (and Jains today invariably filter their water). Wherever he went, he stared fixedly at the ground to avoid treading on bugs; and Jains are mindful of where they step today. At the age of 72, he decided to end his life and he performed upon himself the ritual act of suicide called *sullakana* (self-inflicted death through fasting), which is still permitted to elderly Jains today. Before he died, he achieved supreme enlightenment or *kevalajnana,* and when his soul was released from his body, it is said to have been translated to the top of the world where Mahavira's spirit dwells in omniscience.

Jains have been called "the conscience of India"; and so rigorous are the demands that their faith places on them that they are truly worthy of their name "Jain"—from the word *Jina*, which means conqueror: the idea being that to live life as an ascetic one must first conquer oneself. It is almost axiomatic that a religious group that goes to the trouble of staring at the ground so as to avoid stepping on bugs will have a pacifying effect on others. If the world's religions had more of the Jain philosophy in their creeds, humanity would be the better for it. ✋

R.B.

. . . .

1 Christopher Key Chapple, *Nonviolence to Animals, Earth and Self in Asian Traditions* (Albany: State University of New York Press, 1993).

2 Sramanic: the indigenous, pre-Aryan religion of India, which is non-Brahmanic and which holds that animals are implicated in the cycle of rebirth. Humans can gain release from the cycle through the practice of austerities, ethical vegetarianism and gnosis. Jainism, Buddhism, the Ajivakas and the Sankhya school of yoga are believed to be remnants of

this ancient chthonic religion. Through the reforms of the Jains and the Buddhists, classical Hinduism absorbed many Sramanic doctrines, eg., reincarnation and ethical vegetarianism.

[3] Heinrich Zimmer, *Philosophies of India* (New York: Pantheon Books, 1951), pp. 219, 233.

[4] *ibid.*, p. 219.

[5] Chapple, *op. cit.*, p. 7.

[6] Louis Dumont, *Homo Hierarchichus: The Caste System and Its Implications*, trans., Mark Sainsbury (Chicago: The University of Chicago Press, 1970), p. 149.

[7] See my essay on Taoism.

[8] Albert Schweitzer, *Indian Thought and Its Development*, (Boston: The Beacon Press, 1956), pp. 80-1.

[9] Paul Dundas, *The Jains* (London: Routledge, 1992), pp. 45-8.

MUNI NANDIBHUSHAN VIJAYJI

BORN IN GUJARAT, MUNI Nandibhushan Vijayji was a precocious student, who, at the tender age of fifteen, decided that he wanted to become a *muni* (monk); so he took the vows and underwent the rigorous training that is demanded of any would-be Jain monk. In the Jain community, it is an honor for a youth to enter the Jain priesthood; so his family was proud to learn of his decision. In fact, when his own father had fulfilled his own duties as a husband and householder, he renounced the world and became a Jain muni himself. Today, Muni Nandibhushan minor is highly revered for his wisdom

and for his public speaking skills; he has a fund of colorful anecdotes with which he tellingly illustrates his points, and is very popular in Jain assemblies where he speaks to overflow audiences. A master of many languages, he speaks Gujarati, Marathi, and Hindi, he has a reading knowledge of Sanskrit, Prakrit, and Magadhi (the language of Mahavira and the Buddha), and considerable fluency in English. We met on the top floor of the Swantinath Jain temple, where seven other monks were staying at the time. He was wearing a flowing cotton tunic that looked like nothing so much as a Greek chiton, so that for a moment I fancied myself in the presence of a Pythagorean philosopher in ancient Croton. Although the interview was held in the winter (January), the air that wafted through the balcony windows was warm and heavy with the pungent odors of Bombay; in the hubbub from the streets below, one could hear street vendors hawking pomegranates, sugar-cane, and custard apples; songbirds alighted on the sun-washed balcony and nonchalantly strutted back and forth.

....

BERRY: Do you come from a family of Jain priests?

NANDIBHUSHAN: Yes.

BERRY: How old was your father when you became a priest?

NANDIBHUSHAN: He was fifty-two years old.

BERRY: And you: how old are you now?

NANDIBHUSHAN: I am thirty-nine years old. I was fifteen when I became a priest.

BERRY: Why did you become a priest at such a tender age?

NANDIBHUSHAN: There are two reasons why one would want to become a *sadhu* — one is unhappy with the world and desires to escape from it; one meets a guru who inspires one to follow his example. In my case it was the latter. After school, I used to go to hear a Jain guru who persuaded me through his words and his example that I could only make spiritual progress if I were to become a *sadhu*. So at the age of fifteen I left school and became a *sadhu*. I ceased my formal education, but in a sense my education really began when I left school.

BERRY: Where did you learn to read Sanskrit and Magadhi?

NANDIBHUSHAN: From my fellow *sadhus*: we teach each other.

BERRY: Are women allowed to become priests?

NANDIBHUSHAN: Yes, in fact the majority of Lord Mahavira's followers were women, which was more than two thousand years ago. The Jain priesthood has always been open to women. We call our female priests or monks *sadhuis*.

BERRY: It's funny, I've never seen a *sadhui* address an assemblage of males or even an audience comprising males and females. Are the *sadhuis* permitted to preach to men as well as women?

NANDIBHUSHAN: As a rule the *sadhuis* don't speak in front of men; the *sadhus* (male priests) speak before male and female audiences; however, the Jain *Acharya* or *Guru Maharaj* (head priest) may appoint a woman to speak at Jain assemblies.

BERRY: What is the population of Jains in India today?

NANDIBHUSHAN: About one *crore*, or approximately ten million.

BERRY: Is the population increasing or declining?

NANDIBHUSHAN: In some places it is increasing; in others it is declining. The great thing is that it goes on.

BERRY: In what geographic regions are the Jains concentrated?

NANDIBHUSHAN: The greatest concentration is in Gujarat, Rajasthan and Maharashtra, but there are Jains living in every state.

BERRY: In what ancient languages were the Jain *sutras* and sacred texts composed?

NANDIBHUSHAN: In Prakrit and Magadhi, but they've been translated into all languages, even English.

BERRY: Are the Jains still prohibited from eating such root vegetables as potatoes, carrots and radishes, as well as garlic and onions?

NANDIBHUSHAN: It is a cardinal Jain precept that one should never kill any form of life. It is our belief that while these root vegetables are growing underground, they have an infinite number of organisms attached to them. By uprooting them, one is disrupting their lives and killing them. This is contrary to the first Jain precept against taking life. That's why we don't eat root vegetables. Our stomach is not a burial ground for dead bodies.

BERRY: Are Jain dietary laws stricter than those of Hinduism?

NANDIBHUSHAN: Yes, Jainism is decidedly stricter than Hinduism. For instance, we don't eat before sunrise; nor do we eat after sunset. Many foods that Hindus are allowed to eat such as root vegetables are forbidden to Jains. Furthermore, Hindus are permitted to drink alcohol and fermented beverages, but for Jains this is strictly prohibited. For Jain priests, the dietary rules are stricter still. From the foods that we are allowed to eat we only take the bare minimum necessary to keep the body functioning. The body is like a steam engine; if one puts in more food than is required to run it, it will damage the engine.

BERRY: What about the Jain layman? Is he as strict in his dietary habits as a Jain priest?

NANDIBHUSHAN: No, not everyone is so strict. There are gradations, but everyone is a strict vegetarian.

BERRY: Do Jain priests still carry whiskbrooms when they go abroad to sweep away the insects in their path?

NANDIBHUSHAN: Yes, I am never without my whisk.

BERRY: What is the specific term for this whisk broom that you carry?

NANDIBHUSHAN: It's called *rajoharam*.

BERRY: What does it mean?

NANDIBHUSHAN: *Rajo* is "*karma*," or the reaction that comes from work, and *haram* means "to remove."

BERRY: So it's symbolic then?

NANDIBHUSHAN: Yes, it's symbolic, but it's also an actual *karma*-remover because it enables the *muni* or priest to brush away insects without killing them.

BERRY: The antithesis of the *rajoharam* or "*karma*-remover" is the Western device of the fly swatter, or the insect-bomb. Would you call this a "*karma*-attractor"?

NANDIBHUSHAN: Yes, absolutely. It points up the difference between Jainism and Western thinking. We Jains go to great lengths to avoid killing insects, but for you Westerners with your fly swatters and insect-bombs, killing insects is almost a sport. Not only does it attract bad *karma* but it cheapens the value of life.

BERRY: How do you mean?

NANDIBHUSHAN: You Westerners were diabolically clever to

have invented the insect-bomb, but you have also invented the
atom bomb and napalm. Are they not like insecticides for humans?
The human world and the insect world are fatefully interlinked. We
cannot harm insects without at the same time harming humans. Westerners have invented the atom bomb, but India has invented the
atman [spirit] bomb. So many other countries are bent on destroying the world, but India has always been the home of teachers
who are teaching the world to improve their souls. The West has
given birth to scientific leaders, but India has given birth to spiritual leaders.

BERRY: How do you deal with mosquitoes, termites, bed bugs and
crop-destroying pests such as fruit-flies, locusts and other parasites?

NANDIBHUSHAN: According to Jainism, even these bugs have
souls; so one must deal with them very gingerly.

BERRY: What if you were besieged by a cloud of mosquitoes one
fine night? What action would you take?

NANDIBHUSHAN: I would sweep them away with my whisk
broom. If they really got bad, I would sleep under a mosquito net;
but there is a difference between my killing them and their committing suicide. (*laughter*)

BERRY: Do Jains avoid wearing leather, wool, silk and other animal products?

NANDIBHUSHAN: We never wear leather, but some of our garments are made from wool. We justify that by reasoning that wool
grows on top of the animal; so that to remove it is not causing the
animal any deprivation. Anyway, artificial fabrics are now rendering the wearing of wool obsolete; it's becoming an academic
question.

BERRY: Did the concept of *ahimsa* originate with the Jains?

NANDIBHUSHAN: It began with Jainism, and the genesis of
ahimsa can be found in Jain philosophy. No other religion has
articulated the idea of *ahimsa* so forcefully as have the Jains. For
instance, Mother Teresa says that when you care for another person, you are caring for God; but Jainism says that when you care
for an insect, you are caring for God. That's truly *ahimsa*!

Jainism goes so far as to say that you should be concerned not only for the well-being of people, animals and bugs, but also for the well-being of the soil, the water and the air: *ahimsa* extends to all of nature. Jainism has always been very ecology-minded. We should be unstinting in our efforts to care for all life forms—even stones, soil, trees, water and air contain microscopic beings, which by the lights of Jainism are also sentient beings.

BERRY: Yes, but aren't some beings more sentient than others? How would you weigh the life of a man against the life of a flame spirit or a water being?

NANDIBHUSHAN: Jainism divides the world into five classes of beings whose membership in each class is determined by the number of senses that each being possesses. The highest class is that of the five-sensed beings, which comprises men, gods, hell-beings, and the higher animals such as monkeys, parrots, dogs, horses, elephants, pigs, etc. The next class consists of four-sensed beings who are thought to lack the sense of hearing; they include the larger insects such as flies, bees and grasshoppers; the next class comprises three-sensed beings such as moths, ants, mosquitoes, etc. that lack the senses of hearing and seeing; the fourth group consists of two-sensed beings such as mollusks, crustaceans, worms, etc. who have only the senses of taste and touch; the final group of one-sensed beings includes trees, water-bodies, wind-bodies and fire-bodies—these too are sentient beings and as Jains we have an obligation to treat them with the same respect and care that we accord to any other life form.

BERRY: Do rocks have senses?

NANDIBHUSHAN: No. Rocks are *pudgala*, that is they are matter with neither soul nor sense, but they may contain minute souls in their interior spaces, so we should treat them carefully.

BERRY: What about water and fire?

NANDIBHUSHAN: They are also *pudgala*, but they may contain water-bodies and flame-bodies that live only for a few seconds.

BERRY: What about the doctrine of reincarnation in Jainism? Do the Jains hold the view that one can be reborn in a higher or lower life form?

NANDIBHUSHAN: Basically, your *karma* in this lifetime determines what you will become in your next lifetime. If you've been a slaughterer in this lifetime, then you may be slaughtered in the next lifetime.

There are no levels of incarnation; one life form is not held to be higher or lower than another. All are sacred.

BERRY: Is the Jain concept of *karma* different from, let us say, the Vaishnava concept of *karma*?

NANDIBHUSHAN: There are subtle differences, but basically it is the same. Hindu *dharma* and Jain *dharma* are essentially the same. The goal for both is ultimately to become one with God.

In Jainism, it is important to control your mind and think *sattvic* or pure thoughts. This will affect your *karma* positively.

BERRY: Isn't it equally important that one eat *sattvic* food?

NANDIBHUSHAN: Indubitably. Eating *sattvic* food brings one closer to God.

BERRY: So the theory of the *gunas*, or modes of nature, obtains in Jainism as well as in Hinduism. Did it originate with the Jains?

NANDIBHUSHAN: Yes.

BERRY: Can the *gunas* be referred to colors?

NANDIBHUSHAN: Yes, they can be referred to colors, tastes, thoughts, everything. For instance, *sattvic* thoughts are pure and spiritual; *sattvic* food is pure vegetarian—fresh, unspiced, without dairy products; a *sattvic* color is white, or translucent. On the other hand, *rajasic* thoughts are passionate and worldly; *rajasic* food is highly spiced and piquant; the *rajasic* color is red. Finally, *tamas* refers to dark, destructive homicidal thoughts; the *tamasic* food is flesh and other putrefying foods; the *tamasic* color is black.

BERRY: Do the Jain priests often eat non-dairy, or pure vegetarian (vegan) dishes?

NANDIBHUSHAN: Yes, we call it *amil*; these dishes contain no *ghee*, no spices, no dairy products. Sometimes we eat it every day, because one benefits spiritually as well as physically from eating *amil*; it is the ultimate in *sattvic* food. For most of his life as a *sadhu*, Mahavira subsisted on rice and boiled chickpeas, without spices.

BERRY: Are any vegetables classified as *tamasic* foods?

NANDIBHUSHAN: Yes, garlic, onions and *brinjals* (eggplants) are classified as *tamasic* foods because they are thought to provoke *tamasic* or lustful thoughts in men and women; so Jain priests and many other Jains will avoid them.

BERRY: What is a typical meal for a Jain monk?

NANDIBHUSHAN: The food must be fresh: we cannot eat food that has been stored overnight.

BERRY: Is that because leftover food attracts more microorganisms, more bacteria, hence more life-forms?

NANDIBHUSHAN: That's correct. If I want to eat something, I will go to a Jain home and I will eat the food that has been prepared for me—but as I said, it must be fresh, and it cannot contain root vegetables.

BERRY: So the Jain *sadhus* don't do any cooking themselves? They procure all their food from members of the Jain community?

NANDIBHUSHAN: That's right. It's considered an honor for a Jain family to provide sustenance for a Jain monk. They invariably try to give us more food than we can eat in order to obtain more blessings.

BERRY: Buddhist monks have the same custom, don't they?

NANDIBHUSHAN: Not exactly. Buddhist monks do their own cooking, and they also drink alcohol; whereas, Jain priests depend entirely on the Jain community for their sustenance, and they never touch alcohol. Furthermore, not all Buddhist monks are vegetarians; whereas, all Jain monks without exception are strict vegetarians.

BERRY: Will you be getting your food from one of the Jain households in the neighborhood this afternoon?

NANDIBHUSHAN: Either I or one of the other *sadhus* will go out and collect the food for the group in one of these bowls. We go twice a day—once in the morning and once in the afternoon, and we share the food out among us.

BERRY: You feed a group of *sadhus* from one little bowl? That seems a very meagre ration.

NANDIBHUSHAN: As I said before, we only take enough food to maintain life. You Westerners are accustomed to bolting down big portions; you would be surprised at how little the body requires. Now would you be so kind as to pour me some water—I'm a bit thirsty. Could you also pour some water for the other *sadhus*?

BERRY: Certainly, I would be honored. Are you unable to pour your own water for this same reason that you can't prepare your own food—for fear of killing microorganisms?

NANDIBHUSHAN: That's right. We do our utmost to avoid sin.

BERRY: In the Jain household where I am staying, all the family members drink boiled water because the municipal water is contaminated. Is this water that you and the other *sadhus* are drinking also boiled water?

NANDIBHUSHAN: Yes, it has been boiled for us.

BERRY: You mentioned that it is important that Jains be willing to follow rules. What are some of the rules that govern your life as a Jain priest?

NANDIBHUSHAN: When we travel we must walk barefoot everywhere. We are not permitted to touch a woman; we are not allowed to touch money; we never eat after sunset; twice a year I must pluck out all the hair on my face and scalp. Whatever rules are handed down by my Gurudev, we must follow and stay within the limits of those rules.

BERRY: Why do you pluck out all your facial and scalp hair?

NANDIBHUSHAN: To increase *parishaha* (endurance of pain). There are twenty-two *parishahas*, such as going without food; enduring cold; enduring heat; enduring insect bites; tolerating bad odors; deliberately wearing dirty clothes; sleeping on the ground (sometimes we cannot find a decent place to sleep)—these are all *parishahas*.

BERRY: To an untutored Westerner, these *parishahas* seem like an exercise in masochism; what is their purpose?

NANDIBHUSHAN: *Parishaha* strengthens the spirit and reduces *karma*. In doing *parishahas*, we are following the example of our twenty-fourth Tirthankara, Mahavira Bhagwan, who after undergoing the severest *parishahas* was able to dissolve his *karma* and achieve *kevalajnana*—eternal blissful omniscience.

BERRY: Where does your Gurudev live and what is his name?

NANDIBHUSHAN: His name is Jain Acharya Vijay Bhawanbhanu Surij Maharaj. He is 84-years-old. Right now he is stopping in Surat. He walks barefoot wherever he goes. Within a month he will be here. He is coming here on foot—a distance of some 260 kilometers.

BERRY: Your Gurudev at 84 is amazingly spry; but what happens to a Jain priest who becomes too old and infirm to be able to walk barefoot everywhere?

NANDIBHUSHAN: Still, they don't take vehicles; there are people in the community whose job it is to carry them in a sedan-chair.

BERRY: How far do you walk in the space of a year?

NANDIBHUSHAN: Thousands of kilometers.

BERRY: Do you walk alone, or in groups?

NANDIBHUSHAN: My fellow *sadhus* and I walk together. We sing songs and chant together to beguile the time. We rise as soon as we can see the palms of our hands in the dawn light; and we walk until we reach our destination.

BERRY: This is such a lovely temple; why don't you and your fellow *sadhus* just stay here?

NANDIBHUSHAN: As *sadhus* we strive not to become attached to any person, place or thing. That is why we have no possessions and that is why we keep on the move—lest we become attached to a community or a temple.

BERRY: If I were to write you a card or a letter how would it reach you if you are always on the move?

NANDIBHUSHAN: Send it to me in care of my Gurudev; he will know where I am to be reached.

BERRY: Do you ever fall sick?

NANDIBHUSHAN: Certainly.

BERRY: What do you take for a cold, or any other malady?

NANDIBHUSHAN: We take homeopathic medicine, and some allopathic medicine—whatever works; however, it must contain no animal products.

BERRY: Is it true that Jains tend to live longer than most other Indians?

NANDIBHUSHAN: That's true.

BERRY: Do you carry any money on your walks?

NANDIBHUSHAN: Jain priests are not permitted to touch money.

BERRY: Why? Is money intrinsically evil, or *tamasic*?

NANDIBHUSHAN: No, money has the potential to be either good or evil; but, it is so volatile that we cannot run the risk of touching it for fear of contamination.

BERRY: What about the Hindu priests: are they not permitted to touch money?

NANDIBHUSHAN: Yes.

BERRY: Perhaps that is why there is so much corruption among the Brahmins?

NANDIBHUSHAN: Yes, we have eliminated the potential for corruption among Jain priests.

BERRY: How do you buy your necessities?

NANDIBHUSHAN: People come to us. It is an honor for members of the Jain community to supply our needs.

BERRY: Supposing you needed a book, or some writing material, how would you obtain it?

NANDIBHUSHAN: Every day members of our community come to us to ask what we require. They are eager to serve us.

BERRY: Do the Jains still make it a point to pursue innocent professions such as commerce or teaching in order to avoid having to take a job in the restaurant, leather, or agricultural trades, which are considered cruel because they necessitate killing life forms?

NANDIBHUSHAN: In the old days, this was strictly true; but nowadays many Jains are not so careful about the sort of work they do so long as it pays them a good salary. Unfortunately, they don't realize that if they fail to follow the precepts of their religion, even in the workplace, they will never gain enlightenment.

BERRY: Are Jains permitted to serve in the armed forces?

NANDIBHUSHAN: Not even a Tirthankara, not even Mahavira himself, is permitted to take the life of another being. In the end, whoever takes the life of another being will have to pay for it.

BERRY: What about the Jain ritual of *sallakhana*? At the end of one's life I understand that it is permissible for Jains to commit suicide through fasting to death. Does Jainism condone taking one's own life?

NANDIBHUSHAN: It depends on your intentions: if you give up eating food because you want to make spiritual progress and enter a higher life form—that is permissible. But if you use fasting as a means of escaping the problems of life, then you will be punished for it in the next life.

BERRY: Are there gods in Jainism? Are Tirthankaras considered to be gods? Or is Jainism an atheistic religion like Buddhism?

NANDIBHUSHAN: The Tirthankaras are perfected humans, great teachers who have transcended their *karma*. We consider them to be divine beings, gods, if you will, but not in the Western sense of omnipotent father figures who grant boons to those who pray fervently and who mete out punishments to those who displease them. The Tirthankaras are paragons of human perfection. They dwell in divine omniscience. They exist as examples of what we might become. Remote and impersonal, they don't interfere in our lives just as we don't interfere in the lives of animals.

BERRY: Didn't George Bernard Shaw admire this aspect of Jainism?

NANDIBHUSHAN: That's right. There is an anecdote about Gandhi's son having paid a call on Shaw when he was in London. Gandhi knew that Shaw was a devout vegetarian; so he asked him if he believed in reincarnation. Shaw said that he did; so Gandhi's son asked him if he were to be reborn what religion would he choose to be born into. Without hesitating, Shaw said that he would choose to be reincarnated into the Jain religion. Why not into Hinduism? After all Hindus are vegetarian and their numbers are legion. Whereas Jainism is only a small sect. "Because," Shaw said, "the Hindus have made Ram into a God and Krishna into a God—there's no room for any new gods; whereas, in Jainism the average man can become a god. If I wanted to become a god, Jainism has provided an avenue for me to become a god. I can become a god without having to bow the knee to other gods."

BERRY: When did the first Tirthankara live?

NANDIBHUSHAN: The first Tirthankara of this cycle was Rishabha, but since Jainism has no starting point and no ending point, there have been and will be an infinite number of cycles.

BERRY: Why is the twenty-fourth Tirthankara, Mahavira, the most famous of all the Tirthankaras?

NANDIBHUSHAN: Because he is the closest Tirthankara to us. He is, as it were, the last prime minister.

BERRY: When may we expect the next Tirthankara — the twenty-fifth Tirthankara?

NANDIBHUSHAN: Strictly speaking, he will not be the twenty-fifth, but rather the first of the next cycle, which will be in another 84,000 years. He is waiting in the wings! (*laughter*)

BERRY: Might it not be a female Tirthankara? After all the nineteenth Tirthankara, Malli Kumari, was a woman. She converted six kings and made them renounce the world.

NANDIBHUSHAN: It's possible.

BERRY: Is it true that the earlier Tirthankaras lived in a sort of golden age in which all humans were vegetarian and *ahimsa* was everywhere practiced? And is it true that these Tirthankaras lived longer than the later Tirthankaras?

NANDIBHUSHAN: Since the world has been inexorably declining, life has grown shorter and more difficult for humans as well as for Tirthankaras.

BERRY: A moment ago you said that the Tirthankaras don't interfere in the lives of humans, just as humans shouldn't interfere in the lives of animals.

NANDIBHUSHAN: Yes, that's right.

BERRY: Is that why Jains are not permitted to own pets — because it would be regarded as an intrusion in their lives, a meddling with their *karmic* destiny?

NANDIBHUSHAN: As a rule Jainism discourages the keeping of pets; however, if you decide to keep a pet, you are not really committing any great infraction of the rules.

BERRY: But you say it's not encouraged.

NANDIBHUSHAN: Correct. We don't encourage the keeping of pets, as we feel it is best not to interfere in the lives of animals. They should be allowed to live free and unimpeded. Of course, when animals have been mistreated or abandoned, we believe in looking after them. We have a long tradition of establishing hospitals and rest-homes for animals. In fact, I just received in the post some photographs of an animal sanctuary that we recently opened in Gujarat. Here, take a look.

BERRY: Are these pictures of animals that you rescued from the slaughterhouse?

NANDIBHUSHAN: That's right. Jains all over India make a practice of going to slaughterhouses to try to rescue animals that are about to be butchered. For thousands of years we Jains have operated special institutions that are called *pinjarpols* for the care and protection of helpless and decrepit animals. There is scarcely a single town in Rajasthan or Gujarat that doesn't have a *pinjarpol*. We take care of stray cows, pigs, goats, sheep, birds and insects—all creatures irrespective of economic considerations. We keep veterinarians on hand to look after the animals regardless of cost.

BERRY: I've read that Jainism arose in Magadha in Northeastern India. Is that correct?

NANDIBHUSHAN: Mahavira was born in that region. The language that he spoke was Magadhi.

BERRY: Where were the other twenty-three Tirthankaras born?

NANDIBHUSHAN: Also in that same area—except Aristanemi, the twenty-second Tirthankara; he was born in Palitana in Gujarat.

BERRY: Wasn't Aristanemi also Krishna's uncle.

NANDIBHUSHAN: That's right: his brother was Krishna's father.

BERRY: So could one say that Lord Krishna descended from a Jain family?

NANDIBHUSHAN: Yes, we consider him to be a Jain as well; but it depends on which angle you're viewing him from; people have taken Krishna and formed their own religion—which is wholly divorced from Jainism. The Tirthankaras are the fathers of Jainism; Krishna, Shiva, Vishnu—these are the political fathers.

BERRY: What is the difference between Jainism and Vedic religion?

NANDIBHUSHAN: The difference is that we do not believe in *yajnas* (animal sacrifice) or *himsa* (killing). In the Vedic period, the priests practised *yajnas* and *himsa*. These practices were reformed by our twenty-third and twenty-fourth Tirthankaras—Parshwa and Mahavira.

BERRY: So you regard Hinduism as an offshoot of Jainism?

NANDIBHUSHAN: One might say that Hinduism is a corruption of Jainism.

BERRY: Was Jainism anterior to Hinduism?

NANDIBHUSHAN: Jainism has no beginning point; nor does it have an ending point; whereas, Hinduism has an historical beginning. I leave it to you to decide whether Hinduism has developed out of Jainism.

BERRY: It would seem that the influence exerted by Jainism on Hinduism has been enormous.

NANDIBHUSHAN: Without a doubt.

BERRY: I understand that Mahavira converted many Brahmins to Jainism.

NANDIBHUSHAN: That's right. Mahavira's first student (*ganadhara*) Indrabhuti Gotama, was a high-ranking Vedic priest with 500 students of his own. Gotama was alarmed to discover that many of the younger Brahmins were playing truant and going off to hear a Jain *sadhu* who claimed that he had just achieved *nirvana*; his name was Mahavira. So Gotama Swami and ten other Brahmins decided to put this upstart preacher in his place. They would engage him in a public debate and humiliate him in front of his followers. As it turned out, it was Gotama and his cohorts who were humbled: not only did Mahavira defeat them in debate, but he convinced them to become his pupils.

BERRY: How did Mahavira win them over?

NANDIBHUSHAN: He gave them the *tripadi*, and he explained Jain metaphysics to them. When Gotama Swami asked Mahavira the true meaning of life, Mahavira gave him three words in Magadhi that are known as the *tripadi*. The first word that he gave them was the Magadhi word *upaneyva*, which means "everything gets created." After a pregnant pause, he gave them the second word in Magadhi, *wigmeyva*, which means "everything on this earth gets destroyed;" after another pregnant pause, he gave them the third word in Magadhi, *dhurveyva*, or "everything remains as it is."

BERRY: Was he trying to show them the many-sidedness of the Jain view of the world that you were talking about?

NANDIBHUSHAN: Right, but he was also demonstrating that the world with all its evils and injustices was not created by God but shown by God to be what it is—an endless circle in which the time-wheel will redress all wrongs; replace bad with good, suffering with happiness. He instructed them in such Jain metaphysical doctrines as the paramount importance of *ahimsa*; the imperishable nature of the soul; the impermanence of the physical body; the viscous, sticky nature of *karma*, which clings to the spirit, etc. Gotama and the ten other Brahmins who were Mahavira's first students converted many other Brahmins to Jainism and founded lineages of ascetic disciples among the Jains.

BERRY: I've noticed that in the Hindu religion, the Brahmin performs *puja* (worship); whereas, in Jainism, the lay member performs his own *puja*. It seems more just and proper that the lay member can worship the deity directly as is possible in Jainism; whereas in Hinduism the Brahmins insert themselves between the worshipper and the god.

NANDIBHUSHAN: The Brahmins do *puja* for the sake of money; it's not done from the heart. Just as when you leave the maid in charge of your child instead of caring for it yourself—the care given it won't be the same as if you had done it yourself.

BERRY: Is it important that one do *puja*?

NANDIBHUSHAN: Yes, all Jains do *puja*. Before they can come to me for advice, they must do *puja*.

BERRY: Is there a yoga associated with Jainism?

NANDIBHUSHAN: Yes, as a matter of fact, I'm sitting in a lotus pose even as we speak. In our morning prayers we adopt so many yogic *asanas* (attitudes) that we practice it, as it were, inadvertently. There are three kinds of yoga: that of the mind; that of the body; and that of the spirit. When you gain mastery of all three, then you can gain *samadhi* (the highest state of meditation when the mind is at one with the divine).

BERRY: In your opinion, is yoga a religion?

NANDIBHUSHAN: Unquestionably.

BERRY: Did yoga originate with the Jains?

NANDIBHUSHAN: Yes, as I've said, all Indian religions have developed from Jainism.

BERRY: I've noticed that all Jain priests are *sadhus*. No other religion that I know of has *sadhus* for priests. This is peculiar to Jainism. Doesn't this suggest that *sadhuism* was a Jain idea?

NANDIBHUSHAN: Yes, the original *sadhus* were Jains.

BERRY: What is the difference between Jain *nirvana* and the Buddhist form of *nirvana*?

NANDIBHUSHAN: The Jain *nirvana* and the Buddhist *nirvana* are the same; but the Jain *nirvana* and the Hindu *nirvana* are different: in Jain *nirvana* there is a complete destruction of *karma* and the soul becomes free. In Hindu *nirvana*, there is one *atman* and everyone has a little piece of that *atman*; according to the Jains, we are all separate, but when we achieve *nirvana*, we all become one.

BERRY: Benares is the holy city that is sacred to the followers of Shiva; Vrindavan is sacred to the followers of Krishna. Is there a city in India that is sacred to Jains?

NANDIBHUSHAN: There are many sacred places, but perhaps the most paramount is Palitana in Gujarat. It is believed that if one travels to Palitana, one's *karma* will be dissolved and one can attain *nirvana*.

BERRY: How does Jainism differ from Buddhism?

NANDIBHUSHAN: In Theravada Buddhism, they maintain that it is all right to eat the flesh of an animal if the animal has not been expressly killed for you; whereas we Jains do not approve the eating of flesh under any circumstances. Furthermore, we believe that the soul is continuous and indestructible; whereas the Buddhists believe that the soul is renewed from moment to moment. In other words, your personality today is not the personality that you had yesterday, and it will be completely different tomorrow.

BERRY: Since the Buddha's philosophy bears such a marked resemblance to Jainism, I'm wondering if the Buddha might not have studied with Jain *sadhus,* or perhaps have been a Jain himself before formulating his own religious system.

NANDIBHUSHAN: Yes, I can say quite unambiguously that he did. The Buddha and Gotama (who was the first student of Mahavira) met many times. There isn't a great deal of difference between the Buddha's philosophy and Mahavira's philosophy. *Ahimsa* is paramount in both philosophies; however, Mahavira taught that everything in life gets created, which corresponds to Brahma (creation); everything in life gets destroyed, which corresponds to Shiva (destruction); and everything in life remains as it is, which corresponds to Vishnu (preservation); whereas, the Buddha in his teachings laid too much emphasis on the Shiva principle (everything gets destroyed).

BERRY: Are you implying that this tripartite division of the universe of Brahma, Vishnu, and Shiva, which animates Hindu religion, originally came from Jainism.

NANDIBHUSHAN: Yes, the understanding is that all Indian religions have grown out of Jainism.

BERRY: So the Buddha emphasized the Shiva function (everything gets destroyed) to the detriment of the other two principles of creation and preservation?

NANDIBHUSHAN: Exactly. Buddha emphasized that everything in the world gets destroyed because if you realize that everything will perish, and die, then you are less likely to become attached to them; and the Buddha was advocating a philosophy of non-attachment. But he was magnifying one aspect of life at the expense of all the others. He was viewing life from only one angle; and this is where his philosophy sharply differs from Jainism. In Jainism we call this tendency to view life from one angle *"ekantavada,"* a "one-sided view." We Jains try to view the world from all angles. We call this the philosophy of *"anekantavada,"* or non-one-sided-ness. For instance, Buddhism emphasizes the mutability of the soul; whereas, we Jains recognize that the soul can grow and change while remaining constant and indestructible.

BERRY: Could you sum up by saying that for Buddhists the self is fleeting and transitory, but for Jains it is indestructible?

NANDIBHUSHAN: For Jains the self continues after death, but it can be reincarnated as a human or an animal according to its *karma,* whereas, for the Buddhists the self is dying every minute. It is never the same from moment to moment. The self that you were five minutes ago is now extinct. Buddhism conceives of the *atman* as being a chain of linked selves that dies and is reborn every instant.

BERRY: How do they differ in their view of *moksha* (release from the wheel of rebirth)?

NANDIBHUSHAN: For Mahavira Bhagwan, *moksha* is achieved when *karma* is destroyed; for Buddha, *moksha* is achieved when the linked selves are destroyed.

BERRY: Finally, do you think that Jain ethical principles will spread thoughout the world, or will they always be confined to the ten million or so members of the Jain community?

NANDIBHUSHAN: Jainism is a very deep and demanding religious philosophy. There are only a select group of people who are lucky enough to have it as their religion and are capable of practicing it. Even the "Three Jewels" of Jainism—right thinking, right knowledge and right practice—are too difficult for most people to follow. Jainism is particular to India, which is a very sacred place. In India there is religion in every grain of sand.

BUDDHISM

Tolerant to a degree that a Christian, Muslim, or Jew might find hard to credit—not only has Buddhism been tolerant of others' religious beliefs, it has been tolerant of differing beliefs within its own system; thus within Buddhism there are many subsects such as Tibetan Buddhism, Tantric Buddhism, Ch'an, Nichiren, Shingon, Amida, Tendai and Zen Buddhism—but, generally speaking, there is little rancorous rivalry among them. Buddhism has, in the main, not forced its doctrines on anyone, nor has it waged religious wars to acquire territory or to compel non-Buddhists to convert. Buddhists do not rouse each other with martial hymns like "Onward Buddhist Soldiers" or "A Mighty Fortress is our Buddha." There has never been a Buddhist Inquisition in which heretics have been burnt at the stake, or a Buddhist war of annihilation in which the occupants of a "holy land" have been exterminated. Instead, it has peacefully coexisted with and adapted itself to the indigenous faiths of other lands. Just as by spreading *ahimsa* culture throughout India, Jainism formed the non-violent substratum of the Indian character,[1] so Mahayana Buddhism—which is essentially an exportable Jainism—by spreading *ahimsa* culture throughout East Asia, seems to have formed the non-violent substratum of the character of the East Asian peoples, who until the twentieth century were largely vegetarian.[2] The first precept has given Buddhism the strong ethical foundation—particularly with respect to the human treatment of other life forms—that the indigenous customs and faiths of other countries might have lacked. Therefore, Buddhist missionaries have often been called in to supply this lack. Its flexibility and willingness to adapt have been responsible for its ability to spread to other countries and take firm root. Not so long ago, it was the religion of all East Asia. Now it appears to be going west. Indeed, there are now more Buddhists in America than there are in India, the country of its origin. In the West, its message of non-violent eating and living, embodied in the word *ahimsa* (loosely translated as "reverence for life") is most urgently needed. It was the Buddha's desire to reform the animal sacrifices of the Vedic priests in India during the sixth century BCE that provided Buddhism with its original impetus. At this time the Vedic priests, or Brahmins, engaged in animal sacrifice to appease the old Rg Vedic gods Agni, Indra, and Rudra, who had an insatiable appetite for horses, bulls, and cows. Indra alone is said to have devoured a thousand cows at one sitting.

To pay for these costly sacrifices, the Brahmins imposed crippling taxes on the people. By launching a vigorous attack against the sacrifice of animals on moral grounds, and by asserting that every Buddhist could be his own priest, the Buddha challenged the caste criteria on which the Brahmins based their moral and social superiority. As a direct result of the Buddha and Mahavira's teachings, the rigid caste structure of Brahminism was modified, and animal sacrifice was eventually abolished. The Buddha's reforms improved conditions for animals even as they improved conditions for humans—thus showing in rather striking fashion that the fate of humans and animals are inextricably linked.

The son of a prince of Indian-Mongolian stock in a small kingdom in Northeastern India (Lumbini Garden in what is now modern Nepal), Siddhartha Gautama was born (in 563 BCE) like Mahavira into the *kshatriya* or warrior caste. It is a curious fact that the warrior caste has produced so many ethical vegetarian reformers—Tolstoy, Mahavira, the Buddha, and Henry Salt. (Salt, the son of a British colonel who had helped subjugate India to the British Raj, coined the phrase "animal rights.") Like his contemporary Mahavira, the Buddha renounced the world when he was in his twenties; he gave up the privileged life of a pampered young princeling for the begging bowl and the loincloth of a *sannyasi* (an ascetic seeker). After years of wandering as a mendicant ascetic, he gained the insight that all life is suffering and that we should resign ourselves to that fate by moderating our desires and following the middle way between self-indulgence and self-mortification. Reality itself is illusory; and the self or personality that perceives it is merely a bundle of psychosomatic states that are inherently unstable. Even though this assemblage of psychosomatic states that are called "self" is highly unstable, the Buddha taught that the self could reincarnate, and one's incarnation in the next life would be determined by one's *karma*. Fundamental to the Buddha's *dharma* teaching is the first precept that humans should refrain from killing or causing harm to their fellow creatures. This meant that the Buddha followed a strict vegetarian regimen and that he expected his followers to do the same.

Although the Buddha himself was a strict vegetarian and forbade the killing of animals for food, he predicted that some of his meat-eating followers would manipulate his teachings to make them appear to condone the practice of flesh-eating. Flexible as he might have been in other matters, the *Lankavatara Sutra* makes it plain that when it came to the eating of animal flesh he was fiercely uncompromising:

"For the sake of love of purity, the Bodhisattva should refrain from eating flesh, which is born of semen, blood, etc. For fear of causing terror to living beings, let the Bodhisattva, who is disciplining himself to attain compassion, refrain from eating flesh....

"It is not true that meat is proper food and permissible when the animal was not killed by himself, when he did not order others to kill it, when it was not specially meant for him. Again, there may be some people in the future who...being under the influence of the taste for meat will string together in various ways sophistic arguments to defend meat-eating....

"But meat-eating in any form, in any manner, and in any place is unconditionally and once for all prohibited.... Meat eating, I have not permitted to anyone, I do not permit, I will not permit...."[3]

Another Mahayana *sutra* that clearly condemns flesh-eating is the *Suranangama Sutra*:

"The reason for practicing *dhyana*[4] and seeking to attain *samadhi*[5] is to escape from the suffering of life, but in seeking to escape from suffering ourselves why should we inflict it upon others? Unless you can so control your minds that even the thought of brutal unkindness and killing is abhorrent, you will never be able to escape from the bondage of the world's life....After my *parinirvana* in the last *kalpa*[6] different kinds of ghosts will be encountered everywhere deceiving people and teaching them that they can eat meat and still attain enlightenment....How can a *bhikshu*, who hopes to become a deliverer of others, himself be living on the flesh of other sentient beings?"[7]

The Mahayana version of the *Mahaparinirvana Sutra* sums it all up when it states: "The eating of meat extinguishes the seed of great compassion."

It is quite clear that Buddha was from the same *Sramanic*[8] renouncer tradition as Mahavira. In all likelihood, the Buddha was himself a Jain, and his teachings were a stripped down version of Jainism designed for the export market. Certainly his teaching of the first precept (to cherish all life and to do no harm); his *sadhuism;* his contempt for Vedic religious rituals, especially animal sacrifice; his glorification of *ahimsa;* his carrying of a whisk with which to sweep the path of insects; his use of a water strainer to filter out organisms from his drinking water—all smack of Jainism. In fact, the five ethical precepts of Buddhism are identical to those preached by Mahavira. Significantly, both Buddhism and Jainism give pride of place to the non-injury to all other life forms.

The *Jataka Tales*, which the Buddha himself may have authored,[9] show his ethical vegetarian teachings in action. From these tales— in which animals (some of which, like the deer, were previous incarnations of the Buddha) interact as equals with humans to point a moral—it is evident that Buddhism, after Jainism, was one of the world's first animal protection societies. After reading the *Jataka Tales,* in which the Buddha himself often forfeits his life to save that of an animal, or the *Lankavatara Sutra,* one of the earliest *sutras* of Buddhism, it is impossible to believe that he would have condoned the eating of animal flesh whether it had been killed for someone else or not. Nor is it possible to believe that the Buddha died from eating tainted flesh. In his book, *To Cherish All Life,* Philip Kapleau Roshi has pointed out that this controversy over the Buddha's last meal has been settled once and for all. (It was poisonous mushrooms, "food beloved of pigs," *sukara maddava*, not "pig's flesh," that killed the Buddha.) The Roshi says: "Within the Buddhist tradition, one hears today of Buddhist priests, monks and teachers who do eat meat under certain circumstances. Their justification seems to be that Buddha himself ate a piece of meat at the home of one of his followers rather than hurt the feelings of his host. 'Like Buddha,' these priests may say, 'we gratefully eat whatever is put before us, without preference or aversion;' (The 'meat,' it turned out, was putrid and it poisoned Buddha, causing his death.) And then they may add, 'And are you not also aware that Buddha laid down the rule that one must refrain from eating meat only if one knows, hears, or suspects the animal has been killed specifically for one's own consumption?'

"What they gloss over with respect to the first proposition is the research of scholars, the majority of whom contend that it was not a piece of meat but a poisonous truffle (a species of mushroom) that caused the Buddha's death; and what they ignore with respect to the second are the Mahayana scriptures which unequivocally condemn meat-eating."[10]

I asked Philip Kapleau Roshi, founder of the first vegetarian Zendo in America, how the rumor got started that the Buddha ate spoiled meat at his last supper, and how it was that people thought the Buddha had winked at flesh-eating. Kapleau Roshi said that it was because almost from the start, some very powerful Buddhists have been meat-lovers. Kapleau Roshi believes that just as the gospel accounts of Jesus's having eaten fish were falsified by princes of the Church who were much addicted to flesh-eating, so also did certain early

Buddhists go to the length of corrupting texts and fabricating phony *sutras* to justify their appetite for animal flesh.[11]

As with most religious movements, shortly after the Buddha's *parinirvana*,[12] a schism arose among his followers that split Buddhism into two schools: the Mahayana, or Northern school, and the Theravada, or Southern school. Mahayana literally means "the big raft" or "vehicle," from the same root as the Latin *magna*, "big," and the Sanskrit word *yana*, "raft," or "ferry." *Yanas* were a very important mode of transport in ancient India, where roads were often rendered impassable by rain-swollen rivers and streams. It was necessary, therefore, to use a raft or ferry to make one's way, especially during the monsoon season when it can rain for weeks without stopping. (It is instructive that the word for the great world teachers in Jainism is *Tirthankara*, which means "ford maker" or "crossing maker.") People saw the Buddha's teachings as a raft, or *yana*, that enabled the wary traveler to cross the treacherous waters of life and pass to the other side. However, the Mahayanists regarded the teachings of the Theravada school as self-seeking and egocentric, so they scornfully referred to the Theravadins as the *Hinayana*, or "small raft," because their doctrines were so self-centered that there was room on the raft for only one person—the *arhat*, or monk. On the contrary, the teachings of the Mahayana were all-inclusive; there was room on the big raft for the laity and all creatures, not excluding frogs, snakes, spiders and insects, who also possessed the Buddha nature.

Perhaps the most striking difference between the two schools is their attitude towards the first precept. It is a curious fact that in the Mahayana countries, such as China, Korea, Nepal, Mongolia, Vietnam and Japan, the Buddha's teachings against flesh-eating and animal abuse are faithfully preserved (in the *Lankavatara Sutra*, etc.), but in the Hinayana countries, such as Sri Lanka, Burma, Thailand and Cambodia, the first precept is widely flouted.[13] In Hinayana countries laypeople revere the monks as though they were saffron-robed demigods and there is an impassable gulf between the laity and the priests. In the Mahayana lands, however, priests and laity are treated as fellow-seekers, or comrades. So, if these saffron demigods, the Hinayana monks, are eating animal flesh, which they do unabashedly, it sets a bad example for the laity. To justify their monks' eating animal flesh, the Hinayanists invented the spurious *sutra*, that they attributed to the Buddha, that: "If the animal was not killed expressly for you, then it's permissible to eat its flesh."

In his book, *To Cherish All Life*, Kapleau Roshi loses little time in demolishing this specious argument. It's worth quoting him at length: "How plausible is it that the Buddha sanctioned the eating of animal flesh by his monks in all circumstances except when they had reason to suspect the animal had been killed specifically for them? Aren't domestic animals slaughtered for whoever eats their meat?....So if the Buddha actually uttered the statements attributed to him, what they would mean effectively is that with the exception of the handful of persons who were offered meat from an animal killed just for them—and of course hunters, slaughterers and fishermen—he freely sanctioned meat-eating for everyone, including his monks. Not only does this contention fly in the face of the first precept (which makes the one who causes another to take life equally culpable), it also implies that the Buddha approved of butchering and the horrors of the slaughterhouse. Yet slaughtering is one of the trades forbidden to Buddhists, and with good reason. To say on the one hand that the Buddha sanctioned flesh-eating in all cases except those that are already noted, and on the other that he condemned the bloody trades of slaughtering, hunting and trapping, not only denies the link between the two, it involves one in an absurd contradiction."[14]

Not only do the two main schools of Buddhism differ sharply on their interpretation of the first precept, they differ on other key points as well: The Mahayanists believe that the Buddha's most important work started after he had attained Nirvana. Not content to sit in a lotus position and be a contemplative for the rest of his life, the Buddha made the decision that Arnold Toynbee considered to be more momentous for mankind than the founding of the Platonic Academy: He set out to share his religious system and his hard-won spiritual insights with others. "He attained perfect knowledge and tried to save all sentient beings."[15] Above all else, he sought to reduce the amount of suffering (*dukkah*) in the world not only for humans but also for animals (who are seen as being potential Buddhas). To this end, the Buddha taught that humans, in addition to practicing the cessation of desire, must hold the life of animals to be sacred and inviolable. That is why the first and most important precept is to do no harm to any living creature (not excluding frogs, snakes, spiders and insects). The Mahayana school also preserves the tradition that it was more important for a would-be Buddha to help others to achieve salvation than for a would-be Buddha or Bodhisattva[16] to achieve Nirvana for him- or herself alone.

On the other hand, in the Theravada or Hinayana school, only humans are regarded as possessing the Buddha nature; and only monks are capable of reaching Nirvana. The Hinayana teaches that it was the events leading up to the Buddha's Nirvana, i.e., the fasting, the meditating, the enlightenment, that are important — not what came after. Not the ministry; not the spreading of the doctrine of *ahimsa;* not the Buddha's noble efforts to save all sentient beings. Since, in the Hinayana scheme, it falls to the lot of only a select few to attain Nirvana, theirs (the Hinayana) is a narrowly-focused, elitist enterprise, for priests only. There is room on the raft for the *arhat,* or monk, but not for anyone else, and certainly not for animals, much less for frogs, snakes, spiders and insects. As we've seen, Kapleau Roshi, who is the world's foremost authority on the first precept, has shown us how fatuous it is to say that the Buddha ever sanctioned eating flesh taken from an animal that has not been specifically killed for the eater! How then did this phony *sutra* get into the Pali[17] canon, which the Hinayanists claim is the oldest Buddhist tradition? As Kapleau Roshi reconstructs it, the Hinayanist hierarchy were inveterate meat-lovers, who, to justify their decadent tastes, made up the specious argument and attributed it to the Buddha — "If an animal has not been specifically killed for your benefit, then it is permissible to eat it."

Still, a question remains: How did these words attributed to the

Buddha get into the Pali canon? The answer is simple: monks and scribes still attached to meat-eating put them there. After the Buddha's passing, three councils were held over a hundred years to establish the Buddhist canon, that is, to establish what material was "legitimate" and what was not. Obviously, this entailed much discussion, selection and emendation. Can anyone doubt that throughout this period the utterances of the Buddha or those attributed to him were expanded, subtracted, rewritten, recopied and arranged to suit the tastes, dispositions and interpretations of the elders of the various Buddhist schools who took part in this lengthy process? Leading Buddhist scholars who have spent many years studying and translating the Pali *sutras* into English don't doubt it.

While Oldenberg, Foucher, Rhys Davids, and other respected Buddhist scholars of another generation regard portions of the Pali canon as suspect, a contemporary Buddhologist goes even further. In his *Thirty Years of Buddhist Studies*, Edward Conze reminds us that the Buddha spoke not Pali, but a dialect called Magadhi, and that all his sayings are lost in their original form.[18]

Despite the anti-vegetarian sophistries of the Hinayanists, it is remarkable how the spirit of the first precept still pervaded such Hinayana countries as Sri Lanka, Burma, Thailand, Laos and Cambodia right up to the early 1960s. It is as if the people in those countries, by ignoring the Hinayana priests' finessing of the first precept, were determined to keep from eating animal flesh anyhow. Although Kapleau Roshi witnessed monks guzzling animal flesh when he was a guest at a Hinayana monastery in Rangoon in the early 1950s, he quotes other Western visitors to Hinayana monasteries who noted the monks' vegetarian proclivities: "Alexandra David Neel, who spent many years in Tibet, tells us that while Tibetans in general are fond of meat, many lamas entirely abstain from animal food, and if they eat meat or not, all except followers of Tantric doctrines declare that meat-eating is an evil action which brings harmful results to those who are guilty of it and 'creates a deleterious psychic atmosphere in places where it is habitually eaten.' She also says that in the Sagain Mountains in Burma she has known whole communities of *bhikkus* (ordained members of the Order) who were strictly vegetarian. Surely this shows that even in Theravadin countries not all monks and lay people subscribed to the Pali version of what the Buddha supposedly said about meat-eating. She also points out that there were many pious laymen who imitated them in Tibet."[19]

Another Western traveler, the actor and pacifist Lew Ayres, while filming a documentary on comparative religion in East Asia in the 1950s, had seen so few people eating flesh, even in the Hinayana countries that he concluded (mistakenly) that nearly all Buddhists are vegetarians.[20] More recently, however, a British journalist visited a Hinayana monastery in Burma and was served "pickled vegetables and fried locusts."[21] (Evidently, it's considered okay to eat grasshoppers if they've not been killed specifically for your benefit!) But something far more insidious than this phony Pali *sutra* was at work, undermining the first precept and making flesh-eating suddenly modish and popular.

After the Second World War, the might and power of the Western nations were in the ascendant, and it wasn't lost on the war-ravaged, financially pinched peoples of East Asia that business leaders, film stars and other glamorous trendsetters in the West were avid eaters of animal flesh. So Asians made the grave mistake of trying to copy the Westerners' diet as well as their industrial technology and their fashions with the result that their rates of cancer and heart disease, diseases associated with the Western meat-centered diet, climbed dramatically. Of the Mahayana country, Japan, where he had lived and studied for many years, soy-foods pioneer and former Zen Buddhist monk, William Shurtleff, author of *The Book of Tofu*, says: "The taboos against meat-eating were very strictly observed until 1868, which was when the Meiji Restoration took place....There has been a steady and accelerating consumption of meat there until 1983 when the Japanese started to become aware of the perils of imitating the Western diet."[22]

The *Encyclopedia of Buddhism* points out that prior to the twentieth century, vegetarianism was closely observed in the Mahayana countries of Japan and China: "In China and Japan, the eating of meat was looked upon as an evil and was ostracized."[23] However, as a result of the Westernization that had taken hold there, vegetarianism declined sharply among the common people. Just how far it has declined may be gauged from the fact that in Japan as recently as 1856, when the visiting American ambassador, Townsend Harris, ordered beefsteak, his Japanese hosts—politely kowtowing to the ambassador's decadent tastes—slaughtered the cow with thinly-concealed revulsion and erected a plaque in honor of the murdered creature.[24]

Even fish-eating was looked down upon: As Kapleau Roshi points out, up to the end of the nineteenth century, meat-eating was such a taboo that a term of opprobrium for a Zen monk who ate fish was *namagusu bozu:* "You unholy monk, stinking of raw fish!" And in China at the turn of the century the first precept of Buddhism was such a vital force that the Chinese were shocked to see Westerners tearing and slashing at scorched animal parts with knives and forks.[25]

Now that Buddhism seems poised to establish itself in the West as a major faith, it is important that it reaffirm the first precept and rededicate itself to nonviolent eating, lest Buddhism become just another protestant sect with a utilitarian view of animals. It is instructive to cast back and look into the palace kitchens of the Indian emperor Ashoka (273-232 BCE) who transformed Buddhism from a fledgling sect into a world religion. In Rock Edict One (in the style of the Zoroastrian Persian kings, Ashoka inscribed his royal decrees on huge rock faces) he put an end to the killing and eating of animals in the royal kitchens.[26] In Rock Edict Two, he ordered the setting up of medical facilities for men and beasts.[27] No footling monarch he, Ashoka was the grandson of Chandragupta Maurya, one of the mightiest and most rapacious conquerors in Indian history, who, with the aid of the brilliant Brahmin strategist, Kautilya, author of the *Arthashastra* (a handbook of statecraft and warcraft), piled up more territory than any previous Indian ruler. Jain tradition has it that in his dotage, Chandragupta abdicated his throne and became a Jain *sadhu,* who wandered his kingdom, begging for alms. If the legend is true, then converting to an *ahimsa*-based religion was something of a family trait; for it was at the height of his career as a conqueror that Ashoka sacked his Brahmin strategists, whom he had also inherited from his grandfather, and adopted Buddhism as India's state religion. From then on, his governmental policies were guided by the first precept.

What was it that made one of India's bloodiest rulers do such a *volte-face?* The answer may be found in another of his famous rock inscriptions. In this rock edict he says that it was his conquest of Kalinga, the gateway to the South, which cost over 100,000 lives, that had pricked his conscience.[28] Disillusioned with his Brahmin strategists (who had urged him to take Kalinga to give his empire an eastern seaboard), he turned to the Buddhist sages. They advised him to embrace the first precept, to give up eating animals and to cease waging war. Under their guidance, Ashoka became one of the most enlightened rulers in the annals of humankind. By sending Buddhist missionaries far and wide to preach *ahimsa* and the first precept, Ashoka made Buddhism into a world religion. ✥

R.B.

• • • • • • • • • • • •

[1] Vilas A. Sangave, "Jain Society and National Culture," in *Medieval Jainism: Culture and Environment*, ed. P. S. Jain and R. M. Ladha, (New Delhi: Ashish Publishing House, 1990), p. 10.

[2] Philip Kapleau, *To Cherish All Life: A Buddhist Case for Becoming Vegetarian* (New York: Harper & Row, 1982), pp. 34-8.

[3] *The Lankavatara Sutra*, trans., Daisetz Suzuki, (London: Routledge: 1932). (cited in Kapleau, *ibid*.)

[4] *Dhyana*: "concentration of mind," a one-pointed, concentrated and awakened mind.

[5] *Samadhi:* equilibrium, tranquillity and one-pointedness, a state of intense yet effortless concentration, of complete absorption of the mind in itself, of heightened and expanded awareness.

[6] *Kalpa:* the period of time between the beginning of a world cycle and its extinction; an incalculably long time.

[7] *A Buddhist Bible*, ed., Dwight Goddard, (New York: Dutton, 1952), pp. 264-65. (cited in Kapleau).

[8] *Sramanic*: See essay on Jainism.

[9] Christopher Key Chapple, *Nonviolence to Animals, Earth, and Self in Asian Traditions* (Albany: State University of New York Press, 1993), p. 223.

[10] Kapleau, *op. cit.*, pp. 23-5.

[11] *ibid.*, pp. 39-43.

[12] *Parinirvana: lit.*, "complete extinction," a term usually referring to the passing away of the Buddha.

[13] Kapleau, *op. cit.*, pp. 28-9.

[14] *ibid.*, pp. 30-1.

[15] Beatrice Lane Suzuki, *Mahayana Buddhism: A Brief Outline* (New York: Macmillan, 1969), p. 33.

[16] *Bodhisattva*: a Sanskrit word meaning an enlightened being. In Buddhism: one who seeks enlightenment to help all living beings.

[17] *Pali*: the language in which the scriptures of Theravada Buddhism are written. Known also as Southern Buddhism, the Theravada arose in India and traveled to Sri Lanka, Burma, Thailand, Cambodia, and the West.

[18] Kapleau, *op. cit.*, pp. 39-41.

[19] *ibid.*, p. 35.

[20] Lew Ayres, *Altars of the East* (New York: Doubleday, 1956), pp. 83-93.

[21] Stanley Stewart, "Buddha Without Bowlers," *The Sunday Telegraph*, (The Sunday Review), April 21, 1996, p. 17.

[22] Rynn Berry, *The New Vegetarians* (New York: Pythagorean Publishers, 1993), pp. 33-34.

[23] *Encyclopedia of Buddhism*, ed. G. P. Mahalaskera (Govt. of Ceylon Press, 1963) pp. 1, 2, 291.

[24] Steven Rosen, "Ahimsa: Animals and the East," *The Animals' Agenda*, October 10, 1990, Vol. X, no. 8, p. 21.

[25] Kapleau, *op. cit.*, p. 38.

[26] N. A. Nikam and Richard McKeon, ed. and tr. *The Edicts of Ashoka* (Chicago: University of Chicago Press, 1959), p. 55.

[27] Nikam and McKeon, p. 64.

[28] *ibid.*, p. 27

Conversation/Buddhism

....

ROSHI PHILIP KAPLEAU

FOR THE PAST THIRTY YEARS, the Venerable Philip Kapleau, founder of the Rochester Zen Center, has been one of the most influential figures in American Buddhism. Having served as the chief court reporter at the International Military Tribunal at Nuremberg, and the International Military Tribunal for the Far East in Tokyo, Kapleau Roshi gave up his court reporting business and trained as a Zen monk in Japan and Burma for 13 years under three Zen masters. After being ordained by Zen Master Yasutani Hakuun in 1963, Kapleau Roshi returned to America, and in Rochester, New York, in 1966, he established America's first all-vegetarian Zendo. A prolific author, Kapleau Roshi's books have won him an international readership. His classic, *The Three Pillars of Zen* is in its 30th year of publication and has been translated into ten languages including Polish and Chinese. Other books include *Zen Dawn in the West, To Cherish All Life,* and his most recent, *The Wheel of Life and Death.* A passionate advocate of vegetarianism and animal rights, Kapleau Roshi—in his public addresses, essays and books, such as *To Cherish All Life*—has attempted to reinvigorate the first precept of the Buddha's teaching "not to kill, but to cherish all life." The Zendo in

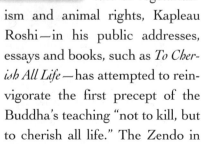

....

57

Hollywood, Florida, where I interviewed Kapleau Roshi, with its profusion of tropical flowers and its dank, mango-scented air was punctuated with birdsong. It seemed an appropriate place to be interviewing a Buddhist sage, as I recalled that the Buddha's birthplace, Lumbini Garden, and the towns in India where the Buddha taught, such as Saranath and Benares, were also rioting with flowers the ambient air, doubtless also mango-scented and punctuated with birdsong.

. . . .

BERRY: As I understand it, the Buddha and his followers were wending their way through the kingdom of Magadha—the present state of Bihar—on what Zen Buddhists call a *takuhatsu*, or "going forth to proclaim the *dharma*," when he was invited to dinner at the home of Chunda, a metalworker. (Metalworkers were held in almost religious awe and enjoyed a high social status throughout the ancient world.) Among the dishes that the Buddha was served by Chunda was the fatal dish that carried him off in his eightieth year; it was called "*sukara maddava*," which can be rendered either as a subjective genitive, "pig's flesh," or an objective genitive, "food beloved of pigs," in other words, a tree mushroom, or truffle, of which pigs are excessively fond.

Is it not customary, even today on a *takuhatsu*, for a Buddhist monk to feel compelled to eat the food that is set before him by an almsgiver, even if the monk is a vegetarian? So perhaps the Buddha was putting protocol above the first precept?

KAPLEAU: As I said in my book *To Cherish All Life*, I seriously question that Chunda, who was a follower of the Buddha, or any other close follower of the Buddha, would ever serve him a meat dish. It was well known how the Buddha felt about this: meat was no part of his diet. There are so many indications that the Buddha adhered to a strict vegetarian diet that it isn't likely that Chunda would have offered him a meat dish.

As you know, there has been a controversy about this matter—

one that I think has now been resolved. Most scholars are now convinced that it was a poisonous truffle that the Buddha ate, and not toxic meat. So I would be loath to accept that story in the manner in which people who want to make a case for meat-eating choose to interpret it.

BERRY: It's ironic that this word *"sukara maddava"* had that curious ambiguity so that it can be quoted to serve the purpose of the meat-eater as well as the vegetarian.

KAPLEAU: Mrs. Rhys David, that fine Buddhist scholar, in her *A Manual of Buddhism*, casts the "pig's flesh" interpretation into further doubt when she observes: "A food compound of pig-flesh *(sukara-mamsa)* does occur once in the scriptures, in a *sutta* of a curiously unworthy kind, where a householder, in inviting Gotama to dine, goes through quite a menu in a refined detail! *Maddava* is nowhere else associated with meat, and I remain of Rhys David's opinion that we have here a root, such as truffles, much sought by swine, and which may have been called 'pigs' joy.' Such a root we actually have—this the critics did not know—in our 'pignut'...the little nut-shaped bulbous roots of which, called also 'earthnuts,' are liked by both pigs and children."

BERRY: Didn't you have a similar experience on a *takuhatsu* in Japan when you were a monk in training? You were developing a strong aversion to meat at that time; however, a well-meaning alms-giver, thinking that you were given to the stereotypical American tastes at that time, served you steak, coffee, and brandy; and your roshi insisted that you eat it.

KAPLEAU: He didn't insist, but later on he explained that these simple villagers think that all Americans like to eat steak. If I didn't eat a little of it, he said, I would hurt their feelings. So I ate most of it and got very sick. Then when I went to the big boss—the abbot—and told him about it, he said, "You don't have to eat anything that doesn't agree with you."

BERRY: Was the abbot a vegetarian?

KAPLEAU: The abbot was a strict vegetarian and a teetotaler—but the assistant abbot was a meat-eater and a heavy drinker; it was the classic case of a teetotaling father with a booze-drinking son.

BERRY: Nevertheless, the abbot did tolerate his assistant's foibles.

KAPLEAU: Yes, he did.

BERRY: Doesn't this say something for Zen training—that it enables one to become long-suffering and forgiving?

KAPLEAU: Since everybody possesses the all-embracing nothing-lacking Buddha nature, you can't condemn anybody. The most you can do is feel bad about one's errant ways; but you know that eventually, given good *karma* and sympathetic treatment, he will turn out to be a fine person in the end. And the assistant did too. He became the head abbot.

BERRY: Did he reform his diet?

KAPLEAU: I wasn't around, so I don't know of my own knowledge, but I was told he did.

BERRY: As I understand it, there are two main branches of Buddhism: the Theravada (or Southern School) and the Mahayana (or Northern School). The Mahayana promotes vegetarianism and holds the first precept in high regard; whereas the Theravada school tends to ignore the first precept and to condone flesh-eating.

KAPLEAU: First of all, we should be clear that the precepts do not compel abstention from meat. The first precept is "not to kill but to cherish all life." The implication, of course, is that one should practice vegetarianism. Still, it's not quite right to say that the Theravada ignores the first precept, and that the Mahayana promotes vegetarianism, though indirectly it does. In the Theravada tradition you can eat meat only if you haven't seen or heard or suspected that the animal hasn't been killed especially for you. But there's no such sanction in any of the Mahayana scriptures.

BERRY: Do you think there was an interpolation of texts in the Pali Canon?

KAPLEAU: Yes, and I say so in my book *To Cherish All Life.*

BERRY: You suggest that there may have been some meat-loving priests who tampered with the texts.

KAPLEAU: That's right. This phenomenon can be seen in several religious traditions.

BERRY: Not excepting Christianity?

KAPLEAU: In the Buddhist canon the doctrines which cover more than the words attributed to the Buddha have not, I believe, been tampered with, but the stories and incidents have certainly been tampered with to suit the preference of the meat-loving priests. In *To Cherish All Life*, I cited several cases where there had been deliberate changes made in the *sutras*, so there isn't the slightest doubt in my mind that this took place.

BERRY: You are talking about the Theravada school?

KAPLEAU: Yes. But it also happened in the Mahayana—perhaps not with respect to meat-eating but with respect to other matters. This is because in the Mahayana *sutras* there are numerous strict injunctions against meat-eating.

BERRY: In the Mahayana, the *Lankavatara sutra* is openly critical of flesh-eating among the followers of the Theravada tradition.

KAPLEAU: To be fair, I should say that when I was in Japan I saw many followers of the Mahayana eat meat, and I am sure they still do.

BERRY: So they are not necessarily holier than the Theravadins.

KAPLEAU: By no means. In the countries that practice Theravada Buddhism they openly eat meat, citing scriptural authority. They cite this apocryphal saying of the Buddha: that you may not eat the flesh of an animal if you know or suspect it was killed expressly for you.

BERRY: In Sri Lanka, which is a bastion of Theravada Buddhism, the Theravada Buddhists hire Christians, Muslims, and Indian Harijans (untouchables) to slaughter animals for their table.

KAPLEAU: When I was in Ceylon in the 1950s I didn't hear about that sort of thing, but certainly Buddhists ate meat there. As I point out in my book on vegetarianism, all the outstanding teachers of the Theravada and the Mahayana traditions condemn the taking of animal life, especially if one is on a spiritual path. How can anyone pretend that any form of life is inferior and that therefore animals have no rights?

One could take it entirely out of the religious sphere and simply put it on the humanitarian plane. It's a matter of justice.

BERRY: Since you trained as a Zen monk in Japanese monasteries and have lived in Japan for a number of years, how would you characterize the Japanese diet?

KAPLEAU: Although Japan is nominally a Buddhist country, the Japanese now eat a great deal of meat and fish. Apart from flesh foods, they eat a great deal of tofu and sea vegetables as well as other vegetables. In addition, they eat a lot of rice. And of course there are many dishes with miso. So their diet can be called a good one.

BERRY: Would you impute this eating of meat and fish to the Western influence on Japan that began with the Meiji Restoration in the mid-nineteenth century?

KAPLEAU: That would probably be true as respects meat. Starting from the Meiji period, when they began Westernizing at a furious pace, trying to catch up with the West, they began adopting a lot of Western manners and customs. At first, however, the Japanese and the Chinese regarded Westerners as barbarians, but then they began to emulate them. The Chinese in particular were shocked by what they called the barbarities of Westerners in regard to flesh-eating. By way of example, let me cite this passage from my book, *To Cherish All Life*: "This Chinese scholar, who had just returned from his first visit to America, was asked 'Are the American people civilized?' 'Civilized? Far from it....They eat the flesh of bullocks and sheep in enormous quantities....It is carried into the dining room in huge chunks, often half raw. They pluck and slash and tear it apart, and they eat with knives and prongs, which make a civilized being quite nervous. One fancies himself in the presence of sword swallowers."

BERRY: This was at the turn of the century in 1906. The Buddhist precepts were still in force in China at that time?

KAPLEAU: Yes, in China and to a large extent in Japan.

BERRY: In emulating the West, they appear to have adopted the flesh-eating practices of the West as well.

KAPLEAU: That's right. Like anything the Japanese do or adopt, they do it so thoroughly that it puts others to shame. I remember one time reading in a Japanese newspaper about these Texas cattlemen who, when they came to Japan, were given a taste of Kobe beef, which was from cattle that had been massaged and fed on beer. The Texans grudgingly had to admit that this Kobe beef tasted better than any beef that they'd ever tasted in Texas. As for fish, the Japanese have always eaten it.

BERRY: When you were training as a Zen monk in the monasteries of Japan, was the food served to the monks strictly vegetarian?

KAPLEAU: Only vegetarian food was served in the three monasteries where I trained. But, sad to say, when the abbot went to town—to Tokyo perhaps—and was going to be gone for a few days, then the monks would surreptitiously go out and buy meat dishes they were fond of. In a certain barn-like structure adjoining the monastery they would furtively devour these dishes.

BERRY: The food in the Zen monasteries—the *shojin ryori*, as it is called—is noted for being bland: rice gruel and pickled vegetables. How would you characterize it?

KAPLEAU: In the Zen monasteries where I trained, the food was very plain. Rice was served three times a day. Now that's not nearly so bad as it sounds; in fact, the rice was exceptionally tasty. It was a long grain rice that is grown in the paddies. Once my body adjusted to it—it took about a year or a year and a half—I began to enjoy it immensely. In the morning we usually had rice gruel with some *umeboshi* (sour plums) and tea. For lunch, which is the main meal, we would have miso soup, a few vegetables, and rice; for supper, the leftovers from the other two meals. However, during special celebrations we ate lots of nourishing vegetarian food, such as mountain potatoes, sesame, black beans, mushrooms, lotus root, tofu, and many varieties of sea vegetables. In the cities, older Japanese ate these same foods, in addition, of course, to fish. I say "of course" because many Japanese regard fish as not a flesh food. Once when I was teaching at our Zen Center in Costa Rica, I was invited by a high Japanese official (who happened to be a member of our Zen group) to stay at his home during my brief visit. I told him that he should be aware that I was a vegetarian. He replied, "You mean you don't even eat fish?" "No I don't eat fish." "Really?" He just couldn't believe it. To he and his wife's credit, during my entire stay they didn't serve meat or fish, nor did they eat any themselves.

BERRY: How often did the monks go on begging expeditions?

KAPLEAU: The English word "begging" is not appropriate in this context because it doesn't begin to describe what's involved in *takuhatsu,* going forth to proclaim the truth of the Buddha's dharma, the Buddha's teaching. The monks on *takuhatsu* exemplify in their own lives the truth of the Buddha's teaching. In return, they are economically sustained by the people who believe in the Buddha's dharma. So when they go on *takuhatsu* they will have a large bag tied around their neck in which people will deposit raw rice, vegetables, and similar foods. Additionally, they will have a bowl into which money usually will be placed. Receiver and giver bow to each other in mutual respect and appreciation. It's a meaningful religious practice that is designed to teach one humility. It could be particularly humiliating to have young pranksters from the village put stones into one's begging bowl, while others more subtly goaded or taunted the monks to provoke anger in them.

However, since I was a *gaijin,* or foreigner, I was spared these pranks and japes. In fact, I received more donations than any of the other monks. All the little children and their parents waited to put donations into my bowl as a way of encouraging me by showing their appreciation. It was a beautiful gesture on their part.

BERRY: Why did you feel that you had to travel to Japan to study Zen in a monastery?

KAPLEAU: When I was in Japan I was asked the same question many times: "Why would you, an American, come to Japan, which after the war is so prostrate and poor? Why would you give up the comforts of American life to endure the austerities of a Zen monastery in Japan?" I said I did it because I actually needed to do it, that it was my *karma*. Very often one must go abroad to learn the truth about oneself.

BERRY: Yes, it was Calvino, I think, who said "A traveler only comes to know a city after he arrives at another."

KAPLEAU: How true. And wasn't it Kipling who said, "What does he of England know who only England knows?" Travel often brings one back to oneself.

BERRY: When did you change your diet once and for all?

KAPLEAU: In 1966, when I opened the Zen center in Rochester, New York, we began getting these wonderful young people of the '60s, the so-called "flower children." They were so idealistic that had I not been a vegetarian at that time I'm sure they never would have stayed. That's when I finally determined to become a strict vegetarian. Up until that time I had been an on-and-off vegetarian.

BERRY: In the Zen monastery the job of *tenzo*, or cook, is one of the most venerated, I understand, and is usually given to a senior monk. Did you ever hold this position at any of the Zen monasteries where you trained in Japan?

KAPLEAU: No, because at that time I was a trainee, a beginner, and therefore not considered to be advanced enough. You've got to be highly developed spiritually in order to be a *tenzo*. My teacher used to say that if a person's mind is not equable, if it is anxious or disturbed, these vibrations seep into the food and have an adverse effect on sensitive individuals. This is why novices are not allowed into the kitchen to prepare the food. I think it's a sound practice.

BERRY: At the tea ceremony, which is at the heart of Japanese culture, and at funerals, too, they serve *kaiseki ryori*, which is elaborately prepared vegetarian food. It's interesting that at these two highly significant cultural events they eat exclusively this *kaiseki ryori*. Wouldn't this suggest that there is a deep strain of vegetarianism in Japanese culture?

KAPLEAU: Absolutely.

BERRY: As you point out in *To Cherish All Life,* as recently as the middle of the 19th century, the first precept and a vegetarian diet were so closely observed in Japan that a monk who ate fish was held up to ridicule and called *"namaguʃu bozu,"* which means "an unholy priest reeking of raw fish." Apparently their devotion to the first precept was much deeper in previous centuries.

KAPLEAU: Much, much deeper.

BERRY: I guess the term *namaguʃu bozu* would be meaningless in the Japan of today.

KAPLEAU: Without a doubt. Rynn, my Japanese dictionary defines the Japanese term *ʃhojin* as "abstinence from animal food;" the verb *ʃhojinʃuru* means "to abstain from animal food: fish and flesh; to observe religious abstinence; to eat, keep, or live maigre."

BERRY: We don't even have an English equivalent for *ʃhojinʃuru;* we have to use a circumlocution. We don't have a verb or a noun that can encompass the meaning of *ʃhojinʃuru*: "to exercise religious abstinence from animal food."

KAPLEAU: That's right, we don't. But what is this English word "maigre?" I have a book in my library titled *Ancient Buddhism in Japan.* In the index there are many entries under *maigre,* which has the meaning of "vegetarian." For example, one entry says that in the year 584 CE a certain Buddhist erected a Buddhist temple, after which he invited three nuns, "and in a great meeting arranged for the *maigre* entertainment." Getting back to the Japanese dictionary, under the entry for *ʃhojin ryori,* it says "of a vegetable; a meatless diet, *maigre.*"

BERRY: If it's a synonym for *ʃhojin,* then maybe we're about to discover an English term for religious abstinence from animal food. We have to use five words to express that thought—which shows that this notion is very foreign to our way of thinking in the West.

KAPLEAU: The English dictionary defines *maigre* as "not consisting of flesh or its juices; Maigre day in the Roman Catholic Church: A day of abstinence on which only maigre food may be eaten." So the Church does have a term for it.

67
• • • • • •

KAPLEAU

BERRY: Yes, but it's a very obscure word. It's certainly not in common usage, and it may be archaic.

KAPLEAU: It's certainly an archaic word. I'm enormously encouraged not only by the growth of interest in vegetarianism, but also by the number of religious groups that are holding ceremonies for the blessing of animals. In the Rochester Zen Center I introduced a very old Buddhist practice of holding animal-release ceremonies. We would buy animals that were destined to be slaughtered and then would chant *sutras* for them and set them free.

BERRY: It's an old Buddhist custom?

KAPLEAU: Yes. In Holmes Welch's book on Buddhism in China he talks about animal-release ceremonies. It's a wonderful practice because, among other things, many children come to watch it. We used to have these ceremonies often at our monastery-center in Mexico. We began doing it when I came back from Japan. Actually, I never saw it done in Japan. It was certainly done in China in the Buddhist monasteries—not in modern times but in ancient times. I thought it would be a great thing to revive the practice.

BERRY: I notice that you've revived a number of these practices that honor the first precept—such as keeping a strict vegetarian Zendo and reinstituting the animal-release ceremony—but they have fallen into disuse.

KAPLEAU: I'm sure there are other Zendos in the United States that are vegetarian.

BERRY: Yes, but most of them are those of your dharma-heirs. Do you believe there was a Golden Age—a time in the annals of humanity when all humans were vegetarian?

KAPLEAU: Probably in the early history of the civilizations in China, Japan, and India, a Golden Age prevailed in which virtually the entire populace was vegetarian.

As far back as the time of the Vedas and the Upanishads—which antedate the Buddha—strictures against meat-eating are numerous. Dr. Koshelya Walli in her book *The Conception of Ahimsa in Indian Thought* points out that while some of the ancient Hindu scriptures do, under certain circumstances, sanction the eating of meat that has been offered for sacrifice, for the most part they condemn the consumption of animal flesh.

We also know that the teaching of *ahimsa* strongly influenced the spiritual climate of the Buddha's day. Mahavira, the founder of Jainism and a contemporary of the Buddha, considered harmlessness to all living things the sublimest of virtues and made it a fundamental tenet of his teaching.

One can judge how deeply the doctrine of *ahimsa* had penetrated into the Indian consciousness from this picture of India given us at the beginning of the 5th century by Fa-Hsien, the famous Chinese Buddhist pilgrim:

> The inhabitants are numerous and happy….Throughout the country the people do not kill any living creature, nor drink intoxicating liquor…they do not keep pigs or fowl, and do not sell live cattle; in the market place there are no butcher shops and no dealers in intoxicating drink….Only the Chandalas (the lowest and most despised caste) are fishermen and hunters and sell flesh meat….

On a pilgrimage to India many years ago I marveled at how few butcher shops and liquor stores one saw. India is a vegetarian's delight. It's not that the Indians can't afford flesh foods, but that every great spiritual figure in India—including, in modern times, Mohandas Gandhi—so emphasized nonviolence and harmlessness to human beings that even wealthy Indians spurn animal flesh. However, nowadays I understand that many more Indians are eating flesh foods, especially those who have lived or traveled extensively in the West.

BERRY: In *To Cherish All Life*, you said that the spreading of the glaciers during the last Ice Age may have been a factor in forcing some peoples to adopt a non-vegetarian diet.

KAPLEAU: My research told me that originally man was not a meat-eater. He was innately vegetarian until the Ice Age set in.

BERRY: But the last Ice Age did not encompass all of humanity. For instance, India, Java, and Southeast Asia were not under the ice cap, and they enjoyed a salubrious climate throughout the pleistocene; so I should imagine that people who lived in these areas would have continued to be vegetarian.

KAPLEAU: Yes, I would think so.

BERRY: Most of the archaeology on Ice Age sites has been conducted by Northern Europeans with a carnivorous bias. Very little archaeology has been done in the tropical lands that persisted throughout the last Ice Age, so our picture of Ice Age man has been distorted. The vegetarian peoples in Southeast Asia have been grossly ignored by Ice Age archaeology.

KAPLEAU: That's a vital point.

BERRY: Right, but let's move on. Originally (back in 500 BCE), Jainism and Buddhism were quite similar. In fact, the Buddha had studied with a pupil of Mahavira—but the Buddha formed his own concept of the soul that sharply diverged from Mahavira's teaching that the soul is eternal and indestructible. What is the Buddhist concept of the soul?

KAPLEAU: What we call our soul, or our self, is actually no more than a current of consciousness comprised of thought moments of infinitesimal duration succeeding one another in a stream of inconceivable rapidity. The speed and progress of this process, although always of lightning-fast duration, can change according to the nature of the stimulation. If the catalyst is slight the process functions without full cognition.

We can compare the process to a movie: the illusion of motion is created by numerous still frames moving in swift progression. It is also like a river: the body of water rushing before us is in reality made up of innumerable droplets of water flowing together.

BERRY: This is quite different from the Jain concept of the soul—to say nothing of the Western concept of the soul.

KAPLEAU: The Buddhist scholar Francis Story explains "soul" more precisely: "Much misunderstanding of the Buddhist doctrine of rebirth has been caused in the West by the use of the words 'reincarnation,' 'transmigration' and 'soul'...." These are ambiguous terms that have never been clearly defined in Western religious thought. Take the word "soul," for example. It is generally taken to mean the sum total of an individual personality, an enduring ego entity that exists more or less independently of the physical body and survives it after death. The "soul" is considered to be the personality factor which distinguishes one individual from another, and is supposed to consist of the elements of consciousness, mind, character and all that goes to make up the psychic, immaterial side of a human being. The Buddha categorically denied the existence of a "soul" in the sense defined above. He recognized that all conditioned and compounded phenomena are impermanent and this makes the existence of such a soul impossible.

BERRY: In ancient Greece the Pythagoreans held it as an article of faith that the souls of men could transmigrate into the bodies of animals [*metempsychosis*] and vice versa—which is similar to the doctrine of reincarnation in Hinduism. The idea that if you mistreated an animal you might be harming a departed relative or friend—this operated to restrain people from abusing, to say nothing of eating, animals. Is that notion also present in Buddhism?

KAPLEAU: Yes, to a certain extent. Buddhism holds that in our ascent and descent through many lifetimes, our lives have taken many forms according to our *karma*.

There's a wonderful cartoon, by the way, that shows a very proper man walking a dog and the dog is thinking, "There's *karma* for you: in a previous lifetime he was *my* dog!"

BERRY: In Buddhism can one reincarnate as an animal?

KAPLEAU: There's some disagreement on that point. Some Buddhist sects say that you adopt a new life form according to the way you've lived your previous life, and that you can take on an animal form in the lifetime following this one. Others say it takes many lifetimes to lose the human form. In Buddhism, one of the things that makes human life so sacred, so precious, is that it is only from the human condition that one can come to enlightenment; animals, so far as we know, cannot come to enlightenment. Never having been estranged from their primal oneness with nature—True-nature—by the self-conscious awareness of themselves as discrete beings, presumably they cannot know the joy of reconciliation.

BERRY: Is human life regarded by Buddhists as the pinnacle of spiritual development?

KAPLEAU: No, it isn't. Unlike Christianity, which in an exuberance of self-deification, elevated man to the summit of earthly existence, with the power of life and death over non-human creatures, as the Bible states, Buddhism places Man midway between an amoeba and a Buddha. Buddhism postulates six realms of unenlightened existence. In ascending scale these are the realms of hell, *pretas* (or hungry ghosts), beasts, *asuras* (or fighting demons), human beings and *devas* (or heavenly beings). You can conceive these different levels, or states, in either a physical or a psychological sense, or both. Take hell: for those who were tortured in the Nazi death camps those places were surely a hell for them. Or take the slave ships transporting blacks from Africa to the new world. The brutalities these blacks were subjected to were certainly hellish. Psychologically, we can say that hell is a state in which a person thinks everyone is his enemy.

Consider *pretas*, or hungry ghosts. They are said to be beings with tiny mouths and bloated bellies who suffer terribly from hunger and thirst. Because of their gluttony they have condemned themselves to a miserable existence. They can perhaps be compared to people who are suffering from ulcers. Psychologically, they can be said to represent unsatisfied passions and unfulfilled desires.

Devas are similar to angels. By reason of favorable *karma* in the past they now lead a life of ease, luxury, and transient pleasures. In Zen it is said that the realm of *devas* should be looked upon as a temporary stopping place from which, if they tarry too long, they may find themselves dropping all the way down to hell after the favorable *karma* that brought them there expires. That's why a Zen adept prefers to live and work in the mundane world where he can help bring distressed people to know the bliss of awakening.

The animal realm is characterized by ignorance and fear, and the human realm by greed, anger, and lust. *Asuras,* or fighting demons, are characterized by a lust for power.

All creatures in these realms are tied to the ceaseless round of birth and death, that is, to the law of causation, according to which existence on any one of these planes is determined by antecedent actions. In Buddhism these planes are depicted as the spokes or segments of the "Wheel of Life." This "wheel" is set in motion by actions stemming from our basic ignorance of the true nature of existence and by karmic propensities from an incalculable past, and kept revolving by our craving for the pleasures of the senses and by our clinging to them, which leads to an unending cycle of births, deaths, and rebirths to which we remain bound.

Buddhism also speaks of four realms of enlightened existence, sometimes called the "four holy states." In ascending order these are the worlds of Shravakas, Pratyekabuddhas, bodhisattvas, and full buddhas. A Shravaka is one who hears the teaching of the Buddha and accepts it into his heart, thereby attaining enlightenment. Pratyekabuddhas ("private buddhas") are those who carry on solitary practice and reach enlightenment without a teacher. At the highest two levels of enlightened existence are bodhisattvas and full buddhas. Bodhisattvas are enlightened beings who, deferring their full enlightenment, dedicate themselves to helping others attain liberation. In his self-mastery, wisdom, and compassion a bodhisattva represents a high stage of buddhahood, but he is not yet a supremely enlightened, fully perfected buddha.

Lastly, speaking of buddhas, there are various classifications of the stages of buddhahood. A buddha in the highest stage is not only fully enlightened but, in the words of Lama Govinda, "a perfect one who has become whole, complete in himself, one in whom all spiritual and psychic faculties have come to perfection, to maturity, to a state of perfect harmony, and whose consciousness encompasses the infinity of the universe. Such a one can no longer be identified with the limitations of his individual personality, his individual character and existence; of him it is rightly said that 'There is nothing by which he could be measured, there are no words to describe him.' "

Full buddhas, when they pass on from this world, reach a state called "*parinirvana*." The Sanskrit word *nirvana* means "extinction" or, literally, "a blowing out," the unconditioned state beyond birth and death that is reached after all ignorance and craving have been extinguished, and all *karma*, which is the cause of rebirth, has been dissolved. The term *parinirvana*, used only in reference to a full buddha, means complete extinction, the state of perfect freedom from bondage reached by Gautama Buddha at the time of his utter passing away. *Parinirvana* is a bodiless state of Pure Consciousness.

Now let us reflect on this pronouncement of the Buddha when his passing away was imminent: "In this hour of joy it is not proper to grieve. Your despair is quite inappropriate, and you should regain your composure. The goal, so hard to win, which for many aeons I have wished for, now at last is no longer far away. When that is won, no earth or water, fire, wind or ether is present; unchanging bliss beyond all objects of the senses, a peace which none can take away, the highest thing there is; and when you hear of that and know that no becoming mars it and nothing ever there can pass away—how, then, is there room for grief in you minds? At Gaya, at the time when I won enlightenment, I got rid of the causes of becoming, which are nothing but a gang of harmful vipers; now the hour comes near when I get rid also of this body, the dwelling place of the acts accumulated in the past. Now that at last this body, which harbors so much ill, is on its way out; now that at last the frightful dangers of becoming are about to be extinct; now that at last I emerge from the vast and endless suffering—is this the time for you to grieve?"

So, you see, the earnest Buddhist does not aspire to rebirth as another human being. Rather, he seeks, first, to become a full buddha, then, upon his *parinirvana*, to achieve the rarefied state of Pure Consciousness, and, finally, to take appropriate form somewhere in the "*saha* world of men and gods," as the scriptures say, where his presence can help relieve the pain and ills of suffering beings.

When you see that man is poised halfway between the lowest and the highest forms of existence, you have something to aspire to. It's humbling, but at the same time it's exhilarating to know that the potential for buddhahood is within each of us.

Understand that from a Buddhist point of view animals are also possessed of the Buddha nature. In our innumerable upward and downward rebirths, dependent on causes and conditions, we've been animals of every species. We ourselves have an animal nature, so to destroy an animal for meat, or for research purposes, is to destroy a part of oneself.

BERRY: Is there *karmic* retribution for one's killing and eating animals?

KAPLEAU: Yes; that's why I would hate to be a vivisector or a butcher; meat-eaters are less culpable when they do not kill the animal themselves.

BERRY: Doesn't this notion of retributive *karma* also pervade Hindu thinking?

KAPLEAU: Yes. However, Hinduism teaches, I believe, that the *guru* can remove your *karma* — that is, take it onto himself; whereas in Buddhism you have to expiate your own *karma*. Nobody can do it for you. You can't depend on God or Christ or Buddha or your *guru* to do it for you. You must take responsibility for your own actions.

BERRY: In propounding his new system of belief, wasn't the Buddha trying to reform the excesses of the Hindu priesthood — the Brahmins — many of whom were engaging in animal sacrifice on a prodigious scale.

KAPLEAU: That is true. Lama Govinda, however, insists that it's a mistake to think of Buddhism as constituting essentially a reform of Hinduism. Buddha was an innovative thinker who developed pragmatic methods for dealing with the universality of suffering by removing the root cause of suffering — namely, desire. His methods for eradicating the cause of suffering are set forth in the Eightfold Noble Path.

Let me say that the Buddha's *dharma* ought not to be considered as a system of philosophic or intellectual thought, much less a system of ethical idealism. Even less is it a religion based upon authority. It is simply a way of life based on what Buddha called the Eightfold Noble Path and The Middle Way, which, he said, would lead one who followed it to emancipation of body, to enlightenment of mind, to tranquillity of spirit, to highest *samadhi* (of heightened and expanded awareness). Furthermore, it is a system of mind control leading to the highest perfect cognition. He did not make it up. It is the record of his own experience under the Bodhi tree, where he himself attained supreme enlightenment.

BERRY: How does Zen relate to all this?

KAPLEAU: Fundamentally, it is the root source of all forms of Buddhism. As a sect it arose as a reaction to the Indian philosophical and intellectual excesses. Indian philosophy in the sixth and seventh centuries was too theoretical, too abstract, too remote. But Chinese Taoists, with their wonderful practicality, brought it down to earth. In their hands, Buddhism was transformed into Ch'an, or Zen. Thereafter, Zen practice became a matter of personal experience and testimony. The Chinese emphasized that one must realize for oneself the nature of the world and thereby transcend birth and death. When the Japanese adopted Ch'an Buddhism, they refined it, and in the process they systematized and rejuvenated the Ch'an, or Zen, *koans*, those baffling spiritual problems. I think it's fair to say that the repository of Zen today is Japan, although Zen originated in China as a fusion of Buddhism and Taoism.

BERRY: The Taoists were vegetarians too; so there was a confluence of vegetarian ideas in Chinese Buddhism—from the Taoist side and from the Hindu side.

KAPLEAU: Yes, the Taoists on the one hand and the Jains and Hindus on the other. The Taoist contribution to Zen was not insignificant.

BERRY: It strikes me that there are also many yogic elements in Zen Buddhism; so I'm wondering if, with many *gurus* of *yoga* insisting that their serious pupils adopt a vegetarian diet to enable them to achieve *samadhi*, you believe that a vegetarian diet would better enable a Zen monk to achieve *kensho* or *satori*?

KAPLEAU: A vegetarian diet is not the *sine qua non* for enlightenment, but there's no question that the clarity and calm that a vegetarian diet induces would help. The outstanding masters in all the major spiritual traditions were not flesh-eaters.

BERRY: There seems to be a cultural interchange taking place between Asia and the West whereby we are adopting the pre-World War II eating habits of Japan, China, and India, and they are emulating us and adopting our worst eating habits.

KAPLEAU: It's ironic, isn't it?

BERRY: It really is. Similarly, Bill Shurtleff, who trained as a Zen monk in Japan, tells me that the spirit of Zen is stronger among idealistic American Zen students than it is among the Japanese. Likewise, Satyaraj Das (Steven Rosen), who is an American Vaishnava, a Hare Krishnaite, informs me that the idealism and fervor of Western Vaishnavas has reinvigorated the Vaishnava *bhakti* tradition in India.

KAPLEAU: To some extent the roles have been reversed: now it's the materialistic East versus the spiritual West.

BERRY: So perhaps when Westerners have adopted vegetarian eating habits via Zen, via Hinduism, via Chinese Buddhism and Taoism, the Eastern cultures in which these religions arose will rediscover the virtues of *ahimsa* and a vegetarian diet.

KAPLEAU: Speaking of cultural distortions, what's really interesting is that when you look at a Buddha figure in every Buddhist country, you will find that the figure has the facial features of the inhabitants of that country. The point is, we can all become Buddhas regardless of race or nationality.

BERRY: I've also noticed that the Buddha figure in every country is androgynous—which suggests that women as well as men can identify with the Buddha on equal terms.

KAPLEAU: That's true.

BERRY: The original Buddhist *sangha* was remarkable in ancient Hindu society because it admitted men and women on an equal footing and promoted them on the basis of merit.

KAPLEAU: During the Buddha's time men and women were

treated as equals in the *sangha*, but only after Ananda, the Buddha's attendant and cousin, pleaded with him to allow women in. The Buddha finally consented, but with certain restrictions.

BERRY: I know that in Japan, China, Thailand, and Southeast Asia today the women are segregated from the men and are often treated as inferiors within the Buddhist community. What about the status of women in your Zendos?

KAPLEAU: In the Zendos that I've founded, whether in Rochester, Canada, Poland, or Mexico, the status of women is absolutely equal to that of men. Actually, in our *sangha* in Mexico not only do we have more women then men, but the extraordinary thing is that most of these women are psychotherapists!

BERRY: As highly educated professionals they're on an equal footing with men in the professional world as well as in the *sanghas*.

KAPLEAU: Right. Here is another fascinating fact: in the workshops I have given abroad, whether in Sweden, Poland, Hungary, Yugoslavia, Germany, Canada, Haiti, Mexico, Costa Rica, whatever — in all these countries the same kind of people are attracted to Zen: middle class professionals. The fact is Zen has always attracted well-educated, sensitive, intelligent, and caring people.

BERRY: Soyfood appears to be a concomitant of Zen Buddhism. When the first Buddhist monks arrived in Japan, they imported tofu from China in the sixth century CE. In the late twentieth century an American Zen monk, William Shurtleff, brought the secrets of making and preparing soyfoods to the West. With the arrival of soyfoods and Buddhism to the Western world, is the stage being set for the spread of *ahimsa*, nonviolent eating, and the dawning of a new Golden Age in the West?

KAPLEAU: That's a fascinating question. I fervently hope the answer to it is "yes!" The grim fact is that thousands upon thousands of children, women and men, are dying of starvation in Africa and elsewhere today, and that unless we stop eating animals and begin growing grain for human consumption on the thousands of acres of land now devoted to feed for animals and simultaneously preserve the tremendous amounts of water required in the slaughter of animals, our species may not survive.

Essay

······················

HINDUISM

OR THE PAST 3,000 YEARS, India has been a much-invaded country. Its wealth;[1] its high culture; its love of display and adornment; and unabashed hedonism have been a magnet to hordes of barbarian conquerors —from the Aryans, to the Scythians, Persians, Macedonians, Huns, Mongols, Muslims, and most recently the British. These truculent, flesh-gorging tribes, with their patriarchal customs and their war-like gods, descended on India like a lion springing on-to the back of an elephant. Sinking its pitiless teeth and claws into the pachyderm, the lion draws blood, but it isn't long before the elephant heaves its shoulders and sends the lion sprawling. Eventually, that's what India does to its conquerors: it is mauled by them, to be sure, but after a few generations it usually ends up absorbing them or shrugging them off. Like as not, the descendants of those fierce invading tribes that pillaged and marauded their way to power, end up seated cross-legged on the floor, eating vegetarian food with their fingers, concentrating on their ingoing and outgoing breaths, intoning mantras, and assuming the attitudes of a *yogin*.

Although Westerners tend to think of Hinduism, the predominant religion of India, as being a single, shaggy, polytheistic behemoth, there are almost as many sects of Hinduism as there are of Christianity—Shaivites, Vaish-navaites, Tantrics, Animists, Suryas, Shaktas, and so on. Over the centuries Hinduism has evolved and adapted. Some scholars say that the earliest manifestation of Hinduism, known as Brahminism, was based on the ritual sacrifice of animals, and was very different from the Hinduism that is practiced today. The Hinduism that we are familiar with—the gentle, all-embracing religion that preaches *ahim-sa, karma*, reincarnation, and forbids the eating of animal flesh is real-ly a product of Buddhist and Jain reforms that began to take hold in the sixth century BCE. Prior to this time, reincarnation, *karma*, veg-etarianism and *ahimsa* were nowhere mentioned in the sacred writ-ings of the Brahmins; according to Professor David Kinsley, the Vedas mocked the very notion of asceticism.[2] However, with the cre-ation of the *Upanishads* and particularly the *Bhagavad Gita* (which is an *Upanishad*), Hindus turned away from the sacrifice of animals and the glorification of the Brahmin caste and began to emphasize the path of devotion as the way to human salvation. In other words, they went from the worship of polytheistic deities to the worship of an impersonal god, Brahman, as prescribed in the *Upanishads* and to the devotion (*bhakti*) of a personal savior God, the most prominent of which was Krishna, an *avatar* of Vishnu.

In the medieval period, the Bhakti movement enjoyed a wide popularity throughout India and bade fair to eclipse Brahminism. As Professor Paul Toomey notes: "During the medieval period (from the thirteenth to seventeenth centuries) a new attitude toward God emerged among Hindus. Bhakti, emotional, passionate devotion to the Lord, replaced the old approaches of sacrificial rite and monistic meditation. The focus of religious attention moved from the great gods and his liturgies to one God and his *avatars*. In this new religious configuration, Vaishnavites were those who followed the Panchara-tra system of ritual. They were thus distinguished from Shaivites and Shaktas, followers of Lord Shiv and Devi."[3]

Hindus have a more intimate relationship with the Supreme Reality than do Westerners. Through meditation and contempla-tion, or the intense expression of love, Hindus seek to unite them-selves with the Supreme Reality. In the West, on the other hand,

Yahweh, the god of Christianity, Islam and Judaism, as He is depicted in the Hebrew scriptures, is such a majestic and mighty god that it would be sheer effrontery, not to say blasphemy, to try to unite with Him.

Troubling for the vegetarian Christian, Muslim or Jew is it that Yahweh is depicted in the Hebrew scriptures as delighting in the odors of the burnt animal sacrifices that are made to Him. After Noah sacrificed animals to him, "Yahweh delighted in their savor." (Genesis 8:21) In this respect, Yahweh is really no different from the Indo-European gods of ancient Greece, Rome, Persia and *Rg Vedic* India who sustained themselves on the smoke from the flesh of animals consecrated to them by priests. Aristophanes' comedy *The Birds* provides an amusing look at how the Indo-European burnt animal sacrifice worked. In the play, the birds blackmail the gods by deflecting the smoke that curls skyward from the animal sacrifices so that the gods can't inhale it.

"Peithetairus: 'There is a corridor in the air between earth and sky. Just as when we want to go to Delphi we have to ask the Boeotians for safe passage through their territory, so the Gods will have to bring you a tribute if they want to receive the savory smoke from the burning haunches of the sacrificial animal; otherwise you'll blockade the corridor between earth and heaven whenever men sacrifice to the gods!'"[4]

Although a satire, *The Birds* shows how implicitly it was believed by the animal-sacrificing peoples of antiquity—the Jews, the Greeks, the Romans, the Persians and the *Rg Vedic* Indians—that the sacrificial smoke and the cooked flesh of the animal victim were nutritious to the gods. The sacrifice concluded, it was customary for the priests to share the leftover flesh with worshippers who had paid for the sacrifices; in this way, sacrificial flesh became a status food that was charged with magical power.

In India, animal sacrifices were abolished by the Buddhists and the Jains as well as by other elements of the *Sramanic*[5] renouncer religion, which Professor Christopher Key Chapple believes is the indigenous religion of India and the source of its ethical vegetarianism and *ahimsa*.[6] Except for a few obscure sects in places like

Bengal, where some Bengali Brahmins still worship Kali by sacrificing goats on the temple altars, the gods in Hinduism today are propitiated with offerings of vegetables and fruit called *prasadam*. In order to become "at-one" with the deity, whether by means of *bhakti* (unstinting devotion), or *jnana* (gnosis), one must become as *sattvic* as possible. *Sattva* (knowledge, purity and brightness) is one of the three strands or *gunas* that make up the continuum of nature. The other two strands are *rajas* (lust, envy, action) and *tamas* (delusion, fear, and inertia). Everything in the world is made up of one of these three energies, or a combination of the three. Each *guna* is mutually suppressive. The *tamas guna* darkens consciousness; the *sattva guna* reveals consciousness; and the *rajas guna* activates the *tamas guna* to suppress the *sattva guna* or vice versa. Cultivation of the *sattva* energy leads to pure consciousness or *moksha*. Foods as well as colors are also associated with the three *gunas*: *Sattvic* food is light and vegetarian and corresponds to the color white; *rajasic* food is highly spiced and stimulative and corresponds to the color red; *tamasic* food such as animal flesh is noxious and decayed, and corresponds to the color black. The theory is that one must eat lightly (*sattvic* food) and live as lightly on the earth as possible so that one can be re-absorbed into the Godhead.

Beginning in the middle of the second millennium BCE, India had been invaded by waves of warlike Indo-European speaking nomads, or Aryans. Without a doubt these Aryan incursions added greatly to the store of human and animal misery in ancient India. To the Aryan invaders, scholars have assigned responsibility for the imposition of the caste system and a pantheon of warlike divinities—Rudra, Indra and Agni—who demanded to be appeased with hecatombs of animals sacrificed on fiery altars. To escape the Aryan depredations, the dark-skinned natives, the Dravidians, scattered in all directions: some fled south to the subcontinent; some renounced their possessions and families and became *sannyasis* in the time-honored pre-Aryan *Sramanic* manner; some fled East into the Gangetic plain which was still a stronghold of the pre-Aryan religion. It was from this region that Mahavira and the Buddha rose up against the Brahmin animal sacrificers and succeeded in abolishing the institution of

ritual animal sacrifice that had been introduced into India by the
Aryan invaders.

Food historian Reay Tannahill credits the Jains and the Buddhists with being catalysts for the spread of *ahimsa*-based vegetarianism throughout India: "So influential was the new religions'
[Buddhism and Jainism's] anti-slaughter campaign that by the
first century BCE, even the Brahmin priests had come round to it.
And it was they, vegetarians themselves by the end of the first millennium BCE, who took their food creed with them when as missionaries they penetrated beyond the Vindhaya Mountains and
laid the heavy hand of Hindu orthodoxy on the South. As a result,
the South was introduced not only to a matured Hinduism, but to
a Hinduism that equated vegetarianism with meritorious living.
Perhaps because of this, South Indian vegetarian cooking remains
today one of the world's most distinguished cuisines."[7]

Two of the early *bhakti* sects that emerged from the Buddhist
and Jain reforms were Vaishnavism and Shaivism. Both celebrated the pre-Aryan vegetarian diet of their forebears. The Vaishnavas stand out as being particularly gifted cooks and some of the
leaders of Vaishnavism have also been notable gourmets—like Sri
Chaitanya and Swami Prabhupada. One of the reasons why
Vaishnavas are such gifted cooks is that as devotees of Lord
Krishna, who is an *avatar* of Vishnu, they traditionally consume
the food that they offer him which is called *prasadam* (food offerings made to a god that are returned to the worshipper imbued
with the god's blessing).[8] This is not strictly true of other sects.
The Shaivites for instance customarily do not partake of the food
after it has been offered to Shiva because Shiva is a capricious and
mercurial god who like the Greek god Dionysos is an apotheosis
of the wild zest of nature. In his fits of temper, Shiva is believed
on occasion to bewitch the food. A mouthful of *prasadam* that had
been bewitched by Shiva could be intoxicating if not fatal.[9] Other
Hindu sects are less democratic than the Vaishnavas, and the
priests take the choicest *prasadam* for themselves and their families. The Buddhists also do not return the food offerings that are
made to images of the Buddha, but feed them to dogs and crows.[10]

Vishnu and his *avatars*, on the other hand, are noted for being expansive, playful and a touch sybaritic. Chaitanya Mahaprabhu—the sixteenth-century Vaishnava saint and devotee of Krishna from whose Bengali tradition the Hare Krishna movement, with its ecstatic dancing and chanting of love for Krishna, springs—was himself a noted gourmet. In fact, Chaitanya's biographer Krishnadas Kaviraj Goswami included a collection of Chaitanya's favorite recipes in his biography of Chaitanya, the *Chaitanya-charitamrita*. Lord Krishna himself had a voluptuary's love of fine food. So, far from being ascetic, Vishnu and Krishna encourage their followers to share in the enjoyment of delicious vegetarian *prasadam*. In return for being fed by humans, the gods infuse the leftover food, the *prasadam* (the God's leftovers), with magical vitamins, as it were. Before they partake of their food, Vaishnavas, or Krishnaites, dedicate it to Vishnu or Krishna; this they do in public temples and in kitchen temples at home. The eating of vegetarian leftovers is a peculiarly *bhakti* form of worship, as the sharing of food with the god brings the worshipper into greater intimacy with the deity. "It is well known that in Hindu ritual food is offered to the gods and is later consumed by the devotees as *prasad*, or leftovers of the offering, which contains divine substance."[11] "Food offerings for feeding the god change into leftovers once the divine person eats a portion of them. These divine leftovers are known and handled as transvalued food (*prasad*) containing the qualities (*guna*), blessings, or 'energy grace' of the god."[12] In Hindu *bhakti* practice, all food is first offered to the household god, and his leftovers received back as his *prasadam*.

Such a concept shouldn't be difficult for Christians to grasp because as Professor Toomey points out when Christians eat of the Eucharist they are contacting the god through their lips—much as in eating *prasadam* Vaishnavas are contacting the divinity of Krishna through their lips. "These properties [of *prasadam*] are not entirely dissimilar to the properties associated with the Eucharist in Western Christianity, in that the reception of God through one's lips constitutes an important mode of spiritual encounter in both ritual systems."[13] In the Indo-European religions of ancient Greece and Rome and in the monotheistic religions of Christianity, Judaism and Islam, the god resided in the animal flesh that was sacrificed to the divinity. What the Greeks called *ieara*—meat barbecued in the temple for the delectation of the god and his worshippers—was the epitome of sacrificial flesh, so that the god was contacted through the lips in the form of animal flesh. Perhaps we should look on the flesh diet of Western Europeans as being the *prasadam* of the Indo-European sky gods, the *prasadam* of Zeus, Odin, Indra, and Yahweh. In its attempt to abolish animal sacrifice with the substitution of Christ for the sacrificial animal, orthodox Christianity was thus a *bhakti* cult that failed. What is needed is a new *bhaktification* of Christianity—or, better yet, of all three Semitic revelatory religions (Christianity, Judaism and Islam) in which we may once again experience a divinity in the *prasadam* of fruits and vegetables.

One of the people who tried to "bhaktify" the West is A.C. Bhaktivedanta Swami, affectionately known as "Prabhupada." As the founder of ISKCON (The International Society for Krishna Consciousness), also known as the Hare Krishna movement, Prabhupada was instrumental in spreading Vaishnavism to the West. He was also a gifted cook. Indeed, he attracted many of the earliest devotees to the Hare Krishna movement with his skill as a vegetarian chef. In this context, Swami Prabhupada was functioning as a Vaishnava cook-*pujari*, or cook priest. Since cooks as creators of *prasadam* serve as intermediaries between the gods and men, it is not surprising that in Vaishnavism, so many inspired leaders have been either cooks, like Prabhupada and Krishnadas Kaviraj, who was Chaitanya's cook-*pujari* in Chaitanya's role as *avatari*, or noted gourmets, like the founder of the Gaudiya Vaishnava sect himself, Sri Chaitanya. It's not for nothing that Vaishnavism has been affectionately called "the kitchen religion." Yamuna Devi, author of *Lord Krishna's Cuisine*, for example, after watching the deft, devotional manner in which Prabhupada prepared *prasadam* for her sister's wedding, was so deeply touched that she implored Prabhupada to teach her how to do it for *him*—almost as though she wanted to become his cook-*pujari*. At Prabhupada's urging, she collected vegetarian recipes from India's regional family kitchens and from Vaishnava temple kitchens that would have been inaccessible to her without Prabhupada's help. His idea was for her to share with the West the culinary treasures of Indian vegetarian cuisine so that more and more Westerners might be enticed into practicing an *ahimsa*-based diet.

In Indian culture the ability to prepare food with flair is not regarded as undignified in an *avatar* of Vishnu or in a Vaishnava scholar, as it would be in a Western intellectual or religious figure. (Try to picture Bertrand Russell with a potato peeler in his hand! Or the Pope slicing and dicing fruits and vegetables with a Whiz-O vegetable grater!) That Prabhupada was a dab hand in the Indian kitchen in no way diminishes his stature as a *pandit* (scholar). For in addition to being a renowned cook, Swami Prabhupada was the author of innumerable translations of the works of Hindu sacred literature, and was a religious leader of genius. Professor A.L. Herman compares him favorably with the two other twentieth-century exemplars of Indian thought—Ramana Maharshi and Mahatma Gandhi.[14] Ramana Maharshi sought to solve the problem of the human condition—which is suffering—through stillness, reflection, meditation, and the identification of the self with the Supreme Reality. Herman sees Ramana Maharshi as being the embodiment of *jnana* yoga (gnosis) or of *advaita* (non-duality). Mahatma Gandhi sought to solve the problem of human suffering through the selfless action prescribed by *satyagraha* (truth force). Gandhi is the embodiment of self-realization through disinterested action (karma yoga). Professor Herman considers Prabhupada, or A.C. Bhaktivedanta Swami, to be the embodiment of *bhakti* Hinduism; Prabhupada sought to treat the human condition through the enamoring of self with Krishna. As Professor Herman phrases it: "Swami Prabhupada is the most well-known missionary of devotional Hinduism in the twentieth century."[15]

An Indian businessman-turned-Vaishnava-monk, Prabhupada traveled to the U.S. in 1965 to spread Vaishnava Hinduism at the behest of his teacher Swami Bhaktisiddhanta, who had charged him to preach *bhakti* to the English-speaking world as early as 1932.[16] In founding ISKCON, Prabhupada was the first religious teacher to found an Asian religion in the West in two millennia. According to noted Indologist, Professor A. L. Basham, the Hare Krishna movement is an authentically orthodox, theistic Hindu movement that represents "the first time since the days of the Roman empire that an Asian religion is being openly practiced by people of Western origin in the streets of Western cities."[17]

Prabhupada certainly was an improbable figure to have founded a religion on Western shores: he arrived in New York almost penniless in 1965. Clad in a flimsy *dhoti* and wearing rubber shoes, his only luggage was a battered portable typewriter, an umbrella, and a trunk of sacred books. When he embarked on his long sea voyage to the United States, he was seventy years old (an age at which many people are checking into rest homes). On the outward voyage from Calcutta, he had several mild heart attacks. Yet he did the impossible: he established a branch of Gaudiya Vaishnavism[18] in America, Europe and Asia—and it seems to have taken root. As noted above, if Krishnaism or *bhakti* Hinduism is one of the most potent proselytizing sects of Hinduism, it's because it is so much more accessible and approachable than are other strains of Hinduism such as *advaita* Brahminism. Since it is comparatively devoid of caste distinctions and since it's not overburdened with Brahmanic *yajnas* (sacrifices) and rituals, it has become a Hinduism for the export market—much as Buddhism was a Jainism for the export market.

It's no deprecation of the sect to say that the Hare Krishnas have won many of their converts through the preparation of food. The cook-*pujari* is a venerable figure in Vaishnavism; so, in a sense it's part and parcel of their work as cook-*pujaris* that the Hare Krishnas run a successful chain of vegetarian restaurants in major cities throughout the world. Even in so seemingly secular a place as a vegetarian restaurant, the diners can contact Lord Krishna through their lips as they taste Krishna *prasadam* in the shape of a succulent *shukta* or a Mung Bean and Mango Salad. In their missionary work in the West, the Krishnaites or Vaishnavaites are without doubt one of the most significant factors in the conversion of the West to a vegetarian diet and the philosophy of *ahimsa*. The *bhaktification* of the West may now be at hand. ॐ

R.B.

············

[1] Even in Alexander the Great's time, India was known to be a fabulously rich country where precious stones were plentiful. Here is a description from Robin Lane Fox's biography of Alexander the Great: "The troops therefore were given leave to plunder the nearby country, no mean privilege in a land where precious stones were theirs for the taking; in a river like the Chenab, jewels were washed to the surface, until no keen eye could miss the Indian beryls and diamonds, the onyxes, topaz and jasper and the clearest amethysts in the classical world." Robin Lane Fox: *Alexander the Great: A Biography*, (New York: The Dial Press, 1974) p. 368.

[2] David R. Kinsley, *Hinduism: A Cultural Perspective* (Englewood Cliffs: Prentice Hall, 1982), p. 31.

[3] Paul Toomey, *Food from the Mouth of Krishna: Feasts and Festivities in a North Indian Pilgrimage Center* (Delhi: Hindustan Publishing Corporation, 1994), p 8.

[4] Aristophanes, *The Birds*, p. 80-85. (Translation mine).

[5] *Sramanic*: See essay on Jainism.

[6] Christopher Key Chapple, *Nonviolence to Animals, Earth and Self in Asian Traditions* (Albany: State University of New York Press, 1993), pp. 1-19.

[7] Reay Tannahill, *Food in History* (New York: Crown Publishers, 1988), p. 109.

[8] Manuel Moreno, "Pancamirtam: God's Washings as Food" in *The Eternal Food: Gastronomic Ideas and Experiences of Hindus and Buddhists*, ed. R.S. Khare (Albany: State University of New York Press, 1992), p. 153.

[9] *ibid.*, p. 153.

[10] Senevirtane, "Food Essence and the Essence of Experience," in *The Eternal Food*, p. 189.

[11] *ibid.*

[12] Moreno, *op. cit.*, p. 152.

[13] Toomey, *op. cit.*, p. 8.

[14] A.L. Herman, *A Brief Introduction to Hinduism: Religion, Philosophy and Ways of Liberation* (Boulder: Westview Press, 1991), pp. 1-36.

[15] *ibid.*, p. 16.

[16] *ibid.*, p. 18.

[17] Steven J. Gelberg, ed. *Hare Krishna, Hare Krishna* (New York: Grove Press, 1983), p. 162.

[18] Gaudiya Vaishnavism: The religious tradition founded by Chaitanya Mahaprabhu, which advocates the devotional worship of Krishna and his consort Radha as the Supreme Godhead.

STEVEN J. ROSEN

S TEVE ROSEN, A BRILLIANT, tough-minded young Jewish intellectual, who had been something of a religious skeptic, attended his first Hare Krishna (Vaishnava) service in 1972 and was captivated by the preaching of its charismatic *leader*, A.C. Bhaktivedanta Swami Prabhupada. After closely examining the sacred texts of the Vaishnavas, Rosen embraced Vaishnava Hinduism and eventually became one of

Swami Prabhupada's disciples. Since then, Rosen (now Satyaraj Das) has become a widely recognized Vaishnava scholar and practitioner.

The author of twelve books on Vaishnavism and related subjects,

Rosen has developed an important voice in the Indian religious community. As a measure of the high esteem in which he is held by Indian scholars, his works have been issued by three of India's prominent publishers: K. L. M. Firma (*Archaeology and the Vaisnava Tradition: The Pre-Christian Roots of Krishna Worship*, Calcutta, 1989); Munshiram Manoharlal (*Passage from India: The Life and Times of His Divine Grace A.C. Bhaktivedanta Swami Prabhupada*, Delhi, 1992); and Motilal Banarsidass (*Vaishnavi: Women and the Worship of Krishna*, Delhi, 1996). Among his other books are *Food for the Spirit* (which has recently been reprinted as *Diet for Transcendence*, Torchlight, 1997);

Om Shalom; and *East-West Dialogues*. He is also the editor-in-chief of the *Journal of Vaishnava Studies*, an academic quarterly that is esteemed and supported internationally by scholars in the field.

I interviewed Rosen in his book-lined apartment, where we sat amid paintings and statues of Lord Krishna. On the stereo in the background one could hear the hypnotic strains of some Krishna devotees softly chanting; for a moment, I fought the urge to blend my voice with theirs and cut a few capers in praise of Lord Krishna. It reminded me of the Indologist A. L. Basham's reaction when, for the first time, at a station yard in Calcutta he witnessed the Chaitanyites performing a *kirtan* — the ceremony of chanting and dancing in praise of Lord Krishna started by the Vaishnava saint Chaitanya Mahaprabhu in sixteenth-century Bengal. Albeit a starchy and proper academic, Professor Basham couldn't resist being caught up in the chanting and dancing, so infectious did it become. Steve Rosen and many millions of other Westerners are joining that irresistible *bhakti* devotional dance.

• • • • • • • • • • •

BERRY: How long have you been a vegetarian?

ROSEN: I became a vegetarian in 1971, after studying the roots of various religious traditions. It started when I began to look deeply into Western religion, especially Christianity, which goes back about two thousand years. I then studied Judaism, which is somewhat older. Both of these religions emphasize the need for love and compassion, but rarely take it to the point of vegetarianism, at least not overtly. Wanting to delve deeper and go further back into the religious history of mankind, I began studying the various Eastern religions, which go back many thousands of years. In the course of my research, I found that common to most of the Asian religions was this sort of *ahimsa* sensibility — this notion of "harmlessness" and "nonviolence," this mood of treating others as you would have them treat you. And that's what led me to vegetarianism quite early on.

Then, taking the religious quest back to its roots, I became interested in yoga and ancient Hindu traditions that emphasized vegetarianism. This was well before I met the devotees of the International Society for Krishna Consciousness [ISKCON]. I was already a practicing vegetarian when I became a practicing Vaishnava, although my commitment to the Krishna religion definitely enhanced my resolve to be kind to all creatures and to be a vegetarian.

But the point I want to make is this: I saw that there was a thread connecting all the religious traditions and, for me, this was best expressed in what is known as *sanatan dharma*, or "the eternal function of the soul," which is to serve God. That's what the devotees of Krishna were purporting to follow. So that's what I started to explore in the Krishna consciousness movement. Now, that particular *sanatan dharma* ideology, that particular point of view—wherever you find it, be it in Christianity or Hinduism or whatever—necessarily insists on kindness to all living creatures. Taken to its furthest and most logical end, it insists on vegetarianism.

BERRY: Larry Shinn, President of Berea College, Kentucky, and an acknowledged expert on the Hare Krishna movement, observed that many vegetarians joined the Krishna movement because it gives them a rationale for their vegetarianism. Did you find this to be true in your case?

ROSEN: Yes. I would say so. Here at last was a religious tradition that provided a clear connection between vegetarianism, kindness to all creatures, and the religious pursuit. As I said, I found this same principle in other traditions, but you had to look really hard for it— it was mainly to be found in the mystical traditions. Mainstream Judaism, Christianity, and Islam, for example, certainly do not stress vegetarian teachings. If anything, they would reject it. But they do stress universal compassion and love, which ultimately leads to vegetarianism, at least if such love is truly universal. Therefore, the mystical traditions that grew up around these religions do support a vegetarian way of life; but their mainstream counterparts lost sight of this. Whereas in Krishna consciousness, whether mainstream or the more mystical side, it is right on the face of it, right there as a prominent teaching.

BERRY: I understand that in 1975 you were initiated by Swami

Prabhupada himself, the founder of the International Krishna Consciousness movement. Did you have a sense that he was a special person?

ROSEN: When I first met Prabhupada in 1972, my immediate impression was that he was a genuine saint, and his saintliness inspired me to want to improve my lifestyle. So I followed his instructions, distributed his books and spread his teachings with a view to becoming his disciple.

BERRY: What were the prerequisites for becoming a disciple of Swami Prabhupada?

ROSEN: One had to follow four basic principles—no meat-eating, no intoxication, no illicit sex, and no gambling. One also had to chant sixteen rounds of Hare Krishna on beads. There are 108 beads on the Vaishnava rosary. So one has to go around sixteen times chanting the Hare Krishna *maha-mantra:* "Hare Krishna, Hare Krishna, Krishna Krishna, Hare Hare, Hare Rama, Hare Rama, Rama Rama, Hare Hare." This was the minimum prerequisite for initiation.

BERRY: Did you have to repeat this refrain constantly?

ROSEN: Sixteen rounds on beads as a minimum—that was for quiet, reflective meditation—and then you would chant aloud in *kirtan,* a sort of joyous, overflowing spiritual exercise wherein you sing and dance with others. You must have seen the devotees singing like this on the streets. It's quite traditional, and it's a well-known practice all over India. There are many Vedic and post-Vedic prayers and chants like this, but this particular one is known as the *maha-mantra,* which indicates that it is all-inclusive and all-encompassing. It's said that all other mantras are contained in this one mantra. It's *that* powerful. So it has a soteriological function, its meaning is very deep, and it is extremely purifying.

You see, most prayers or incantations ask for something in return. "Give us our daily bread," or something of that nature. Or, in the latter-day Buddhist tradition, you have *nam-myoho-renge-khyo*—supposedly, if you chant this incessantly, you'll get whatever you want, any material acquisition. But this Hare Krishna prayer is totally selfless. It asks for nothing in return. So its power comes from its selflessness, its purity, and it puts you in touch with the supreme pure, God.

BERRY: How would you translate it?

ROSEN: "O Lord! O divine energy of the Lord! Please engage me in Your service!" It means, essentially, "Whatever You want, O Lord, that's what I want!"

BERRY: The great Indologist A. L. Basham said that Swami Prabhupada, in founding the International Hare Krishna movement, had established the first Asian religion in the West since the days of the Roman Empire. Harvey Cox, Professor of Divinity and Chairman of the Department of Applied Theology at Harvard Divinity School, said of Prabhupada: "There aren't many people you can think of who successfully implant a whole religious tradition in a completely alien culture. That's a rare achievement in the history of religion. Eventually, he planted this movement deeply in the North American soil, throughout other parts of the Europe-dominated world and beyond. The fact that we now have in the West a vigorous, disciplined, and seemingly well-organized movement—not merely a philosophical movement or a yoga or meditation movement, but a genuinely religious movement—introducing the devotion to God that he taught, is a stunning accomplishment. So when I say 'he was one in a million,' I think that's in some way an understatement. Perhaps he was one in a hundred million."

ROSEN: Yes, that's a wonderful quote.

BERRY: He certainly was an improbable figure to have founded a religion on Western shores: he came to New York without any money. Wearing an Indian *dhoti* and rubber shoes, his only luggage was a battered typewriter and an umbrella. He was seventy years old (an age at which many people are retiring from active life) and yet he did the impossible: he established a branch of Gaudiya Vaishnavism in America, Europe and Asia—and it seems to have taken root.

ROSEN: That's true—it was a phenomenal accomplishment! But he was not really "an improbable figure," as you say. In many ways, Swami Prabhupada was the most likely person to do it, chiefly because, as his biographers tell us, he spent a lifetime in preparation. He was born to devout Vaishnava parents of the Chaitanyaite school; he studied Vedic texts for most if not all of his life; he knew Sanskrit; he knew Bengali; in college, he majored in economics, philosophy and English (interestingly enough, studying these things would later enable him to run a worldwide institution and explain complex Vaishnava theology to Westerners); and he lived a pure life of loving God from the very beginning. So these things really prepared him for coming West, and for the monumental success that followed.

BERRY: But he was an unlikely figure in another sense. Come to think of it, Mahatma Gandhi was an improbable figure as well. *Dhoti*-clad like Prabhupada, he weighed about 125 pounds soaking wet; yet he drove the British out of India and is considered, in some respects, the father of modern India. So that's a consideration: very often even the most unlikely figure triumphs. The weak overcome the strong when they have truth on their side—that's the whole idea of *satyagraha*.

ROSEN: Ultimately, Prabhupada's greatest strength lay in his dedication and faith in his spiritual master, Bhaktisiddhanta Sarasvati Thakur. There were several people who had been given the instruction by Bhaktisiddhanta to come West and to deliver the esoteric teachings of Krishna consciousness; but they considered it to be totally impossible because they'd been given to understand that people in the West were meat-eaters, alcoholics and sex-mongers. So they backed off. On the other hand, Prabhupada rose to the challenge, saying, "They declared that it was impossible…but I was determined to try it anyway." (*laughter*)

BERRY: Do you think the Krishnaites [Vaishnavas] have been responsible for the spread of vegetarianism and the doctrine of *ahimsa* in America and Europe?

ROSEN: Yes, very much so. In ISKCON vegetarianism is a requirement for practitioners, whereas, generally in other traditions it is optional. Thus it is an actively promoted philosophy; ISKCON has opened vegetarian restaurants in every major city of the world. They are immensely popular, opening people up to a broader conception of the vegetarian lifestyle. There are, of course, Jain and Buddhist denominations who have contributed to the popularity of vegetarianism, and certain Christian sects like the Seventh-Day Adventists have contributed as well. Perhaps I'm biased, but I would say, comparatively speaking, ISKCON has had a broader influence.

BERRY: In fact, Bill Shurtleff told me that, when he was training as a Zen monk in Japan and working on *The Book of Tofu*, he met Swami Prabhupada, who had come to Tokyo in the late sixties to open a branch of ISKCON. So thanks to Prabhupada's zeal it has become a worldwide phenomenon.

ROSEN: Vaishnava restaurants, which are strictly vegetarian, or, I should say, lacto-vegetarian, have been thriving all over Europe, Japan, Australia, China, India, and Hong Kong, and, of course, in America as well.

BERRY: India? I should think that opening a Krishnaite restaurant in India would be like taking coals to Newcastle.

ROSEN: ISKCON has its own particular style of cooking and preparing sacred food that's offered to Krishna. In addition to the interest created by the mere fact of seeing Westerners preparing traditional dishes, devotees sometimes take traditional recipes from the culture and give them a distinctive Western flourish. Thus the popularity is twofold.

BERRY: What characterizes that style of cuisine?

ROSEN: *Bhakti.* The love and devotion of the devotee—this is the main ingredient. You see, in Vaishnava devotional cooking, there are three concepts that one should be aware of: first, there is *bhoga*, or "mundane enjoyment," and this refers to unoffered food. Then you have *naivedya*, or the food that is brought before the Deity. Finally, you have *prasadam*, literally, "the Lord's mercy," which refers to the food after it is offered to the Deity with love and devotion by a qualified priest. This food is spiritually purifying and is always *sattvic*, or vegetarian and health-giving.

BERRY: Is Yamuna Devi's cookbook *Lord Krishna's Cuisine* representative of *prasadam* preparation?

ROSEN: Yes, in the sense that her mood in this book is devotional, but, in addition, it is a masterpiece of traditional Indian culinary art. For many years Yamuna was Prabhupada's personal cook; he taught her his own cooking secrets, helped her collect recipes and specifically asked her to compile a cookbook. That was a great impetus for her; that's why she did it and doubtless that's why it turned out to be the award-winning cookbook that it is.

BERRY: Prabhupada wanted her to do it for the West?

ROSEN: For the world—even for India—because he wanted her to perpetuate traditional Vaishnava vegetarian cooking.

BERRY: I understand that Prabhupada saw to it that his protégé Yamuna was given access to temple kitchens to which non-Westerners and non-Hindus had never been admitted. Have you, as a Vaishnava scholar, penetrated any of these temples?

ROSEN: Yes, I've entered the sacred precincts of some temples that are off-limits to Westerners and non-Hindus. I've been to Tirupati, Guruvayur, Shri Rangam, and others. But, in actuality, they're easing up on the restrictions for foreigners. I think this is also due, in part, to ISKCON's presence.

BERRY: In your book *Om Shalom* [a collection of dialogues with Rabbi Jacob Shimmel, who has studied and traveled extensively in India], you discussed a temple in South India, Pakshi Tirtha, where they have a time-honored custom of feeding two white eagles at precisely the same time every day. Can you tell me about that?

ROSEN: That's a Shaivite temple [where Shiva is worshipped] near Mahabalipuram in southern India. An amazing place. The temple sits atop an enormous hill. To reach the top, one has to climb a seemingly endless flight of steps that are carved into the mountainside. You have to time your journey so that you arrive before the feeding of the two eagles, which takes place at 12:30 P. M. sharp every day.

To climb these steps takes about an hour or an hour and a half. At this time of day, the sun is positively scorching. It beats down piteously on the stone steps—which have to be climbed barefoot because one must remove one's shoes upon entering a sacred place. So to climb these steps is quite an austerity.

As soon as you get to the top, amidst throngs of pilgrims, the first thing that you see is a *pujari*—a priest who worships the deity and presents *prasadam* (sacred food) to the deity as well. Around twenty-seven minutes after 12:00, the *pujari* takes out a pot of *prasadam* and places some in his hand. Soon after he does this, at exactly 12:30, one sees two black dots in the sky, moving in from quite a distance. It's the two white eagles! This ritual has been going on for thousands of years. It's even mentioned in the *Puranas*, where there's a story that refers to two devotees of Shiva, two *yogis*, who were cursed to take birth as birds perpetually, birth after birth. It's also briefly mentioned in the *Chaitanya-charitamrita*—the most authoritative and canonical of the biographies of Lord Chaitanya, which was composed in the early seventeenth century. [Chaitanya Mahaprabhu was the founder of Gaudiya Vaishnavism, of which ISKCON is a branch.] So there is evidence that something has been going on here for a long, long time.

BERRY: Rabbi Shimmel, who is a keen but not uncritical student of Hinduism, was very impressed by the whole Pakshi Tirtha incident.

ROSEN: That's right. He witnessed it, and for centuries European travelers who visited this Pakshi Tirtha temple have left accounts of it. For instance, in 1908 the Archaeological Survey of India published interesting findings in the annual report of the *Madras Epigraphist*. It seems that ten Dutch army officers had inscribed their names in the Pakshi Tirtha area in the year 1664, attesting to the fact that they had witnessed the noontime meal.

So the two black dots appear in the sky just after noon, flying in from across the subcontinent. As they get closer, one can see that they are actually two white eagles. They swoop down, seize the *prasadam* from the *pujari's* hands, and eat it. Then they fly around the mountain to clean their beaks on the alternate mountainside. What's more, since these birds (and, perhaps, their ancestors) have been cleaning their beaks after lunch for millennia, there are large indentations in the mountain where they clean their beaks. So this is the story of the two Shaivites who were cursed to take birth as eagles....

BERRY: Cursed or blessed? It's not such a bad existence, is it? Flapping about merrily while feeding on tasty vegetarian dishes prepared by a temple chef...

ROSEN: One man's curse is another man's blessing. (*laughter*)

BERRY: It's also rather extraordinary that eagles, which are thought of as being exclusively carnivorous, should be so taken by this vegetarian food that they appear at 12:30 on the dot every day for at least two thousand years.

ROSEN: India is filled with such inexplicable enchantments and paradoxes. You'll find many truly sacred places with uncommon marvels that defy the imagination.

BERRY: Can one interpret this metaphorically I wonder? That these two white eagles should feed on the *prasadam*—isn't that almost symbolic of the way that devotees of Shiva and Krishna sustain themselves on the gods' *prasadam*?

ROSEN: It's a little different here because this is Shiva *prasadam*. Shiva is a demigod, and so feeding on his *prasadam* can only bring material benefits. Whereas devotees feeding on Krishna *prasadam* are feeding on food that is consecrated to the Supreme Personality of Godhead; the result of this kind of feasting is that it frees you of sin, brings intense happiness, and ultimately liberates you from material existence, situating you in love of God.

BERRY: Do you yourself feed on *prasadam* at home? Do you consecrate your food to Krishna before you eat it?

ROSEN: Yes. I offer my food to Krishna. At the same time, I try to remember that the energy I get from this food is to be used in Krishna's service. This is another aspect of honoring *prasadam*.

BERRY: Is it Krishna's teaching that He will not accept animal flesh? Does He only accept vegetarian food as *prasadam*?

ROSEN: Exactly. That's based on various passages in the Vedic literature. Prabhupada was fond of quoting one particular verse from the *Bhagavad-gita* in which Krishna says, "If one offers Me with love and devotion a leaf, flower, fruit or water, I will accept it." Prabhupada points out that Krishna doesn't ask for meat, fish, or eggs in this verse. Of course, this *Gita* verse is not in and of itself conclusive; but there are many other parts of the Vedic literature that also point in this direction, as well as those that state it overtly. For example, in the *Mahabharata* [anu. 115.47], it is said, "He who desires to augment his own flesh by eating the flesh of other creatures lives in misery in whatever species he may take his birth." Or, also in the *Mahabharata* [anu. 114.11], "The meat of animals is like the flesh of one's own son, and thus the foolish person who eats meat must be considered the vilest of human beings." So the *Gita* verse taken in tandem with these other texts inescapably points to vegetarianism. Moreover, the Vaishnava tradition has been emphatically vegetarian since ancient times. In later literature, such as Krishnadas Kaviraj's *Chaitanya-charitamrita*, vegetarianism is an implicit and recurring theme.

Actually, in that mammoth work, Krishnadas Kaviraj does something quite remarkable: in addition to delineating an incredibly complex theological system and systematically revealing Lord Chaitanya's prevailing hagiography, he describes hundreds of dishes that Lord Chaitanya favored. Many of them, incidentally, appear in Yamuna Devi's cookbook.

BERRY: Could you give some idea of Chaitanya's favorite recipes according to Krishnadas Kaviraj?

ROSEN: Well, various forms of *shak* are described, that is, green leafy vegetables with interesting combinations of *ghee* and spices. All kinds of exotic rice preparations are there as well; and delicious forms of *dahl* too; the list really goes on and on.

BERRY: But they're not vegan recipes...

ROSEN: No. There *are* some that involve the use of milk and *ghee*, as I've said. But many of the recipes are vegan-oriented—simple but tasty vegetarian fare that would appeal to all connoisseurs of good food. You can ask Yamuna about the specific recipes. Basically, there are two food groups: foods called *kacha*, which are grains, vegetables, and various foods that are boiled in water (wherein you will actually find thousands of vegan recipes). Then there are foods called *pakka*, which are prepared with cow products—again, there are thousands of recipes. These are the two basic categories. Paul Toomey, in his excellent work, *Food From the Mouth of Krishna*, explains these various types of *prasadam*.

BERRY: So Chaitanya would dine on these vegetarian meals, dished up by temple chefs in the sixteenth century. How fascinating to have these culinary artifacts preserved so faithfully by his biographer!

ROSEN: Well, there's an esoteric reason for that. An interesting thing about Krishnadas Kaviraj, which would kind of explain why he peppers an intensely philosophical work like the *Chaitanya-charitamrita* with lists of food preparations, has to do with his ontological form; it has to do with who he is in the spiritual realm. He is a maidservant named Kasturi Manjari. Appropriately enough, this maidservant assists Radharani in the kitchen when she prepares food for Krishna. Since this is his eternal activity in the Spiritual Sky, it is quite natural that in his bodily form as Krishnadas Kaviraj he has a preoccupation with recipes and has a predilection for listing foodstuffs and feasts in his *Chaitanya-charitamrita.*

BERRY: Interesting. You are suggesting that Chaitanya's biographer, Krishnadas Kaviraj, was the reincarnation of a sous-chef in the kitchen of Krishna Himself!

ROSEN: In a manner of speaking, yes. In his original spiritual form, he is the assistant of Radharani in the kitchen. And so this affects the way in which he approaches his service as a writer of Chaitanya's biography in this world. This is even brought out more clearly by the fact that Chaitanya's other biographers—and he's had several—don't delve into the recipes or give a detailed listing of the preparations at all. But Krishnadas sure does! He's obsessed with describing all the different kinds of feasts that Lord Chaitanya attended; he tells how to prepare the various dishes, and he lingers lovingly over every detail of its preparation.

BERRY: I should think that after having been Radharani's kitchen assistant, Krishnadas would have achieved *moksha,* or liberation from the wheel of rebirth. Wouldn't being reincarnated as Chaitanya's biographer have been a bit of a comedown?

ROSEN: Not at all. Here's the first thing that needs to be understood: as Radharani's assistant, there is no higher goal—he was already beyond *moksha* and established in his natural constitutional position in the spiritual world. He's one of the inner circle of Krishna's associates and so he is considered eternally liberated. That's the first thing. Closely linked to that is another, related idea: his incarnation as Sri Chaitanya's biographer can be seen as *lila,* or pastime, enacted merely for the Lord's pleasure.

You see, people are born into this world for diverse reasons. Conditioned souls need to learn certain lessons and are forced to take birth as a reaction to their *karma,* or materialistic activity. Through proper conduct and the Lord's mercy, they ultimately achieve *moksha,* or liberation. However, liberated souls also take birth in our world, but their reason is different: they come to help others and to assist the Lord in His mission. So this is one way to answer your question. Krishnadas came here for the Lord's purpose, not for achieving perfection.

From another perspective, it can be seen like this: Lord Chaitanya is considered the most confidential and powerful *avatar* of Krishna. The Gaudiya Vaishnava tradition proclaims that Chaitanya *is* Krishna, but in His most intimate feature as Radha and Krishna combined. So, since Krishnadas was Chaitanya's intimate devotee and biographer, he moved closer to the Godhead. Direct service to Lord Chaitanya is the ultimate form of *moksha*, even for souls who are already liberated. So this is seen as a very exalted thing. This ultimate form of liberation—*seva*, or service to God—is delineated in *Bhagavad-gita.*

BERRY: I see. So his incarnation as Krishnadas is actually a blessing. That resolves the issue quite well. But I want to ask you something about the *Gita,* since you just mentioned it. In the *Gita* there are several passages which stress *ahimsa* as one of the eternal verities. Would you say that the *Gita* is a seminal work for the Vaishnavas?

ROSEN: Yes. The *Gita* comprises chapters 25 through 42 of the *Bhishma-parva* section of the *Mahabharata,* and the *Mahabharata* is considered one of Vaishnavism's main texts. In regard to *ahimsa,* the *Mahabharata* says *ahimsa paro dharmo:* "nonviolence is the highest duty." This emphasis on nonviolence can be found in all major religions as well.

BERRY: You've become something of a scholar in the field of comparative religion, too, having written *Food for the Spirit, Om Shalom, East West Dialogues, inter alia.* As a spokesperson in the field of comparative religion, how would you account for the fact that the Indic religions of the East, such as Buddhism, Jainism, Taoism, and Hinduism tend to promote *ahimsa* and vegetarianism, whereas the Semitic revelatory religions of the West, such as Christianity and Judaism, condone, if not encourage, the taking of animal life and the eating of their flesh?

ROSEN: I think it's because in Western religion there tends to be an emphasis on *loka-hita.* This is Sanskrit terminology; it means "kindness to one's own species."

BERRY: This would include Islam as well.

ROSEN: Especially Islam. Western religions emphasize *loka-hita* more than Eastern religions. The newer religions emphasize *loka-hita* more than the ancient religions. Islam is only 1,300 years old. Since it's a newer religion, it accentuates *loka-hita*, which is a fundamental, beginning spiritual ethic: "First you have to be kind to yourself and your own kind; then you can extend it to others." Now, in the older religions, and especially in the East, they stress *sarva-bhuta-hita*, which means "kindness to all living things." It's a more inclusive ethic—it includes one's own kind as well as all other living entities. This is the compassionate sensibility that is stressed in ancient India's Vedic texts, and especially in the *Puranas* and the *Gita*. This is one of the things that attracted me to Vaishnavism: it promotes this more inclusive, embracing ethic. It encourages love for all creatures; vegetarianism is implicit.

Furthermore, the Eastern religions, especially the various forms of what has come to be called "Hinduism," also stress the principle of *aham brahmasmi*—"I am not this body but, rather, I am spirit soul." This very spiritual perspective includes a sense of bonding with all that lives, an interconnectedness with all life forms. They are spirit, and so are we. So we have much commonality with all creatures in God's creation. People who adhere to an Eastern religious tradition will tell you in all candor that "I am not this body—I am something beyond this body." Of course, this notion can be found in the Western religious traditions as well; every spiritual path will include some sense of experiencing our identities as different from the body. But it's a question of emphasis. In the East, it is a rigorously elaborated upon and highly valued sensibility. Especially among Brahmins, these spiritual ideals are markedly evolved.

BERRY: By chance, as I was making my way here this afternoon, I was reading Norman Lewis's book called *A Goddess in the Stones*—it's about his travels in Eastern India. In it, he recounts an incident that vividly illustrates the point you are making. He describes the reaction of a little Hindu girl on learning that there are people in the world who actually eat fish. Let me read it to you: "Fish had been introduced and ingenious wicker traps were offered for hire in which several, not exceeding two inches in length, had been caught and transferred to tins full of water. These were being examined by a pretty and expensively-dressed little girl, who I was to learn, had

never seen a live fish before. 'And what will they do with them?' she
asked her father. 'They will eat them.' he told her. She seemed to
turn pale with horror, and was on the verge of tears. The father
explained smilingly, 'She is very gentle by nature. You see, we are
Brahmins. We do not eat living things.'"

ROSEN: Yes. Instinctively, she realizes that the only difference between her and this poor fish, who is going to be eaten, is the body;
spiritually she realizes that she and the fish are one, parts of God,
and should not be exploited or abused in any way.

The interesting thing to me is that in the West this would be considered an esoteric teaching, whereas in the East this is a most *exoteric*
teaching. As Prabhupada would often say, "The common street-
sweeper in India knows that he is not the body." By contrast, in the
West, people are generally not conscious of the distinction between
body and soul in their everyday life.

BERRY: This may be related to the Indic idea or belief in *samsara*
or the transmigration of souls. The Western religions do not support such a belief. Is that a fair statement?

ROSEN: No, this is not really an accurate assessment. In my book,
*The Reincarnation Controversy: Uncovering the Truth in the World Reli-
gions*, I argue that just as with *ahimsa*, the principle of reincarnation
is accepted by both Eastern and Western traditions. Although practitioners are generally unaware of it, Western religion for the most
part accepts the doctrine of transmigration, even if it's only religious
mystics, or those who study the "esoteric teachings" of Western religions, who would admit this to be true. In the East, transmigration
is common knowledge and is pretty much accepted across the board.
But make no mistake: *samsara* is definitely there in Western religion.

You have the example of orthodox Judaism—generally those who
adhere to this system of religious belief will deny the doctrine of
reincarnation. However, those Jews who know their own mystical
tradition, Kabbalah, will inevitably come up against texts that lend
support to the idea of transmigration, and they will even become
acquainted with a lengthy work known as *Sefer-HaGilgulim*, which
is largely devoted to elucidating the truth of reincarnation. The Has-
sidim and other orthodox Jewish sects are aware of this, and they

accept that a person can be reincarnated in the shape of a stone, an insect, a plant, an animal, and so on, until one perfects one's life and learns one's lessons. But the mass of Jewish people do not know that transmigration plays a role in Jewish teaching.

In Christianity, the idea of reincarnation was consciously suppressed. If one studies the twenty-five ecumenical councils one will find that at the Second Council at Constantinople, in 553 CE, Emperor Justinian, with the approval of Pope Vigilius, ordered that all references to reincarnation be stricken from the Bible and from post-biblical Christian literature. So most Christians are unaware of Christian reincarnationist teaching.

BERRY: Weren't they trying to stamp out Origenism—the teachings of Origen of Alexandria? The emperor and the pope made common cause against Origen because his teachings on reincarnation threatened the establishment.

ROSEN: That's right. The pope was afraid that if Christians in general believed that they had many lifetimes in which to perfect themselves, they would not treat death as such a grave issue. (Forgive the pun.) If they had more than one life, they might not be serious about following Christian directives and scriptural injunctions. In a word, they couldn't be threatened with hellfire and damnation after a single life. With this in mind, the powerful leaders of that period decided to tell the mass of people that they had only one life—and that after this they would go to heaven or hell. Finished. This, they hoped, would make serious Christians.

BERRY: You were saying that *ahimsa* and *samsara* are esoteric doctrines in the West but are known to the man-in-the-street in the Orient. What about vegetarianism? It strikes me that this has also been an esoteric practice in the West, but commonplace in Asia.

ROSEN: Until recently, one had to go to a specialized, metaphysical bookstore to find information about vegetarianism or reincarnation; they are considered countercultural subjects in the West, or at least they were up until the last twenty years or so. But in India these have long been topics with which the common man is conversant, and speaks about very easily.

BERRY: This is a bit off the point, but I was wondering if you've read Jeremy Rifkin's popular book, *Beyond Beef*.

ROSEN: Yes. It's an excellent work.

BERRY: Do you agree with his view of Indian history?

ROSEN: No, not exactly. For the most part, he seems to accept textbook Hinduism, the kind that was popularized by Indologists who were largely Christian missionaries—biased, with a secret agenda, to say the least. In chapter five of Rifkin's work, he mentions that Hindu Brahmins were largely performers of animal sacrifices, and that it wasn't until the rise of Buddhism that *ahimsa* principles were adopted by the Hindus. This is simply untrue. Rifkin's main reference is Marvin Harris, an anthropologist who does not draw on primary sources. If one studies the original texts, in Sanskrit, one finds that *ahimsa* was promoted in the earliest portions of the Vedic literature. This can be found in the *Rg Veda* (10.87.16), for example, "One who partakes of human flesh, the flesh of a horse, or any other animal, and deprives others of milk by slaughtering cows, O king, if such a fiend does not desist by other means, then you should not hesitate to cut off his head." Or consider the *Yajur Veda* (12.32), which says, "You must not use your God-given body for killing God's creatures, whether they are human, animal, or whatever." Or the *Atharva Veda* (17.1.4): "One should be considered dear, even by those in the animal kingdom." So, contrary to popular belief, most scholars would support the idea that the *ahimsa*-principle can be found in the earliest Vedic texts.

Now, it is true that the Buddha refuted the hypocritical Brahmins of his time who were engaged in needless animal sacrifices in the name of religion. But other Brahmins spoke out against these hypocrites as well. It's not that *ahimsa* was peculiar to Buddhism; it was there in Hinduism all along. Only misled, bogus Brahmins bastardized the tradition and taught that it was appropriate to conduct animal sacrifices in Kali-yuga. But this was an aberration that was not condoned by Vedic texts.

You see, in India, there are eighteen Puranas, ancient scriptures— six for those in the mode of goodness, six for those in the mode of passion, and six for those in the mode of ignorance. The scriptures for those in the mode of goodness adamantly eschew the use of flesh foods—*and* animal sacrifices. Only the scriptures for those in passion and ignorance condone meat-eating and, rarely, animal sacrifices—and both in regulated fashion only. It is meant to wean practitioners off of these things. A similar phenomenon exists in the Bible, for example, in the section where koshering laws are described.

So while I feel that Rifkin's book has a lot to offer, I think he didn't really do his homework in regard to Asian religions. The history of Indian religion in relation to vegetarianism is quite complex, and in order to understand it one needs to delve into the early Sanskrit texts. So Rifkin's analysis is not surprising.

BERRY: It would appear that Westerners become vegetarians largely for narcissistic or health reasons; whereas, in Asia, especially in India, people seem to be vegetarians for spiritual and ethical reasons. Is that a correct assumption?

ROSEN: Not entirely. Practitioners in the East are also aware of the health benefits conferred by a vegetarian diet, and, conversely, Westerners often become vegetarian for spiritual reasons. But to focus on the Eastern religions: if one studies ancient Ayurvedic texts, one will find it very clearly stated that it is better to be a vegetarian not only for religious, ethical, and moral reasons but also for medical and nutritional reasons. It is always better to do things in full knowledge than to do things without knowing the purpose. That's acknowledged in all Indic traditions. But the central reason for Asian vegetarianism, especially for Vaishnavas, is twofold: first, a Vaishnava cannot bear to see the suffering of others. They feel an intense love for all living beings, and cannot harm anyone—not to speak of eating them! Secondly, a Vaishnava only eats foods that are offered to Krishna, and as we've mentioned earlier, Krishna will only eat vegetarian foods. These two reasons are deeply ingrained in Vaishnava culture, and have been an integral part of Vaishnava consciousness long before the rise of Buddhism. So, yes, the two main reasons are basically ethical and spiritual.

BERRY: You were raised in a non-practicing Jewish family, and after converting to Vaishnavism, you've become something of an expert in the field of comparative religion. Has your interest in Judaism been rekindled by your study of other religions?

BERRY: Can one be a practicing Jew and a devoted Krishnaite at the same time?

ROSEN: The average Jewish theologian would say no. They would say that it's not possible because Hinduism is idolatrous and polytheistic. But the conception of *sanatan dharma* that is set forth in the Vaishnava literature is quite monotheistic in that it sees Krishna as the supreme God—the *same* supreme God that is mentioned in biblical literature. And, as far as idol worship goes—there is a huge difference between worshiping a Deity of the Supreme and worshiping an idol of some lesser god, fashioned by one's own imagination. I've actually written quite extensively on this. You see, what Vaishnavism, or Krishnaite religion, emphasizes is this: getting at the essence, finding God, and this is the same basic idea that is there in Judaism and in all major world religions. So, I would say, yes, one can actually be a good practitioner of any faith and still be a Vaishnava. But one must dig deep, and must look into the essence of one's religion. In fact, if one does so, one will find that the practice of Vaishnavism can enhance one's faith in many ways, whatever one's sectarian affiliation may be.

BERRY: Actually, in *Om Shalom*, you and Rabbi Shimmel discuss a small colony of Jews living in India who can trace their lineage back over one thousand years.

ROSEN: That's a different issue because these people are actually practicing Jews; they're not following Krishnaite religion.

BERRY: Have they retained their Jewish customs and dietary habits? Or have they assimilated and become vegetarians?

ROSEN: It really varies, because Judaism teaches that it's a *mitzvah*, or a "good thing," to eat meat on the Sabbath. Or at least it teaches that one should rejoice and eat luxuriant foods on the Sabbath—and most Jewish authorities interpret this as a mandate to eat meat. But by and large I'd say that the Jews in India have assimilated and become vegetarians. Many of them speak Hindi or, rather, Tamil, and they wear *saris* and *dhotis;* so it is difficult to distinguish them from Hindus, and although their practices are distinctly Jewish they have imbibed many Indian customs. For many of them this would include the vegetarian diet.

BERRY: Can you draw any parallels or connections between Judaism and Vaishnavism?

ROSEN: That's the subject of a whole book, and your readers can turn to *Om Shalom*. But, as an example, the word *judaism* comes from *judah*, which means "to exalt the Lord" or "to glorify God." So if one could, for a moment, divorce Judaism from its ethnological dimension, the essence of Judaism is to glorify God. The connection to Vaishnavism, then, is obvious, for the goal of Vaishnavism, too, is to glorify God. In this way, if one looks at the essence, one can find great harmony in these traditions.

BERRY: Although many Jews observe koshering laws, only a small minority are vegetarians. If a Jew wanted to become a vegetarian, what passages could he cite from the Bible to justify his conversion?

ROSEN: Well, this is more Robert Kole's subject, but I would say that one could begin with the first book of the Bible, in Genesis 1:29, where a non-flesh diet is forthrightly recommended; in this text, God actually describes the vegetarian diet as "very good," whereas later diets containing meat are given as an emergency measure, and are usually clearly described as such. The meat-oriented diets mentioned in the Bible are generally referred to as "a concession to human weakness." If one studies the Bible closely, one can see a distinction between God's preferred will and His permissive will.

BERRY: Why did God make these concessions and why did He permit Noah and his descendants to eat animal flesh?

ROSEN: The crucial thing here is to try to understand exactly what was taking place at the time of Noah. Actually, man had become so depraved that he would eat a limb freshly torn from the body of a living animal. The situation had become so degraded that God decided to create a great flood—incidentally, the flood that is depicted in the Bible would doubtless have wiped out all vegetation, leaving scant alternatives to animal foods.

In any case, God did give a concession at that time for the eating of animal flesh. This occurs in the ninth chapter of Genesis, where God gives permission for man to eat anything that moves. Soon after this verse, God says that man should not eat the blood of animals (it is for this reason that the Jewish koshering laws came into play). And not long after that, I believe it's in Genesis 9:5, God reveals the *karma* that awaits those who slaughter animals: "By their own hands shall ye be slain." This is translated variously in different versions, but this is basically what it means.

BERRY: What about this matter of God's having given man dominion over the animals?

ROSEN: Dominion was never taken to mean "one who enslaves" or "one who exploits"—at least not according to traditional biblical usage. Rather, the original Hebrew for the word "dominion" is *yirðu,* and it connotes a sort of stewardship or guardianship. In other words, we are given the command to care for our more humbly endowed brothers and sisters—the animals—not to eat them. A king may have dominion over his subjects, but he doesn't slaughter them and feast on their remains. Not generally.

It should be added, too, that Genesis 1:26, the verse that gives us dominion over the animals, is followed, only three verses later, by the verse that clearly recommends a vegetarian diet. In other words, God gives us dominion over the animals and only three verses later prohibits their use for food. Implicitly, the dominion He gives us does not include using animals for the satisfaction of our tastebuds.

BERRY: You've touched on the Jewish tradition with respect to vegetarianism. Could you briefly outline the Christian tradition vis-a-vis vegetarianism and animal rights?

ROSEN: Well, many of the arguments given for the Jewish side of vegetarianism would apply to the Christian tradition as well—they're both based on the Bible. But Christians claim to adhere to a new covenant, set in place by Jesus and his unique spirituality. Basically, over the centuries, there have arisen two distinct schools of Christian thought: the Aristotelian-Thomistic school of thought and the Augustinian-Franciscan school.

BERRY: How do they differ in their view of animal rights?

ROSEN: The Aristotelian-Thomistic view has, as its basis, the premise that animals are here for our pleasure—their purpose in this world is only to serve us; that's what animals are for. Period. We can eat them, torture them in laboratories, and do anything to them we please. This is almost Cartesian in scope. Unfortunately, much of modern Christianity seems to take its cue from the Aristotelian-Thomistic school.

The Augustinian-Franciscan view, on the other hand, teaches that we are all brothers and sisters under God's fatherhood. Based largely on the world-view of St. Francis, and being essentially Platonic in nature, this school emphasizes love and compassion and, consequently, lends support to the vegetarian perspective. There is clearly a spirit of the law that is missed when one neglects the Augustinian-Franciscan view. Modern Christians would thus benefit greatly by exploring the philosophical teachings of St. Augustine and St. Francis.

In summation, I think you'll find that in all religious traditions some form of these two antithetical strains exist—the Cartesian rationalist view versus the compassionate empathetic view. It is the judgment of the mystics, and I quite concur, that those who are more spiritually evolved tend to be attracted to the latter strain, though lest one lapse into total sentimentalism one should have a healthy regard for the rationalist approach as well. Perhaps it's the Libra in me, but I feel that there must be a balance of these two approaches if the practitioner is to be successful in his spiritual quest.

BERRY: This brings to mind religious schisms in general, a problem which is reflected in attitudes toward vegetarianism, among other things. For example, Muslims and Hindus in India have such divergent views on vegetarianism, don't they?

ROSEN: Sure. And you can even see such differences of opinion in the various Hindu sects, too. You have Shaivites and worshippers of Kali, for example, who often sacrifice animals and eat flesh—they call this animal sacrifice *bali*—and then you have the Vaishnavas, who are scrupulous vegetarians and who are kind to animals. Sometimes worshippers of Kali offer a goat to the goddess in sacrifice, for she is said to be propitiated only by red blood. Vaishnavas who enter Kali temples often bring an offering of red flowers to appease the goddess by the similarity in color. To this day, there is an unscrupulous class of Kali priests who run a lucrative slaughterhouse business in the name of religion. Not so for the Vaishnavas.

BERRY: Would you say that a goodly number of Hindus indulge in meat-eating as a result of this form of Kali worship?

ROSEN: Well, animal sacrifice, or *bali,* is now on the wane. Thankfully. There's evidence that Calcutta's most famous Kali temple, known as Kalighat, now sacrifices fewer goats per year than ever before. This is setting a standard in the less popular temples, too. All Kali temples that are associated with the Ramakrishna Mission have prohibited animal sacrifice, and it is prohibited by law in the temporary shrines erected throughout Calcutta during Kali Puja. So there is something of a "vegetarianizing" of the Goddess going on. Rachel Fell McDermott, a Harvard scholar now teaching at Columbia University, has been doing a good deal of research on this subject.

BERRY: But in the Vedic texts—is there ever an allowance for meat-eating?

ROSEN: Well, certain medicines include animal products, so, yes, for medicinal purposes—but a true Vaishnava, and especially a Brahmin, would never ingest these things. Also, in Vedic culture, there was some allowance for a *kshatriya,* a member of the warrior class, to eat meat, but this was only in very special conditions—when he was living in the forest, preparing for battle. And even then, he would do so only under certain regulations, and then he would have to kill the animal himself, uttering the *mamsa mantra* in the animal's ear. This *mantra* basically says, "As I eat you now, in a future life, you may eat me." This was to inculcate in the meat-eating *kshatriya* a sensibility of karmic or causal truth. There is a severe reaction for killing animals, or eating meat, and this was widely known in ancient India. Actually, in India, it is still widely known, and meat-eating is frowned upon by most believing Hindus.

BERRY: What about the Ashvamedha, or the horse sacrifice, that one reads about in histories of ancient India?

ROSEN: The Ashvamedha was one of many royal sacrifices. Three were most prominent: the Rajasuya, the Vajapeya, and the Ashvamedha. Again, this was for *kshatriyas,* and they were very complicated sacrifices that would ensure entrance into heavenly planets, although not necessarily into the kingdom of God. There were scriptures to guide those in passion and ignorance through these complex rituals—*kshatriyas* especially, but never Brahmins. Those in goodness, the uncorrupted brahminical class, were generally beyond these sacrifices—they tended to focus more on direct spiritual pursuits—it is they who attained the ultimate destination.

Anyway, the Ashvamedha involved a complex series of events that lasted over one year. Essentially, it called for over one hundred horses, but only one was chosen as the main object of sacrifice. What is not generally mentioned in relation to this sacrifice, however, is that the horse was not only killed but was immediately brought back to life—immediately rejuvenated by the power of the *mantras* that were chanted by the priests. If the priests could not produce a young horse out of the sacrificial fire, then they were forbidden to perform the sacrifice at all or to kill the older horse in the first place. Incidentally, the whole ceremony is off-limits in this age, since there are no qualified priests who can properly chant the *mantras*.

BERRY: Wasn't there some sort of sexual ritual between the horse and the queen?

ROSEN: (*laughter*) Well, some scholars have assumed as much. The ceremony called for the Queen, or Princess, to lay down behind a drawn curtain with the horse that was to be sacrificed. This was to soothe the horse, to calm the poor animal. Sexual innuendoes are not really there in the texts, and there is no evidence that any perverse activity was part of the ritual. Anyway, I must reiterate that these sacrifices are not recommended for this age. However, some sects say that it can still be done. It should be pointed out, though, that the vast majority of practitioners and Vedic scholars insist that the Ashvamedha and similar sacrifices were for a previous age, and that the modern sacrifice is the chanting of the holy name. This is the recommended process for our current age.

BERRY: Speaking of schisms, what about the rift between Advaita philosophy and non-Advaita philosophy? According to Indologist A. L. Basham, when he visited Benares, which is the sacred city associated with Shiva worship and Advaita religious philosophy, the Advaita Brahmins who pride themselves on having gone far on the path of Raja yoga and Shankarite meditation tend to be very arrogant and self-important because they feel that they have successfully merged their *atman*, their soul, with Paramatman, the supreme soul, or God. Basham notes that they strut about the streets of Benares like *dhoti*-clad gods. Far from exhibiting a fading away of self, they display a refined egotism that reminds him of the self-absorption of the Theravada Buddhists.

On the other hand, Basham says that when he visited Vrindavan, which, as you know, is that city in northwestern India that is associated with Krishna worship and non-Advaita or theistic Hinduism, he found the Vaishnavas to be friendly, unassuming, and forthcoming. Basham ascribes their friendliness and lack of holier-than-thou attitude to their being dualists who worship a personal God, holding themselves separate from God (unlike the Advaitavadis of Benares, who see themselves as one with God). Identifying with God, however one rationalizes it, seems to run counter to humility.

So we have these two cities—impersonalist Advaita Benares and personalist non-Advaita Vrindavan—representing the polarity that exists in Indian religious philosophy. Do you agree with Basham's critique?

ROSEN: Yes, to a certain degree. I think it's very well stated, too. Advaita philosophy is very much akin to Theravada Buddhism. Chaitanya Mahaprabhu preferred the non-Advaita or dualist system because under the Advaita system there is no opportunity for rendering service to God. He prefers being distinct from God and thus being able to pay his adoration to a personal deity. Thus, Vaishnavas would rather *taste* sugar than *become* sugar...

BERRY: (*laughter*) What about reincarnation and liberation? Do these various systems perceive the ultimate goal in different ways?

ROSEN: There are various nuances of difference in these things, depending on which Advaita group you are talking about and which Vaishnava group you are talking about. Generally, in the Advaita system you continually reincarnate until you achieve *moksha,* "release," which, for them, means becoming "one with God," a position from which one generally falls. For Buddhists, the goal is *nirvana,* or enlightenment, but this, again, is not really an ultimate goal: what do you do in your enlightened state? The Vaishnavas say that the ultimate liberation is developing love for Krishna and, after death, attaining His supreme abode. This is the perfection of *moksha* and *nirvana.*

You experience release from material bondage and are situated in your eternal constitutional position. What's more, you exist in eternity, knowledge, and bliss, so you have enlightened activity in Krishna's service and relish it for all time.

TAOISM

TAOISM IS ONE OF THE three main religions of China, and is the most ancient of the three. (The other two are Confucianism and Buddhism.) It has survived—with characteristic resiliency—the Chinese Communist Party's attempts to tear it out of the Chinese cultural soil, root and branch—perhaps the greatest challenge that Taoism has had to face since Kublai Khan ordered the burning of all Taoist books (save the *Tao Te Ching*) in 1281 CE. There are some who hold that Taoism in Maoist China was strengthened through persecution and adversity, much as bamboo is said to draw its strength from the winds that buffet it.

Furthermore, the orthodox Taoist monasteries, in keeping with the Taoist affinity to nature, are sited on remote mountain fastnesses. These beautiful mountain temples are designed to merge with their craggy surroundings. Consequently, they are not easy to get to. Some of these hermitages are so out of the way that doubtless they were spared the worst depredations of the Cultural Revolution because of their very aloofness.

Like Buddhism, its archrival among Chinese religions for almost 2,000 years, Taoism has always required a vegetarian diet of its closest followers. The Taoist lay vegetarian societies, which since the Maoist takeover in the early 1950s have had to operate secretly, have long promoted vegetarianism among the Chinese peasantry and middle class. Writing in his *History of Chinese Religions*, D.T. Smith says: "Yet Taoism still maintained some hold through its lay vegetarian societies, promoted for mutual encouragement in the religious life; meditation; study and good works in its secret societies among the peasants giving a sanction to revolutionary activity in times of trouble."[1]

Like many other Eastern religions such as Buddhism, Zen, Hinduism and Yoga, Taoism is becoming increasingly popular in the West. Since Taoism is a religion with a strong vegetarian imperative, this augurs well for the future of vegetarianism (to say nothing of Taoism itself) in the West.

As a measure of Taoism's growing popularity in the West, there are over twenty-five titles in print that begin with the three magic words "The Tao of..." *The Tao of Health, The Tao of Peace, The Tao of Longevity, The Tao of Power, The Tao of Pooh.* Certainly the word "Tao" seems to have a magical effect on sales. Any book with the word Tao in its title seems destined to become a bestseller; so perhaps the word Tao does have talismanic powers after all.

The extraordinary thing about the first "Tao of..." book—the *Tao Te Ching*—is that shorn of its mystery, and its cryptic language, it is essentially a manual of yoga. Although the date is uncertain, it was probably written in the third century BCE by a Chinese sage named Lao Tzu (which means literally "the old boy").

Scholars consider the *Tao Te Ching* by the Chinese sage Lao Tzu to be a "Warring States" work, because it was composed from 700-300 BCE. It is called the time of the Warring States because China, which had hitherto been a fairly placid place, had degenerated into a collection of petty kingdoms that were constantly at war with each other. It had become a time of unimaginable brutality and cruelty. The warrior princes who had always conducted warfare in a chivalrous manner, had been replaced by upstarts and usurpers who would stop at nothing to gain their ends. They were not above poisoning rivers, invading without warning, breaking treaties or betraying friendships and alliances at a whim. Whole cities were sacked and all their male inhabitants were put to the sword. To enhance their prestige, these warriors would boil their foes in a cauldron and gulp down the broth.[2]

Despite the tendency among the upstart princes of this period to make a wonton soup of their fallen enemies and toss it off with gusto, the princes were not without cultural pretensions; they read widely, and they wrote and commissioned poetry; many of them plumed themselves on being patrons of the arts. World-weary and often bored to extinction, the Chinese nobles used warfare and hunting as an antidote to boredom. It is worth quoting Professor Jacques Gernet on this point: "Apart from its religious activities, the noble class devoted its time to hunting and warfare. In the archaic period no distinction was made between the two. The weapons used were the same, and the great hunting parties were useful for training troops. Even the assembly places were the same. Captives and game were treated identically and consecrated to the ancestors and the gods. Some of the prisoners were in fact executed at the moment of triumph, or else kept in reserve as sacrificial offerings."[3]

The Warring States period occurs some time after this; but the attitudes of the nobility towards animals and peasants hadn't changed; only the weapons had gotten better: the invention of the composite bow and iron slashing swords made both hunting and the game of warfare at once deadlier and more intoxicating. Gernet calls the noble classes of this period "carnivorous by preference."[4]

How to persuade the warrior princes to stop waging war and rending the country—that was the task that Lao Tzu had set himself. He decided to do the same thing that another great political thinker would do some 2,000 years later—Nicolo Machiavelli in Renaissance Florence—and that was to write a treatise on statecraft. Machiavelli called his little how-to book, *The Prince;* Lao Tzu called his, the *Tao Te Ching,* "The Book of the Way and Power." Whereas Machiavelli urges the prince to be a combination of the lion and the fox—a tellingly carnivorous pair—Lao Tzu urges the prince to be like water whose strength paradoxically resides in its passivity, plasticity and downward pull. Water embodies Lao Tzu's concept of how an enlightened ruler should govern—through *wu-wei,* or effortless action. "Water is of all things most yielding and can overcome rock, which is of all things most hard." Instead of instructing the prince on how to make another conquest or commit a fresh chicane, Lao Tzu urges the prince to look inward, adopt a contemplative manner, meditate on his ingoing and outgoing breaths—in a word, to study yoga. And the first precept of any classic system of yoga is the same as that of Buddhism and Jainism—to do no harm to any other life form, in essence to become an ethical vegetarian. Having become a vegetarian and learned to practice breath control, the ruler could look forward to achieving yogic trance, ecstasy and longevity. By thus cultivating his interior life, and ruling over his people with effortless action or *wu-wei*, he could become the ideal ruler, the yogic sage-king.

Scholars are divided on the question of whether the trance state that these Taoist yogins achieved was ecstatic. But Henri Maspero, the great Taoist scholar, asserts that ecstasy was routinely achieved by the Taoist adepts. Moreover, he also says that Lao Tzu and Chuang Tzu were quite energetic in promoting a yoga of ecstasy.[5] Indeed, a psychotropic payoff was one of the enticements for a young Chinese ruler to take up yoga in the first place. How else could Lao Tzu and his disciple Chuang Tzu have turned the heads of the young warlords for whom their works were written other than by offering them an ecstatic experience and the promise of a long life—for increased longevity was the other prospect that the practice of Taoist yoga held out for the young prince?

Little is known about the life of Lao Tzu (born circa fourth century BCE in Ch'en). As nearly as it can be pieced together, the evidence suggests that he was a librarian in the royal library of the kingdom of Hu. Apparently, he was of a retiring nature and was rather solitary in his habits. Legend has it that at the age of 160[6] he was on the point of embarking on a permanent retreat to some remote and secluded hermitage when he was persuaded by a minor government functionary (some reports say that it was a customs official), to set down his message to the world before withdrawing from it. It may be an apocryphal story; yet it is interesting in and of itself because it throws light on the nature of Taoism.

First of all, there is Lao Tzu's predilection for anonymity—which is rather fitting because Taoists tend to be reclusive, and they don't give a fig for celebrity or fame; in fact, they have a horror of it. There is also something quintessentially Taoist about Lao Tzu's honoring the request of a humble customs official to interrupt his journey and dash off one of the world's great literary masterpieces in impromptu fashion. For Taoism teaches that one must seek knowledge and contentment in the lowliest places (like water that flows downward and seeks the lowest level). Taoism sets its face against the social climbing and mindless striving after high office of the Confucians.

Taoist, too, is the quickness and spontaneity with which Lao Tzu dashes off the great work. It illustrates the Taoist concept of creation through spontaneity (*tzu-jan*) that one can see exemplified today in the lightning brush strokes of the great Chinese calligraphers and *sumi-e* painters. That the "old boy" could produce one of the greatest masterworks of world literature "off the cuff" is the ultimate act of *tzu-jan*.

Significant as well is Lao Tzu's age at the time he is supposed to have written the *Tao Te Ching*. Legend has it that he was from 160 to 200 years old. Since long life is one of the chief aims of Taoism, the fact that its historical founder was mentally adroit enough to compose the *Tao Te Ching* at such an over-ripe age is a good advertisement for the Taoist way of life—and for the diet that propelled the "old boy" through the vagaries of life for 200 years and more. In all probability, his diet was a vegetarian one, as Taoists have eaten vegetarian food since the inception. Even today, the food eaten by Taoist monks and nuns in Taoist monasteries and by reclusive lay Taoists is exclusively vegetarian as the eminent sinologist, Dr. Michael Saso, points out in his book *A Taoist Cookbook:* "Taoist monks, nuns, and recluses, who follow the strictest rules of Taoist cooking, observe an almost pure vegetarian diet."[7]

Although it has been some 2,400 years since Lao Tzu composed it, the *Tao Te Ching* is still the fundamental text used by the conservative Taoist monasteries in China. Taoist monks study it, invoke it, debate it and endlessly reinterpret it, much as Christian monks do scripture. Despite its brevity, it's a very slender volume of only 4,000 Chinese characters; it is so profound, multilayered and mystical that the commentary on the Tao is voluminous. Indeed, there are commentaries on commentaries. However, beginning with Arthur Waley's key work *The Way and Its Power*, scholars have finally cracked the code of the *Tao Te Ching*. The most recent confirmation that Waley's theory was correct, that the *Tao Te Ching* is a covert manual of yoga, comes from Professor Victor Mair, who in his new translation of the *Tao Te Ching*, has lent color to Waley's findings.

With Arthur Waley, whose insight it first was, Mair believes that the *Tao Te Ching*, in addition to being a guide to statecraft, is also a manual of yoga that gives specific instructions on how to induce a yogic trance: "There are so many correspondences between yoga and Taoism even in the smallest and oddest details—throughout the history of their development—that we might almost think of them as two variants of a single religious and philosophical system."[8] Among some of the more striking parallels that Mair points out are that both the yoga of the Upanishads and the yoga of early Taoism lay stress upon the vital breath, and both conceive of it as flowing through channels in the body. He points out that yoga and Taoism "share a close association with external and internal alchemy. Both resort to the use of charms, sacred syllables and talismans as aids in meditation and for conveying secret knowledge." He also mentions that both yoga and Taoism claim that those who become adepts can easily achieve supernatural powers such as clairvoyance, clairaudience, and, of course, longevity. He concludes his lengthy list of correspondences between Indic yoga and Taoism with the following summation: "By now it is hoped that even the hardened skeptic and the most ardent Chinese isolationist will admit that Yoga and Taoism bear such striking affinities to each other that they must be related in some fashion.

"In most instances, however, what the founders of Taoism absorbed from Yoga were radically new ideas concerning man and his place in the universe and a complementary physiological regimen (meditational discipline, dietary practices, flexing exercises and so forth). Considering the immense linguistic, social and philosophical differences between China and India, it is astounding that the kindredness of the *Bhagavad Gita* and the *Tao Te Ching* shines through so conspicuously."[9]

It is important to note that among the "radically new ideas" the founders of Taoism absorbed from yoga were "dietary practices." Although Mair doesn't spell it out for us, the new dietary practices associated with Yoga could only have meant one thing—vegetarianism. For it is obligatory on the serious student of Yoga that he be a strict vegetarian. In his book *Light on Yoga,* B. K. S. Iyengar, one of the world's foremost experts on yoga, observes: "A vegetarian diet is essential to the practice of yoga." Let's face it, yoga without a vegetarian component would be merely a system of stretching exercises. It is the meditation and the vegetarian regimen that make of yoga something more than just a set of preposterous-looking postures, and help raise it to a metaphysical plane.

Not only does a flesh diet interfere with meditation, but some yogins have even gone so far as to say that a flesh-eating yogin runs the risk of being accosted on the psychic plane by the disembodied spirits of the animals that he or she may have dined on the night before. Meeting the disembodied soul of a cow, a fish, or a chicken from whose carcass one's dinner was plucked could seriously disrupt *samadhi!* Apropos of this, one is reminded of Theosophist Annie Besant's vivid account of her train trip to Chicago, when Chicago was "Hog butcher to the world." As her train chugged towards the city looming in the distance, "a profound sense of desolation oppressed her spirit" because from the South Chicago stockyards she received astral messages of reproach from thousands of slaughtered beasts, suspended between the physical world and the thought world.

Although Taoist yoga appears to have derived from India, its goal, according to Taoist scholar J. C. Cooper, was very different from that of Indian yoga. Whereas the Indian yogin tried to reach a state of *samadhi* (ecstatic trance), the Taoist yogin's objective was to achieve *samadhi* as well as immortality. As Cooper writes in *Chinese Alchemy, The Taoist Quest for Immortality:* "This goal of immortality marks a difference between Indian and Chinese yoga; the former is concerned with the control of the body as a preparation for meditation and other religious exercises for the sake of the spirit, while the Chinese cult of immortality in some cases made the achievement of immortality a goal in itself."[10]

Thus, one of the most irresistible features of Taoism was its promise of—if not immortality—then the prolonging of life beyond the normal compass. The implication was that this could be done by practicing yoga and eating *sattvic*, or healthful, vegetarian food.

Although most Western scholars disparage the mystical quest for immortality in Taoism—they regard it as a corruption that crept in during the Three Dynasties Period—Henri Maspero, the French Taoist scholar who made the study of Taoism his life's work, believed that the concern for prolonging one's life and increasing vitality were present in Taoism from the very start. He writes as follows: "From the fourth and third centuries BCE, the Taoists were seekers of immortality; from its origin, Taoism has been a doctrine of individual salvation which claimed to conduct the adept to immortality. The methods must have varied: each master had his own, which he kept secret and transmitted only to certain chosen disciples; from this time on we see most of these which were to be current at the time of the Six Dynasties and Tang."[11]

What part did vegetarianism have to play in the Taoist quest for immortality? Here is what Professor Maspero has to say: "The prohibition of eating meat had nothing to do with the similar Buddhist prohibition. In Buddhism, it is the consequence of the interdict upon killing living beings; for the Taoists, it is because the spirits of the interior of the body have a horror of blood, the Breath of which wounds them, causes them to flee, and thus shortens life."[12]

In sum, the Taoists were compassionate towards animals and forbade scientific experiments on them. Indeed, the Taoist doctrine of *wu-wei*, or "non-interference" has much in common with the Jain concept of not interfering in the lives of other beings. Taoists have always been vegetarians for reasons that were unabashedly health-conscious; the main purpose of the Taoist religion is to increase vital energy and prolong life; they believed that a meatless diet would help them attain physical immortality, and the quest for the *elixir vitae* has been the consuming passion of Taoists from time out of mind.

To judge how strong this passion was, one has only to consider the strange case of the otherwise savvy Chinese emperors who were gullible enough to swallow lethal doses of mercury and lead and other heavy metals in the mistaken belief that they were quaffing the *elixir vitae*. One of China's most despotic emperors, the Napolean of China, Qin Shih Huang Ti (circa 215 CE), perished in this manner. Although he had many great accomplishments to his credit, such as the building of the Great Wall, he earned the undying enmity of Chinese scholars because he burned all the Chinese literary and philosophical classics—sparing only the *materia medica*, which he hoped to use to procure his immortality. After launching an ill-fated expedition to find the magic potion of immortality on the Islands of the Immortals, he browbeat his Taoist physicians into concocting a golden pill of immortality. They did, and after taking it, he died.

Besides the golden pills that poisoned a few gullible despots, many other useful byproducts have emerged from the Taoist quest for immortality. To list but a few: the discovery of the pulse; the science of acupuncture; herbology; the martial arts; alchemy as the precursor of chemistry; and the discovery of gunpowder and metallurgy. Their sampling of almost everything edible in their attempt to find the *elixir vitae* led them to collect the wide range of spices and herbs used in Chinese cookery; it also, in all likelihood, led them to the discovery of tofu and other soy foods, whose anti-carcinogenic and anti-angina properties have recently been confirmed scientifically in the West.[13] To the indefatigable Taoist quest for eternal life, the Chinese also owe their vast *materia medica* which boasts the world's earliest and most sophisticated pharmacopia. The history of Taoism shows there are moral as well as utilitarian benefits to being a vegetarian for health reasons. ☯

R.B.

[1] D. Howard Smith, *Chinese Religions: From 1,000 B.C. to the Present Day*, (New York: Holt, Rinehart and Winston, 1971), p. 111.

[2] Holmes, Welch, *Taoism: The Parting of the Way* (Boston: Beacon Press, 1965), p. 19.

[3] Jacques Gernet, *Ancient China: From the Beginnings to the Empire* (Berkeley: University of California Press, 1968), pp. 58-9.

[4] *ibid.*, pp. 50-51.

[5] Henri Maspero, *Taoism and Chinese Religion* (Amherst: University of Massachusetts Press, 1981), p. 30.

[6] Welch, *op. cit.*, p. 2.

[7] Dr. Michael Saso, *A Taoist Cookbook*, (Rutland: Charles E. Tuttle, 1994), p. xviii.

[8] Lao Tzu, *Tao Te Ching*, trans. by Victor Mair (New York: Bantam Books, 1990), p. 145.

[9] *ibid.*

[10] J.C. Cooper, *Chinese Alchemy, The Taoist Quest for Immortality* (New York: Sterling, 1990), p. 109.

[11] Maspero, *op. cit.*, p. 33.

[12] *ibid.*

[13] Leon Jaroff, "The Man's Cancer," *Time*, April 1, 1996, p. 65.

DR. MAOSHING NI

D R. MAOSHING NI, AUTHOR of *The Tao of Nutrition*, was born into the 38th generation of a family of Taoist healers. For a man who has written so many books, and who is weighed down with so many degrees, Dr. Ni seems remarkably youthful for his years. His boyish good looks are his own best advertisement for the rejuvenative properties of the Taoist health secrets that he purveys. His father, Master Ni Hua-Ching, is an esoteric Taoist who lived as a hermit in the monasteries and mountain fastnesses of China for over thirty-five years and is a prolific author of books on Taoist medicine and metaphysics. Some

of Master Ni's books include his translations of Lao Tzu and such other titles as *Esoteric Tao Teh Ching; The Taoist Inner View of the Universe;* and *Internal Alchemy: The Natural Way to Immortality.* Under his father and other Taoist masters, Dr. Ni studied Taoist philosophy; the martial arts (which had their origin in Taoism); Tai Chi Chuan; Taoist nutrition; and such Taoist healing arts as acupuncture, herbology and acupressure. With his father he is the co-founder and Vice-President of Yo-San University of Traditional Chinese Medicine in Santa Monica, California. We met in Dr. Ni's office in Santa Monica, which was less than a hundred yards from the craggy cliffs (*yang*), soaring above smooth beaches (*yin*), that Taoist *sumi-e* painters love to depict.

·············

BERRY: There seems to be a growing awareness of the Tao in the West. There's a plethora of books that have been published with the title, The Tao of...—everything from *The Tao of Pooh*, to *The Tao of Baseball*, to *The Tao of Cooking*.

NI: It's all so mysterious because the Tao can't be effectively rendered into words.

BERRY: There's that famous aphorism of Lao Tzu's that the Tao that can be described is not the real Tao.

NI: Exactly. So it has a mysterious appeal, but the simple truths that Taoism purveys are actually difficult for most people to grasp because their thought processes have become too convoluted. If they would quiet themselves down and try to take their mind back to its original simplicity, then they would be able to grasp immediately the truth of the Tao.

BERRY: Is Taoism making a comeback in China? I know that it was driven underground by the Maoist persecutions.

NI: It has made a comeback under the guise of *ch'i-kung*. You know in the 70s, before the openness, before the government loosened the reins on religion, one thing that really seized the popular imagination was *ch'i-kung*, and in fact the government even established the study of *ch'i* in government research institutes—that was their way of getting around the religious prohibitions. So through *ch'i-kung*, Taoism has already experienced a revival, and it's become so popular that it's estimated that 100 million people from China practice *ch'i-kung* every day.

BERRY: In what form? "Tai Chi?"

NI: There are so many different styles of *ch'i-kung*. The important question is: "What is the principle in this?" The underlying philosophy of *ch'i-kung* is to enable one to achieve balance, harmony with the universe, and a calm; these effects are achieved through Taoism and they've been presented in such a way that it's not offensive to the government. Strangely enough, it doesn't pose a threat to the government when twenty-thousand people gather in the arena to listen to a *ch'i-kung* master preach about *ch'i* and then demonstrate it, while engaging everybody in this practice. So, whilst they don't openly worship Taoism, they observe Taoism in the guise of *ch'i-kung*. China is such a deeply religious society that even the Communist officials secretly practice Taoism. Within the next decade I predict that folk Taoism as a full-blown religion will be restored to its pre-Maoist pre-eminence. It's inevitable. It's already started in the rural areas among the peasants, and it's slowly drifting back into the cities. Eventually the government will have to bow to the inevitable and allow Taoism to reenter people's lives.

BERRY: In his book, *Chinese Religions*, D. Howard Smith remarked that vegetarianism has been preserved in China through the lay Taoist organizations.

NI: Yes, that's very true.

BERRY: Many Taoist monasteries were destroyed during the Cultural Revolution; are they also being restored?

NI: Yes, Taoism is being revived through the monasteries and vice-versa. In fact, I subscribe to a Taoist journal that is published in China; five years ago, it would have been impossible for this magazine to have been published. In its pages one can read about new temples that are being constructed and about people who are dedicating their lives to being Taoist monks and priests. Resplendent in their robes, they are shown preaching and presiding over religious ceremonies. Just a few short years ago, this too would have been unthinkable. So the return of Taoism in China appears to be unstoppable.

BERRY: The White Cloud monastery in Peking was one of the most famous Taoist monasteries in China. Was it destroyed during the Cultural Revolution, or is it still thriving?

NI: No, it survived the Cultural Revolution, and many of the Taoist temples that were destroyed by the Red Guards have been rebuilt. You see, even the Communist leaders recognized the historic value as well as the tourist value of these temples.

BERRY: In his book, *Facets of Taoism*, Holmes Welch published the memoir of a Japanese scholar, who had been invited to undergo training as a Taoist monk in the White Cloud Monastery before the Maoist regime took over. What I found particularly fascinating was his observation that not only was exclusively vegetarian food served at the White Cloud, but that there were two tiers of vegetarian food (reflecting the social division within the monastery)—a very palatial vegetarian food was served to the abbot and the higher ranking monks, but the lower ranking monks had to content themselves with *congee* (rice gruel) and pickles. I was somewhat dismayed to find this distinction in the quality of the food based on rank. Surely, the food at China's premier Taoist monastery should not have been based on rank.

NI: It's always been hierarchical. Rank has always been very important in Taoist temples and monasteries.

BERRY: I guess that's why Mao and his minions tried to wipe it out. How far did they succeed?

NI: Well, the White Cloud is as thriving a monastery as it ever was. Does that answer your question?

BERRY: As a strict vegetarian, could I make my way through China by dining at Taoist monasteries and temples?

NI: When I have friends or patients who are traveling in China, I recommend that they stop at the Taoist monasteries for their meals as often as possible, because Taoist cuisine is undoubtedly the cleanest, the tastiest and the most economical cuisine to be had in China. In flavor and cleanliness, restaurant food cannot compare with Taoist temple cuisine.

BERRY: In China, is there a difference between Taoist and Buddhist cuisine?

NI: Yes, there is a distinct difference between Taoist and Buddhist cuisine. What really separates these two types of cuisine is the extensive use of herbs. Taoist cuisine is a therapeutic cuisine. Taoist dishes are created not just to please the palate, but to heal the body and the spirit. Consequently, you will find that Taoist dishes are seasoned with herbs in such a way as to promote the diner's well-being. So a Taoist cook must know the medicinal value of the foods, herbs and spices that he uses; whereas this is not the case with Buddhist cooking.

BERRY: Since Taoism has taken root in California, I'm wondering if there are any restaurants serving Taoist cuisine out here?

NI: Yes, there used to be a Taoist restaurant in San Francisco called the Emperor's Restaurant. It was unique in that when people would come in for a meal they would be greeted by a Taoist herbalist who would feel their pulse, look at their tongue, and then recommend the dishes on the menu based on his diagnosis. The menu contained all sorts of exotic vegetable dishes seasoned with medicinal herbs. It closed, I believe, because it was slightly ahead of its time.

BERRY: Is it customary for Taoist chefs to be herbalists and to know the medicinal value of foods?

NI: Yes. Quite early on, Taoists realized that food should be and could be our best medicine; so they developed a system of nutrition that utilized food as a healing agent.

BERRY: Does this tradition go back as far as Lao Tzu?

NI: I think it precedes Lao Tzu, because there is mention of it in the very first *materia medica*, which was written in China by an emperor named Shen Nung. By the way, Shen Nung was considered the father of herbology as well as other technologies. But in this particular work, the first *materia medica*, he talks about three categories of herbs, one of which would strengthen one's vitality, and increase one's longevity. So these herbs were classified as herbs of immortality.

BERRY: Is this peculiar to Taoist religion, or doesn't Buddhism also have access to the same *materia medica* and herbal remedies?

NI: In Buddhism, the emphasis is more on sustenance; whereas, in Taoism, the emphasis is placed upon the therapeutic and life-prolonging properties of foods. Keep in mind that the Taoists were after one thing—the secret of immortality—so they were constantly testing the life-prolonging properties of foods.

BERRY: Unlike today's pharmaceutical houses, these Taoist wizards appear to have experimented on themselves rather than on guinea pigs or laboratory monkeys. Did the doctrine of harmlessness to animals in Taoism keep them from experimenting on animals?

NI: That's right—they were their own guinea pigs, if you will.

BERRY: Didn't quite a number of these Taoist wizards poison themselves in their attempts to find the *elixir vitae*?

NI: Yes, that's true. These early Taoists were alchemists; they experimented with such heavy metals as lead, arsenic, mercury, etc., in the hope of finding the elixir. By ingesting these chemicals in minute doses, they thought they could prolong their lives.

BERRY: (laughter) These Taoist wizards were considered to be the world's first alchemists, were they not?

NI: Precisely. Ko Hung, the author of the classic work on alchemy (circa 312 CE), was the outstanding Taoist alchemist of his time.

BERRY: In his book, *The Way and Its Power*, Arthur Waley advanced the theory that the early Taoists, in the early part of the first millennium BCE, may have been influenced by the philosophies of India that had been imported to China by Chinese merchants who traveled back and forth between the two countries. How do you feel about that?

NI: My studies confirm that there was indeed commerce in ideas between India and China during this period, but that it flowed in two directions. Sure, Taoism was tinged with Indian philosophy, but then I believe that Indian philosophy was also tinged with Chinese ideas. The influence was not all one way. In fact, Lao Tzu had talked about going to a place up in the foothills of the K'unlun mountains—the range of mountains in the Himalayas that borders Pakistan. This is the place to which Lao Tzu retreated when he finally left China by mounting a water buffalo and riding West. So I think that this legend of Lao Tzu's journey to India may well symbolize how the Taoist teachings have crossed the Himalayas into India.

BERRY: In the appendix to his translation of the *Tao Te Ching*,

Professor Victor Mair confirms the findings of Arthur Waley by showing the correspondences between the *Bhagavad-gita* and the *Tao Te Ching.*

NI: Yes, these texts were probably composed at about the same period, and given the lively commerce in ideas between the two countries, it's easy to see how these mutual influences might have taken place. Buddha, Lao Tzu, and Pythagoras were all contemporaries, and they were expounding similar philosophies.

BERRY: The great thing is that they were all preaching a doctrine of *ahimsa* or harmlessness to animals, as well as techniques for putting this doctrine into operation, such as yogic breathing, yogic *asanas*, and even yogic diet.

NI: Yes, that's right.

BERRY: It was Arthur Waley who pointed out that there were some elements of yogic instruction in the *Tao Te Ching.* Waley's theory was that Lao Tzu was trying to instruct the princes of the Warring States Period in yogic practice as a way of pacifying them, and enticing them away from war-making onto a more spiritual path. He saw the *Tao Te Ching* as a disguised manual of yoga, which was based on Indic doctrines.

NI: In the Taoist tradition we call all these practices "Dao-In"— to conduct and to move the *ch'i*, which is the energy in the body. These "Dao-In" exercises bear a similarity to the exercises of the Indian yogic tradition. I know that some scholars may argue that those practices came from India; however, they have a unique Chinese origin. It is true that Lao Tzu advocated that the rulers adopt his philosophy during the Warring States period as a way of bringing about peace, but it was a distinct Chinese philosophy of *yin-yang* balance that he was expounding.

BERRY: Wouldn't the Sanskrit word *prana* [breath] be the counterpart of the Taoist *ch'i*?

NI: They are similar.

BERRY: *Pranayama*, or the yogic breathing exercises, would probably correspond to the Taoist yogic breathing exercises that Waley and Maspero talk about, wouldn't you say?

NI: Yes, they are quite similar, but as I said before, they have a unique Chinese quality.

BERRY: An integral part of yogic practice in India is the observance of a vegetarian diet. Is that true of Taoism as well?

NI: That's generally true. Many of the serious Taoists of the past lived in caves, and in remote places, high in the mountains; so they had very little access to animal flesh. Consequently they did mostly subsist on herbs and grains and seeds.

BERRY: In his book, *Tao: The Parting of the Way*, Holmes Welch cites a book called *The Monastery of Jade Mountain*, which had been written by an Anglo-Russian businessman who had traveled extensively throughout China. Prior to the Maoist regime, Peter Goulart (the author of *The Monastery of Jade Mountain*), had spent months-at-a-time in various Taoist monasteries. Some of the laxer monasteries served non-vegetarian as well as vegetarian food; but at the Jade Mountain monastery they served only strict vegan food, that is, strict vegetarian fare containing no animal products. Would this have been typical of the cuisine served at the pre-World-War-II Taoist monasteries in China?

NI: Yes, here I'd just like to note that there are two large branches of Taoism—folk Taoism and esoteric Taoism; the folk Taoists, as the name implies, are the common people; whereas the esoteric Taoists disassociate themselves from the world and keep themselves aloof from it as much as possible.

BERRY: They would be the counterparts of the *rishis* and *sadhus* of India.

NI: Exactly, they are the reclusive holy men and hermits who live alone. In fact, that's the tradition that our family comes from. My father has written extensively about that in his books.

BERRY: Did he ever live in a monastery?

NI: Yes, he spent about thirty years in the mountains of China living as a hermit and also dwelling in different monasteries.

BERRY: How does folk Taoism differ from esoteric Taoism?

NI: The folk Taoists have monasteries and temples, and they have the hierarchy of monks and priests just like the Buddhist tem-

ples. Folk Taoism does bear a striking similarity to Buddhism; its
purpose is to facilitate public worship.

BERRY: Did folk Taoism precede the arrival of Buddhism in
China, or is it a synthesis of Taoism and Buddhism?

NI: Taoism is an indigenous religion of China—there's no question about that. However, folk Taoism has been influenced tremendously by the arrival of Buddhism in China. On the other
hand, esoteric Taoism has tried to maintain the purity of the
indigenous tradition, and has preserved its original simplicity.

BERRY: Have the esoteric Taoists been vegetarian as well?

NI: Again, as I said, the esoteric Taoists were the hermits and
recluses up in the mountains cultivating their *ch'i*, and their
immortality, and so forth; so they probably were—they were vegetarians. Herbs played a huge part in their diet. But again, it
needs to be stressed that vegetarianism was not a religious belief.
Not even in folk Taoism was it a religious belief. However, eating
animal flesh didn't make health sense; so the Taoists, being such
pragmatic people, were vegetarians for health reasons.

BERRY: The Chinese scholar Yi-Fu Tuan has written on this
point. In his book, *Morality and Imagination* that addresses this
issue he writes:

"Unlike Greece, Rome and India, China did not produce
thinkers who pondered on the suffering of animals. The vast
majority of people in China were poor, and the poor in China, like
those in other civilizations, never had the opportunity to slaughter animals and eat meat. The well-to-do, including Confucius and
the Confucians, certainly ate meat, but they all seem to have done
so with an easy conscience. If certain foods were proscribed as in
religious Taoism, it was done as a hygienic measure and as a tech-
nique for attaining immortality. No doubt all Chinese abhorred
violence and bloodshed: the profession of butcher, was, after all,
held in disesteem."

NI: The Taoists, who were mostly meditators and *ch'i-kung* practitioners, didn't exert themselves physically, so they tended to
stick to light foods, such as fruits, vegetables, light grains, seeds.

BERRY: Peter Goulart, the Anglo-Russian traveler whom I mentioned earlier, observed that many of the abbots and priests in the Taoist monasteries were strict vegetarians and that they looked thirty or forty years younger than they were chronologically; they were also able to perform prodigious feats of strength and endurance. So perhaps there is something to the notion that the Taoist mode of living enables one to achieve a measure of immortality.

NI: Certainly they achieved an uncommon state of good health; my own research reveals that herbs played a huge part in the diet of these long-lived Taoists—such herbs as lotus seed, fox-nut and wild yam, that are rich in various vitamins, mineral adaptagens and nutrients.

BERRY: Does tofu play an important role in Taoist cuisine?

NI: Yes, tofu is made of soybeans, which is tonic to the *ch'i* and strengthens the spleen.

BERRY: The Taoists were using tofu in their cuisine long before the arrival of Buddhism in China?

NI: Yes, after Buddhism arrived in China, tofu became an essential part of Buddhist cuisine.

BERRY: When Buddhism, or I should say Ch'an Buddhism, traveled from China to Japan in the 6th century CE, didn't the art of tofu-making accompany it?

NI: Precisely.

BERRY: Would you say that tofu-making is an indigenous art of China just as Taoism is an indigenous religion?

NI: Yes. Certainly.

BERRY: Did the Taoists discover tofu-making?

NI: It's highly possible. The making of tofu has a long history in China that goes back thousands of years.

BERRY: Since tofu-making is associated throughout Asia with the ethical vegetarianism of Buddhism and Taoism—with tofu being used as a meat-substitute in vegetarian cooking—I'm wondering if the great antiquity of tofu-making in China doesn't suggest that the vegetarian tradition in China may be a very ancient one.

NI: It probably is very ancient, but it's very hard to pinpoint when tofu-making began, because the first authoritative cookbooks were not compiled until the Zhen Dynasty, which was the Mongol era.

BERRY: Confucianism and Taoism are quite contrasted, are they not?

NI: Yes, they've always been contrasted throughout Chinese history. With its rules, regulations and rigid hierarchical structure, Confucianism did not appeal to the Taoists, whose belief it was that nature should dictate and not man. Confucianism places the family and social obligations above the individual; whereas Taoism encourages individualism and self-unfoldment. Taoism offered a sanctuary from the rigid confines of Confucianism. As you know, Confucianism is very dogmatic and authoritarian. Just as the emperor was the absolute ruler in Chinese society, so the father was the absolute authority within the family; if he were to die then the mantle of authority would pass to the eldest son — not the mother; the son could actually order the mother around. In fact, according to Confucian dogma, the father or male head of household has the power of life and death over his family. For the Confucians, the essence of life is order and structure; whereas for the Taoists, the essence of life is naturalness and spontaneity. Confucians are politically ambitious; whereas Taoists despise social climbing and shun politics. Although Confucianism held the fabric of Chinese society together, it was also a source of tension and stress. In order to relieve this tension people turned to Taoism.

BERRY: It's curious that they've coexisted for centuries; they almost seem to be inseparable and complementary like Yang and Yin.

NI: That's right. When a Confucian is weighing a decision, he will often invoke the principle of *Yin* and *Yang* to make the right decision and find the middle way.

BERRY: In other words, he might consult the *I-Ching*?

NI: Yes, exactly. In fact, Confucius himself used and commented upon the *I-Ching*, which is clearly a Taoist text.

BERRY: Is Taoism a pacifist religion like Jainism?

NI: Throughout its history Taoism has kept itself above the political fray and in the background; however, there have been several times in its history when Taoists have been at the forefront of popular uprisings against the State. Notable among these insurgencies was the Yellow Turban Rebellion, which took place in the third century CE. But that had more to do with the political ambition of this Taoist leader, and did not stem from the philosophy of Taoism itself, which is inherently peaceful and teaches that one should remain in harmony with one's environment. So those few political uprisings that were led by Taoists were very much the exception to the rule.

BERRY: How do you reconcile the Taoist dream of harmony and peace with the martial arts tradition that has arisen from Taoism?

NI: I really don't see that there is a contradiction. The martial arts tradition arose in Taoism for two purposes. The martial arts were developed in Taoism as a series of exercises that were designed to promote vigor and health among sedentary monks who sat on their backsides all day in meditation and whose health deteriorated because they weren't getting enough exercise. Later, the monks at certain monasteries found that these exercises could be used defensively against soldiers and brigands who had been sent by capricious rulers to attack the monasteries and suppress Taoism.

As in Lao Tzu's teachings that one should be like water and yield to aggression, the Taoist martial arts are softer and more yielding than are those of other martial arts systems. Typically, the Taoist martial arts practitioner will yield to his opponent's aggression and turn his own violence against him.

BERRY: How did the science of acupuncture arise out of the Taoist tradition?

NI: The Taoist sages meditated and observed the workings of nature and the body and they recognized that the human body is a small universe. It responds and reacts to all the laws that govern nature. There is a vital energy that flows through the body. Just as energy courses through rivers and streams and oceans in nature, there are similar concentrations and conduits of *ch'i* in the human body. Again, in nature, when the river becomes clogged, it causes flooding in adjacent farmlands.

BERRY: I notice you frequently refer to the Taoist symbol of water.

NI: Yes, water symbolizes energy within the body. So, when there is disease, the disease arises from a blockage in this flow of energy; there are dikes along these channels or canals through which the energy flows that can relieve the congestion or blockage and restore the energy flow. So the acupuncturist channels the energy away from the blockage and directs it to a place where there is a deficit. He relieves all blockages so the energy is continuously flowing; just as in nature, wherever the water flows, it sustains life. Although it's a very simple philosophy, the science itself is very complicated because the acupuncturist has to learn all the acupressure points, and he has to learn the techniques for their application, and he has to learn different points for different purposes and different ailments. If you can, try to understand this very simple picture: the human body is the universe; when you lie down, here is the mountain; there is the river and all the indentations where the *ch'i* flows. It's a fascinating study.

BERRY: Is there a relationship between the acupuncture points and the pressure points in the martial arts?

NI: Sure..Let's take *ch'i-kung* first because *ch'i-kung* is closely related to acupuncture: in *ch'i-kung* you learn where the channels are and how to move the energy mentally, without needles. You learn to guide the energy flow through your body with your mind. Likewise, in the martial arts, you attack your opponent's pressure points; you can choke off his energy flow and cause an illness, or disable him on the spot.

BERRY: So, the same principles that operate in the healing arts of acupuncture also operate in the martial arts.

NI: Yes, the same principles apply. So, one cannot say that Taoism is a pacifistic religion. If it were utterly passive and pacifistic, then one would only learn the constructive applications of this *ch'i*. On the contrary, you learn how to defend yourself against an assailant and how to disable him. Even though you may be defending yourself, from an absolute pacifist viewpoint, you're still committing a belligerent act. A true pacifist would let people run roughshod all over him. So this is the *yin-yang* of the thing. The

Taoist can see both sides of the issue and accepts them. For the Taoist the purpose of life is to create, to protect and nurture life. Therefore, he puts his knowledge at the service of the healing arts. But in times of political strife and social turmoil, in which he may need to defend himself, he uses his knowledge to achieve the opposite effects: instead of making his assailant's energy flow, he blocks the energy and disarms him. Martial Arts also owes a great deal to the esoteric Taoist tradition. The esoteric Taoists lived alone in caves and mountain retreats as hermits; they often had to travel alone, and on their journeys they would occasionally encounter brigands, or ferocious animals. So they had to be able to defend themselves. Martial arts training was part of their philosophy of complete self-sufficiency.

BERRY: Would knowledge of Taoist martial arts have enabled a Taoist hermit to fend off an attack by a wild animal? Could choking off the energy flow at a pressure point, for instance, disable a bear or a tiger?

NI: Certainly. But, quite apart from that, the study of the martial arts is excellent training for the mind; it imposes a rigorous self-discipline. That's why I myself recommend that the youth of this country study the martial arts. It teaches humility, self-respect, respect for others and self-discipline.

BERRY: Lin Yutang states that "every Chinese is a Confucian when he is successful and a Taoist when he is a failure." He might have added that when they are not being either Taoists or Confucians, they are often Buddhists. The great thing to me as a Westerner is that people in China were free to be all three. There is no imperative in any of the Chinese religions that one must follow a particular faith exclusively as there is in the Semitic revelatory religions of the West — Christianity, Judaism and Islam.

NI: That's very true. Even Buddhism, when it entered China, was transformed by Chinese culture and Taoism into a distinctly Chinese Buddhism. Under Huineng, who was the sixth patriarch of Chinese Buddhism and the founder of Zen Buddhism, it later evolved into Ch'an or Zen Buddhism and was adopted by the Japanese as their state religion. So, as a Confucian scholar, one would study not just the Confucian scriptures but also the Buddhist and Taoist texts and be able to incorporate all of them into a certain practical application in his life. So I would say that the three pillars of philosophy in China—Taoism, Confucianism and Buddhism—coexisted very peacefully for many centuries.

BERRY: However, they were quite competitive. Weren't there periods when Taoism was the religion of the state; then Buddhism took its turn; then Confucianism. They often seemed to alternate with each other. But wasn't the period of the T'ang dynasty one of Taoist hegemony?

NI: Yes, there was a Taoist hegemony during this period because the T'ang emperors were wise to follow the natural course—which was to allow all schools of thought to flourish. Therefore the T'ang dynasty was considered to be the most progressive and prosperous in both the arts and commerce. There was minimal interference in people's lives and thoughts.

BERRY: It sounds as if the T'ang rulers practiced the Taoist principle of *wu-wei*.

NI: Precisely; it's a Taoist precept that governments ought to follow in contemporary times.

BERRY: Another commentator on the Tao, Raymond Smullyan, refers to the Tao as "The Valley Spirit that never dies; it is named the mysterious female. The generic female is something dark, formless and vague, just like the Tao." Smullyan's theory is that the Tao was a maternal energy, a mother goddess, if you will.

NI: Taoism recognizes that without the *yin* energy, the *yang* could not be formed; but without the *yang* energy the *yin* would be useless. First there was the *yin*—the solid mass, the void, and passive, absolutely quiet tranquillity. This was the feminine principle, fertile with latent power. From this latent fecundity arose the masculine, creative energy—the strong movement that characterizes the *yang*. So the *yin* gives rise to the *yang*, and the *yang* mobilizes the *yin*; both of these energies are essential to each other. But it should be emphasized that Taoism pays special reverence to the feminine principle. Femininity, or receptivity, is inherent in the philosophy itself. Throughout Lao Tzu's teachings, such feminine attributes as yielding and receptivity are key words. Water, which we consider to be a feminine element, is used a great deal to symbolize or epitomize the Tao. Many of the Western commentators on the Tao invoke the image of water.

BERRY: As in Alan Watts's pithy work *Tao: The Watercourse Way*?

NI: Exactly. But it doesn't mean that it is weak or meek, but rather that it has so much latent power that it doesn't need to display it. Its *yang* power is enveloped within the *yin*.

BERRY: If one could analyze countries in terms of *yang* and *yin*, then the West would seem to be very *yang*.

NI: (laughter) Yes, that's very interesting; it's just the reverse. It's *yang* on the outside—it's very strong and very tough— yet it's *yin* on the inside.

BERRY: I wonder if one could press the analogy further and say that *yang* nations eat *yang* foods, such as animal flesh, and yet are inwardly weak because they die of degenerative diseases, such as cancer and the diverticular diseases that result from lack of dietary fiber, which are basically *yin* diseases.

NI: Yes, I agree, but that's not to say that the West is weak—it's just a different approach to life. Outwardly, the West is more forceful, but Asians are just the opposite: outwardly, they are much more indirect and subtle.

BERRY: Are Western women more *yang* than women in Asia?

NI: Without a doubt. Speaking as one who was born and educated in China and who has lived here in the States for fifteen years, I straddle the two cultures. So I can say with some authority that Western women on the whole tend to be more *yang*; Asian Women, more *yin*. The nuances are quite striking.

BERRY: The principle of *wu-wei* is a fundamental precept of Taoism. Could this be compared to the Jain precept of "non-interference" in the lives of other creatures as well as of other humans?

NI: Initially when the term *wu-wei* first caught on in the West it was during the "hippie generation" in Berkeley in the 1960s. But the term was widely mistranslated and misunderstood. "Non-doing," "non-action," was the popular mistranslation that gained currency at that time, and the hippies used it to justify their sitting back, making love, smoking grass, and being non-productive. But that was a gross distortion of the meaning of *wu-wei* as the Taoists understood it. "Non-interference" is a much better translation because it implies that one doesn't meddle with the natural process. One should allow the natural process to unfold in every moment of life; but that doesn't mean that one should take a passive approach to the process of living. Taoism really advocates a pro-active approach to living. One should strive for excellence, one should be ambitious, but one should not force anything. One should be patient, allow events to unfold, and learn to discern the right moment for taking action.

BERRY: That closely parallels the Jain view of "non-interfering"; they make a point of extending that principle of non-interference to other forms of life as well. They have a *laissez-faire* attitude towards animals and other life-forms including insects and even rocks. Their strict vegetarianism grows out of their policy of not-interfering with other life processes. In fact, it strikes me that their idea of *ahimsa* — of doing no harm to any other creature — is *wu-wei* raised to its highest power.

NI: Yes, and I think that is increasingly becoming a potent concept in the West as we see the ecological balance of the West being disrupted. People have started to realize that they have interfered so much with nature and the life forces that they must energetically practice *wu-wei*. So we're coming to a Taoist view of nature in the West.

BERRY: Taoism has been described as one of the most ecology-conscious religions. Would you agree?

NI: That's very true. Over thousands of years, the Taoists have developed techniques for living in harmony with nature, *wu-wei* being one of them.

BERRY: Is there a concept of reincarnation in Taoism?

NI: Very much so. Right from the beginning, we recognize that life itself is a manifestation of energy. Energy and spirit combine to form being. At the end of the physical life, the energy is scattered, and the spirit will become reincarnated, depending on the level of your spiritual inclinations at that moment. What you've done in your life to refine and cultivate yourself will certainly have an impact on the form into which you are reincarnated. Therefore, the Taoists work very diligently to cultivate and refine their spirit to gain control of their spirit, so that when the physical body dies, the spirit becomes immortal. So achieving spiritual immortality means to transcend reincarnation—a point at which the spirit dwells outside of the cycle of reincarnation.

BERRY: That's very close to the Hindu view of *moksha*, in which the spirit is released from the wheel of rebirth; or the Jain view of *kevalajnana*, in which the enlightened spirit dwells in omniscience at the top of the world.

NI: Yes, except with the difference that Taoist immortals will become spiritual beings who can materialize themselves anywhere at any time.

BERRY: Theoretically, one could come back as a lower form of life?

NI: Theoretically, yes, but in Taoism there is no concept of accumulating bad *karma* in a sort of spiritual bank account which will be paid out in the next life. Let's say you slaughter a cow that had incarnated the spirit of your mother—there is no concept of having to atone for that in your next life. Rather, in Taoism what you do in life will affect the quality of your *ch'i*.

BERRY: That's not *karma*?

NI: No, that's not *karma*; we call it "subtle universal response." It's similar to *karma*, but in Taoism, with the concept of "subtle universal response," you don't have to wait until your next life for rewards and punishment. It happens right now [claps loudly for effect] in this life! In other words, don't wait until the next life to improve your behavior, or to make your resolutions. Do it now! Because this subtle universal response can manifest itself at any moment, your behavior, your thought patterns, will provoke an immediate response.

Essay

················

JUDAISM

ALTHOUGH SMALL IN THE number of its adherents, Judaism is one of the most influential religions in history. Both Christianity and Islam, whose followers number in the hundreds of millions, owe their existence to this small desert religion. Jews consider themselves to be a singular race who were selected by their god Yahweh to be his chosen people. They trace their beginnings to the covenant that God established between himself and Abram, the patriarch of their religion, sometime in the second millennium BCE. Under the conditions of the covenant, Abraham (as Abram was thereafter known) was obliged to stop practicing polytheism, and to worship Yahweh alone. For his part, Yahweh promised to bring forth a mighty race from Abraham's loins and lead him and his descendants into a promised land where they would dwell forever. As a pledge of his willingness to keep the covenant, Abraham and his descendants would have to circumcise themselves, a rite that is still observed today. Yahweh reaffirmed his covenant with the Children of Israel when he led them out of slavery in Egypt, using Moses as his spokesman. In Egypt, by way of showing his power, Yahweh afflicted the Egyptians with plagues of frogs and insects and with a pestilence

············

that wiped out the livestock of the Egyptians, but not the Children of Israel. Since Pharaoh still would not let Yahweh's people go, Yahweh then "smote" every Egyptian first-born, "both man and beast."[1] Fearing any further demonstrations of Yahweh's wrath, the Pharaoh, Rameses II, let the Children of Israel leave his country; but having second thoughts, Rameses sent his army against the fleeing Jews; Yahweh, however, to protect his people, drowned the Pharaoh's pursuing cavalry, "the horse and his rider,"[2] in the Red Sea.

During their years in the wilderness, the people grew famished and implored Yahweh to supply them with food; Yahweh showered them with a type of wonderfood called *manna*; it could instantly satisfy one's hunger and could take on whatever flavor one desired. But the people were not content with *manna*, and cried out for animal flesh, for which they had acquired a taste in Egypt — "When in the Land of Egypt we sat by the flesh pots."[3]

Yahweh sent them quail, which the people promptly devoured, but within a short time they came down with a plague-like illness that thinned their ranks. (One scholar has interpreted this as the second vegetarian attempt,[4] which humans characteristically flunked; the first being in the Garden of Eden.) Atop Mount Sinai, Yahweh gave Moses the Torah or laws and let the Children of Israel live in Canaan (the Promised Land) so long as they obeyed the laws and kept the covenant. But the Promised Land would not be bestowed on the Children of Israel as a gift; it would have to be taken from the Canaanites by force. Yahweh assumed a militaristic aspect and authorized the Children of Israel to slay the Canaanites mercilessly. After they had taken the land from the Canaanites, the Children of Israel began to pay worship to the local Canaanite deities and went so far as to forget Yahweh. Feeling that another *tour de force* was needed to show the power of Yahweh, the prophet Elijah challenged the Canaanite priests of Baal (the indigenous fertility deity) to a bullock-eating contest. Pitting Yahweh against Baal to see which god could consume the bullock faster, Elijah and the priests of Baal placed a bullock on an altar on Mt. Carmel. Fifty priests of Baal prayed and flagellated themselves to make their god send down fire to consume the bullock, but to no avail; then Elijah called on Yahweh to devour the bullock; and within seconds the bullock was consumed by fire.[5]

In 586 BCE, however, Yahweh's strength would again be tested. In that year the Babylonian king Nebuchadnezzar, in retaliation for the Children of Israel's refusal to pay him tribute, invaded Palestine, laid waste the land and destroyed the Temple of Yahweh; as further punishment, he abducted wealthy Jewish families from Canaan, and forced them to live in Babylon. The prophets took this as a sign that the Jews had been disobedient to the laws. Their forced exile caused a crisis in their faith; for if Yahweh were all-powerful, how could he have permitted the Babylonians to rape Palestine and demolish Yahweh's temple? Many Jews renounced their faith, but others remained steadfast. Those who remained faithful were rewarded; for at length the Persians under Cyrus conquered the Babylonians.

The Persians, Zoroastrian monotheists who worshipped a Wise Lord, Ahura Mazda, were benevolent towards the Israelites. It is believed by many scholars that out of gratitude towards the Persians, under whose rule they thrived for over two hundred years, the Israelites adopted many Zoroastrian ideas. Among them were the concept of personal immortality; a concept of an evil principle at large in the world that the Persians called Angra Mainyu and the Israelites called Satan; and perhaps most important of all—a concept of humans being expelled from paradise through erring dietetically. In the Persian version of the expulsion from Paradise, humanity falls from grace because the primeval parent King Yama gives the forbidden food, beef, to his subjects.[6] At Cyrus's behest, the Israelites were allowed to return to Canaan, where they rebuilt the Temple, which had as its focus the sacrificial altar on which the choicest animals from their herds were sacrificed to Yahweh.

This is the picture of Israelite life as it is painted in the Pentateuch or the Torah, the five sacred books of Judaism that were edited in the sixth century BCE by the Yahwist editor, Ezra, to make it appear that Yahweh alone had been the sole god of the Jews since time immemorial. In point of fact, prior to the Yahwist reforms in the sixth century BCE, the Jews were henotheistic and Yahweh was only one among many gods. Max Weber speculates that he may have originally been a god of natural catastrophes and thunderstorms like Indra,[7] who was called by the *Rg Vedic* Aryans "the releaser of waters." After the Temple was restored by Nehemiah with the backing of the Persians, Yahweh was installed as the sole God of Israel; although, like a husband with a roving eye, Yahweh's people were tempted to worship alien gods — which was bound to incur Yahweh's wrath.

Why should this have been so? Why were the Israelites so prone to worship other gods? Why did they pray to golden calves and prostrate themselves before images of Baal? One of the reasons that Professor John Armstrong gives for the continual lusting of the Hebrews after other gods, was the increasing remoteness and unapproachableness of Yahweh.[8] As the Yahweh-alone party prospered under Persian rule, Yahweh was elevated into a high and mighty dweller on mountain tops; he becomes increasingly remote from his people. This left a void that was filled by the *dei loci* of Palestine, the Baals of fertility, and other less powerful but more intimate deities. Yahweh as he is conceived by the redactors is a lonely and aloof god who, as he gains in potency, became isolated and elevated. Curiously, Professor Armstrong points out, as Yahweh's power grows, the lives of animals become less important in the scheme of things; they become foreshortened into emblems of Yahweh's mighty procreative powers; as evidence of his divine handiwork; in a word, they become *jeux d'esprit*, divine playthings, which humans as the Lords of Creation in the image of Yahweh, are free to do with as they wish.[9]

In his essay, "Golden Calf or Holy Cow? Animals and the Sacred,"[10] the Reverend Gary Kowalski points out that the famous episode of the Golden Calf, whether historically true or not, illustrates the Israelites' deep-seated hostility toward representing the divine in zoomorphic or non-human form. In Western thought, the divine is opposed to the bestial; the heavenly to the earthly. Thus, it is not surprising that an anthropomorphic god should call forth a zoomorphic devil or anti-God. For centuries the Christian Church has referred to the anti-God as "the Beast," which is traditionally represented as having hairy haunches, cloven hooves, curling horns, *et al.* The fact is, Georges Cuvier, the first scientist to classify animals according to their anatomical characteristics, declared that as he is popularly depicted (with cloven hooves, curling horns, etc.) the devil is a vegetarian.[11] Is it any wonder that Jews, Christians and Muslims (all sons and daughters of Abraham), have made the easy inference that non-herbivores and non-vegetarian humans are closer to God and that herbivores and vegetarian humans are closer to Satan, or at least to the principle of evil? Perhaps this is why these faiths boast so few vegetarians.

The Old Testament or Torah has many affecting human-animal stories, such as Rebecca's fetching water for Abraham's servant's camels, the story of Balaam's ass, and of course Noah's ark (although after Noah emerged from the ark, he built an altar on which he sacrificed to Yahweh some of the very animals he had saved; and Yahweh is reported to have "smelled the soothing savor."[12])—it also has compassionate sayings such as "Thou shalt not muzzle the ox when he treadeth out the corn,"[13] or "He that killeth an ox is as if he slew a man; he that sacrificeth a lamb, as if he cut off a dog's neck".[14] But ethical vegetarians are perplexed by the Torah. Animal rights activists view it with alarm because the very covenant between Yahweh and humans was sealed with the blood of a sacrificial animal—bulls are brought to the sacrificial site, and then they are slaughtered; their blood is drained into basins; half the blood is splashed on the sacrificial site, and the other half is tossed on the people: "Then he took the account of the covenant and read it into the ears of the people. They said: 'All that Yahweh has spoken, we will do and we will hearken.' Moses took the blood and tossed it on the people, and said: 'Here is the blood of the covenant that Yahweh has cut with you by means of all these words.'"[15] If the covenant between God and the people of Israel wasn't extended to animals (and many animal activists wonder why it wasn't)—perhaps it's because it's a little tricky to make a covenant with animals if you seal it by dousing them with bulls' blood! It is dismaying to ethical vegetarians that Yahweh demands burnt offerings, and when he destroys a city, he "smites" the animals in it as well. Ethical vegetarians rejoice in the first book of Genesis which envisions a vegetarian paradise, but they are distressed when Yahweh revels in the odor of animal sacrifices, and (in I Kings,18:38) when he engages in a bull-eating contest with the Baal of Palestine and wins!

Furthermore, it is more than a little disquieting when Yahweh divides the animal kingdom into clean and unclean, and gives humans permission to eat specific animals that Yahweh deems to be clean.[16] Prior to Yahweh's permitting humans to eat animal flesh, the portions of meat burnt on the altar were called the Lord's food and bread;[17] the sacrificial altar was called Yahweh's table;[18] and the basins used to catch the blood of sacrifices were referred to as "Yahweh's vessels and pots." Pacifists are put out because Yahweh dons battle-dress and calls for wars of annihilation against his foes. "Proclaim ye this among gentiles. Prepare war...the Lord also shall roar out of Zion."[19] Could this be why so many Jews have gone over to other religions, particularly the Eastern religions of Buddhism, Hinduism and Jainism that honor the first precept that all life is sacred and that one must never do violence to any life form? In fact, two of the interviewees in this book were born into Judaism; one was born into Catholicism, and all three have gone over to Eastern religions that revere the first precept — Steve Rosen (Satyaraj Das), Philip Kapleau (now the Ven. Philip Kapleau Roshi), and Joan Campanella (now Yamuna Devi).

It is important to note that although the Jews sacrificed all manner of animals to Yahweh in the restored Temple, they were not alone in making "vain oblations." The followers of other religions in ancient Palestine propitiated their gods with burnt offerings of sacrificed animals, so it was not a singular practice. In fact, the religion that most closely competed with Yahwism in Judah were the Baal worshippers whose deities received and demanded copious animal sacrifices. Throughout the Near East, animal sacrifice was customary. Even Yahweh's covenant with the Jews was sealed with the blood of a sacrificial animal, because that's how important contracts were sealed. The Israelites were no more reprehensible or praiseworthy in this regard than were the worshippers of Baal or the worshippers of Zeus or the worshippers of Moloch, or any of the other competing faiths in the Near East during this period. However, the lamentable feature of it is that the sacrificial rites that were sanctioned and advocated in Exodus, Deuteronomy and Leviticus (books of the Torah that were virtually manuals of sacrifice) were codified in Jewish Law, so that these unedifying practices were perpetuated via both Christianity and Islam—which are in Heine's phrase "Jewish heresies." For almost two thousand years Christians and Muslims took these books of the Torah as a moral Baedeker on how to treat animals.

Much of the meat that was consumed in the ancient Near East was consumed as part of an animal sacrifice. Professor Morton Smith in his book *Palestinian Parties and Politics That Shaped the Old Testament* writes in this connection: "In the ancient world religious observances were attached to most acts of everyday life; any festivity or misfortune was an occasion of sacrifice and the meat of most sacrifices was used for food."[20] In order to interact socially with others and to hold public office and participate in the affairs of the city, one had to be willing to worship other people's gods. Professor Smith's further point is that the followers of Yahweh alone were singular in that they refused to eat the sacrificial meat of other gods—only Yahweh's god-food would do. In this way, they were setting themselves apart from other peoples of the ancient world who were syncretistic. Indeed, the cult of Yahweh had been syncretistic prior to the restoration of the second temple under Persian auspices. So the sacrificial meat of Yahweh was especially sacred; its consumers could not share it with aliens nor could they partake of the meat of other sacrifices. Professor Smith concludes that they were preparing the ground for the exclusivity that marks not only Judaism, but also its heretical offspring—Christianity and Islam.

It is instructive to compare the Hindu Vaishnava practice of *prasadam*, dedicating an offering of food to the god Krishna—with the sacrificial offerings rendered up to Yahweh and other divinities of the Near East in the first millennium BCE. Whereas the god

Krishna receives offerings only in the shape of vegetarian foods, Yahweh and the gods of the Indo-European pantheon received offerings in the shape of animal flesh. At a typical temple sacrifice, the entrails were burned on the altar, which at the Temple in Jerusalem was essentially an ever-burning barbecue pit; the thighs and other portions were shared out among the priests and the people who paid for the sacrifice. Yahweh's palate was tickled by the sacrifice of not thousands but millions of animals. Birds had their necks pinched so that the priests could squirt their blood out on the altars and roast them on the fire, feathers and all, for the delectation of Yahweh and his worshipers.[21] During the seven days of the Sukkoth festival, the law required that 98 lambs, 70 bulls, 14 rams and 7 goats be sacrificed.[22] The Talmud records that King Agrippa once had the paschal (Jewish Passover festival) lambs counted and found that six hundred thousand had been sacrificed. At every Jewish festival (and the calendar is crowded with them) a similar number were sacrificed.

Nonetheless, it would be erroneous to think that all the Jews in ancient Palestine ate sacrificial flesh; the practice was limited to the upper classes. It was they who had the financial wherewithal to be able to pay for the animals to be barbecued and offered up to Yahweh. For the cost of buying sacrificial animals such as bulls for a temple sacrifice would have been prohibitively expensive; goats and lambs were not cheap either. Here is what Professor Kantor has to say about the practice: "Near Eastern diet, then as now, did not critically involve beef; so the cumbersome problem of kosher slaughtering of cattle was a modest one, as it is also not a big issue in Israel today. Lamb was a precious commodity privileged for the rich or for ritual occasions at the Temple in Jerusalem. The staple diet of the Near East then and now is rice and other grain topped off with a little bit of fowl (easily slaughtered by kashrut method), or fish, supplemented by a lot of vegetables and fruit. Only when Jews came to live in the northern world of Europe did the observance of kashrut become a difficult thing in that much more carnivorous beef-eating environment. Observant Jews serving in the Roman army in the second century CE were less bothered by dietary restriction than Jews serving in the American army today."[23]

The Jews like the other peoples of the ancient Near East were mostly vegetarian; like the Romans and the Greeks they ate flesh if at all on sacral occasions; and then it was only the rich and well-to-do who could afford to purchase animals and have them sacrificed. As Professor Kantor points out, it was when the Jews prospered in the carnivorous nations of Northern Europe and America that they could afford to buy butchered animal flesh.

Doubtless the recurring cycle of defeat, exile, destruction and restoration that marked early Judaism may have fostered Judaism's dietary idiosyncrasies; for in order to preserve their identity in exile they persisted in their characteristic rites of circumcision, keeping of the Sabbath, self-segregation,[24] an attitude of hostility towards gentiles[25] and the eating of approved animals that had been slaughtered in a kosher manner—these and other cultural specificities kept the Jews from being readily assimilated into the country of exile. Among these dietary peculiarities was their fastidiousness in eating some animals as distinct from others, animals that they felt were clean, i.e., those that had cloven hooves and chewed the cud; and scaly fish, or birds that flew. Unclean animals, which did not have these features, were declared unfit to eat. Other curious Jewish punctilios, such as the prohibition on seething (cooking) a kid in its mother's milk, which is at the root of the kosher laws of separation of milk and meat, while supposedly done for humane reasons was in fact only less inhumane in degree. Why eat a kid at all? Or the sophistry of eating flesh that has been bled out when it is physically impossible to remove all the blood from flesh without destroying it. So while the emphasis on these traits reinforced their identity, and increased their self-confidence—it also served to perpetuate dietary practices that were less than salutary and less than humane.

Judaism, it should not be forgotten, while small in itself, has had a disproportionate influence via its heretical progeny—Christianity and Islam. For while these religions display many of the admirable qualities that one associates with Judaism, i.e., its re-

spect for learning, its desire for justice, its concern for the poor —
the dietary imperatives that Judaism has bequeathed have been
an ethical, physiological and ecological disaster for the West and
for the world. Both Christians and Muslims look back to the Old
Testament books of Leviticus and Deuteronomy for their dietary
cues. Fundamentalist Christians can find ample justification for
eating animals in passages such as: "And the fear of you and the
dread of you shall be upon every beast of the earth, and upon
every fowl of the air; with all wherewith the ground teemeth, and
all the fishes of the sea, into your hand they are delivered. Every
creature that lives and moves shall be food for you; I give you
them all as once I gave you green plants."[26] "When Yahweh your
God broadens your territory, as he promised you, and you say: I
want to eat meat because your appetite craves eating meat according to all your appetite's craving, you may eat meat."[27] "You are
to sacrifice your offerings up, the meat and the blood on the
slaughter site of your God: the blood of your slaughter offerings
you are to pour out on the slaughter site of Yahweh your God, but
the meat you may eat."[28] — that are unequivocal in advocating the
eating of animal flesh. The Jewish vegetarian's dilemma is how to
become and remain a vegetarian without flouting the Torah, which
is Judaism's most sacred book. Some have done it by harking
back to Genesis and taking their dietary cues from the original
fruitarian couple; others have simply become Jewish Buddhists
or Jewish Hindus while combining the best of both faiths.

Some social critics and historians, such as Arnold Toynbee of
London University, Professor Ian McHarg of the University of
Pennsylvania and Professor Lynn White of Stanford have been
wont to see the second book of Genesis as the source of all bad
things in the world. It is their contention that it was the concept
that God gave man dominion over nature and the animals that has
led the West particularly to exploit the natural world without
regard to the consequences. Here is what Professor McHarg has
to say about it: "Whatever the earliest roots of the western attitude to nature it is clear they were confirmed in Judaism. The
emergence of Judaism had as its corollary the rejection of nature;

the affirmation of Jehovah, the God in whose image man was made, was also a declaration of war on nature.

"The great western religions born of monotheism have been the major source of our moral attitudes. It is from them that we have developed the preoccupation with the uniqueness of men, with justice and compassion. On the subject of man-nature, however, the biblical creation story of the first chapter of Genesis, the source of the most generally accepted description of man's role and powers, not only fails to correspond to reality as we observe it, but in its insistence on the dominion and subjugation of nature, encourages the most exploitative and destructive instincts in man rather than those that are deferential and creative. Here can be found the sanction and injunction to conquer nature—the enemy, the threat to Jehovah."[29]

Arnold Toynbee is also very explicit about calling monotheism to account; he longs nostalgically for the pre-monotheistic *Weltanschauung* of the Greeks and the Romans. When he traveled to Japan it reminded him of this pantheistic world view in which nature was revered, not held in contempt. East Asia, with its reverence for nature such as one finds in its religions of Taoism, Buddhism and Hinduism, made him feel at home; he believed that Judaism and Christianity must be re-animated with this respect for nature that monotheism has corroded. "If the cogent evidence for divinity were really power, Dionysos and Demeter and Zeus and Poseidon, who are now reasserting their power, would be more credible gods than Yahweh, for they are demonstrating to present-day man that he cannot pollute soil, air and water with impunity. Moreover, the monotheistic disrespect for nature has survived the weakening of belief in monotheism in the ex-monotheistic parts of the world, and it has invaded that major portion of the world in which monotheism has never been established. When a native of the monotheistic portion of the present-day world travels eastward beyond the easternmost limits of Islam, he finds himself in a living pre-monotheistic world, and if he has had a Greek and Latin education which he has taken seriously, the religion of present-day East Asia will be more familiar to him and also more congenial to him than the religion of the West, in which the traveler himself has been brought up. For instance, when I myself visit Japan, I find myself being constantly reminded, by present-day Japanese religious sites and shrines, of Saint Augustine's pre-Christian religion of the Romans."[30]

If we extend this a bit further, does it apply to the treatment of animals as well? Are monotheistic cultures more exploitative of animals than are those of the Eastern religions? Toynbee would seem to think so. However, when Toynbee talks about the ethical superiority of the pre-monotheistic world of Greece and Rome, he fails to mention the institution of animal sacrifice in those countries, which was no less bloody than in the Temple at Jerusalem. All the Indo-European religions practiced animal sacrifice with flesh-eating as a consequence. *Do ut des* was the operating principle in the sacrificial rite: I give that You (the God) may give back to me in return. The return was a thick, juicy barbecued steak that was shared out among the priests and the congregation. Classicist Bernard Knox points out that "The calendar of the Athenian year was studded with festivals great and small. The Athenian citizen enjoyed not only spectacle in the form of dances, tragedies and comedies, athletic, musical and literary contests and processions, but also public feasts for all these events involved sacrifice to the gods. And sacrifices meant the distribution of that rarity in the Athenian diet — meat.

"At the annual celebration of the victory over the Persians at Marathon, 500 goats were sacrificed; at the Dionysia in 330 BCE, 240 bulls went under the knife; and at the Panathenea, the sacrifice was a hecatomb — 100 animals."[31] For every instance of animals being sacrificed among the Jews there were manifold atrocities among the Greeks and Romans. While it is clear that the Jews were not ethically superior in the matter of animal sacrifice to the pagans, it is also true that the pagans, in spite of Toynbee's protestations to the contrary, were not ethically superior to the Jews. Indeed, as Archibald points out in *The Origins of Christianity:* "The Deuteronomists were clearly pioneers, too, in the abolition of human sacrifices. Human victims were slain in Phoenicia and its colonies down to the fall of Carthage in 146 BCE, and even occasionally in Greece and Rome until the time of the Roman Empire. Rationalists who are weak in historic sense often deplore the intolerance of the Deuteronomists towards rival cults. But would Rationalists tolerate a cult which offered children in sacrifice to idols? Civilization owes a debt to those who first fought against the burning of children in the fire of *balaam*."[32]

Although, as we have seen, there are so many instances of animal sacrifice in the Torah—the books of Deuteronomy and Leviticus are cookbooks of animal sacrifice—there is much in Judaism that lends itself to a vegetarian interpretation. For instance, there is God's first dietary law as it is set forth in Genesis 1:29. Before the flood and the Noachian age—when God permits humans as a concession to their weakness to eat animals—humans were vegetarian. Every precaution was taken by the Temple priests and their successors, the *shochets* of today, to minimize the animals' suffering. To that end, only a knife with the keenest blade was used, and the animal's throat was cut with surgical celerity and precision. The prophets such as Hosea, Micah and Isaiah were notable for the fervor with which they denounced the sacrificial cult that had concentrated its power among the priestly elite. Passages from Isaiah such as his famous execration of animal sacrifices: "To what purpose is the multitude of your sacrifices unto me? saith the Lord: I am full of the burnt offerings of rams, and the fat of fed beasts; and I delight not in the blood of bullocks, or of lambs, or of he goats. Bring me no more vain oblations;"[33] or even before Isaiah, the gentle Hosea's prophesying a true covenant between humans and the animals: "And in that day will I make a covenant for them with the beasts of the field and the fowls of heaven, and with the creeping things of the ground: and I will break the sword and the bow and the battle out of the land, and will make them lie down safely."[34]—all go to show that like the proverbial thin man within every fat man, there is an ethical vegetarian in the Hebrew scriptures struggling to get out. Perhaps the jeremiads that these prophets had hurled against the sacrificial cult found their mark: for the destruction of the second

Temple by the Romans and the dispersal of the priestly sacrificers spelled the end of institutional animal sacrifice in Judaism.

Moreover, after the destruction of the second Temple in 70 CE, a number of vegetarian sects that had existed on the margins of Judaism began to attract followers from among Jews, who in their grief at the loss of the Temple, took the occasion to convert to vegetarianism. This alarmed many of the rabbis of the period who were distressed at losing so many meat-loving Jews to these reclusive and ascetic sects. The argument of these ascetic Jews, which is recorded in the Talmud, ran as follows: "When the Temple was standing, our joy was in eating meat, as it is written, 'Thou shalt kill of thy peace offerings and eat them there and rejoice before the Lord thy God.' Now, when the temple is destroyed, we rejoice only in the drinking of wine."[35] Conspicuous among these vegetarian Jewish sects were the Essenes, the Therapeutae, the Ebionites, and the Nazoreans, of which there is strong circumstantial evidence that Jesus himself may have been a member. In the first century of its existence, it is not unlikely that Christianity may also have been a fledgling vegetarian sect to which many Jews converted.

Despite the emphasis on flesh-eating and animal sacrifice in the Torah, many modern Jews have become strict vegetarians. Notable among them are two Nobel Laureates in literature: S.Y. Agnon and Isaac Bashevis Singer. Singer was the son of a rabbi and had always wanted to be a vegetarian, but had bowed to parental pressure and remained a secret vegetarian until 1966 when the death of his pet parakeet Matzi prompted him to renounce the eating of animals. Singer was outspoken in his criticism of the glaring ethical inconsistencies in Judaism with respect to the treatment of animals. It bothered him that the Torah was bound in animal hide and that the phylacteries were made of leather. In his novels, such as *Satan In Goray* and in his short stories, such as "Blood" and "The Slaughter," the *shochet* or ritual slaughterer is often depicted as an agent of evil; although in an interview with the author, Singer made it clear that butchers and ritual slaughterers are no more reprehensible than the people who eat animal flesh; he admitted, however, that he liked to portray them as ruffians.[36]

The first book written by a Jewish author urging vegetarianism was *Thou Shalt Not Kill or the Torah of Vegetarianism*, which was written by Aaron Frankel in the nineteenth century. One of the first modern spokesmen for the cause of animals rights, and a devout vegetarian, was Lewis Gompertz. A non-practicing Jew, Gompertz founded the first modern animal protection society in England.

Rabbi Abraham Isaac HaCohen Kook, the first Chief Rabbi of pre-State Israel, predicted that when the Jews entered the Messianic age, they would become vegetarian. It was Rav Kook who also said that Jews can help to accelerate the arrival of the Messianic Age by becoming vegetarian. Echoing Rav Kook, vegetarian writer Jo Green said that Jewish religious ethical vegetarians are leading lives that herald the Messiah and make his coming more likely.[37] There are many Jewish vegetarian societies throughout the world, and their number is growing. There are even, as this interview will make plain, a number of Jews who observe an Edenic diet of raw fruits and vegetables and count themselves among a small but thriving number of vegetarian rawfoodists.

For a description of what life was like before humans fell from dietary grace, one can do no better than quote from the great Jewish scholar of comparative religions, Robert Eisler. Imprisoned at Dachau and Buchenwald, Eisler lectured at Oxford until 1949 when he died from the after-effects of his mistreatment in the German concentration camps. Toward the end of his life he came to realize that humans were morally and physiologically destined to be vegetarians. "The African and South Asiatic core-tools—the so-called handaxes, eminently suitable for root grubbing and crushing—are the remains of the original innocuous vegetarian herds of early man, whose mothers accidentally discovered gardening and agriculture when like squirrels they buried grain and their seeds or roots in the ground to store them up for the hungry winter season and found them sprouting and multiplying in the womb of the earth.

"These vegetarian herds are the ancestors of the recent wholly peaceful food-gathering tribes and of the primitive grain-and-fruit growing populations."[38] ✡

R.B.

[1] Exodus 12:11-12.

[2] *ibid.*, 15:1-2.

[3] *ibid.*, 16:3.

[4] Jean Soler, "The Dietary Prohibitions of the Hebrews" in *The New York Review of Books*, 23:10, (June 14, 1979), pp. 24-30.

[5] I Kings 18:38.

[6] James H. Moulton, *Early Zoroastrianism* (Amsterdam: Philo Press, 1972), pp. 307-8.

[7] Max Weber, *Ancient Judaism* (New York: The Free Press, 1952), p. 128.

[8] John Armstrong, *The Idea of Holiness and the Humane Response: A Study of the Concept of Holiness and its Social Consequences* (London: George Allen & Unwin, 1981), p. 21.

[9] *ibid.*, pp. 40-41.

[10] Reverend Gary Kowalski, "Golden Calf or Holy Cow? Animals and the Sacred," in *Between the Species*, Vol. 4, No. 4 (1988), pp. 263-67.

[11] Herbert Wendt, *In Search of Adam* (Boston: Houghton Mifflin, 1956), p. 149.

[12] Genesis 8:20.

[13] Deuteronomy 25:4.

[14] Isaiah 66:3.

[15] Exod. 24:3-8.

[16] Leviticus 11:1-12:1.

[17] *ibid.*, 3:11; 21:21; Numbers 28:2.

[18] Ezekiel 44:16, Malachi 1:7.

[19] Joel 3:9-17.

[20] Morton Smith, *Palestinian Parties and Politics That Shaped the Old Testament* (New York: Columbia University Press, 1972), p. 30.

[21] Lev. 1:15.

[22] Numbers 29:12-34.

[23] Norman F. Cantor, *The Sacred Chain: The History of the Jews* (New York: Harper Collins, 1994), p. 64.

[24] Smith, *op. cit.*, p. 145.

[25] Cantor, *op. cit.*, pp. 40, 106-7.

[26] Genesis 9:2-3.

[27] Deut. 12:20.

[28] *ibid.*, 12:27.

[30] Arnold Toynbee, "The Religious Background of the Present Environmental Crisis," in *Ecology and Religion in History*, ed., David and Eileen Spring (New York: Harper & Row, 1974), pp. 137-49.

[31] Bernard Knox, "A Duty to Act," in *Civilization*, Vol. 2, No. 2 (1995), p.44.

[32] Archibald Robertson, *The Origins of Christianity* (New York: International Publishers, 1961), p. 31.

[33] Isaiah, 1:10-17.

[34] Hosea 2:18.

[35] Quoted in Louis A. Berman, "The Dietary Laws as Atonements for Flesh-eating" in *Judaism and Animal Rights*, ed. Roberta Kalechofsky, (Marblehead, Massachusetts: Micah Publications), 1992, p. 151.

[36] Isaac Bashevis Singer in an interview with Rynn Berry, *The New Vegetarians* (New York: Pythagorean Publishers, 1993), p. 76.

[37] Quoted in Richard Schwartz, *Judaism and Vegetarianism* (Marblehead, Massachusetts: Micah Publications, 1989), pp. 11-12.

[38] Robert Eisler, *Man into Wolf* (New York: Philosophical Library, 1952), p. 37.

Conversation/Judaism

....

DR. ROBERT KOLE

A SHAKESPEAREAN SCHOL-ar engaged in teaching Renaissance literature at Queens College, Dr. Kole recently served as a consultant on the film about the making of the film *Richard III*, "Looking for Richard." When I inter-viewed Dr. Kole at his apartment, I was taken aback to see that his stove was serving as a makeshift bookshelf. Books were neatly piled on gas burners, and when I o-pened the oven, I beheld a verita-ble literary feast. Didn't this pose a fire hazard? No, Dr. Kole assured me: as a vegan rawfoodist, who es-chews cooked food, he'd had the gas turned off and was using the stove for non-culinary purposes.

His 100% raw food diet struck me as being appropriately Edenic, and it cast my mind back to those intrepid Jewish vegetarian raw-foodists of antiquity—the Ebion-ites and the Nazoreans, who ate much of their food in its un-cooked state, to say nothing of Banus, the Jew-ish rawfood an-chorite with whom the Jewish histori-an Josephus lived for three years. For three years at least, from the ages of 18 to 21, Jose-phus himself became a practicing rawfoodist: "As I had heard that there was a man named Banus who stayed in the desert...and who took as food only what grew by itself (thus rawfood)...I decided to try his system." (*Vita Josephi*, 2,

....
163

11). It also put me in mind of the vegan rawfoodist imperative in Genesis (1:29) "Here I give you all plants that bear seeds that are upon the face of the earth, and all trees in which there is tree fruit that bears seeds—for you they shall be for eating."

· · · · · · · · · · ·

BERRY: Forgive me if this sounds snide, but from time immemorial Jews have been noted for their high intelligence. How is it that only a fraction of them have perceived the wisdom of following a vegetarian diet?

KOLE: Tradition, at least the tradition that I belong to—the Ashkenazic Jews, or European Jews—may indeed be noted for intellectual ability, but our tradition, in terms of food, is very meat-oriented. Among my Grandmother's dishes, for example, there was always a meat meal or a dairy meal: the notion of a vegetable meal just didn't exist. It's not part of the tradition, not part of the culture. (For dinner, my mother would make roast beef, London broil, or lamb chops. Without meat, it wasn't a meal. For lunch, the next day, we would have leftover meat in sandwiches or tuna fish; so like most Jews in America, we lived very much in a meat culture, like Eastern Europe.)

We can see this tradition in the delicatessen—the New York deli is very much a Jewish institution. It's part of being a Jew in an urban environment—and it is very meat-oriented. Cured and smoked meat and fish in different flavors—pastrami, corned beef, smoked salmon (or lox, as it is called) are important dynamics of urban Jewish life in America.

BERRY: That marks quite a contrast with your present diet. I understand that you're a vegan rawfoodist.

KOLE: That's right.

BERRY: You don't even eat bread, the staff of life. Why not?

KOLE: That's right; bread the staff of life is not natural; it's been baked, kneaded, yeasted, etc. All the original nutrients have been refined and cooked out of it. In Western cuisine, we cook out the good stuff and cook in the bad stuff. Nuts that have been roasted in oil and salted are terrible for you; whereas raw, unsalted nuts are great. Cooked fruit and fried vegetables lose their natural goodness. Even pasta is too far removed from its natural state. The grains have been turned into a paste then dried and cooked again before eating.

BERRY: What about spices? Do you season your food?

KOLE: No, as a rawfoodist of the T.C. Fry and Herbert Shelton school, I would not. Because when you cook the flavor out of foods, you have to put spices on top of the cooked foods. If you just eat the natural raw food, with its innate flavor and goodness, you don't need spices.

BERRY: So Indian and Chinese cuisine, which are considered the haute cuisine of vegetarianism, would be studiously avoided?

KOLE: Yes. Exactly.

BERRY: It certainly does run counter to mainstream vegetarian practice! Have you known any rawfooders who've reverted to cooked foods?

KOLE: Well, they slip. Sometimes they're seduced by the aromas wafting from an Indian vegetarian restaurant, but they eventually return to their base, which is rawfoodism.

BERRY: I have friends who eat 80% raw vegan food during the summer and 60% raw during the winter.

KOLE: That's probably the direction in which I'm heading as well. I'm sure there will come a time when I'll go to a vegetarian restaurant, and I won't be able to resist the cornbread with nutbutter or something wonderful like that. But I'll regard it as a splurge, a rare treat, which shouldn't be indulged in too often. Other people go to a typical vegetarian restaurant, and they eat overcooked vegetables or grains, and they assume that they're having a very healthy meal. Or they go to a Chinese vegetarian restaurant and order mock chicken and mock beef with all kinds of spices and they consider that a healthy meal; I'm saying it's not. I'm saying a healthy meal is a raw mango: That's healthy. Raw lettuce: That's healthy.

BERRY: Could a raw mango be the substance of a meal for you?

KOLE: Each time I eat a piece of fruit, it's a meal, but I don't call it a meal. I call my salads the meal.

BERRY: Has there been an upsurge in your energy?

KOLE: I need half the amount of sleep. I can exercise intensively and no longer need naps. I'm alert and energetic the entire day. It's remarkable.

BERRY: Did you become a vegan rawfoodist for health reasons or for ethical reasons?

KOLE: For health reasons, but the ethical considerations filtered in as I was deciding.

BERRY: Getting back to the reasons why Jews seem to be preternaturally attached to a non-vegetarian diet; you were about to give another reason when I interrupted you.

KOLE: The second thing besides the diet would be our strong identification with the modern medical profession. Jewish doctors have helped create the medical paradigm that primarily focuses on diagnosis and treatment—not on prevention. Medical research primarily wants to come up with new and better ways to diagnose and treat illnesses people already have, rather than teach prevention of disease through nutrition and exercise. Training in nutrition is simply not emphasized in medical schools.

BERRY: Yes, it's curious that the dynasties of Sephardic Jewish physicians, stretching back to the early Middle Ages, and the great modern Jewish physicians of America and Europe, haven't seized on a vegetarian diet as the panacea that it undoubtedly is.

KOLE: Since the medical community in general has been so slow to come around to it, I don't see any reason why the Jewish doctors would be any better able to break through their own institutional prejudices.

BERRY: I wonder if the concern with Talmudic purity among Jews and the dietary laws that condone meat-eating as a way of preserving Jewish identity, haven't served to perpetuate meat-eating among Jews who might otherwise find the practice abhorrent?

KOLE: I agree that the preservation of Talmudic purity is an important element of Jewish identity. The first five books of the Hebrew Bible are simply called the Torah or Law, and Moses is known as "the Lawgiver." Among those who study the Talmudic laws, the controversy about whether meat should be eaten or not is not a primary focus. Instead, they focus on how the Kosher laws should be interpreted and enforced. For example, they decide if the modern methods of slaughtering animals conform to the original laws in the Torah.

So the concern is not whether eating meat is immoral or not; it's whether the meat from a particular butcher fulfills the requirements of the kosher laws as set down in the Torah and interpreted through the Talmud up to the present day. Being an orthodox Jew requires strict adherence to the laws. However, along with that acceptance comes a continuous questioning of how those laws are to be interpreted, of what actions constitute proper adherence to the Torah.

BERRY: But somehow the dietary laws are not so openly questioned.

KOLE: Not really. One of my classmates in college, who had been to *yeshiva*, repeated an expression he had heard that "no matter how kosher you are, you can always be more kosher." Dairy and meat cannot be served together; separate sets of plates and utensils are required as well. And if two kitchen sinks are necessary in a kosher home—one for dairy and one for meat—then, just for Passover week, one could have a third sink that no leavened food would touch. There's a continuous re-examination of what constitutes keeping kosher, but among the Orthodox there is no question that kosher laws must exist and must be followed.

BERRY: So the morality of meat-eating is never questioned?

KOLE: Right, at least among the mainstream Talmudic scholars. For them, as long as the meat is officially kosher, then the meat is good. You can then eat it with a good conscience.

BERRY: Of course, kosher meat may still be full of salmonella, phosphorine, putrescine and other pathogenic bacteria.

KOLE: Right. I don't think there's any injunction against the microorganisms in the meat, but there are injunctions against fillers and against excess refrigeration, and how long after an animal has been killed that its flesh can be eaten. But all of that, as spiritual as it may be in practice, does seem to have some basis in human hygiene. However, since the process has become somewhat sanctified, it is not dealt with as a human health issue, but as an official religious one. The result: as long as it's kosher, it obeys the Law.

BERRY: Wouldn't the conversion of Jews en masse to vegetarianism be a threat to the *kashrut* ceremony and to the keeping of kosher laws?

KOLE: No, not at all, because being a kosher vegetarian fulfills the requirements. All fruits and vegetables, grains etc., are kosher. They do not have to be picked or grown in any special manner that I know of to be kosher.

But you're right in one sense; there would be hesitation within the Jewish community itself to dispense with an entire tradition of laws that deal with the production of kosher meat. But if the demand for meat, kosher as well as non-kosher, declines, there would be less and less meat to inspect both by the secular authorities and the religious ones.

BERRY: Wouldn't it be easier to keep kosher as a vegetarian? For one thing you wouldn't have to use two sets of dishes.

KOLE: That's right, you wouldn't. Since you really only have to separate meat from dairy: If you were a lacto-vegetarian, or even a vegan, you would just need one set of dishes. Even to be superkosher, you would just need one sink. It would indeed be simpler, but perhaps that goes against the very idea of being kosher: you're supposed to go to some trouble to be kosher; there seems to be some pride, deservedly, in maintaining an adherence to tradition—to the laws. Therefore, I don't think that would be a good selling feature—"Oh, it will be easier!" A much better selling point to help Jews convert to vegetarianism would be to stress that being a vegetarian is healthier. Life is especially sacred to Jews. Our celebratory toast is "La Chaim," which means, "To life," and next to the star of David, the most widespread Jewish symbol is the "Chai": the first letter of the word for life. It's also important to realize that the existence of kosher laws implies a separation of foods into clean and unclean, acceptable and unacceptable. Whereas the Christian religion permits all animals to be eaten, the kosher laws are restrictive. And this idea of dietary restriction lends itself, I feel, to further restrictions that could promote vegetarianism. And since most Jews who keep kosher do so not for hygienic reasons but for religious or spiritual ones, another way to promote vegetarianism is to argue that not eating animal flesh makes one even more spiritually pure, more kosher, closer to the tradition of life and humanity, which is what being a real Jew is supposed to mean.

In fact, I've noticed that many Jews are embracing Eastern religions and Eastern philosophies even within Judaism, and that leads them to a vegetarian lifestyle—either within Judaism or as converts to Eastern religions.

BERRY: It's very difficult for non-Jews or non-Muslims to criticize the cruelty inherent in ritual slaughter without appearing to be anti-Semitic. In England, for example, the movement to ban both Jewish and Muslim ritual slaughter was stopped in its tracks by cries of anti-Semitism.

KOLE: Public criticism from outside any group, no matter what your group is, is a very sensitive issue. I think it's natural that most Jews would resent anyone's singling out for criticism our kosher laws concerning ritual slaughter. I think there are several reasons for particular sensitivity on this issue: It's a real source of pride—it seems to me—to have maintained kosher laws in modern society. The struggle not to assimilate and lose one's Jewish identity is an important one. I once heard a rabbi talk about the intermarriage of Jews in America as a second holocaust—because if Jewish men marry non-Jewish women, their children cannot be officially Jewish, because their mothers would not be Jewish.

BERRY: So Judaism is not a proselytizing religion. That is to say, it doesn't seek converts?

KOLE: No, definitely not. It's very much not the case. Even the Hasidic Lubavitcher movement only proselytizes actively among other Jews. Their street ministry, if you could call it that, consists of getting Jews to practice the Laws. On the street, they ask people, "Are you Jewish?" They're only going to work with people who have the birthright of being Jewish. And among the Orthodox only certain conversions are recognized.

BERRY: You pointed out the paradox that koshering gives meat a patina of wholesomeness in spite of the fact that it may be crawling with bacteria.

KOLE: Yes, and the animals suffer tremendously in the slaughter! And because of a dreadfully ironic conflation of two different regulations—a kosher one and a modern hygienic one—their suffering is even greater. The kosher laws require that an animal must be conscious when it is slaughtered and a modern hygienic law requires that no animal be slaughtered in the blood of another animal. This has led to the hoisting of fully conscious animals on conveyor belts in our modern mechanized slaughterhouses. This situation was not intended by those who created the kosher laws or by those who issued the hygienic injunction against mixing the blood on the slaughterhouse floors. It's a terrible irony that the kosher laws, which seem to imply a much more humane slaughter of animals for food, has now led to this terrible suffering of animals hoisted on conveyor belts, fully conscious. And you're right: there is a seal of approval on the food because it's kosher, but there's also a seal of approval on non-kosher meat from the Department of Agriculture. Or the implied seal of approval that's conferred on all meat by virtue of the way it's packaged so neatly by the meat packers. The bulk of the commercial meat packers aren't kosher, yet virtually all meat appears packaged in a wholesome manner that implies social approval. So I think for most people the kosher packaging is just another label, another seal of approval.

BERRY: It's another veil of sanctity.

KOLE: Your point assumes a very religious and spiritual attitude on the part of people who eat meat. Certainly all orthodox Jews who eat meat will buy only kosher meat, but many people who buy kosher meat simply like it for one reason or another. My father, for example, who is not kosher, likes kosher chicken. Maybe it's because it's prepared in a certain way, or maybe he gets the feeling that since he's paying a bit more for kosher, he must be getting something better.

BERRY: Are ritual forms more important in Judaism than they are in Catholicism?

KOLE: No. Certainly the rituals of the Catholic Mass, for example, are very important and precisely observed. The priest must put on his cassock just so, but the rituals are continually re-edified by Rome, such as the recent switch from Latin into English or whatever the vernacular might be. You can eat meat on Fridays now; the Pope has reinterpreted that. So too with Judaism—religions continue to recodify themselves; it's possible for there to be modifications and reforms. But the re-evaluation of the kosher laws are not necessarily in the direction of vegetarianism. Those responsible for Talmudic purity in the modern age must adapt ancient laws governing food preparation to the modern age, showing how the modern mechanized slaughterhouse can replace the village butcher.

BERRY: Since it's been codified in the Law, it would seem to be almost ineradicable.

KOLE: But the Law doesn't say, "You have to eat meat." The Law says that when you eat meat, it must be slaughtered and prepared in a specific manner, and that you can't mix meat and dairy.

BERRY: In my book *The New Vegetarians*, the Nobel Laureate Isaac Bashevis Singer lamented the fact that the phylacteries were made of leather and that the Torah was bound in animal-skin. He regarded this as a sacrilege.

KOLE: Yes, but that whole problem could be solved in the future the way the Gandhians deal with the issue of leather; they use only the skin of animals who have died on their own of natural causes. But, you know, the killing of animals for their fur and their flesh is widespread in the Torah. Jacob prepares venison for his father, Isaac, and wears fur to disguise himself as his older brother. In the light of these and other passages in the Torah, it would be a difficult thing to argue that the eating of meat inhibits spiritual growth as defined in the Torah.

BERRY: A Jewish man once told me that meat-eating was an integral part of Judaism, and that at Passover it's mandatory that an observant Jew eat meat.

KOLE: Not anymore, as far as I know. We no longer celebrate Passover the way it is defined exactly in the Torah. The Torah does tell you that you have to eat barbecued lamb at the end of the meal; the men have to stand up and eat it and then burn the leftovers. Nowadays, we have Passover desserts made without any leavened products and most American families have turkey; the turkey is the centerpiece of the big family dinner in America. The dinner itself turns into a sort of Thanksgiving—except that there is no bread and that before people can eat they have to follow the Seder ritual, which commemorates the liberation of the Jews from slavery in Egypt as detailed in the book of Exodus. Eating lamb is simply no longer required and is, in fact, in my experience, not that widespread. On a special Passover display plate, which is a Talmudic requirement instituted after the Torah, different items are placed on that plate, and these items must be shown to everyone at the table. The shank of a lamb is one of the items. But you do not have to eat it and even a picture of one might suffice.

BERRY: The image of the turkey as festal bird reminds me of the incident during Exodus when the children of Israel were being supplied with *manna*. Every day the amount of it doubled. But it wasn't long before they began to pine for the fleshpots of Egypt. So they demanded meat and God answered them by sending down quail, whose flesh stuck in their teeth and shortly thereafter they were carried off by plague.

KOLE: Well, as I recall, they did not kill the quail; they found dead quail; and that is specifically non-kosher: To eat animals that you find already dead certainly violates the dietary laws; which makes sense, since flesh from dead animals will turn rancid, especially in the desert conditions of the Middle East.

BERRY: It's been suggested by some Jewish vegetarian scholars that *manna* was a vegetarian food; and in preferring to eat the flesh food the Jews were erring dietetically and thus brought the plague down on themselves as a sort of condign punishment.

KOLE: Certainly, it's healthier to eat vegetarian—not only for the basic health reasons that you are going to eat better food, but also to avoid the dangers of disease. So the children of Israel wandering in the desert, like everyone else, would be better off eating vegetarian; and perhaps since we already have these kosher laws whose original basis seems rooted in a health code, it could be a logical progression to say that true kosher would be totally vegetarian. But if you're going to have to eat meat, as the people demanded, then you should eat only the meat from animals that you have killed yourself. Don't eat the meat from animals that you find already dead on the ground, like a scavenger, a hyena or a coyote. That would be incredibly detrimental to human health. I'm hesitant to make the story of the *manna* and the quail into a vegetarian parable because I don't see the necessity for it. I don't take my own vegetarianism from the authority of ancient texts.

BERRY: Many Jews, Fundamentalist Christians and Muslims do take their dietary cues from ancient texts. Isn't there a sort of bibliolatry that prevents them from thinking for themselves and looking at their diet objectively?

KOLE: Well, Judaism is a very text-driven religion. Moses delivered the Torah, the Law, to the people. This is the great gift from God, the Torah, which codified the Law. This document created the religion and helped sustain it. In many ways, this document, the Torah, created the Jewish people. So it's difficult for many Jews to separate out the bibliolatry, as you call it. But speaking for myself, I became a vegetarian simply because I felt better, and Judaism does teach us (at least in the way that it's been received by me) to value one's health, to take care of oneself. Your life is a gift from God. If you know something is good for you, then you should do it. However, as I said before, I'm not sure that the Bible lends itself to being interpreted as a vegetarian parable. We've seen how the story of Jacob and the dying Isaac involves the slaughter of deer. The blood of the sacrificial lamb at Passover spares the first born of the Jews from death in Egypt. Another example is when Abraham, ready to sacrifice his son Isaac at God's command, substitutes a ram. The Torah, in many places, replaces human sacrifice with animal sacrifice.

BERRY: What about the first dietary law in Genesis when God says, "Behold I have given you every herb-bearing seed which is upon the face of the earth, and every tree which is the fruit of the tree-yielding seed..."? Wouldn't you say that there are passages in Genesis that lend themselves to a vegetarian interpretation?

KOLE: One can interpret that to mean that it's the number one food that God gave us—fruits and vegetables; but it's hard to get away from the fact that there's so much in the Bible describing how to eat meat. The children of Israel were weak because the *manna* did not satisfy them and so they demanded meat. As a concession to their weakness, God gave them the laws that make it possible to eat meat without destroying themselves entirely. So the kosher laws do in fact accomplish that—they give the regulations for the preparation of meat in the least unhealthy manner. And the acceptable animals can be considered those that are least offensive to human health: cows, deer, goats, birds, fish, rather than pigs, insects, reptiles, crustacea. I do not see these laws for the eating of meat as separate or alien to the spirit of the Torah.

BERRY: Unfortunately, for the lot of animals in Western civilization, Yahweh, who is the God of Islam and Christianity as well as of Judaism, looks pleasingly on animal sacrifices, and delights in them.

KOLE: As inhumane as this may seem—and we have to keep in mind that this is from an earlier era—Yahweh replaces human sacrifices with animal sacrifices. The surrounding tribes worshipped gods that demanded human sacrifice—gods such as Baal and Moloch. The Torah celebrates the victories of the Israelites over these other gods who demanded human sacrifice from their adherents. So taking the Torah as a kind of middle way, we've been moving in a more humane direction. Preserving human life on earth is our sacred duty as Jews. Life above all. And as you know, human life will never be assured on earth until we cease the mass consumption of meat, which destroys the environment through misuse of precious and limited resources. Eventually, the human race will be forced to give up meat just in order to survive. And if our survival is part of God's plan, then the next millennium, the next eon, will see us as a species moving away from the slaughter of animals for food. To a large extent we've already moved away from religious sacrifices. Only a few religions on the fringes still practice animal sacrifice. I don't know any Jews who still sacrifice animals to God. Although some extremists say that when the Temple is rebuilt in Jerusalem, they will re-institute animal sacrifice.

BERRY: Isn't it still being done by proxy, when the *schochet*, or the slaughterer, draws his blade across the animal's throat?

KOLE: Well, he's not really sacrificing. He's making sure that you eat the meat kosher so you don't get sick. And he's seeing to it that the laws are obeyed.

BERRY: Isn't it true that since the destruction of the Second Temple, the *shochet* attempts to establish the cultic setting in which the animal was sacrificed according to the dictates of the Law? Isn't this what the Mishnah recommends as a way of restoring the significance of the Temple sacrifice after the Romans destroyed the temple in 70 CE?

KOLE: I don't see it that way, because there's no gathering of the community to watch that; there's no special holiday to celebrate it. When a farmer decides that his cow is big enough to be slaughtered for the winter, he takes it to the person who's going to slaughter it in the proper manner. But the whole village doesn't come out to watch; it's not a public religious ceremony as it was in the Temple. You see, for the orthodox observant Jew, everything is a religious ceremony. Plates are washed according to religious laws in the proper sink: dairy or meat. There are hundreds of laws in the Torah. I reject the idea that the ritual slaughter of animals to produce kosher meat is analogous to the sacrifice of the animals to God, which was definitely a very religious ceremony carried out by priests in the Temple.

BERRY: You mentioned that it was Peter Singer who first prompted you to look at the ethical aspect of your diet?

KOLE: In his book, *Animal Liberation*, Peter Singer says that animals suffer gradations of pain based upon the development of their nervous systems. Singer discusses it at some length. When he was discussing the sea animals, I was struck that the animals who swarm and crawl are not kosher. So let's say that animals that appear to be like insects and actually are insects and reptiles are not kosher; and these are the animals that according to Singer feel less pain as humans understand pain. And so it seems ironic and it bothers me more than a little bit...

BERRY: ...that kosher animals experience the most suffering when they are killed for the table?

KOLE: Yes, but not just from that; they're capable of suffering more throughout their lives than other animals not as close to us in terms of evolutionary development. Many mammals are kosher and they live in family units that experience loss and grief. They bleed when they're cut, and they have nervous systems that are very similar to ours. This bothers me a lot. It seems a shame that the kosher laws sanction the eating of mammals because the kosher laws purport to be more humane, and are in fact more humane than the traditions they replace. But they're still obviously part of a very speciesist tradition. Mankind is given dominion over the animals and the earth; we're created in God's image, but the animals aren't. The purpose of the universe according to the Bible is human progress. When the Bible was written, it was thought that the earth was the center of the universe. We now know that we're *not* the center of the universe; we now know about the delicate interaction of the ecosystem on earth. We're beginning to realize that our dominion over the earth had better improve or we're going to destroy the planet's ability to sustain human life.

BERRY: Since the Torah has been revised so many times by priestly scribes who condone hunting and animal sacrifice, do you think there might have been a vegetarian version of the Torah? For instance, Roshi Kapleau believes that the teachings of the Buddha were corrupted by meat-loving priests.

KOLE: No, I don't. Not in the Torah. The big shift from the polytheistic tradition which precedes the Torah to the monotheistic tradition of the Hebrew scriptures is one from human sacrifice to animal sacrifice. If any documents were rewritten during the time that the Hebrew scriptures were produced, it would have been an excision and revision of anything condoning human sacrifice.

BERRY: What about the Genesis sagas, which indicate that there was a prelapsarian vegetarian paradise? The first dietary law that Yahweh hands down is to observe a vegetarian diet, a raw food vegetarian diet at that.

KOLE: Perhaps. That's one way to interpret it in order to teach people that being a holier Jew requires keeping to a vegetarian diet. A vegetarian rabbi once said to me that meat-eating is to Judaism what sex is to Catholicism. In other words: you *can* have sex in the Catholic religion, but you're a holier Catholic if you don't. And you *can* eat meat in the Jewish religion if you follow these particular laws, and eat these particular animals killed in these particular ways, *but you'll be a holier Jew if you don't eat meat at all.* Of course, in the Asian religions, you're a holier Buddhist, a holier Jain, or a holier Hindu if you don't eat animals, and I myself believe that a vegetarian diet is an important prerequisite for spiritual growth.

BERRY: I've noted that the Asian religions that follow the first precept also have a doctrine of reincarnation. Is there a doctrine of reincarnation in Judaism?

KOLE: There's more of a doctrine of pre-incarnation, which says that the soul of every Jew was present at Mount Sinai when Moses received the Torah, that my soul was there centuries before my birth.

BERRY: Is there any connection between the Hebrew scriptures and the European dietary paradigm that views the eating of animal flesh as a status symbol?

KOLE: I don't see one. One could just as easily say that the Homeric epics shaped the European paradigm. In the *Iliad*, they use any excuse to sacrifice a bullock to Zeus so that they can have a feast. Certainly, the Hebrew scriptures are in keeping with that tradition, but without any incidence of human sacrifice, as when King Agamemnon sacrifices his daughter in the *Iliad*. But you can make the point that the Judeo-Christian Bible is a fundamental document of Western Civilization. And Western Civilization does seem to have a great meat-eating tradition. I just don't view it as cause-and-effect, that the Bible caused a greater dependence on meat-eating in the West.

BERRY: Do you think that the Essenes were Gnostics?

KOLE: There seems to be some evidence of that. The Gnostics were not so well organized. There was probably no organized Gnostic movement, but rather a number of small sects like the Essenes who were searching for their own answers.

BERRY: They tended to be largely vegetarian.

KOLE: Yes, because of their Eastern world view, which was more in the Buddhist tradition.

BERRY: Some scholars have suggested that Christ may have been a Gnostic.

KOLE: I would be very much surprised if he weren't a vegetarian.

BERRY: That's what many vegetarian Christians also believe. The Catholic religious, Brother Ron Pickarski and Dr. Conrad Latto of the Order of the Cross, both of whom were interviewed by me, say that they believe he was a vegetarian. In the event that there should be a mass-conversion of Jews to vegetarianism, do you envision a time when Jews may wish to edit the Torah and re-interpret it as a vegetarian text?

KOLE: Reinterpret it, yes. But I strongly doubt that it will ever be re-written. I would not favor altering the ancient text no matter how many revisions it went through centuries ago. It would certainly be more legitimate to revise and rewrite the prayers that were written after the Torah. Certainly the Haggadah for Passover—the Seder instructions on how to conduct a Passover dinner—has been through many revisions. But they are a more recent construction, and more obviously man-made. The concept of the holy Torah, though, is another matter. From the archeological evidence that we have, the Torah has been preserved by generations of scribes almost exactly as it was written. It's been through the Diaspora; it's survived all the assimilation by the Jewish people in all the nations we have settled throughout the centuries.

BERRY: Although it's clear that there have been many redactions.

KOLE: Yes, but the Massoretic text, the standard Hebrew text, is a solid thousand years old, and older scrolls as they are discovered reveal an astonishing consistency with the more recent text. I favor reinterpretation, but not revision. I would rather study what

"J" wrote in Harold Bloom's sponsored translation, coupled with a continuous re-examination of the text—studying how it was written, who wrote it, at what stage different sections were written. That, to me, is of tremendous interest. But not a rewriting of this vital document, which is a holy text to many and of tremendous significance to most of the human race.

When vegetarianism as a universal phenomenon does happen, and I hope it will (and believe it must), it will not take place in a Jewish way, or a Christian way, or even a Buddhist way. I believe, rather, that it will take place in a Western cultural way, due to concerns about the environment, human health, and unfortunately, due—only in a peripheral way—to concerns about the suffering of non-human creatures.

BERRY: Rabbi Abraham Isaac HaCohen Kook, the first Chief Rabbi of pre-State Israel, predicted that when the Jews entered the Messianic age, they would become vegetarian.

KOLE: To me, the Jewish idea of the Messianic Age implies the same change in the world that the Christians refer to when they talk about the Second Coming of Christ. Life will change as we know it, and if the lion does lie down with the lamb, and no carnivorous activity takes place in the animal kingdom, then nutrition itself as we know it will change and the dead will come back to life. It's almost impossible to speak of a mass conversion to veganism at such a time. It will be like entering a different dimension, a different state of existence. All the old rules will cease to apply.

BERRY: It was Rav Kook who said that Jews can help to accelerate the arrival of the Messianic Age by becoming vegetarian; they're priming the pump, so to speak.

KOLE: That makes good sense because spiritual growth is implied in the search for the Messiah. The late Lubavitcher Rebbe, Menachem Schneerson, whom many of his followers consider to be the Messiah, said that the desire for the Messiah represented the hope for a perfect world. Without such desire there is no reason to live, no reason to expect progress. The Rebbe said that a general improvement in the spiritual forces of the universe can help bring about the Messianic Age: the perfect world. I believe in a more secular version of that progress, that if people increase their spiritual awareness in any kind of mass way, it is possible to have a form of the Messianic age without the Messiah. To be sure, there would still be brigands and criminals, and the dead would not come back to life, but there would be an end to state-sponsored war, environmental destruction, and enmity among nations and races. And, of course, lions would still be killing other animals for food.

BERRY: So, in Jewish eschatology, the last days would resemble the first days. There would be a return to Edenic diet and Edenic peace.

KOLE: Yes, in the way you put it: it would be the day when the tigers are not eating the lambs.

BERRY: Or when humans are not eating the lambs. Could there be a collective instead of an individual manifestation of the Messiah?

KOLE: I believe there can be. In fact there must be a collective movement toward spiritual awareness if my secular version of the Messianic Age will come to pass. Let's put it this way: I don't believe that the human race will mature as a species or fulfill its potential until the mass consumption of meat is over.

BERRY: Are you familiar with Arnold Toynbee's thesis that the concept of dominion as it was put forth in Genesis in which humans are given dominion over animals and nature is responsible for the exploitation of animals and the plundering of the planet?

KOLE: It's a very complex philosophical and cultural idea, but I see a greater connection there. We can consider what happened to the Native Americans when the Europeans settled in North America. The Europeans brought the Old and New Testaments in one hand and deeds and wills in the other; whereas, the American Indians had no concept of the ownership of land in that sense. The Western idea of dominion certainly has led to environmental exploitation.

BERRY: Is that because the term "dominion" has been misconstrued?

KOLE: "Caretaker" would have been a better term. We're supposed to be caretakers of what we've been given.

BERRY: The common conception seems to be that we can do whatever we like with the animals; we can lord it over them?

KOLE: Yes, we are in God's image, and they are not. The Torah definitely specifies our holiness over them. They are not sacred the way we are.

BERRY: Roshi Philip Kapleau, in my interview with him, made the point that in the Indic religions such as Buddhism, Jainism and Hinduism, the first precept forbids killing; whereas in the Western religions, the commandment against killing is only the sixth.

KOLE: Well even the sixth commandment, "Thou shalt not murder," refers only to other human beings. The killing of animals is not included.

BERRY: Unlike Jainism or Buddhism, where the injunction against killing in their first precept is extended to all living creatures.

KOLE: Right, because the Torah says humans are holy; we are in God's image—we were created last, in a special way. Our species is, in a sense, God. The first precept of the Torah is not to have any other gods. You could say that the purpose of the Torah is to codify the monotheism of Moses in Israel.

BERRY: Isn't that rather narcissistic of God in the Torah?

KOLE: Well, he's considered a jealous god. The daily prayer of the Jews, the holiest sentence you can say—the *Schma*, as it's called—the most sacred thing you can say as you're dying is, "the Lord is one," or as it's been recently translated, "the Lord alone."

BERRY: Yahweh, alone?

KOLE: Yes. "The Lord Our God, the Lord Alone." Again, this was in reaction to the polytheism that preceded Moses.

BERRY: It was Philip Pick, the founder of the International Jewish Vegetarian Society, who pointed out that permission was granted Noah to eat meat by Yahweh, but that it was given with a curse: "The blood of your lives will I require" [Genesis 9:5], and that the fear and dread of man would be upon the animals [Genesis 9:2]—so that humans were not permitted to eat the flesh of animals with impunity.

KOLE: It says "Whoever sheds the blood of man, by man shall his blood be shed, for in the image of God was man created." As I said earlier, human blood must be reckoned with. If you shed blood, then there has to be an expiation of that blood.

BERRY: Pick's interpretation is that "the blood of your lives will I require" is retributive. You cannot eat the flesh of animals without paying a forfeit of some kind.

KOLE: It's an interesting idea, since it stresses the importance of blood, and you should not eat flesh with its lifeblood in it.

BERRY: Well, it's almost impossible to eat flesh — no matter how much it's been bled out — without taking in some residual blood from the meat. No matter how kosher it is, it's physically impossible to remove all the blood from the flesh. So if Pick's interpretation is correct, there's no way of eating meat without suffering the consequences.

KOLE: Perhaps. However, the text goes right on to talk about murder. It's one thing to say that the text deconstructs itself; but on the other hand, God goes on for about four or five lines here about not shedding the blood of another human being, and affirming the regulations about the eating of animals. So I'm not sure that Mr. Pick and others aren't grasping at straws here — in pushing the biblical text to fit the modern vegetarian-animal rights orientation.

BERRY: Wouldn't you say that he's forcing the text to yield this interpretation?

KOLE: Perhaps, but either way, I'm not sure that it's productive. Certainly, in the Essene Gospels, we have Christ quoted as saying not to eat animals, but in the Torah, where human sacrifice is pointedly excluded, Noah is being given permission to eat animals. He specifically slaughters and burns, and makes offerings to God of all the kosher animals.

BERRY: What does this say about the god to whom he would offer these animals?

KOLE: That he's a god who demands obedience in every aspect of life. Life, at that time, as it does now, included eating animals. God asked for the sacrifice of grains too. He demands offerings to him of everything that passes your lips. Before you put it into your mouth, God gets thanks. That's neither a vegetarian nor an anti-vegetarian idea. It's a monotheistically powerful idea.

BERRY: Isn't that an anthropomorphic idea? Isn't God behaving like a fallible human when he seems to want everything for himself?

KOLE: Perhaps, but we are in his image. He cannot be so different from us.

BERRY: Doesn't it diminish Him to say that He is subject to these human desires?

KOLE: Perhaps. He may be a jealous god. But he's jealous for a purpose: He doesn't want anyone to stray from the straight and narrow path of monotheistic worship. I don't see the God of the Hebrew Bible as being carnivorous; I see Him as demanding fealty to himself, to a monotheistic ideal, and requiring ethical treatment among humans. This was the main intention of the authors of the Hebrew Bible; so I would not look for any chink in the armor of the text as being pro- or anti-vegetarian. Rather, it's an anti-murder text; it's an anti-human-sacrifice text, and it's very much a pro-establishment text, which supports the theocratic state established by Moses and the Elders of Israel.

BERRY: Many feminists and not a few Jewish vegetarians are troubled by the depiction of Yahweh as a cruel and warlike God. As a result, many vegetarian feminists have begun to postulate a Hebrew Goddess, who may have been deposed by the followers of Yahweh. There are even some Hebrew scholars who believe there is a hidden goddess in the Torah. In view of the fact that the mother goddesses of other ancient religions seem to have been more compassionate towards animal and human life than male gods who supplanted them, there is a movement afoot to try to restore the ancient Hebrew goddesses and to connect them with vegetarianism and animal protection.

KOLE: I would rather move forward than to try to re-write the past, especially when the past is encoded in text. I don't allow the authority of original texts to govern my actions. We don't need a different Torah before we can grant equality to women and to stop exploiting animals. As a Shakespearean textual scholar, I'm not going to go back and re-write the First Folio of Shakespeare because I want it to be more adaptable to television. I'll interpret it as I see fit, without changing the original. So I'm more supportive of the feminist attempts to glorify biblical figures like Miriam and Sarah, and other women in the Bible who haven't been given their due. I'd rather reevaluate them than to extrapolate a goddess from a text which seems very patriarchal, and very warlike, when dealing with anyone who opposes Israel and Yahweh. Why not move forward and accept the text as it is?

BERRY: To be fair, Jack Miles in his book, *God: A Biography*, remarked that the female goddesses of the ancient Near East were "utterly ferocious."

KOLE: So, in that sense as well, Yahweh may represent an ethical advance on the surrounding pagan cultures that practiced human sacrifice and worshipped truculent female goddesses.

BERRY: In your view, can one at least find justification in the Torah for vegetarianism and for compassion towards one's fellow creatures.

KOLE: To me, it's the most natural progression to go from compassion for fellow humans, which the Torah demands, to a vegetarian lifestyle and compassion for animals. Such a progression would be a sign of the maturing of the human species. But, as I've said, the Hebrew Bible is an old document, and if we are moving forward to the fulfillment of the Hebrew Bible, then we are moving away from it, away from human sacrifice, certainly, and away from animal sacrifice, and toward a new age in the West when we do away with the slaughter and consumption of meat.

BERRY: So the document may become obsolete?

KOLE: In a large measure it's already obsolete. We have no Temple. The instructions on how to sacrifice to Yahweh are no longer valid. In those terms it's already obsolete. But many of its teachings, such as monogamy, criminal justice, charity for the poor, are intensely relevant today. However, it is true that as we move away from the modes of worship in the Hebrew Scriptures, the Bible will be treated the way we treat Homer, as a literary document.

BERRY: Of course, that would be anathema to the fundamentalists who believe that it's the word of God, that it was dictated by God to Moses.

KOLE: Right, but that's not what the Reform Jews say. They acknowledge that the Torah was written over an extended period of time long after Moses died. So it could not have been the direct testimony of Moses.

BERRY: Do they recognize that it was the work of many hands?

KOLE: Yes. But the Orthodox don't. *They* accept the text as literal truth. For them, these are the words God said to Moses. However, the introduction to the edition of the Torah sponsored by the Reform Jewish movement speaks of the four authors of the Torah—"J", "E" "D and "P"—and of an historical figure, Moses, who lived hundreds of years before the long centuries of writing took place.

As a textual scholar, and as an editor of Shakespeare, I'm aware that the form that you place a work in predetermines its meaning. So if you inscribe a text on parchment scrolls and keep it in a holy ark before an eternal flame in the synagogue, it is predetermined to be the truth as God said it. However, if it is published in printed volumes and translated into other languages, in as many new translations as each new editor or publisher desires, then the original Hebrew text is reinterpreted every time it is re-published, or re-examined.

BERRY: So it's an evolving text.

KOLE: Its meaning evolves as its editions evolve. Different editions have different purposes, different audiences. But the original text, as far as we can determine the original text to be, remains unchanged. It is not being re-written as it was by J, E, D, and P in those centuries after Moses.

BERRY: At the time of the destruction of the Second Temple, there were many vegetarian sects among the Jews—such as the Essenes, the Zadokites, the Ebionites, the Nazoreans and the Therapeutae in Alexandria. Both Josephus and Philo of Alexandria talk about them at length. You also mentioned the Gnostics; some of these groups were Gnostic.

KOLE: The suppression of any group outside the mainstream seems to have been done in order to maintain the power of the mainstream bureaucracy, the mainstream hierarchy. Anybody not adhering to the laws would be a threat to those who were administering the laws.

BERRY: The outside cults such as the Nazoreans and the Therapeutae tended to be abstemious and vegetarian. Perhaps the priesthood in reaction to these outside cults reinforced their meat-eating tendencies in order to set themselves apart from them. Food in Judaism is a potent symbol; so what better way to stress their apartness than by eating flesh while the renegade sects practiced vegetarianism and fruitarianism?

KOLE: Perhaps. Then the priest class could dispense the rules and permission to eat meat down to the masses. But the big reason was that there should be no competing source of spiritual purity. The source of spiritual purity would then be monolithic with the mainstream organization. The priests would be the ones to decide what was spiritual; what foods could be eaten and what foods were unclean; they would be the ones to choose the documents that would become the scriptures. They did it for the same reasons that the early Christian Church put down the Gnostic groups—to maintain a monolithic source of power.

Power lay in the decisions of what is holy. So if you belonged to a group that did not have to worry about the Temple, and you could become holy just by joining one of these groups—this was a direct threat to the power of those who controlled the Temple. Since the Temple was engaged in ongoing animal sacrifice, you may be correct in saying that the success of the Temple priests over any outside groups did lead to wider consumption of meat; because the idea of holiness through abstention was associated with those outside groups—the Essenes, the Gnostics and the Therapeutae—and was therefore discouraged. But the purpose was not to encourage meat-eating as an end in itself, but to suppress these outside groups and gain a monopoly on spiritual authority.

BERRY: There's a sprinkling of stories in the Hebrew Scriptures that lend themselves to a vegetarian interpretation. Take the story of Daniel, for instance. The first book of Daniel has it that Daniel and two of his companions were in the palace of Nebuchadnezzar, and they didn't want to eat of the king's meat or wine, which they felt would not be kosher, so they said "Give us water and pulse (beans)." And the king's servant was very frightened because he feared that they would waste away, and that the king would blame him. But Daniel and his companions tried to allay his fears, and said that he should try them on this diet for ten days. And sure enough after ten days their countenances were far fairer than were those who had been eating the king's meat. So the servant of the king ended up putting all the others who were waiting for the king on the same diet.

KOLE: Well, it's hard to know whether that's a pro-vegetarian polemic or a pro-kosher polemic because, throughout the Bible, the hint is that if you obey the laws you will live longer and better.

BERRY: So it's simpler for an observant Jew to be a vegetarian in cases where he is uncertain about the purity of the food; he should eat beans even in the palace of the king.

KOLE: Definitely, and that's really the point of the story: even the King of Persia was eating unkosher meat. He thinks he's having the finest food there is, but the simplest Jew eating kosher food is eating better and holier than the king. Obey the laws and you get rewarded. Disobey the laws and you get sick.

BERRY: The Maccabees, when they fled to the mountains, became vegetarians since kosher food wasn't readily available. Would you interpret that story in the same way?

KOLE: Yes. There's a book called *The Hasidic Tales of the Holocaust*, which talk about Orthodox rabbis in Nazi death camps being offered on Yom Kippur huge slabs of flesh, and plates of food. The Nazis had them on a starvation diet all year, and on a day when the rabbis were obliged to fast, the Nazis tried to tempt them with plates of food. The point is: under duress, stick with what's kosher. When should you be rewarded for obeying God's laws? When it's difficult to obey God's laws.

BERRY: And the Maccabees?

KOLE: The Maccabees were fleeing to the hills and couldn't find any kosher food; so they survived as best they could by eating fruits and vegetables. By remaining holy, they remained strong in order to conquer their enemy. They drew their spirituality from God, not from a vegetarian diet. He's the source of spirituality in the Hebrew Scriptures.

BERRY: It's similar to the Jain idea that everyone is his or her own priest. There are no religious intermediaries in Jainism because Mahavira and the other Tirthankaras realized that priesthoods are self-aggrandizing and corrupt.

KOLE: This was also the guiding principle of the Gnostics and the Essenes and many of the other Asian sects of this period, who were destroyed by the Church so that the Judeo-Christian tradition as we have received it could thrive.

BERRY: In reading the Renaissance scholar Stephen Greenblatt's *Learning to Curse*, I was struck by the image that the Amerindians had of the European invaders. They perceived the Europeans as being book worshippers. Their power seemed to reside in their libraries. Greenblatt cites Shakespeare's caricature of an Amerindian, Caliban, as warning of Prospero, his slave master. "Remember first to possess his books, for without them, he's but a sot as I am." It was as if the Europeans were impelled to commit atrocities against the Indians by their books, which they were constantly peeping into. In the eyes of the Indians, the Europeans were dehumanized and de-animated by their books. Text insulated them from feeling and kept them from empathizing with the Indians. For Indians, substitute "animals"—I'm wondering if book culture may not also be responsible for Western civilization's shocking lack of empathy for animals. Or is that just a coincidence?

KOLE: It's a very difficult question because oral cultures have plenty of cruelty and hierarchies too. And the West, with its written culture and history of imperialism, is also the source of individual liberty and democratic institutions throughout the world. Consider the American Declaration of Independence and all it represents.

BERRY: But Asian religions in which the first precept is emphasized have emerged from oral culture; they practice vegetarianism, have a theory of reincarnation, and identify closely with animals. Whereas, the cultures of the West, which are literate and text-driven, are the most warlike and animal-exploitative on earth.

KOLE: I admit that there does seem to be some connection between the text and the exploitation of animals, but I'm not sure that it's causal. Western civilization is a written culture; we're also the most warlike and carnivorous. But I'm not sure if there's a cause and effect there; I certainly can't envision moving back to an oral culture, or that there would be much point.

In Shakespeare's day the big bestsellers were books that showed the reader how to be a rich merchant and still get into heaven.

BERRY: How does it differ from the how-to-do-it books that are on the bestseller lists today?

KOLE: Now the Asian idea of personal growth and self-improvement is becoming paramount and it's permeating Western culture. Whereas in Shakespeare's time the emphasis was on how to make money, have a good death, and go to heaven.

BERRY: So the idea now is how to achieve Nirvana on earth.

KOLE: Yes, progress toward Nirvana, which for me definitely implies ethical vegetarianism. But even people who are moving in that direction without following a vegetarian diet are laying the groundwork for a vegetarian world. This idea of spiritual growth as opposed to simple dominion or material success leads towards real spiritual progress, of which vegetarianism is an important prerequisite.

BERRY: It will be in the first chapter or genesis of every personal growth book in the future.

KOLE: Yes, new Bibles will be written, so we won't have to rewrite the old one.

BERRY: The New Genesis?

KOLE: Right, the New Genesis. We'll start with—not a Garden of Eden—but a real world in which we leave the animals to their own devices, even though by then we may have to artificially preserve the habitats they need to survive.

BERRY: So, in a sense, the final days will resemble the first days. The Garden of Eden will resurface and humans will feast on the fruit of paradise, as in the beginning, as fruitarian rawfoodists?

KOLE: As Genesis described it, or as the Messianic age will bring it to pass.

Essay

ROMAN CATHOLICISM

THE OLDEST FORM OF Christianity extant is Roman Catholicism. It is hierarchically organized with the Pope as the head of the Church, and with cardinals and bishops ranked immediately below him. Tradition has it that the Church was founded by one of Jesus's disciples, Saint Peter. Jesus, of course, is the central figure of Christianity. It is significant that Jesus was born, lived and died as a practicing Jew; and his teachings resembled those quietist, vegetarian sects of Judaism that were prevalent in the Jewish world during the destruction of the Second Temple in 70 CE —the Essenes, the Nazoreans, the Ebionites, and the Therapeutae. That Jesus may have preached the sort of ethical vegetarianism that one associates with the Indic religious teachers, Buddha and Mahavira, is a tantalizing question that Christian vegetarians have long cogitated upon. Were these teachings suppressed by the Church? Can they ever be recovered?

The answer to both these questions is yes. The Church did suppress the true teachings of Jesus, and they are only now, at the dawn of the new millennium, just coming to light. It really began with the discovery in 1945 of the Nag Hammadi gospels near the Nile delta in Upper Egypt. Large stone jars that had been buried for two millennia yielded up a whole library of lost gospels, such as an *Apocalypse of James* and a *Gospel of Thomas* whose existence orthodox Christianity and Judaism had consigned to oblivion—by simply refusing to acknowledge that they had ever existed.

How many other gospels have been buried by the Church under a blanket of silence? Was there an ur-gospel on which the canonical gospels were based that was too radical, too revolutionary for the Church to accept? Through the work of the Jewish religious historian Hans-Joachim Schoeps (a non-vegetarian), and others, the original gospels of Christianity have been partially restored. Called by Schoeps "the Jewish Christian gospels,"[1] they have been partially reconstructed from scraps and fragments in the works of other writers, such as the *Panarion of Epiphanius* and the *Clementine Homilies*. The extraordinary thing about these gospels is that they depict a vegetarian Christ. Professor Ron Cameron notes in his book, *The Other Gospels*, that both Jesus and John the Baptist were presented by the Ebionite gospels as vegetarians. He writes: "Their Gospel makes both John the Baptist and Jesus vegetarians: John's diet is said to consist exclusively of wild honey, and Jesus is made to say that at the Passover meal with his disciples, he does not desire to eat meat."[2] The vegetarian sect of which Jesus was a leader, the Nazoreans, who were later to become the Ebionites, were in the words of Professor Schoeps, "dogmatic vegetarians."[3] They based their vegetarianism on the injunction in Genesis 9:3 not to eat flesh with the life blood therein. Since the ritual incision doesn't completely drain the blood from slaughtered animals, they realized that it was impossible to eat flesh without at the same time ingesting blood. So Jesus and his followers practiced a strict vegetarianism that Schoeps says extended to fish.[4]

Like the Egyptian Therapeutae and the Essenes, the Ebionites and Nazoreans were an anti-sacrificial sect that practiced vegetarianism because the eating of flesh was a concomitant of animal sacrifice. As Professor Morton Smith observes, "In the ancient

world, religious observances were attached to most acts of everyday life; any festivity or misfortune was an occasion of sacrifice
and the meat of most sacrifices was used for food."[5] No less a
church father than Clement of Alexandria bears him out when he
said: "Sacrifices were invented by men to be a pretext for eating
flesh."[6] Some modern writers have questioned the relevance of
ancient animal sacrifice to present-day vegetarianism,[7] but if
flesh-eating grows out of animal sacrifice, as Porphyry believed,[8]
then it is of the utmost relevance. When people eat animal flesh
even today, they are unwitting participants in an ancient blood
ritual; for it was the ancient blood sacrifice that endowed the act
of eating what is essentially carrion or dead flesh with sacral
value. Today people may think they are eating meat for its pro-
tein, or for its amino acids, but it is really *"mana"*[9] or "the god
itself" that they are taking in when they eat the flesh of animals.

Ernest Renan, in his biography of Jesus—which was the first
modern biography to treat Jesus as a man rather than as a god—
was the first modern authority to declare that Jesus was an
Essene. Opposed to the sacrifice of animals, he sought "the abolition of sacrifices that had caused him so much disgust," and said
that "the worship he had conceived for his Father had nothing in
common with scenes of butchery."[10] Since then, there is mounting
evidence to suggest that he may have belonged to the Nazoreans,[11] an anti-sacrificial vegetarian sect of whom the Essenes were
the forerunners. Both groups held many doctrines in common,
such as ritual bathing, vegetarianism, the communal sharing of
property and their opposition to animal sacrifice. The Catholic
Bishop Epiphanius of Constantia in Cyprus (d. 403 CE), himself
of Jewish origin and an important authority on Jewish sects, also
tells us that the Nazoreans differed from other Jews in that they
did not sacrifice, nor did they eat, flesh.[12]

Eyewitness accounts of the practices of the Essenes have been
left to us by Josephus; he was to the Jews of antiquity essentially what Thucydides was to the Greeks. In his *Jewish Antiquity*,
Josephus tells us that the Essenes "lived the same kind of life as
that which Pythagoras introduced among the Greeks,"[13] which is

to say that they were vegetarians. (In antiquity the word "Pyth-agorean" was a synonym for "vegetarian.") Josephus certainly knew whereof he spoke, because he actually became an Essene when he was an adolescent. He also tells us that the Essenes "did not make sacrifices,"[14] and since, as we've seen, animal sacrifice was the chief source of animal flesh in the ancient world, this observation alone would suggest that they were vegetarians. This is confirmed by Philo Judea, who said that "the Essenes did not sacrifice living creatures, but preferred to sanctify their minds."[15] Josephus also noted that the Essenes lived long lives (*makrobioi*) on their vegetarian diet. "Generally, they live long lives; most of them reach an age greater than a hundred years. That I believe is because of their simple way of living and their strict morality."[16] After spending a few years in an Essene community, Josephus went on to live with an Essene anchorite, a man named Banus who lived on raw fruit and vegetables. For these three years at least, from the ages of 18 to 21, Josephus himself became a prac-ticing raw foodist. "As I had heard that there was a person by the name of Banus, who stayed in the desert, who got his cloth from trees (thus he refused fur, camel hair and wool!) and who took as food only what grew by itself (thus raw food), and who repeated-ly bathed by day and night in cold water in order to sanctify life, I decided to try his system."[17]

The sect of which Jesus was the leader was called the Nazore-ans, probably, as Schoeps suggests, from the Hebrew word *Nezer*, "to keep," meaning that they kept the true spirit of Mosaic law.[18] But because they were so absolute in expressing their criticism of the sacrificial cult, the Nazoreans fell afoul of the orthodox Jew-ish community as well as the Roman state. After the Sadducaic high priest Annanus the Younger condemned Jesus's brother James to be stoned—James was a practicing vegetarian,[19] and the first Jewish Christian Nazorean Pope[20]—the Nazoreans fled Jerusalem in 63 CE and settled in Pella in the Transjordan. This region was home to a number of other anti-sacrificial, vegetarian sects who practiced ritual baptism.[21] The Nazoreans settled out-side the cities in wilderness areas because they regarded the wilderness as a state of grace. Anti-sacrificial prophets whom they admired, such as Jeremiah and Micah, as well as the Rechabites (an early anti-sacrificial group), had also taken to the wilderness in protest.[22]

After settling in the Transjordan, the Nazoreans, or Jewish Christians, started calling themselves the Ebionites, from the word *ebio,* which means "poor," and refers to the voluntary poverty that the Judaic Christians took upon themselves—like the Jain *sadhus* or the mendicant Buddhist monks, who took a vow of poverty, and who, as active missionaries in the Near East from the time of the Indian emperor Ashoka, may actually have influenced the Essenes, the Nazoreans, the Ebionites and the other anti-sacrificial Jewish sects.[23]

With the Ebionites it was an article of faith that the Torah had been tampered with. They believed that the Torah had been falsified with each recension, and that very little remained of the pure text. All the depictions of God in the Hebrew scriptures they believed to be false because they show God as being anthropomorphic and anthropopathic—with all the sins and appetites that human flesh is heir to. Therefore, it is not God whom the Torah is portraying but a human-formed monster who is fallible, cruel, vindictive, jealous, lives in a tent, thunders, and is hungry for sacrifices. The real God, as envisaged by the Ebionites, was kindly and loving. The Ebionites also despised the kings, Solomon and David—Solomon because he built the original Temple, which was the seat of the sacrificial cult; and David because he was an adulterer and a warrior. Missing from the Ebionite testimonies is any reference to Jesus as being a descendant of David—because David's being a warrior offended their pacifist sensibilities.[24] They also deplored the priestly redactors' depiction of some of the more famous Biblical characters in a less than flattering light, such as Adam as a fallen man, Noah as a drunkard, and Abraham as a priapic polygamist. Just as scholars like Schoeps have pieced together a lost Ebionite New Testament with a vegetarian Jesus at its center, the Ebionites had reconstructed a lost Torah that had originally been innocent of bloodletting and animal sacrifice—

with a genial creator god at its center. Jesus they believed had come to restore the true law and the original teachings of the Torah that had been suppressed by the sacrificial cult. Unlike the Gnostics, such as Marcion, who wanted to abolish the Hebrew scriptures as the work of an inferior demiurge (Yahweh) whose creation was evil, Jesus and the Ebionites wanted to fuse the Hebrew scriptures with the Christian scriptures and purge the Torah of its false excrescences.

It is worth quoting Schoeps directly on this point: "The Ebionites (Judaic Christians) of the second and third centuries have sharpened the Mosaic law considerably and made it more extreme with their principled vegetarianism, the command of poverty and the community of goods, as well as their rigorous cathartic—they eliminated as being false pericopes [verses] first the bloody animal sacrifices, then the institution of the Israeli kingship, then the false prophecies in scripture, those which had not occurred and finally the anthropomorphic descriptions of God, which had been pushed in afterwards into the Torah of Moses."[25] "Their [Judaic Christian] hostility toward the cult of animal sacrifice clearly manifests their tendency to restore the original Pentateuch [the Torah], purged of false pericopes. Whether or not they actually created such a purged Pentateuch or employed it in their congregations cannot be demonstrated from the available sources."[26] Charles Vaclavik says that one of the great losses to humanity might have been Jesus's own revision of the Torah that had been purged of its false verses.[27]

In the ancient novel that is one of the richest sources of material about the Ebionites, *The Recognitions of Clement*, Saint Peter, the protagonist of this work, says that the Babylonian captivity of the Jews came about as a punishment for the Jews' sacrificing and eating animals. Believing that the sacrificial cult had been instituted by Josiah's reforms and inserted into the Mosaic law by Ezra, which falsified the Torah,[28] Peter says that the Jewish Christians were expecting a Messiah who would reform the dietary laws of the Jews. Peter goes on to say that Jesus was sent to preach against the eating and the sacrifice of animals; he sub-

stituted the ritual of baptism for the sin offering or the scapegoat
ritual. With the waters of baptism, Jesus would wash away the
blood of sacrificial animals in the Temple.[29]

Sadly enough, Jewish Christianity's most revolutionary features
were lost when the apostle Paul colored up the doctrines of Jewish
Christianity to make them palatable to the Gentiles. (Opposition to
the apostle Paul was a common motif of these Jewish anti-sacrificial groups.) Paul's perversion of Jesus's true teachings was held in
particular abhorrence by the Ebionites. They detested Paul and regarded him as an impostor, an opportunist, and an interloper.
Echthros ("the enemy") was merely the mildest of the epithets that
they flung at him; *pseudapostle* ("false apostle") and *apo tou Museous*
("apostate from Mosaic law") were more typical. They believed
that he was involved in the plot to assassinate Jesus's brother
James,[30] the first Pope of the Jewish Christian Church, and that
Paul had invented the episode of his having met the risen Christ on
the road to Damascus. The Ebionites believed that Paul had con-
cocted this "tall story" in order to lend authority to his claim to
being the thirteenth apostle. They especially castigated him for suppressing Jesus's anti-sacrificial and vegetarian teachings—teachings that were reminiscent of the Buddha's teaching of the first precept, which Jesus may have absorbed directly from the Buddhist
missionaries that were actively proselytizing in the Near East.[31]

Although the gospels of the Jewish Christians and their religious
literature were quashed by the Catholic Church, scholars believe
that Jewish Christianity survived in Syria and in Arabia. Schoeps
has speculated that the Ebionites may have occupied all of Syria
by the third century CE, meaning that Syrian Christianity had its
roots in the Jewish Christian Church of which Jesus's brother
James, a rawfood vegetarian who lived on seeds and fruit,[32] (and
not Peter) was the first bishop, or pope. Indeed the ascetic aspects
of Syrian Christianity that gave rise to the desert mysticism of
Simeon Stylites and Saint Anthony the Great who practiced a
rawfood vegetarianism—and that also gave rise to the ascetic *hanifs* of Arabia of whom Muhammad may well have been a member—serve to remind us what Christianity might have been like

had the Apostle Paul not distorted its message, and had the Church authorities not ruthlessly suppressed Jesus's true teachings, which were to restore the true Mosaic law and to annul the animal sacrifices performed at the Judean Temple. Here is Margaret Smith's description of Syrian Christian ascetics of the second century CE. "We find asceticism in Syria and Palestine at an early date. During the latter part of the second century, Narcissus, Bishop of Jerusalem, gave up his see and retired into the wilderness; and in documents of the third century related to south Syria, are found exhortations addressed to wandering ascetics, urging them to asceticism and the celibate life. As we have noted in Syria the ascetics carried their austerity of life to an extreme. Such extremists were the grazers (*boskoi*), who ate only grass, herbs and roots, and exposed themselves almost naked to bitter frost in winter and scorching heat in summer."[33]

Palestine at the time of Jesus's birth was a hotbed of religious movements. Jewish Christianity was but one of the many Judaic anti-sacrificial cults that had risen up to oppose the killing and eating of animals in the Temple. What was the source of all these Jewish heresies and why was there so much opposition to the sacrificial cult in Jerusalem? As I noted in my essay on Judaism, Professor Armstrong contends that Jews hankered after other gods than Yahweh because of Yahweh's increasing remoteness from his people.[34] Add to this Yahweh's insatiable appetite for animal sacrifices, as it is depicted in the Torah, and the elitism of a priesthood, the Levites and the Aaronites, whom the Jewish Christians believed had falsified scripture, and one can see why so many heresies proliferated. Although these heretical sects didn't worship the golden calf, the creeds of the Therapeutae, the Essenes and the Judaic Christians may have owed something to the cow worship of the Hindus and the veneration of animals among the Pythagoreans and the Buddhists. For, this anti-sacrificial movement was not peculiar to Israel. There had been similar anti-sacrificial uprisings in other countries. Buddhism and the Jainism of Mahavira arose as protest movements that were launched against the priestly elite of India—the Brahmins. Like the Aaronites and the Levites of Jerusalem, the Brahmins in India were a privileged hereditary caste of priests, who imposed heavy taxes on the people to pay for costly animal sacrifices. Likewise, in Greece, the Pythagorean order sprang up to set its face against the animal sacrifice and flesh-eating sponsored by the state religion. In China, the Taoists and Buddhists protested the state sponsored animal sacrifice cult, sanctified by the state religion— Confucianism. It is perhaps helpful to think of Jesus as a Jewish Buddha or Jewish Mahavira bent on reforming the sacrificial practices of the Jewish counterpart of the Brahmins—the Aaronites and the Levites.

According to Theologian Carl Skriver, as an enemy of the sacrificial cult in Jerusalem, Jesus placed himself squarely in the Old Testament prophetic tradition of Jeremiah, Amos, Micah, Hosea, and Isaiah who were vociferous in their denunciations of animal sacrifice in the Temple. Skriver writes: "The fame of Israel's prophets derive from their revolt to settle accounts with the idea of sacrifice. Their revolutionary thought was: God's demand is not sacrifice but ethical behavior. In order to be fair it should be noted that the protest against the bloody sacrifices was not a special achievement of the prophets only but also of Mahavira, Buddha, Zarathustra, Pythagoras, Jesus, Apollonius, the disciples of Buddha, the Pythagoreans, the Essenes and the Nazoreans."[35]

Unhappily, Jesus paid for his anti-sacrificial views with his life. Perhaps it was because he wasn't content to prophesy and rail against the sacrificial cult from a safe distance, that he actually went to the Temple in person to set free the sacrificial animals. All four gospels say that he drove the animals from the Temple. "And the Passover of the Jews drew near, so Jesus went up to the Temple. In the Temple he found people who were selling oxen, sheep and pigeons, and the moneychangers sitting at their tables. And making a scourge out of rope, he drove them all with the sheep and oxen out of the Temple, and scattering the coins of the moneychangers, he overturned their tables. To the pigeon sellers, he said 'Take those pigeons away from here! Stop making my father's house into a meat-market!'"[36] If the chronology in the

canonical gospels is correct, then it was shortly after Jesus overturned the tables of the moneychangers in the Temple and drove
the sacrificial animals outdoors that he was condemned to death
by the Sanhedrin (the Judaic high court). He had done the unthinkable: Jesus had profaned the Temple in Jerusalem by interfering with the sacrifice of animals; it was a brazen act of defiance against Yahweh who, the sacrificers maintained, actually
lived in an inner sanctum of the Temple, in a compartment called
the Holy of Holies where Yahweh inhaled the smoke from the
burnt offerings. It was for this act of defiance and desecration that
Skriver and Schoeps believe that Jesus was condemned to die,
like one of the very sacrificial animals that he had liberated. For
as Vaclavik graphically describes the Temple, parts of it that were
used for holding the sacrificial animals must have looked and
smelled like a stockyard or an abattoir.

Vaclavik writes, "We learn from the Bible that the altar of the
ancient Judaic temple was a slaughter house, butcher shop and
barbecue pit, not at all like the ornate altars of our churches of the
twentieth century, with lace or linen table cloths, silver candelabra
and chalices, and a wooden bookholder with an elaborate Bible
opened upon it. It was the practical center to receive the animals for
sacrifice. Certain areas of the temple probably resembled our mod-
ern-day stockyards with hundreds of animals waiting in fenced-off
areas waiting to be slaughtered. These large holding areas in the
temple where animals could be fed and cared for, had to have a
large staff whose duties were specifically designated in caring for
the animals. One could presume that large amounts of manure had
to be removed from the temple area, and it is probable that some of
the altar assistants were no more than attendants of the cattle,
sheep and goats, and spent their whole day hauling manure out of
the Temple, hauling in hay and grain to feed the animals, and keeping them clean for the ceremony of the altar. One can also imagine
the odor that one would experience when approaching the Temple
during major festivals: a combination of the stench of a stockyard,
and the captivating odor of the barbecuing beef." [37]

Vaclavik goes on to describe what the Temple would have looked like on a typical festival day: pilgrims would be thronging its corridors with their freshly purchased sheep and goats. The air would be pierced with the cries of animals, sensing that they would be barbecued on the altar for the Levites and the Aaronites and their families to feast on. After upsetting the tables of the moneychangers, Jesus must have followed the pungent odor of cow and sheep dung, and made his way into the stockyards of the Temple and set free some of the sacrificial animals, rather like the zealous animal activist who liberates the "sacrificial"[38] animals from being experimented on in the laboratory. Only Jesus was delivering them from being committed to the flames on the Temple altars. Clearly this Christ, the Ebionite Christ, was to be a savior for animals as well as for humans. In the *Ebionite Gospel*, Jesus says "I am come to annul sacrifices, and if you will not cease to sacrifice, the wrath will not turn from you."[39] A few decades later, the Temple was destroyed in 70 CE when the Roman armies razed it.

Professor Schoeps says that like the Essenes and the Therapeutae, the Ebionites practiced water mysticism. What does he mean by the term "water mysticism"? Essentially what he means is that these sects practiced ritual baptism, made famous by Jesus's kinsman, John the Baptist. Through baptism, or immersion in water, they sought to wash away the sins of the penitent. This was in sharp contrast to the atonement sacrifice that was practiced by the priests at the Temple in Jerusalem. There, a penitent could purchase an animal, usually a goat, and pay the priest to kill, cook, and eat the animal sacrifice. The penitent would then be absolved of his sins. Jewish sects like the Essenes, the Nazoreans and the Ebionites sought to substitute water purification rituals for the flame roasting of animals in the Temple. They emphasized "water" because water puts out fire; and it was the professed objective of Jesus and many of the other pacifistic sects of Judaism to extinguish the ever-burning sacrificial flame in the Temple with the water of the baptismal rite. As Schoeps phrases it, "Here the sacramental character of Ebionite baptism is evident; it is the soteriologically necessary substitute sought for the age-old Temple sacrifice. The power of the baptism in living spring water lies therefore in the extinguishing of the fire, the superseding of the sacrifice and the purifying of the man who receives it in becoming an Ebionite. Similar beliefs may have been held in other baptismal circles as well."[40]

The waters of the flood had ushered in what the Reverend Dr. Carl Skriver calls "the Noachitic age of sacrifice."[41] To repay Yahweh for having saved him and the Ark filled with animals from being drowned in the flood waters, Noah built a sacrificial altar and barbecued some of the animals that he'd saved from the flood "and Yahweh smelled the sweet savor."[42] Thus in a sense, the flame at the sacrificial altar was kindled by Noah. So it's fitting, one might almost say poetically just, that the Ebionites and the other Jewish baptismal sects sought to extinguish the sacrificial fire that was kindled by Noah after the flood with baptismal water.

If *ichthus,* the fish, was the premier symbol of Christianity, then the other symbol that runs it a close second is *udor*—water. The image of water is rife throughout the New Testament. Jesus walks on water, he turns water into wine, he points to a man carrying a jug of water on his back (the "waterbearer" was an Essene symbol that runs through the gospel);[43] he washes his disciples' feet with water; he serves and drinks water (not wine) at the Last Supper. It's worth noting that water in the ancient world was a vibrant element that was imbued with magical powers. Water, like animal flesh in our culture, has been desacralized and stripped of its value. From the primal element of God's creation—the waters of life—water has been debased into an inert liquid—tap water, dishwater, ditchwater—just as the cow's flesh and the cow's mammary secretions have been debased into the banality of beefsteaks, hamburgers, ice-cream and milkshakes. As we've seen, according to Schoeps, Jesus and the Jewish Christians practiced a sort of water mysticism, as did many of the other sects in the periphery of Judaism such as the Essenes and the Therapeutae. With baptismal water Jesus would put out the fire of sacrifice at the Temple. Skriver believes that Jesus was the fulfillment of the prophecy in Isaiah that a messiah would come who would put an end to animal sacrifice, as surely as water puts out fire.

Evidence for Jesus's vegetarianism in the canonical gospels is circumstantial, but nonetheless compelling. Ethical vegetarians find it inconceivable that such a potent religious figure and moral teacher could have slit the throat of an animal, or have eaten the cooked body parts of an animal. Apart from the moral impropriety of such a diet, flesh (not excluding the flesh of fish) was an extremely scarce commodity in the ancient world and would have been considered a luxurious food; it would have been out of character for a man who stressed simplicity and frugality in living to be eating such opulent food. Flesh remains a luxury food amongst the poor in most non-Western countries today; it only seems commonplace to Westerners because of the mechanized methods of assembly-line slaughter that have put the cost of flesh within the means of even the poorest European or American.

First of all, there is the nagging question of the Lord's Supper or Last Supper. Was it a typical Passover meal at which it would have been obligatory to eat the Paschal Lamb? As early as the nineteenth century, NT scholars such as F.C. Conybeare (who was no vegetarian) were saying that the Last Supper was more like an Essene or Therapeut sacred meal in which the main course would have been bread and water rather than the carnivorous feast of the Passover, at which the main course would have been lamb.[44] Tellingly, there are no references to lamb (or any other type of animal flesh) in connection with the Last Supper in any of the gospels. Furthermore, the synoptic gospels got the timing all wrong. John deliberately corrects the synoptic gospels when he says that the Last Supper took place two days before Passover, which fell on the Sabbath (Saturday) that year. Even if the Last Supper had been a Passover Meal, there is nothing to say that Jesus would have eaten the Paschal lamb. On the contrary, the non-canonical Ebionite gospel says that Jesus emphatically refused to partake of lamb at a Passover meal.[45]

Moreover, the references to Jesus's having eaten meat are based on mistranslations of Greek words such as *bromos* (food), *sitos* (bread or grain), that actually describe plant-based foods. The Greek words for meat, *kreas* and *iera* (sacrificial flesh), are never used in connection with Jesus's feeding habits. Therefore, the true *theobromos* or god-food would appear to be *artos* and *tou genemastos tes ampelou* — or "bread" and "the fruit of the vine" — that Christ served his disciples at the Last Supper. Significantly, in none of the gospel accounts of the Lord's Supper is the Greek word *oinos* (wine) used; it's always the phrase *genemastos tes ampelou*, or "the fruit of the vine." Had it been wine, it strikes me that they would have said so directly, using the word *oinos* rather than this cumbersome circumlocution, "produce of the vine." Abstinence from wine and from animal food are traits that Jesus appears to have had in common with Pythagoras, who is described by Iamblichus in his life of Pythagoras as having abstained from animal flesh and strong drink. At a last supper, what could have been more impeccably vegetarian than *artos* and *genemastos tes ampelou*?

Except perhaps *artos*, *udor* and *als* (salt)! For, according to the Ebionite teachings, the ingredients of the sacred meal were bread, water, and a sprinkling of salt: bread because it was the staff of life, salt because it symbolized incorruptibility,[46] and water because it was the primal element with which god had created the world. Water was also the element, the Ebionites believed, that God had ordained for the rebirth of mankind.[47] In Jesus's world (i.e., the Nazorean-Ebionite world), water was regarded as being more potent than wine, which was merely spoiled grape juice on its way to being vinegar.

Not only have the Greek words been inaccurately translated but the English word "meat" has changed its meaning since it was first used in the version commissioned by King James, published in 1611. In Elizabethan times, "meat" was a synonym for "food." According to Skeats' etymological dictionary,[48] "meat" derives from the Latin *mandere*, to chew. (*Mandere* gives us our word "mandible" and "masticate" as well.) In King James's time, "meat" denoted that which is chewable or edible — hence the word "sweetmeat" or "nutmeat." In short, it had not yet acquired the meaning that it now has of animal flesh exclusively. Thus the *Authorized* or *King James* version has translated the passage *"echete brosimon enthade?"*[49] as "Have ye any meat?" This is the question that Christ asks of his disciples in *Luke* after his resurrection. What it means literally in contemporary English is "Do you have any food here?"[50]

What about Jesus's having eaten fish? There is the famous passage from the gospels in which Jesus is purported to have fed the multitudes with the loaves and fishes; and throughout the gospels, fish imagery is rife. Jesus's disciples become "fishers of men;" Peter plucks a coin from the mouth of a fish in order to pay his tax; and in John 26, there is the miraculous draft of fishes. One of the most familiar of the early Christian symbols, the fish could be found emblazoned on the catacomb walls and carved into rings and gemstones. It became a secret symbol of Christ, originating with the famous acrostic in which the first letters of the Greek word for fish, *ichthus*, form the letters for *Iesous Christos Theou Uious Soter:* "Jesus Christ Son of God Savior."

To the early Christians, the fish was a mystery term and it was employed in this sense by Clement of Alexandria and Tertullian, when the latter refers to Christians as "fishes bred in the water, and saved by one great fish,"[51] and when Tertullian writes: "We little fish after the image of our *Ichthus* (fish), Jesus Christ, are born in the water." Or when one scholar with a mystical turn of mind has said that the fish symbolism in the New Testament may be an allusion to the precession of the equinoxes from the constellation Aries into the Constellation Pisces the fish—an astronomical event that occurred at about the time Jesus was born. Another scholar with a culinary bent has even suggested that Jesus may have fed the multitudes from bread that was baked in a fish-shaped baking dish. To buttress his point, at his lecture he brandished fish-shaped baking dishes of the period. All of this is by way of showing that there are a number of alternative interpretations—some of them, admittedly, too clever by half—to the passages in the New Testament that supposedly portray Jesus as having eaten fish. Perhaps the most creditable explanation is that the references to Jesus's having eaten flesh and fish may have been interpolations or textual corruptions deliberately put there by meat-loving priests. That this is a far from implausible hypothesis is evidenced by Kapleau Roshi in his study of the Buddhist scriptures: He argues quite cogently that both the Buddhist and the Christian scriptures have been tampered with by a meatatarian clergy.[52] Of course, this was also the teaching of the Ebionites, the Jewish Christians. Like the Mahayana Buddhists who believe that the Hinayana priests had suppressed the vegetarian teachings of the Buddha, the Ebionites believed that the Torah had been falsified by the priestly caste, the Aaronites and Levites, to promote flesh-eating and animal sacrifice.

But let us suspend disbelief for a moment, and assume that the miracle was true—that Jesus actually did feed the multitude with five loaves or seven loaves and two fishes. The fourth gospel's account of this event is slightly at variance with the synoptics'. Matthew, Mark and Luke say that he fed the multitudes with seven loaves or five loaves and two fishes, using the Greek words *duas icthuas* (two fish) or *oliga ixthudia* (a few little fishes), but John (the fourth gospel) says five loaves and *dua opsaria*. Where the others say that Jesus multiplied the two fishes, John says that he multiplied the two *opsaria*. Now, most translators render *opsaria* as sardines or little fish, but *opsaria* which comes from the Greek *opson* (relish) also meant "relish;" so it's possible to translate it as five loaves and two "relishes," "dainties" or "tidbits." Eaten as a condiment with bread, *opsarion* is similar to the Latin word *companaticum,* which means an accompaniment of bread. As Professor Robert Lopez has noted, "One fact is certain: in the form of bread porridge or mush, cereals were almost everywhere the basis of human alimentation, in the middle ages as in classical antiquity—so much so that in low Latin and in most of the vernaculars everything else is called *companaticum,* 'the accompaniment of bread.'"[53] People would have bread as their main dish and on top of it they would spread a relish or *opsarion* much as we spread peanut butter or chopped pickle on bread today. In Jesus's time, they dipped their loaf in relish or they tore off pieces of bread from the loaf and dipped it in the *opsarion,* or relish, which might have consisted of finely chopped olives with spices or ground sesame paste. It strikes me that *opsarion* is a more accurate term gastronomically because even if the multitude had eaten fish with their bread, it would have had to be cooked or turned into a pickle before they could have eaten it. Raw fish, or *sashimi*, popular in trendy New York sushi bars, was not a delicacy in the ancient world. Yet there is no mention in any of the Gospels of Jesus's having cooked the fish. Since the example of Jesus's feeding the multitude with loaves and fishes is often quoted by non-vegetarians as proof that Jesus couldn't possibly have been a vegetarian, it's interesting to have this word *opsarion* in John to use as a riposte.

Moreover, it's believed by some New Testament scholars that John's gospel may have been written for the Essene community,[54] who have been characterized as being anti-sacrificial and vegetarian; therefore, the *dua opsaria* may have been more palatable to them than *duas ichthuas*. Elsewhere in John's gospel, he uses the term *opsarion* instead of *ichthus*, as though he were carefully distinguishing between the two. In John 26, for instance, he uses *opsarion* in one sentence and *ichthus* in another, as though he were opposing *opsarion* to fish; relish or dainty to animal flesh. According to Carl Skrivers, John's gospel is the most accurate of the four and should properly be called the first gospel. He writes: "It can also be assumed that he gave to his favorite disciple and friend John more revelations than he gave to the synoptics, so that John's gospel is properly the first and chief gospel and not the fourth one." [55] It's also worth noting that Jesus himself is not said to have partaken of the feast of the five thousand. He increased the amount of food on offer, but didn't necessarily partake of it. Nowhere in any of the gospels, in fact, does Jesus as a living person partake of animal flesh.

Furthermore, Vaclavik points out that when one of the earliest of the Catholic Fathers, Irenaeus, in his book, *Against Heresies*, described Jesus's feeding of the multitudes, Irenaeus doesn't say anything about Jesus's having fed the crowd fish—he only mentions bread.[56] Since Irenaeus was writing 150 years after Jesus's death, Vaclavik concludes that the reference to the two fishes in the canonical gospels was a later interpolation, placed there by one of those overfed, flesh-loving clerics in which the Western Church seems to abound.

However, there is one place where Jesus is alleged to have eaten fish that seems on the face of it rather damning: in Luke 24, when after his death the risen Christ appears to his disciples and they feed him *meros optotou ichthou,* a piece of broiled fish. Here Luke is gastronomically accurate, because the fish is described as being *optotou,* or cooked, and it's a piece of fish (*meros ichthou*). Again, raw fish was not highly favored in the ancient world, then as now, and so Jesus or almost anyone else would not have eaten a whole raw fish.

Not only is Luke the first instance in which Jesus is alleged to have eaten animal flesh; it's the first important instance in which he doesn't feed others, but is fed *by* others. At the Last Supper and the feeding of the multitudes, Jesus does the feeding. Now after his death, he seems singularly passive and will-less; he lets his disciples feed him. And what do they feed him? The roasted flesh of a dead fish. An insensitive wag might ask, "What else should one feed a ghost who has returned from the dead than dead flesh?" Reverend Holmes-Gore[57] has I think the most cogent explanation when he says that the disciples were trying to underscore that Jesus had survived the crucifixion by showing him eating broiled fish. It was simply a literary device that they employed to make Jesus seem more human and alive—when in point of fact it makes him seem more wraithlike and insubstantial, a ghostly presence.

Eating fish, eating *ichthus,* the symbol of Jesus, has resonances with the Eucharist in which the worshippers eat the body and drink the blood of Jesus at the communion mass. But eating the flesh and drinking the blood of a victim smacks of the very blood sacrifice that Jesus had come to annul. Indeed, as we've seen, it is suggested by the gospels that Jesus was executed for trying to interfere with the Temple sacrifice when he drove the moneychangers and the sacrificial animals from the temple. How then did Jesus become the ultimate sacrifice, the lamb whose blood would wash away the sins of the world? How did Christians come to drink Jesus's blood and eat his flesh at the communion meal, which from all indications was, for the first century or so, celebrated as a vegetarian banquet in which the poor were fed from the table of the Lord?[58]

That the Ebionites were unaware of Paul's concept of vicarious atonement in which the blood of a savior god redeems the world is attested by Schoeps. Since they were an anti-sacrificial sect, it would have been morally inconsistent for the Ebionites to have proffered Jesus as the ultimate blood sacrifice. Schoeps writes: "Jewish Christianity clearly knows as little of a supernatural birth as of a soteriological interpretation of Jesus's death on the cross, such as the view that regarded Jesus as a vicarious atoning sacrifice. Since they rejected bloody sacrifices altogether, the Ebionite Jesus can neither have taught this nor by his death have put his seal on it—in contrast with the tradition of the primitive church preserved in I Corinthians 15:3."[59] As it developed, the Ebionites were right to be wary of Paul because it is Paul who is credited with having turned Jesus into a dying and reviving god like Osiris, Adonis, or Tammuz. This is less astonishing when one considers that the city where Paul grew up, Tarsus, had its own cult of the dying-and-rising savior god Sandan and Baal-Tarz,[60] as well as a Mithraeum in which Mithras saves the world by slaying a cosmic bull and bespattering the earth with bull's blood.

Indeed, Carmichael points out that it was Paul who made the death of Jesus into a criobolium, or taurobolium, in which the blood of a sacrificial animal redeems the worshipper.[61] In the taurobolium of Mithraism the naked worshippers, standing in a grotto beneath a grillwork, would be showered with the sin-cleansing blood of a bull. It's no coincidence that Mithras and Jesus were both said to have been born in a manger on December 25th during the Saturnalia or that the chief pontiff of Mithraism, the Mithraic Pater, had his seat on the Vatican mount. (Carmichael says the Crucifixion was also much like a he-goat sacrifice,[62] the criobolium from *crios* (goat), and *boleo*, to slaughter.) The goat was sacred to the wine-God Dionysos; in the Dionysiac "Eucharist," the *omophagia*, people would devour living animals that were sacred to Dionysos. This and other sacrificial rites in which the blood and flesh of the victim were eaten to enthuse (*entheos*) the worshippers have obvious analogies with the Christian Eucharist. By introducing the Eucharist in which the blood and body of the savior god were eaten, Paul was grafting the goriest sacrificial rites of pagan religion onto the life of a man who gave his life to protest the animal sacrifices in the Judaic temple—the cruelest of ironies.

The Eucharist, as Reay Tannahill points out in her study of cannibalism, *Flesh and Blood: A History of the Cannibal Complex*, has been invoked to justify human cannibalism. A striking example of this is furnished by "The Old Christians," the ironic name of a rugby team, some of whose members survived a plane crash in the Andes in 1972. The survivors kept themselves alive in the most adverse circumstances by eating their dead teammates, the dead pilot and assorted other deceased passengers. To justify their cannibalism, one of the "Old Christians" said to a reporter, "If Jesus in the Last Supper offered his body and blood to all the disciples, he was giving us to understand that we must do the same." Another said: "We swallowed the little bits of flesh with the feeling that God demanded it of us. We felt like Christians."[63] Tannahill points out that it was the apostle Paul who first gave the Last Supper the semblance of a cannibal feast by saying that the wine was the blood and the flesh was the body of Christ;[64] but this could always be rationalized by saying it was "symbolic."

However, in the year 1215, at the Fourth Lateran council, Pope Innocent III decreed that when the priest at the altar pronounced the formula *hic est corpus meum* that the bread and wine *were* changed into the body and blood of Christ. In other words, the bread and wine were no longer symbolic of Christ's flesh and blood; rather, they were to be regarded as the actual flesh and blood of Christ! Anyone who doubted it would be declared a heretic. This was the famous doctrine of transubstantiation. With this Papal decree, transmuting the Last Supper into a human sacrifice, the Church negated everything that Jesus the anti-sacrificial Ebionite had stood for. It is significant that the word for the wafer that transubstantiates the body of Christ is "host," from the Latin word *hostia*, meaning "sacrificial victim."

If the Church was vegetarian for the two centuries after the death of Christ, how and why did it lose its original Ebionite-inspired vegetarianism? One likely answer suggested by Geddes

MacGregor in his study of reincarnation in Christianity is that the Church frowned upon vegetarianism for the same reason that it frowned upon reincarnationism, which was a widely held belief among members of the early Church[65]—that the Church's rivalry with the Gnostic sects was so fierce that competition with Manicheism and the other Gnostic sects brought vegetarianism and reincarnationism into bad odor with the Church authorities.[66] In order to set itself apart from the Gnostic heresies that preached the doctrine of reincarnation and advocated a mainly vegetarian diet, the Church began to stigmatize vegetarianism, glorify flesh-eating and suppress reincarnationism. One can find the Church's anti-Pythagoreanism exemplified in the life of Saint Augustine (354-430 CE) who had been a Manichean for ten years prior to his conversion to Christianity. (He became a Christian at 29.) Since the Manicheans were vegetarians, in all probability Augustine had been a vegetarian before his conversion and continued to be one afterwards; however, it is clear from his writings that after his conversion he became an anti-Pythagorean in spirit.[67] Whereas Pythagoras had taught that since animals are rational beings whose souls reincarnate in humans eating them is a form of cannibalism, Augustine adopted the Aristotelian and Stoic view that since animals lack rationality their *telos* (purpose) was to gratify human appetites. Unfortunately, Augustine's anti-Pythagorean influence in the Church has been a pernicious one, as Thomas Aquinas, the architect of Roman Catholic doctrine, later drew on Augustine's works to justify the killing and eating of animals.

How the Church might have looked had it followed the *Via Gnostica* can only be conjectured, but in fact a thriving branch of the Gnostic Christian Church survived into the thirteenth century in the heart of Catholic Europe. The Cathars in the Languedoc region of France were believed to have been a remnant of early Christianity before the New Testament was written and bound with the Old. They were renowned for their simple living and their asceticism. Members of the Cathar Church, those who received the Consolateum, swore to abstain from eating animal flesh (except for fish) and to abstain from sexual intercourse.

Despite the ban on sexual intercourse, the Cathars multiplied to such an extent that their swelling numbers began to alarm the officials of the Church of Rome. One would think that a religious group that called for its members to forgo sexual intercourse and to abstain from eating meat would be rather sparsely peopled, but the opposite was true: They multiplied and were fruitful and they attracted a large number of converts.

Even members of the aristocracy were drawn to the faith. Count Henry VI of Toulouse was a key figure in the resistance to the Catholic Church and many other members of the nobility in the Languedoc region were surprisingly abstemious. The Cathars believed that the devil planted the vine in paradise as a temptation to Adam. They abstained from procreating because they regarded flesh—whether of animal or human origin—as being intrinsically evil; so to create more children, more malignant envelopes of flesh, was to be avoided like the plague. Despite their exacting creed, the Cathars posed such a threat to the Church who were losing members to Cathars and Bogomils at an alarming rate, that Pope Innocent II (a singularly inapt title for a Pope with so much blood on his hands) launched a crusade to exterminate the heretics. The Albigensian Crusade was the first internal crusade (the others had been hurled at Muslim "infidels" in the Near East). Some of the tenets of Albigensianism or Catharism are very interesting and are almost antithetical to those of the Church of Rome. For instance, they taught that Christ was a phantom; that the God of the Old Testament, Yahweh, was Satan himself; and that the Book of Moses was an evil work. They believed that flesh was evil, hence their abstention from animal flesh and from procreation. As dualists, they believed that the earth was the battleground between the forces of good and the forces of evil. Many Cathars survived the slaughter, and escaped to other countries. Not a few simply went underground and pretended to be Christians. It was to root out these pseudo-Christian Cathars that the Pope dispatched St. Bernard to set up an Inquisition in Languedoc. One of the tests administered to see whether a person was a true Christian or a crypto-Cathar was "Are you a meat-eater?"

Since the Cathars were what might be called "pisco-vegetarians," or vegetarians who eat fish, those who signified that they were vegetarians were branded as heretics and burned at the stake. Ironically enough, if the same question had been put to St. John Chrysostom or members of the first Catholic order of monks, they wouldn't have passed it; for they were all strict vegetarians, as were many of the Church fathers, such as Tertullian, Clement of Alexandria, and Origen, among others.

What of the orders today? According to Brother Ron Pickarski, who is a former monastery chef at a Franciscan monastery, none of the Catholic orders is now vegetarian. He himself was rebuked by his order for trying to put vegetarian alternatives on the menu. This certainly runs counter to the popular notion of monks and nuns as living an ascetic existence. To be sure, there is a vegetarian strain in the Catholic Church, but it has long been obscured from view.

Vegetarian too have been some of the greatest mystics and saints of the Church, such as Basilius the Great, Elisabeth Von Thuringen and St. Hedwig of Schliesien, as have been mystics such as Simeon Stylites and Saint Anthony the Great. Many of the monastic orders, such as the Augustinians, the Franciscans and the Trappists, as they were originally constituted, were vegetarian, but during the early Middle Ages, they began conspicuously to fall away from their early asceticism. Indeed, they became notorious for their gourmandizing! Apparently, monks were even bigger trenchermen 500 years ago than they are today. As early as the fourteenth century, Langland, the author of *Piers Ploughman*, remarks on the luxurious food of the friars, and contrasts their diet with that of the average laborer: "While the friars feast on roast venison, they [the poor] have bread and thin ale." According to Barbara Harvey, an Oxford University don, the Benedictine monks at Westminster Abbey in 1500 consumed more than 7,735 calories per day. This included up to three pounds of meat for lunch. Since the monks were sedentary, it's not surprising that most of them were calamitously overweight. Says Dr. Harvey, "I think a lot of them were probably obese."

Nor were the monks teetotalers. To wash down all that greasy animal flesh, the monks quaffed one gallon of ale a day, supplemented by a quart of wine on feast days. This means that twenty per cent of a monk's diet was pure ethanol—five times the amount consumed by the average male today.

Breakfast for the monks was frugal enough. It consisted of bread and ale. But it was at lunch that they started dining spaciously. On the monastery's bill of fare, a monk could choose from veal, mutton, beef, pork or goose. If this didn't satisfy his appetite, he could look forward to gorging himself on a hot supper of meat and cheese. Despite the copious quantities of meat and ale they consumed, the dyspeptic monks pored over the monastic menus like famished friars, and woe betide a monastery cook who underegged a pudding, or overcooked a goose! "Every detail of a monastic meal was and always had been a topic of absorbing interest to the participants," Professor Harvey says. "Nothing could save the kitchener if something was wrong with the sprats at dinner."[68]

While the monasteries in this period were not all corrupt, the more egregious ones could easily be mistaken for dens of iniquity: "The Abbot of Thame was accused of scandalous relations with a boy, running the estates in the interests of his favorites, letting his buildings decay, keeping too many servants and too good a table. He also let women into the monastery, and failed to prevent his monks (many of whom showed total ignorance of the monastic rule) enjoying themselves in the town."[69]

Not surprisingly, the overindulgence in rich food and the general moral laxity in the monasteries led to an erosion of faith: "The life of the ordinary monk had got easier over the centuries with the gradual relaxation of the prescription of the Rule in the matter of fasting and abstinence, a relaxation not in itself directly evil, but indicative of a weakness of faith and spiritual purpose...."[70]

Five hundred years later, Brother Ron Pickarski incurred the wrath of his brother monks when he tried to put vegetarian entrées on the menus at his Franciscan monastery. He wanted to revive the vegetarian diet of the original Franciscans (1209 CE) and Augustinians (circa 390 CE), who were abstemious vegetarians, but the monks at his monastery seem to have been more in the style of Cardinal Wolsey and other princes of the Church who were notorious gourmandizers, and Brother Ron was given short shrift. Brother Ron's chilly reception by the other members of his order after his conversion to vegetarianism is reminiscent of the way those Franciscans who were trying to follow St. Francis's teachings were treated in the sixteenth century. As historian C.S.L. Davies notes: "The dedication of Franciscans to a life of absolute poverty had passed away. (Indeed those who had clung to St. Francis's own ideals found themselves being condemned as heretics.)"

It is interesting to note that St. Francis grew up in the Cathar regions of Italy. Some historians attribute his humanitarianism and his identification with animals to the influence of the Cathars in the regions—those Cathars who had survived the Inquisition in the underground Cathar church.[71] There are some scholars who believe that it was the Cathars who kept alive the original spirit of Christ's teachings. The Cathars believed in reincarnation; vegetarianism; that each man or woman should be his or her own priest; compassion for animals; that animals have souls—indeed the very doctrines that were suppressed by the Church of Rome.

For the past 700 years, there have been two philosophical strains within the Church. They are represented on the one hand by the abstemious Cathar-inspired Francis of Assisi who treated animals as fellow beings with immortal souls and on the other by the gluttonous Thomas Aquinas (1225-1274), who in his *Summa Theologica* treated animals as imperfect beings who could be cheerfully killed and eaten.[72] This is the more lamentable as Thomas's brilliant synthesis of theology and Aristotelian philosophy— which slights both women and animals—is recognized as the cornerstone of Roman Catholic doctrine. Renowned for his excellent appetite, Thomas was nicknamed "the ox" for his immense fatness, and some scholars have suggested that it may have been Thomas's love of animal flesh that led him to justify the killing of animals for the table.[73] This seems farfetched, for it is clear that he got his anti-vegetarianism from Christian thinkers like Saint Augustine whose anti-Pythagoreanism derived from the Stoic and

Aristotelian view that, since animals are irrational beings, it is permissible for humans to sacrifice and eat them. A glance at the Catechism, which enshrines Thomas's derisory view of animals, makes it painfully obvious which of the two schools has been in the ascendant.

That so many of the original orders—the Franciscans, the Augustinians, the Benedictines, among others—started out as vegetarian, gives one cause for hope that in a time of growing awareness of the sentiency of animals, and the rights and souls of animals, that the monastic orders and the Church itself may rediscover their vegetarian roots. Many individual Catholics are becoming vegetarians. Many of my Catholic friends in North America, Europe and South America are turning vegetarian. It is to be hoped that the Church may soon follow their lead and grope its way back to the ethical vegetarian teachings of Jesus, who said "I have come to annul sacrifices [flesh-eating], and if you will not cease to sacrifice [eat animal flesh], the wrath will not turn from you."[74] ✝

R.B.

· · · · · · · · · · · · · ·

[1] Hans-Joachim Schoeps, *Jewish Christianity: Factional Disputes in the Early Church*, trans., D. R. A. Hare (Philadelphia: Fortress Press, 1969), p. 14.

[2] *The Other Gospels: Non-Canonical Gospel Texts*, ed., Ron Cameron (Philadelphia: Westminster Press, 1982), p. 103.

[3] Schoeps, *op. cit.*, p. 100.

[4] *ibid.*

[5] Morton Smith, *Palestinian Parties and Politics That Shaped the Old Testament* (New York: Columbia Universtiy Press, 1971), p. 30.

[6] Clement of Alexandria, "On Sacrifices," Book VII, cited in J. Todd Ferrier, *On Behalf of the Creatures* (London: The Order of the Cross, 1983), p. 19.

[7] For instance, Keith Akers, in his excellent essay on Christianity and Vegetarianism in *The Vegetarian Sourcebook*, says, "That is because the question of animal sacrifice is remote. It is a question, at best, for scholars of ancient history." On the contrary, I would argue that when a person eats animal flesh today, he is inadvertently participating in a ritual sacrifice that is all the more powerful for being unconscious.

[8] Porphyry, *De Absentia II*, p. 27.

[9] "Mana": a term taken from Melanesian religion that has become a *terminus technichus* of comparative religion; it means "supernatural power."

[10] Ernest Renan, *The Life of Jesus* (New York: Doubleday, n.d.), pp. 173, 169.

[11] Schoeps, *op. cit.*, pp. 99-101.

[12] Glenn Allen Koch, "A Critical Investigation of Epiphanius's Knowledge of the Ebionites: A Translation and Critical Discussion of 'Panarion' 30," Unpublished Dissertation, University of Pennsylvania, 1976, p. 198.

[13] Josephus, *Jewish Antiquity*, 15, 10, 4.

[14] *ibid.*, 18, 19.

[15] Philo, *Quod Omnis Probus Liber*, paragraph 12. Translation mine.

[16] Josephus, *History of the Jewish War*, 2, 8, 10.

[17] Josephus, *Vita Josephi*, 2, 11. Cited in Carl Skriver, *The Forgotten Beginnings of Creation and Christianity* (Denver, CO: Vegetarian Press, 1990) pp. 97-8.

[18] Schoeps, *op. cit.*, p. 11.

[19] "The Jewish Christian legends reported by Hegessipus and preserved by Eusebius in his *Ecclesiastical History* (2:23:6) made him a vegetarian, a teetotaler, and an ascetic." Quoted in Schoeps, *op. cit.*, p. 20.

[20] *ibid.*, p. 40.

[21] *ibid.*, p. 29.

[22] *ibid.*, p. 119.

[23] Martin A. Larson, *The Religion of the Occident* (London: Peter Owen, Ltd., 1960), pp. 136-154.

[24] Schoeps, *op. cit.*, p. 87.

[25] Schoeps, "Die ebionitische Warheit des Christentums," *Deutsches Pfarrer blatt*, 1,2, 1953, p. 50. Cited in Skriver, p. 147.

[26] Schoeps, *Jewish Christianity*, p. 84.

[27] Charles Vaclavik, *The Vegetarianism of Jesus Christ* (Three Rivers, CA: Kaweah Publishing Co., 1990), p. 123.

[28] Schoeps, *Jewish Christianity*, p. 82.

[29] *ibid.*, p. 82.

[30] *ibid.*, p. 45.

[31] Larson, *op. cit.*, p. 291. Larson says "During this period of reorientation, he may well have come under the influence of a Buddhist proselytizer."

[32] Augustine, *Ad Faustum* XXII, 3: "James, the brother of the Lord, lived on seeds and plants and never touched flesh or wine."

[33] Margaret Smith, *The Way of the Mystics* (Oxford: OUP, 1978), pp. 19, 21.

[34] John Armstrong, *The Idea of Holiness and the Humane Response: A Study of the Concept of Holiness and its Social Consequences* (London: George Allen & Unwin, 1981), p. 21.

[35] Skriver, *op. cit.*, pp. 97-8.

[36] John 2:13-17. Translation mine. NB: I've translated the Greek word *emporion* as "meat market," which is singularly apposite here.

[37] Vaclavik, *op. cit.*, p. 22.

[38] It's curious how medical researchers refer to the animals they kill in the name of science as "sacrifices."

[39] Ron Cameron *op. cit.*, p. 106.

[40] Schoeps, *op. cit.*, p. 105.

[41] Skriver, *op. cit.*, p. 67-79.

[42] Genesis 8:21.

[43] Skriver, *op. cit.*, p. 121.

[44] F.C. Conybeare, *Myth, Magic and Morals* (London: Watts & Co., 1910), pp. 271-3.

[45] "The Gospel of the Ebionites," in Cameron, *op. cit.*, p. 106.

[46] According to Schoeps, page 62, salt symbolized the incorruptibility of God's covenant with Israel.

[47] Schoeps, *Jewish Christianity*, p. 105.

[48] The Reverend Walter W. Skeat, *A Concise Etymological Dictionary of the English Language* (New York: Perigee Books, 1980), p. 321.

[49] Luke 24:30.

[50] Translation mine.

[51] Quoted in Reverend V. A. Holmes-Gore, *These We Have Not Loved* (Essex England: C.W. Daniels Co. Ltd., 1971), p. 87.

[52] Philip Kapleau, *To Cherish All Life: A Buddhist Case for Becoming Vegetarian* (New York, Harper & Row, 1981), pp. 39-43.

[53] Robert Lopez, *The Commercial Revolution of the Middle Ages, 950-1350* (Cambridge: Cambridge University Press, 1982), p. 37.

[54] Michael Grant, *An Historian's Review of the Gospels* (New York: Scribners, 1977), p. 189.

[55] Skriver, *op. cit.*, p. 122.

[56] Vaclavik, *op. cit.*, pp. 143-4.

[57] The Rev. V. A. Holmes-Gore, *These We Have Not Loved* (England: The C.W. Daniels Co. Ltd., 1971), p. 87.

[58] Conybeare, *op. cit.*, p. 273.

[59] Schoeps, *Jewish Christianity*, p. 62.

[60] Joel Carmichael, *The Birth of Christianity: Reality and Myth* (New York: Dorset Press, 1992), p. 92.

[61] *ibid.*, pp. 87-95.

[62] *ibid.*, pp. 91-4.

[63] Reay Tannahill, *Flesh and Blood: A History of the Cannibal Complex* (New

York: Stein & Day, 1975), pp. 174-6.

64 *ibid.*, pp. 57-9.

65 Geddes MacGregor, *Reincarnation in Christianity* (Wheaton, IL: Quest Books, 1989), p. 21.

66 *ibid.*, pp. 43-4.

67 Augustine, *De Moribus Ecclesiae Catholicae et De Moribus Manichaeorum* 2. 17.54-59.

68 Paul Beckett, "Eat Pounds of Meat, Drink Gallons of Ale, and Be a Very Merry Monk," *The Wall Street Journal* (November 23, 1994), p. 1a.

69 C.S.L. Davies, *Peace, Print and Protestantism 1450-1558* (London: Paladin, 1984), p. 140.

70 David Knowles, *The Religious Orders in England* (Cambridge, 1959) vol. 3, p. 463.

71 Adolf Holl, *The Last Christian: A Biography of Francis of Assisi* (New York: Doubleday, 1980), p. 209.

72 Thomas Aquinas, *Summa Theologica* 2.2 q. 64, a. 1.

73 Steven Rosen, *Food for the Spirit: Vegetarianism and the World's Religions* (New York: Bala Books, 1987), pp. 19-20.

74 "The Gospel of the Ebionites" in Cameron, *op. cit.*, p. 106.

BROTHER RON PICKARSKI, OFM

OSTRACIZED FROM HIS Franciscan order for trying to introduce vegetarian dishes on the menu when he was the monastery chef, Brother Ron Pickarski is now a member of the Franciscan third (secular) order. The orders seem to have changed little from circa 1500 CE, when as noted, monks would consume huge amounts of meat and were calamitously fat. Brother Ron is a

throwback to an even earlier time, when men such as St. Augustine and St. Francis founded orders in which the monks were strict vegetarians. Separated from his order, Brother Ron is not one to let the wheat grass grow under his feet. A certified executive chef who prepares gourmet foods without animal products or refined sugar, Brother Ron is the author of two bestselling vegan cookbooks, *Brother Ron's Friendly Foods* and *Eco-Cuisine.* He is the only vegetarian chef certified by the American Culinary Federation. With his own money he has trained and organized teams of vegan chefs to compete in the International Culinary Olympics. An Olympiad ago, his team won gold, and Brother Ron took a silver medal. Last Olympics, at the 19th *Olympiade der Koche* in Berlin, Brother Ron himself won a gold in the Alternative category and a bronze in food presentation. I interviewed Brother Ron during a vegetarian conference in Portland Oregon, for which he was the supervising chef—much to the detriment of my waistline. From the balcony of his hotel suite, we could see the afterglow of a Pacific sunset; as the sun sank into the West, and darted its dying rays back at us, I pondered the phrase *Ex Oriente Lux*. From the East—from the Japan, China and India of two centuries ago, before Westernization set in—like rays of light from a distant star are filtering in the doctrines of reincarnation, *karma* and *ahimsa* that Brother Ron believes will gradually combine with and reinvigorate a moribund Christianity.

· · · · · · · · · · · ·

BERRY: At the time you became a vegetarian, you were a Franciscan brother. What does that signify exactly?

PICKARSKI: Saint Francis wanted to live the way Christ had lived, which means being poor, celibate and obedient. The Franciscan aspires to follow Francis, who in essence aspired to follow Christ. I model my life after Christ and Saint Francis. It's the inspiration that I get from them—not stale doctrines and outmoded beliefs and laws—it's in love that I want to live and it's that love that drew me to St. Francis and to Christianity.

BERRY: Was St. Francis a vegetarian?

PICKARSKI: It can't be proved or disproved, but I feel that in the end he was. In the beginning, he was leading a very lascivious and luxurious lifestyle.

BERRY: Rather like St. Augustine, who prayed, "Give me chastity, but not yet."

PICKARSKI: Well, I don't think he was ever so dissolute as Augustine. Augustine was really a wild man! Francis was a little more subdued. Remember too: Francis didn't have someone like Saint Monica praying for him for thirty years as Augustine did. Whereas

Augustine lived a debauched and dissipated life that persisted for decades, Francis had a taste of this lifestyle and very quickly realized the futility of it. So instead of giving himself up to debauchery, he gave himself up to his new calling, which was to follow Christ. At first, he wanted to be a knight-errant, a crusader for Christ, who would take up arms and fight for Him, but gradually, he evolved into the gentle, pacifistic, animal-loving friar that he is renowned for being; so in view of the gentle spirit that he transformed himself into, it's logical to think that he might have become a vegetarian. But the evidence is too inconclusive for me to say without fear of contradiction that he was a vegetarian. However, my sense is that we tend to use a saint such as Francis, or a great spiritual leader such as Christ, to justify a contention or an ideal. That is a weak argument for vegetarianism. Rather, we should focus on how we can live in harmony with creation and the nature of our being. Humans have a tendency to go to extremes on issues, and to try to set up absolutes; rather, we should focus on putting the issues in perspective. Vegetarianism should be the chief component of our lifestyle, but it should never be made into an absolute.

BERRY: What about the legends that have it that Francis of Assisi would purchase live fish from fishermen so that he could release them? Or the incident, narrated in "The Little Flowers of Saint Francis," in which he insisted that a friar fling a bowl of ashes in Francis's face as penance for Francis's having eaten animal flesh and drunk meat broth during his illness? Don't these stories suggest that he might have been a vegetarian, at least while he was living the ascetic life of a mendicant friar?

PICKARSKI: Yes, Francis probably *was* a vegetarian, but I would rather err on the side of caution and say that he was *probably* a vegetarian, rather than to say he was indisputably a vegetarian. In the *Omnibus of Sources*, a sick friar was told by Francis that if he were to eat a vegetarian diet, he would be healed. The friar obeyed, was cured, and went on to live a healthy life as a vegetarian.

BERRY: What do you make of that strange about-face that he did at the end of his life when he regretted his asceticism as having "offended my brother the body," as he put it?

PICKARSKI: It's contradictory: That's why I can't put it any more strongly than to say that he *probably* was a vegetarian. The great thing about Francis was that he loved animals and lived in harmony with nature.

BERRY: The religious order that he founded in 1209 CE, the *fratres minores*—the Franciscans—are they vegetarians?

PICKARSKI: Again, it would make eminent sense that Franciscans should aspire to be vegetarians. Unfortunately, they don't: There are very few Franciscans who are vegetarians; however, there are some.

BERRY: I was going to ask you about the status of vegetarianism within the monastic orders. A Roman Catholic friend of mine assures me that monks are lacto-vegetarians. Is that true?

PICKARSKI: Far from it! I wish it were true! Unfortunately, vegetarianism within the orders is greatly lacking. Even the Trappists eat fish. From my own experience, I've not seen any trend towards vegetarianism in any of the major orders. There were a great many more monks living as vegetarians in the early days of the Church because the orders were impoverished and the diet of the poor folk was primarily vegetarian. Modern religious and monastics live as middle and upper class folk, and that unfortunately connotes a diet that is high in cholesterol and high on the food chain (meats and rich fare): that's the reason why so many monastics and religious are overweight and out-of-shape. St. Augustine was a man of high principle; so it's quite possible that his order was vegetarian. I personally believe that religious orders will find their way onto the vegetarian path in time.

BERRY: Compared with the svelte and trim-figured clergy of the Eastern religions, the Western clergy are conspicuously fat. Look at the portraits of popes, cardinals, bishops and other princes of the Church dating back to the early Renaissance and you'll seldom see one that isn't corpulent; whereas, I defy you to find a Taoist priest or a Jain monk, or a Buddhist priest, who isn't scrawny by comparison.

PICKARSKI: That's a fair point. By and large the Western clergy are overweight. I myself was 70 pounds overweight when I entered the seminary, tipping the scales at 200 pounds. Today, I weigh 125 in the summer and 135 in the winter.

BERRY: You're one of the few Western clergymen, of recent vintage, who have become a vegetarian after entering the seminary.

PICKARSKI: That's right: one month after taking my solemn vows, I became a vegetarian.

BERRY: Not to belabor the point, but I'd like to compare the diet of Cardinal Thomas Wolsey, who in the early sixteenth century was the most powerful (and the most venal) prelate in Christendom with the diet of his contemporary in India, Lord Chaitanya Mahaprabhu, who is one of India's most revered saints. To celebrate the betrothal of the Princess Mary to the Dauphin of France, Cardinal Wolsey gave a dinner party that like most of his meals was almost wholly carnivorous. (Foremost among the guests was that great trencherman, Henry VIII.) Wolsey feasted his guests on "beeves and mutton, porkers and fat hogs, capons and chickens by the dozen; six salmon; fifteen swans; four peacocks; fifty-four dozen larks; lashings of butter; green ginger, marmalade, quinces; gallons of cream and 'frumenty.'"

Now compare this with a feast presided over by the Hindu saint Lord Chaitanya, which took place at about the same time in Bengal in Northeastern India: The feast is described by Chaitanya's biographer Krishnadas Kaviraj Goswami: "Among the various vegetables offered were newly grown leaves of nimba (neem) trees fried with eggplant." At a gigantic feast that was held to celebrate Lord Chaitanya's cleansing of the Gundicha temple, Chaitanya saw to it that each of the hundreds of his followers who assembled there was served his favorite vegetarian dish, which was a simple Bengali soup, Laphra Vyanjana, which means "mustard-flavored vegetable soup." You know, it's funny: I can't imagine Cardinal Wolsey, or Henry VIII, or any contemporary prince of the Church, dining on Chaitanya's simple vegetarian fare—but I can picture Christ eating it with relish!

PICKARSKI: There's no doubt about it: Cardinal Wolsey's diet was certainly unbalanced, but I wouldn't want to lay all the blame for his spiritual shortcomings at carnivorism's door. My point is that diet is not the sole factor in determining whether one is corrupt or pure. It's a material factor, but not the sole determining factor. Furthermore, I think it's a little unfair to compare Cardinal Wolsey, who was more of a Church politician than a spiritual leader, with a bonafide Hindu saint. A better comparison would be between the Hindu saint and a Christian saint like Saint Francis, or Saint Anthony the Great, or Saint Hedwig, who followed a vegetarian diet.

BERRY: This reminds me of my conversation with Steven Rosen, in which he pointed out that vegetarianism and reincarnation are esoteric doctrines in the West; whereas, they are exoteric doctrines in the East. Traditionally, in the West, only saints and mystics have tended to be vegetarians, practise *ahimsa*, and have transmundane experiences; whereas in the East, the common street sweeper is a vegetarian, believes in reincarnation and *ahimsa*, and routinely has transmundane experiences.

PICKARSKI: Yes, I agree, but I think that's changing.

BERRY: In my own research, I've noticed that one of the hallmarks of a religion that sets a high value on human and animal life is that it teaches a doctrine of reincarnation. This is true of Jainism, Hinduism, Taoism, Buddhism and of the Order of the Cross (the only sect of Christianity that requires its members to be vegetarians): How do you as a vegetarian Catholic brother feel about reincarnation?

PICKARSKI: I believe in it, and I believe that we are reincarnated in order to work out our *karma*; in other words, we reincarnate to allow God to teach us the lessons of the past life that we failed to learn. When we pay off our *karmic* debt, so to speak, then we don't have to come back. In point of fact, I believe that Christ's resurrection was a form of reincarnation.

BERRY: That's a fascinating concept! If Christians could be persuaded that resurrection equals reincarnation, then the slaughter of animals for food would end tomorrow—especially if they were to entertain the possibility that Christ might have been reincarnated as an animal, and vice versa. We'd have an ethical basis for vegetarianism within the Church.

PICKARSKI: That's right.

BERRY: The theologian, Geddes McGregor, in his book *Reincarnation in Christianity,* points out that the doctrine of reincarnation has never been officially condemned by the Catholic Church. Among the early Christians, reincarnation was a widely held belief until the second ecumenical council in Constantinople abolished it in 553 CE. Were the reasons for the Church's suppressing it anything other than political?

PICKARSKI: It's my recollection that one of the main reasons for the Church's frowning on reincarnationism is that they were afraid that if people thought they could come back in another life, they would behave licentiously and live loosely in this life. To the Church, reincarnationism seemed like a license to live a dissolute life and get away with it; that's why they did away with it.

BERRY: Do *you* think that the Western Church may reinvigorate the doctrine of reincarnation as more and more Christians come over to vegetarianism?

PICKARSKI: I think so: it may not be in my lifetime, but someday the Western Church will adopt many of the features of Asian religions such as *karmic* doctrine, reincarnation, vegetarianism, *ahimsa*, etc.

BERRY: Tell me what it was specifically that prompted you to become a vegetarian.

PICKARSKI: I must talk a bit about my transformation here. Odd as it may seem in view of my religious aspirations, I became a vegetarian for health reasons. Twice during my life, I've had bouts of acute bronchial pneumonia. The first, which was almost fatal, struck me when I was five months old. The second was a near-fatal relapse that I had when I was in the third grade. In spite of my weak lungs, I started smoking in the sixth grade and didn't quit until I was in the eighth grade. To make matters worse, my parents opened a fast-food restaurant, and they stuffed me with

burgers, milkshakes, hot dogs and french fries. My weight bal-
looned to 200 lbs. When I entered the seminary at age 18, I was
overweight and ailing. Not long after becoming a Franciscan brother, I attended a seminar given by Dr. Wesserman. He talked
about the uric-acid-forming properties of meat, and how it causes
the health problems that had been dogging me most of my life. His
talk was so cogent that the very next day I turned vegetarian.
Ironically enough, I had my last dinner with meat at my own
solemn vows, which was my final initiation into religious life.

BERRY: When did you become a vegan?

PICKARSKI: I became a total vegetarian or vegan in May 1977. I
had been experimenting with raw-food, macrobiotic, and dairyless vegetarian diets. As soon as I eliminated dairy foods, my system began to clear up even more; so I made the transition to veganism, or total vegetarianism. Now I jog five miles a day, sleep
four hours a night, and breathe easily. I learned that an important
part of knowing how to live is learning how to eat.

BERRY: So for the last four years of your life in the monastery,
you were a vegetarian?

PICKARSKI: That's right; I was also the monastery chef at St.
Paschal's Friary.

BERRY: Did you use your position as monastery chef to try to influence the other monks to become vegetarians—through your
cooking?

PICKARSKI: Yes, I did, and they gave me a lot of hell for it!

BERRY: How did you go about it? Did you use a heavy hand, and
yank meat dishes off the menus?

PICKARSKI: No, not at all. I was very low-key and subtle in my
approach. They just took it amiss. The very idea that I was a vegetarian bent them out of shape.

BERRY: One would think that they might have admired you for
imitating the founder of the order, St. Francis.

PICKARSKI: No, just the opposite: it was a thorn in their side because they felt that I was making a statement.

BERRY: They felt that by becoming a vegetarian you were taking a holier-than-thou attitude towards them?

PICKARSKI: Precisely.

BERRY: Did they drum you out of the order?

PICKARSKI: In a manner of speaking. They made it very uncomfortable for me to stay there.

BERRY: So you now function independently of the order?

PICKARSKI: Yes.

BERRY: Why didn't you just quietly become a vegetarian, keep it to yourself, and retreat into the splendid isolation of a monastery like Thomas Merton's Our Lady of Gethsemani?

PICKARSKI: I had a mission, a calling that I could not ignore.

BERRY: How did you discover your calling?

PICKARSKI: God in His omniscience knew what I needed: I was given all the tools. While I was a Franciscan brother, I entered culinary school and trained as a meat-cutter; but strange as it may seem, my experience as a meat-cutter helped lay the foundation for me to become a vegetarian chef.

BERRY: Did you go to culinary school while you were in the monastery?

PICKARSKI: Yes, I wanted to become a monastery chef; so I had to go to culinary school and, among other things, become certified as a meat-cutter.

BERRY: What would a typical dinner be like in a Franciscan monastery?

PICKARSKI: They had two entrées, such as Coq au Vin, Chicken Cacciatore, etc. I gave them a lot of vegetarian options though.

BERRY: How did you feel about handling meat in the monastery kitchen after you had become a vegetarian? Did it disgust you?

PICKARSKI: To some extent it bothers me even now, as I still have to handle it in my work.

BERRY: When would you have occasion to handle it now?

PICKARSKI: When I'm working with a restaurant project, or working with food technologies, I've had to develop dishes that have meat in them. Unhappily, it's not something that I've been able to eliminate from my repertoire as a professional chef. Perhaps I'll be able to do it in a decade or so, but I doubt it. You see, because of the nature of the work that I do as a professional chef and food consultant, there's no way that I'm going to be able to cook for the masses and totally dispense with meat in my cooking. My rationale for this is that cooking a little bit of meat will give me the chance to educate hundreds of thousands of people about vegetarianism; whereas if I were to be absolutist and purist, I would be cooking only for myself and a select group of friends. Therefore, I've adopted a gradualist and transitional approach, and I don't feel that I'm compromising my own vegetarian principles by doing it.

BERRY: Can you give me a specific instance of when you'd have occasion to work with meat?

PICKARSKI: A good example was a dinner that I recently prepared for the Nissan corporation in Chicago. They wanted to have vegetarian entrées, but they also wanted me to provide a flesh option for those who might want it. "Fine," I said, "I will give them Sole Bonne Femme. So, out of the ninety-six people present, six ordered Sole Bonne Femme; the other ninety ate the vegetarian entrée. If I had been uncompromising and inflexible about it, I could have refused to cook anything but an exclusively vegetarian meal. That would have infuriated the client, and I would have missed my chance to influence the ninety people who enjoyed the vegetarian meal. Quite the opposite, there would have been ninety-six seafood dinners consumed that night instead of only six — you see, I'm pragmatic in my approach.

BERRY: Speaking of seafood (the only type of flesh that Christ is seriously alleged to have eaten), The Reverend Todd Ferrier, among others, insists that the references to Christ's eating flesh in the gospels are not to be taken literally. Do you believe that Christ was a vegetarian?

PICKARSKI: I certainly think that he was. If he wasn't a vegetarian, then he was the nearest thing to it. Bear in mind that there was very little meat in the diet in those days. In Biblical times, meat was scarce, and people subsisted on figs and nuts and fruit and grain. Once in a great while, they killed an animal for a feast—but that was a rare occasion.

BERRY: What about Ferrier's contention that the fish imagery in the Gospels is largely symbolic?

PICKARSKI: I think there may be a good deal of truth in that.

BERRY: We've been discussing what Christ may have eaten; now I'd like to discuss "the eating of Christ" in the shape of the Eucharist. Do you believe that the person who takes communion is actually ingesting the body and blood of Christ?

PICKARSKI: It's the sacramental reality. What makes an apple an apple? Is it the skin? Is it the seed? Is it the stem? The apple is more than the sum of its components. If Christ can be in a rock, or a tree—can he not also be in a host?

BERRY: Do you believe in transubstantiation?

PICKARSKI: I believe in transubstantiation. God said He had the power to enter into a rock; God can manifest Himself wherever he wants; He's in us! Eating is a form of transubstantiation in that our food, through the digestion process, transforms and transubstantiates itself into us.

BERRY: The Aztecs, the Vedic Aryans, the priests of ancient Rome—all practiced a rite of transubstantiation in which bread was turned into the body of the god and then eaten in a communion ceremony not unlike the Catholic Mass. For this reason the classicist-turned-anthropologist, Sir James George Frazer, implies that the Eucharist is a semi-barbaric rite that smacks of cannibalism. Do you think he's making a valid point?

PICKARSKI: On the contrary, I think he's missing the whole point. Physically, it's a piece of bread, but it is in reality the body of Christ; and the idea is not to become a cannibal, but to become more like Christ, and to let Christ enter our body. Each time I receive the Eucharist through transubstantiation, I am eating the flesh of Christ; and it is empowering me to become more and more like Him.

BERRY: But isn't that same process at work in the mind of certain primitive meat-eaters who admire the animal and eat its flesh so that they can become more like the animal?

PICKARSKI: No, the Eucharist is purely vegetarian.

BERRY: I understand that in the past Popes have granted dispensation to members of the Church who've committed cannibalism in dire circumstances.

PICKARSKI: That's right. He granted a dispensation to that team of rugby players who were stranded in the Andes after their plane crashed and they were compelled to eat their teammates.

BERRY: You mean the Old Christians?

PICKARSKI: The Old Christians?

BERRY: "The Old Christians" was the name of the rugby team that committed cannibalism in the Chilean Andes. I've read the Piers Paul Read book, *Alive*, which was a riveting account of the whole ordeal. By the way, Ron, what would you have done, if you, as a total vegetarian, had been one of the team?

PICKARSKI: I think I could have fasted through it; I've fasted for as much as twenty-eight days on a diet of liquids; if I'd had some nourishment for the first three weeks or so, I think I could have maintained a fast for seven or eight weeks longer. At all events, I would never have eaten human flesh.

BERRY: It seems to me that the Eucharist is a ritual that lends itself to misinterpretation. Prior to the Eucharist taking its present form during the late Middle Ages, people used to celebrate the mass with a vegetarian meal that was shared out with the poor, much as they do in Hindu temples today.

PICKARSKI: That's fascinating. Do you have a reference for that?

BERRY: Yes, Henry C. Lea discusses it in his *History of Sacerdotal Celibacy in the Christian Church.*

PICKARSKI: I'd like to use that in a paper that I'm giving.

BERRY: Was it Pope John Paul who absolved the Old Christians for having committed cannibalism?

PICKARSKI: No, it was Pope Paul.

BERRY: What are some of the other instances in which the Pope has granted dispensation to Catholics for acts of cannibalism?

PICKARSKI: Well, a friend of mine did his Ph.D. thesis on the Crusades. He told me about the siege of Antioch in which the crusaders, after having laid siege to the city for many weeks, ran out of food, and started devouring the Islamic soldiers whom they had killed.

BERRY: Usually, it's the people inside the besieged city who suffer from famine—not the besiegers. Why this strange turnabout?

PICKARSKI: In one word: they didn't have a supply train. They had been marauding their way through Europe until they got to the Middle East; along the route, they pillaged the countryside to feed their massive army; they lived off the hard work of the European peasants until they got to the Middle East, but the Muslims denied them food with a scorched-earth policy. By the time the crusaders reached Antioch their food supply was completely exhausted; so they fell upon the Muslims whom they had slaughtered and lived off their flesh until the city fell to the Crusaders.

BERRY: How long did this go on? How long did the besiegers live on human flesh?

PICKARSKI: For a few months.

BERRY: So am I to understand that the Pope granted them a special dispensation, pardoning their acts of cannibalism?

PICKARSKI: Yes.

BERRY: I wonder if some future Pope will grant a dispensation to the countless generations of Christians who have eaten animal flesh?

PICKARSKI: (*laughter*) I think so, someday; I sense that the Church will come around to it eventually, and when it does I will be waiting to help them; but large institutions move slowly.

BERRY: How would you reconcile the paradisal vegetarian world that God created in the Genesis sagas with the other books in the Bible such as Leviticus and Deuteronomy that serve as manuals of animal sacrifice?

PICKARSKI: These texts have been so corrupted by editors and translators who had an axe to grind that they can only be taken as allegorical.

BERRY: Even so mundane and skeptical a personage as Frederick the Great gave it as his opinion that prior to the third century CE, Christ was widely believed to have been an Essene, and hence a vegetarian. Do you think that the church may again come around to the view that Jesus may have been a vegetarian?

PICKARSKI: Obviously, if the Church becomes more open to vegetarianism, it will be more hospitable to these ideas.

BERRY: Why did the Church suppress the evidence of Christ's vegetarianism—if you believe it did?

PICKARSKI: In my opinion, it's because by the fourth century CE, meat-eating was becoming a symbol of status associated with the upper-classes. As the Church prospered, more and more Church officials took on the airs of the upper classes, they suppressed any teachings that would hinder their leading the high life, which involved eating liberal amounts of animal flesh.

BERRY: A Taoist friend complained that when he attended Western church services, he missed the vegetarian temple cuisine that followed the services in the Taoist temples in China. Buddhist and

Hindu friends have voiced similar complaints. Indeed, there is evidence to suggest that the early Christian Eucharist was a substantial vegetarian meal that was shared out among the poor (as is the practice in Hindu temples today). In Christianity, Judaism and Islam there is no tradition of an ethically-based vegetarian temple cuisine such as one finds among the Eastern religions of Jainism, Buddhism, Taoism, and Hinduism.

PICKARSKI: Within Christianity there is not a real consciousness about diet. But someday the Church will wake up and realize that an ethical diet is necessary to a moral way of life.

BERRY: Have you had any success in changing the eating habits of the members of your order?

PICKARSKI: Oddly enough, I've converted more American chefs to vegetarianism than I have members of my own order.

BERRY: Are you disappointed that the Church hasn't lent more support to your activities?

PICKARSKI: Yes, I've had to move away from the order to do what I'm doing; they approve of the favorable media attention that I'm getting, but they don't really understand what I'm about. In a sense, they've put me out to pasture.

BERRY: Do you tithe your royalties and earnings to the Church?

PICKARSKI: Yes, but by the time I've deducted all my expenses, there isn't much left for the Church. Last year I had well over a hundred thousand dollars in expenses.

BERRY: I understand that you've spent a lot of your own money to train and send a team of vegetarian chefs, headed up by you, to compete in the culinary Olympics in Frankfurt.

PICKARSKI: That's right. The international Culinary Olympics is held in Frankfurt, Germany every four years. It's always held in conjunction with the athletic Olympics. I took a ten-member team over last year. We won a silver and a gold medal.

BERRY: The International Culinary Olympics must be a great showcase for your skill as a vegetarian chef.

PICKARSKI: You bet it is: that was my reason for doing it in the first place. My Natural Foods Team is the only team of chefs to have presented exclusively vegetarian dishes at the International Culinary Olympics and at other cooking competitions around the world. Our purpose is to inspire chefs worldwide to learn about and to cook more vegetarian foods. It's to be hoped that they in turn will inspire the public to adopt vegetarianism as a dietary lifestyle.

BERRY: I understand that the dishes that you presented at the Culinary Olympics were organized around two themes: Eco-Cuisine and Grainology. Could you expand on that a bit?

PICKARSKI: That's right: "Eco-Cuisine" is the term that I coined for the plant-based diet that is designed to nurture the physiological health of the body as well as the ecological health of the planet. "Grainology" was the other theme in our presentation at the culinary Olympics in which we attempted to show the range of delicious dishes that could be made using twenty lesser known grains such as teff, quinoa, kalmut, spelt and sorghum.

BERRY: Have you educated a lot of the judges at these culinary competitions.

PICKARSKI: Yes. Most people have had a misconception about vegetarianism; they think it's boring and bland—you know: endless iceberg lettuce salads and boiled greens. But through the International Culinary Olympics, I've been able to show that vegetarian food can be truly a gourmet cuisine that can more than hold its own against Europe's so-called *haute cuisine*. When the judges first saw my vegetarian dishes at the Culinary Olympics in 1988, they were overawed by them; they had never seen anything like this before; they pulled out their cameras and started snapping pictures of the dishes, as if they were photographing something utterly new and exotic, which, at the time, it was. Since then they've taken a keen interest in what I've been doing with vegetarian food. Last year marked the first year that they've had special dietary categories for the competition—not specifically vegetarian—but for special diets, low cholesterol, low-fat, sugar-free, etc. It's encouraging that they've opened up to that extent. The next stage will be the creation of a separate vegetarian category in the competition. It's already happening in some competitions. For instance, at the recent American Classic in Chicago, there was a vegetarian dish in just about every exhibit that I saw. So, gradually, it's coming to the fore.

BERRY: Do you have a favorite vegetarian dish in your repertoire?

PICKARSKI: My tofu Swiss steak is one of my favorites: quite often I make it with seitan.

BERRY: I notice that you use a good deal of seitan in your recipes.

PICKARSKI: Yes, I'm trying to show people how to use it; it's an excellent meat substitute.

BERRY: It's widely used in the Buddhist and Taoist temple cuisine in China. Was that your inspiration for using it?

PICKARSKI: Yes, indirectly, through my training in macrobiotic cooking.

BERRY: Your dietary views are so much at variance with those of the Church, I'm wondering if your views on human beings' second most powerful appetite also differ from those of the Church. How do you feel about the Church's position on sex, birth control and celibacy?

PICKARSKI: On the matter of birth control, I think that the Pope and the Church need a strong dose of reality. There's nothing in the creed or dogma of the Church that says we can't practice birth control. Birth control is a solid solution to the population explosion that threatens to engulf the world. If we want to check it, we need to start practicing birth control. Although it's contrary to Catholic doctrine, I fully support birth control, and I always will. Contrary to the Church's teaching, sex isn't only for procreation —sex is a pleasure: It's an expression of one's deepest love. The idea that you should have sex only for the purpose of procreation is the Church's way of trying to propagate the world with Christians. (*laughter*)

BERRY: But you, yourself, have taken a vow of celibacy. If, as you say, sex is a positive pleasure and an expression of love, then why are you denying yourself that pleasure?

PICKARSKI: The purpose of sexual congress between two people is the communion of souls; the body is a vehicle for that communion. However, if you can realize it in the spirit, as I can, then you really don't need to actualize it in the body. In that sense, the spiritual sense, I've had great sex all my life. I love women; I have a wonderful connection with them; at one point, a woman was my spiritual director; so, I have a lot of affinity for them. When a woman gives me a big hug, it makes my day.

BERRY: It doesn't have to be consummated—this love that you have for women?

PICKARSKI: No, it's not something that I need. I would be very happy to spend the rest of my life as a celibate.

BERRY: What about the celibacy laws of the Church? Do you feel that they're draconian?

PICKARSKI: The celibacy laws in the Church arose out of economic considerations. They made celibacy mandatory—not because Christ was celibate, but because the bishops wanted to control all the wealth. In the early days of the Church, priests were allowed to marry; monks and bishops had children; Peter himself was married.

BERRY: For all we know Christ himself may have been married.

PICKARSKI: That's right. I would argue that he wasn't, but I wouldn't rule out the possibility that he might have been.

BERRY: Some scholars have suggested that Buddhism, with its celibate priests and monks, may have served as the prototype for celibacy within the Church; other scholars have propounded the theory that the early Church was trying to imitate the Manicheans, who, like the Buddhists, practiced celibacy and vegetarianism. Unfortunately, the Church seems to have placed practically all its emphasis on abstaining from sex and little or no emphasis on abstaining from the eating of animal flesh.

PICKARSKI: That might have been true for the Eastern orders, but celibacy wasn't officially adopted by the Church until Pope Gregory VII made it mandatory in 1085 CE. Up until then the Church permitted bishops, priests and monks to marry, and have children, as I mentioned. There was a lot of resistance to the celibacy laws, and they were honored more in the breach than the observance; it's still a hotly debated issue. Your point about dietary abstinence is well-taken: I think that celibacy and fasting go together. I like to quote Thomas Merton, who said "If you want to become celibate, you must learn how to fast."

BERRY: Celibacy, then, is a sort of sexual fasting.

PICKARSKI: That's exactly the point that Merton is making.

BERRY: But doesn't fasting quicken the appetite.

PICKARSKI: It enables you to control and deepen your appetite without becoming enslaved to it.

BERRY: Was Merton a vegetarian?

PICKARSKI: I really couldn't say.

BERRY: It would surprise me if he weren't: he was steeped in the traditions of Eastern religions. He wrote authoritatively on Zen, Taoism, Mahayana Buddhism, Hinduism and the mystical aspects of Christianity. I believe he was a Trappist monk.

PICKARSKI: His being a Trappist doesn't necessarily mean that he was a vegetarian. As I said earlier, the Trappists eat fish and meat, as do the members of my own order, the Franciscans. I've never found a greater resistance to my vegetarianism and to my starting Eco-Cuisine than I have among members of my own order. Even though Saint Francis was the patron saint of animals and the environment, and even though Franciscans are heavily involved in anti-nuclear and other issues, they don't see the connection between vegetarianism and the environment.

BERRY: If the order is unsympathetic to your ethical vegetarianism, and it doesn't support you financially, or morally, then what's the point of belonging to the order?

PICKARSKI: That's just it: that's why I'm weighing the decision as to whether I should leave the order or not. In the community of friars, I've always been treated as a maverick and an outsider.

BERRY: But I think part of the attraction that you hold for many people is that you are a monk. If you were to renounce that, you would lose one of your most attractive features. There's something decidedly special about a master vegan chef who is also a Roman Catholic monk. It's quite a curiosity.

PICKARSKI: Yes, but I can't let that be the sole consideration for my remaining in the order.

Essay

. . . .

ISLAM

IN A SENSE THE HISTORY OF Islam, the second most populous religion in the world after Christianity, is rooted in foodstuffs; for it grew up in the city of Mecca, which is at the crossroads of two major spice routes: from Southern Arabia to Syria and from Persia to the Nile Valley. The Bedouin, who were the middlemen in the overland spice trade plied these routes with their camels ferrying rice, pepper, incense, silk, cotton and slaves from Asia to the West. Muhammad, the founder of the faith, was a camel driver and caravan leader who trafficked in spices, incense, perfume, and agricultural produce along these ancient caravan tracks. He was born in the year 570 CE in the city of Mecca, in modern Saudi Arabia. Ideas, philosophical and theological, tend to follow the trade routes, and Muhammad who had a quick and comprehensive mind was far more interested in ideas than he was in the goods that he bartered. He was particularly intrigued by the monotheistic religions of Christianity and Judaism that were spreading like prairie fires even in the parched lands of Arabia Deserta. Syrian Christianity, with its mystical-ascetic bent, held a particular attraction for Muhammad, as it did for many other Arabs of his time who emulated the Syrian Christian monks by swearing off meat and drink and becoming wandering ascetics, or *hanifs*, as they were called. In becoming such radical renunciants, the *hanifs* remind one of nothing so much as the Indian *sadhus* who strip themselves of their possessions and their clothes (save for the fig-leaf of a loincloth) and live as frugally as possible. About Muhammad, biographers say, there was the air of the self-abnegating *hanif*. Yet he was far too responsible and sensible of his familial obligations (which after the death of Khadijah, his first wife, included a harem of ten more wives whom he had to look after) to chuck his business affairs and become a desert contemplative, but his mystical propensities never left him; and when he turned forty he took to retiring to a cave on the crags of Mount Hira (near Mecca) and giving himself up to the spiritual reveries that culminated in the oral composition of the Quran.

Dismayed by the bloody sacrificial cults that were swirling around him, Muhammad immersed himself in the study of Syrian Christianity and Judaism. This he did by drawing out wandering *hanifs* and itinerant merchants who belonged to those faiths, not by reading, as it is widely conjectured that Muhammad was unable to read and write. Fortuitously, his wife's cousin, Waraka, was a scholar who had translated sections of the Torah into Arabic. At Muhammad's request, Waraka would read to him.[1] Perhaps the debt that Islam owes to Judaism can be laid to those quiet days when the future prophet of Islam squatted on his haunches, and like a curious child, listened with head cocked as Waraka read to him the gripping biblical stories from the Torah and the New Testament. They would provide the germ for his own religious system, which owes so much to Judaism and Christianity that different scholars have described Islam by turns as a Jewish heresy and a Christian heresy. So besotted with the god of Abraham did Muhammad become that he was given to falling into a trance and dictating his ruminations to bystanders who took them down as the very words of God uttered by a latter-day Moses.

To the Muslims, that is precisely what Muhammad was: the Moses of their faith, the founding prophet whose religious system bore a striking resemblance to the two monotheistic religions that he revered; because Muhammad was unlettered, it was necessary that bystanders scribble down his God-inspired utterances on anything that was handy. So the first edition of the Quran was a mosaic of sayings, compiled a few years after his death from "scraps of parchment and leather, tablets of stone, ribs of palm branches, camels' shoulder blades and ribs, pieces of board and the breasts of men."[2] In his visions, it was revealed to Muhammad that the Arabs were, like the Jews, descended from Abraham, only (unlike the Jews) it was out of Ishmael, Abraham's outcast son. In spite of the mutual hostility that has sprung up among these three Abrahamic faiths, Muhammad felt only the deepest reverence for the Torah and the New Testament, as they had played such a part in shaping his own singular monotheism.

It is perhaps helpful to see Muhammad as a theological middleman, a canny spice importer who brought a piquant mixture of Christianity, Judaism, Zoroastrianism and Gnosticism to the peoples of the desert. With characteristic humility, he would have been the first to admit this; for he made it plain to his followers that he didn't want to be deified or taken for a savior. He was just a humble spice trader-turned-prophet whose mission it was to direct people to the one true god Allah, which is simply the Arabic word for the god of the Hebrew Bible (and corresponds to the Hebrew *elohim*). As a measure of his success, when he arrived on the scene the Arabs were polytheists who worshipped holy date palms, sacred stones, demonic jinns and a bevy of mother goddesses who had to be appeased with sacrificial blood and flesh. By the time of his death (in 632 CE), Arabia was solidly monotheistic.

Besides being a thriving commercial center, Muhammad's birthplace was the site of a sacred stone of meteoric origin. (Pre-Islamic Semites often worshipped stones;[3] the Syrian Arab Elagabalus scandalized the old Romans when he transported his sacred stone to Rome and built a temple for it on his becoming Emperor in 219 CE.) Legend has it that this celestial rock was brought to Mecca by Abraham, who had it built into the Kaaba ("cube"). Pre-Islamic pilgrims and tourists from all over Arabia traveled to Mecca to touch and kiss the hunk of black meteorite that had tumbled from the sky. To it and the gods that surrounded it, they sacrificed sheep and camels. At first, the Meccans stoutly resisted Muhammad's religious reforms for fear that they would be bad for the tourist trade. Their fears were misplaced, however, because more pilgrims than ever now visit Mecca to kiss and touch the sacred rock in the Kaaba, which is now the cynosure of the Hajj, the obligatory pilgrimage to Muhammad's birthplace that every Muslim must make at least once in a lifetime. Next day, at Mina, pilgrims on the return leg of the Hajj sacrifice camels and sheep to commemorate Abraham's sacrifice of a ram in place of Isaac. Regrettably, much of this sacrificial flesh is simply discarded, which violates Muhammad's instruction that if an animal is to be sacrificed at all, its flesh should be distributed to the poor.[4]

The pre-Islamic Arabs were a tough, feral people who settled their scores with summary justice. Although they lived chiefly on dates and camel's milk—like the Jews, the Greeks and the Romans—they had a taste for the flesh of sacrificial animals; they ate pigs, dogs and camel (camel's hump lard was a particular delicacy)[5] but they were not always chary about how they sacrificed their beasts for the table. They often butchered them while they were still living, tearing off limbs and devouring them while the animals suffered unspeakable agonies. "When the Holy Prophet migrated to Medina from Mecca in 622, people there used to cut off camels' humps and the fat tails of sheep. The Prophet ordered this barbaric practice to be stopped. The temptation for the people to perform this sort of vivisection on animals was that the juicy humps and fatty tails could be eaten while the animal remained alive for future use. To remove this avidity, he declared: 'Whatever is cut off an animal, while it is still alive, is carrion and is unlawful (*haram*) to eat.'"[6] Renowned for his honesty in business matters (his nickname was *al-amin,* the trustworthy) Muhammad was also noted for his compassion towards animals; many of the *Hadith* (oral traditions pertaining to him) deal with animal abuse and his attempt to mitigate the suffering of animals:

> The Holy Prophet Muhammad prohibited the use of the skins of wild animals.[7]
>
> The Prophet condemned those who use a living creature as a target.[8]

God's messenger forbade inciting animals to fight each other.[9]

He who takes pity, even on a sparrow, and spares its life, Allah will be merciful on him on the Day of Judgment.[10]

Realizing that it would be futile to try to abolish the slaughter of animals for food (so deeply was it ingrained in the Arab culture), he adopted, with some modifications, many of the methods of ritual slaughter, or *kashrut,* that were being employed by the Jews. What the Jews call *kashrut,* or kosher, Muhammad called *halal,* "fit for human consumption." Like the Deuteronomists, Muhammad divided the clean from the unclean animals, the *halal* from the *haram.* In Muhammad's time Islamic ritual slaughter was certainly a more humane method of dispatching an animal than cutting off a camel's hump while it was still alive. Under *halal,* the animal (supposedly) is killed as painlessly as possible. The slaughterer turns the animal to face Mecca and recites the formula "In the name of God, God is great," as he takes the animal's life. Nevertheless, the whole notion of ritual slaughter has been called into question by ethical Muslim vegetarians. Muslim theologian, Al-Hafiz B. A. Masri has pointed out that as it is currently practiced it is no longer all that humane. The animals are now intensively reared and killed by the factory-slaughter methods of the West. He says, "If only the average simple and God-fearing Muslim consumer of such food animals knew of the gruesome details about the Westernized food industry in their own Islamic countries, they would become vegetarians rather than eat such sacrilegious meat."[11]

Muslims have the same horror of blood as do the Jews. Every precaution must be taken to avoid eating blood; therefore, if an animal is to be slaughtered for the table, its blood must be removed by hoisting the carcass and letting its blood drip out. (Like the Jews, Muslims argue that animal flesh is fit to eat after it has been killed and bled out.) But as it is physically impossible to remove all the blood from an animal's carcass, the eating of animal flesh can never be a bloodless act. To pretend otherwise is pure moonshine.

A better solution to the moral conundrum of eating animal flesh has been proposed by the vegetarian Sufi *shaikh*, M. R. Bawa Muhaiyaddeen; he would require every person who would eat an animal to first look into its eyes while slaughtering it, and to keep on looking into its eyes until the life goes out of them. If every Muslim, or indeed, if every meat-eater looked into an animal's eyes while killing it, doubtless there would be few human flesh-eaters on the planet.

Like orthodox Judaism and Christianity, Islam is not a religion that boasts many vegetarians. But on the theory that the esoteric, mystical branches of Christianity and Judaism are more favorably disposed to vegetarianism, one might think that Sufism, the mystical branch of Islam, would be more hospitable to vegetarianism than the other sects. This was certainly true of the early Sufis. In her book, *The Way of the Mystics*, Margaret Smith tells us about one of the best known of the early Sufis, Rabia al-Adawiyya of Basra (d.801), whose diet was so strict that she regarded fresh dates as a sybaritic luxury; and of another female Sufi, Zaynab, who had been called before the Caliph, Abu Bakr, for refusing to eat flesh. Smith points out that the early Sufis were rebelling against the growth of materialism of the first century of Islam and were trying to recover the simple ideals of the Prophet Muhammad and his companions.[12] The first Sufi spiritual leader with whom I have come into contact, M. R. Bawa Muhaiyaddeen, was a practicing vegetarian, and many of the members of his fellowship (but by no means all) were influenced by him in that direction.

Although Sufism is an Islamic mystical movement that arose in the seventh century, some scholars like Idries Shah say that Sufism is a syncretistic religious sect that combines features of pre-Islamic Mediterranean religions such as Gnosticism, Pythagoreanism, Essenism, and Buddhism.[13] Others say Sufism was influenced by Neoplatonism. Still others have detected in Sufism traces of Syrian Christianity. Doubtless all these observations have some validity; after all, that is what a syncretistic faith does—it blends the thought currents of different belief systems. To achieve their aim which, as with most forms of mysticism, is the *unio mystica*, or the union of self with God, Sufis are willing to put up with a great deal of personal discomfort. They believe that they can achieve salvation through asceticism, through prolonged fasting, through effusive outpourings of love, and

through personal union with Allah. If this sounds like the *bhakti* tradition of Hinduism, in which the devotee strives through intense expressions of love to achieve personal identification with Krishna or Shiva, or Rama, it's not difficult to see why. In the thirteenth century, the Islamic empire extended its rule into Northern India, and there was a great deal of commerce in ideas between the Indic religions and Islam. In fact, from this fusion of Hinduism with Islam another thriving religious sect emerged—Sikhism. It too combined elements of Hinduism, such as the belief in reincarnation, *karma*, *moksha* and vegetarianism, with elements of Islam, such as a fierce monotheism and a martial spirit.

Another striking similarity with Hinduism is the reliance in Sufism upon a spiritual guide, or *guru*, known as a *shaikh* (pronounced "shake"). The *shaikh* or spiritual director guides the student on the path that leads ultimately to *marifa*, *gnosis*, or "wisdom." To prepare himself for the passage to *marifa*, and knowledge of the ultimate reality, the student must surrender himself to the *shaikh*, and learn how to use a variety of contemplative and soul-purifying techniques. Along the way, on the spiritual plane, the student may converse with the original founder of the order, the *Pir*, and even the Prophet himself.

Like the female *mathematakoi* of the Pythagorean orders of ancient Greece and the *bhikshunis* (female monks) of the Buddhist *sangha* in fifth-century BCE India, women are admitted to the Sufi orders on an equal footing with men. Indeed, Sufism was the one area in Islam in which a woman could attain the level of a master teacher and become a *shaikh*. One of the most famous and influential female *shaikhs* was Rabia el-Adawiyya, who set a standard of devotion by her selfless love for God.

Although the Indian and Persian influence was strong in the second phase of Sufism, in the early phase (from 820 to 1090) there is much evidence to suggest that Sufism was shaped by Syrian Christianity. As H. A. R. Gibb writes in *Mohammedanism: an Historical Survey*: "In trying to trace the sources and development expounded in the religious ideas of the Quran (a question be it remembered not only

meaningless but blasphemous in Muslim eyes), we are still confront-
ed with many unsolved problems. Earlier scholars postulated a Jewish source with some Christian additions. More recent research has
conclusively proven that the main external influences (including the
Old Testament materials) can be traced back to Syrian Christianity."[14] Even the woolen robes—the Prophet himself often donned
woolen clothes—from which the Sufis may have taken their name
(*suf* is Persian for wool) were probably first worn by Syrian Christian ascetics. The strain of Christianity practiced in Syria had been
heavily influenced by Gnosticism, Jewish Pythagoreanism and Hinduism. From a vegetarian point of view this is significant because the
Syrian Christians were more ascetic and mystical than were the Western Christians. Syrian Christianity, or more precisely the Christianity of Syria, Egypt and Arabia in the fourth to the sixth century CE,
gave rise to such notable desert mystics as Simeon Stylites and St.
Anthony the Great. Sitting naked atop pillars, or cloistered in cliff-
side cells, and eating only raw vegetarian food, these desert-dwelling
Christian saints bore a closer resemblance to Jain and Hindu *sadhus*
than anything else. That Muhammad may have been inspired by the
doctrines of Christian desert mysticism might also suggest that he
could have imbibed the vegetarian dietary practices of these abstemious Desert Fathers.

Furthermore, the Jewish religious historian Hans-Joachim
Schoeps has advanced the intriguing theory that the vegetarian, anti-
sacrificial sect of which Jesus was the leader, known as the Ebionites, or Jewish Christians, lives on in attenuated form in Islam. Per-
secuted and harried by their fellow Jews for their anti-sacrificial
views, these Jewish Christian sects had fled into Eastern Palestine in
68 CE. Schoeps says that by the end of the second century CE, these
quietist vegetarian Jewish sects occupied all of Syria. Like Jesus,
Muhammad saw himself as the True Prophet who had come to restore the true law of Moses. It is quite possible that Muhammad may
have absorbed many of Jesus's original teachings from the *hanifs* or
Syrian Christians, who were the cultural and spiritual descendants of
the Ebionites.

Was the Prophet Muhammad a vegetarian? That is the burning

question. It's not improbable that he might have been. The founders of all the great religions of the world have been vegetarians—the Buddha, the Nazorean Christ, Mahavira, Lao Tzu. Why should Muhammad have been an exception? His biographers attest that as his faith deepened, his asceticism increased. Professor Charles J. Addams asserts that he was a *hanif*,[15] who, as mentioned above, were the monotheistic forerunners of Islam noted for their simple diet. Whether the founder was a vegetarian or not is a question that is of greater moment in Islam than it might be in other religious traditions because in Islam the Prophet's example is scrupulously studied and imitated. The fact is, an entire spiritual practice has grown up around imitating his behavior, which it is incumbent on other Muslims to follow; it is called *adab*. In *adab* people try to do everything exactly the way they feel the Prophet might have done it, from pouring out a glass of water just so, to the attitude he assumed when he said his prayers. Therefore, if it could be firmly shown that Muhammad was a vegetarian, then in Islamic countries there would be mass conversions to vegetarianism overnight. Yet evidence for Muhammad's vegetarianism is not far to seek. In fact, if his biographers are to be credited (and the great thing about Islam is that it is such a young religion that eyewitness accounts of the Prophet's doings have survived), he was something of a rawfood vegetarian, subsisting as he did for weeks at a time on his favorite fruits of pomegranates, dates and figs. For breakfast he favored a drink of soaked, crushed dates.[16]

Muhammad's Arabia abounded in fruits such as Syrian apples, figs, dates, grapes, raisins, olives etc. For someone who had even a modicum of reverence for animal life, it would have been an easy matter to have been a vegetarian. Why then if Muhammad may have been a vegetarian did he not enforce vegetarianism on his fellow Muslims? Like Yahweh in the Old Testament, who allowed humanity to eat animal flesh as a concession to human weakness, Muhammad is thought to have recognized that the weakness and fallibility of humans was so deep-seated that it was almost impossible for him to make them give up flesh-eating.

If there is an animal that is most favored by Muslim meat-eaters, it is the sheep. Since, as A.C. Bouquet has observed, Islam is a hot-belt religion[17] (it makes most of its converts in Equatorial countries —"the hot belt," but few converts in Northern climes), the food animal that is most suited to the rough terrain and arid climate that Muslims favor is the sheep. Economical and easy to herd over vast distances, the sheep is Islam's flesh meat of choice. Sheep are butchered for food and leather, milked for cheese and milk, and sheered for wool. At Ramadan and other sacral events in the Muslim religious calendar, the pick of the herd are sacrificed. Indeed, many religious pilgrims sacrifice their sheep on the road to Mecca, their carcasses "left to decay and putrefy until offensive smell comes out of them, causing the Muslims much discomfort and danger to their health."[18] The Muslim theologian, Al-Hafiz B. A. Masri has rebuked his fellow Muslims for their carelessness in carrying out these viatical sacrifices.[19]

On the other hand, to its credit, Islam is responsible for the reduction of the consumption of pigflesh in many Middle Eastern countries. It is only countries at the margins of Islamic influence, such as Indonesia and China, that indulge in pigflesh consumption in defiance of the ban. There the pig is declared an honorary sheep to circumvent the ban.[20]

Furthermore, according to the economic geographer Xavier de Planhol, this ban on pigflesh has had the effect of turning many Muslims into vegetarians, or at least to increase the proportion of vegetables and fruit in their diet. "On a more general plane, the proscription of pork has driven Muslims to seek in the world of vegetables for their principle sources of fats; they have cultivated sesame, peanuts, and, above all, the olive tree."[21]

Although the Quran says that it is permissible for Muslims to eat animal flesh slaughtered by the people of the Book (i.e., Christians, Jews—other religions that hold the Bible to be a sacred book), Masri argues that the eating habits of Christians and Jews have changed since Muhammad's time, so much so that he urges that Muslims not buy their flesh from Christian or Jewish slaughterhouses. For instance, Christians no longer obey the Mosaic injunction against eating pork; they blithely eat pigflesh and increasingly so do Jews, even in Israel; so there is a danger of cross-contamination, or else of pigflesh being inadvertently fobbed off on unsuspecting Muslims. Masri also admonishes Muslims against buying flesh from Jewish slaughterers because they run the risk of buying inferior meat, such as the hindquarters of animals that haven't been *porged* (had their nerves and veins removed) — or spent hens (hens that are past their egg-laying prime) that the Jewish slaughterers consider unfit for Jewish consumption.[22]

According to Masri, Islam recognizes that all animals have psychic force, even if they don't have full-blown human souls;[23] therefore, Islam imbues animals with more spiritual significance than does orthodox Christianity, which hasn't yet conceded that animals have souls. Nonetheless, it is debatable whether Muslims treat animals any better than do their Jewish or Christian cousins.

Another positive influence of Islam has been the inhibiting effect that it has had on cynophagy, or the eating of dogflesh in the lands (from North Africa as far as Bahrain) where Islam holds sway. Prior to the Islamic takeover in these regions, dog had been a highly prized food item. According to Planhol, in Djerba dogs fattened on dates were favored by women who wanted to acquire a plumpness that was much admired by the natives.[24] Islam was instrumental in banning this practice, not alas because it was intrinsically inhumane, but rather because the dog is considered to be an unclean beast, *haram* — an unfit food for human consumption. Would that the reasons for the ban had been more humane! But in this case the end very much justifies the means. To the pet-owning cynophile, the very idea of eating dogflesh is abhorrent; yet surely, it is no worse than hippophagy (horse meat is a Belgian delicacy), taurophagy (eating mangled cow's flesh in the form of hamburgers is an All-American pastime), or even anthropophagy. As the vegetarian, Bronson Alcott (father of Louisa May), once jocularly remarked to Ralph Waldo Emerson when he visited the Saturday Club, "If we are to eat flesh, Mr. Emerson, why not eat of the best?" Indeed longpig or human flesh was a delicacy in many south sea islands. Doubtless if those countries were under Muslim sway, "longpig" would have been considered an unclean flesh on the same grounds that pigflesh is considered unclean.

Muslims are such voracious flesh-eaters, like the other "People of the Book," that it would be all-too-easy to be pessimistic about the prospect of their becoming ethical vegetarians. But the example of Al-Hafiz B.A. Masri is cause for hope. Masri, a Muslim theologian who had committed the Quran to memory (the name Hafiz denotes one who has memorized the Quran), converted to vegetarianism for ethical reasons and worked tirelessly to persuade his fellow Muslims to reexamine their attitude towards animals and to try to get them to rediscover in the Quran and the *Hadith* the zoophile teachings of the founding Prophet, for whom, like Jesus, a case can be made for his having been an ethical vegetarian. ☾

R.B.

• • • • • • • • • • •

[1] Joseph Gaer, *How the Great Religions Began* (New York: Signet, 1958), p. 194.

[2] H.A.R. Gibb, *Mohammedanism: An Historical Survey* (London: Oxford University Press, 1962), p. 46.

[3] Maxime Rodinson, *Mohammed* (New York: Pantheon, 1971), p. 39.

[4] Al-Hafiz B.A. Masri, *Animals in Islam* (Petersfield: The Athena Trust, 1987), p. 23.

[5] Rodinson, p. 61.

[6] Masri, *op. cit.*, p. 121.

[7] Narrated by Abu Malik on the authority of his father. Abu Dawud and Tirmidhi as recorded in *Garden of the Righteous-Riyad as Salihin of Imam Nawawi*; translated by M. Z. Khan, Curzon Press, London, 1975; (hereafter referred to as Riyad); Hadith No. 815, p. 160.

[8] Narrated by Abdullah bin 'Omar. Bukhari and Muslim. [Recorded in Riyad]

[9] Narrated by Abdullah bin Abbas. Bukhari, Muslim, Tirmidhi and Abu al Darda; recorded in Riyad (ref. no. 28); Hadith No. 1606; p. 271. Also, 'Robson' (Ref. No. 15); p. 876.

[10] Narrated by Abu Umana. Transmitted by Al-Tabarani.

[11] Masri, *op. cit.*, p. 26.

[12] Margaret Smith, *The Way of the Mystics* (New York: Oxford University Press, 1978), pp. 154-62.

[13] Idries Shah, *The Sufis* (New York: Doubleday, 1964), pp. 33-55.

[14] Gibb, *op. cit.*, p. 37.

[15] Charles J. Addams "Islam" in *Religions of the World: From Primitive Beliefs to Modern Faiths*, ed. Geoffrey Parrinder (New York: Grosset & Dunlap, 1971), p. 392.

[16] Steven Rosen, *Food for the Spirit* (New York: Bala Books, 1987), p. 59.

[17] A.C. Bouquet, *Comparative Religion* (Harmondsworth: Penguin, 1962), p. 283

[18] Masri, *op. cit.*, p. 118.

[19] *ibid.*, pp. 114-125.

[20] Xavier de Planhol, *The World of Islam* (Ithaca: Cornell University Press, 1979), p. 57.

[21] *ibid.*, p. 65.

[22] Masri, *op. cit.*, pp. 140-6.

[23] *ibid.*, p. 11.

[24] Planhol, *op. cit.*, p. 59.

Conversation/Islam

....

DR. REHANA HAMID

D R. REHANA HAMID IS THE daughter of a Jewish mother and a Muslim father. In her person she embodies the hope of peaceful coexistence between these faiths. A devout Sufi, she nonetheless has studied Judaism and is currently reading the Torah in Hebrew. She began her Sufi training under the guidance of Shaikh Muzaffer Ozak, head of the Turkish-based Halveti-Jerrahi order of dervishes. She is also a member of the Bawa Muhaiyaddeen Fellowship, founded by Shaikh M.R. Bawa Muhaiyaddeen, with whom she also studied for many years. When I visited Dr. Hamid in Philadelphia, she took time off from her thriving chiropractic center to give me a tour of the Fellowship's beautiful mosque. Carefully removing my shoes and bathing my feet and hands, I took part in the prayer service that was being led by the Imam. After the service, the other worshippers and I hugged each other and clasped hands. Although we were of different nationalities and races and had been together but a short time, I was moved by the fellow feeling and camaraderie that had sprung up among us. We then descended to a dining area where the staff were bustling about in the kitchen preparing a bountiful Sufi repast. My mouth watered at the delicious odors wafting from the

....
255

kitchen. Would I care to stop for lunch? I was sorely tempted, but there was work to be done, and Dr. Hamid had to get back to her patients; so Dr. Hamid and I returned to her office where she sat for this interview while plying me with tofu burgers and other treats in a further demonstration of hospitality for which the Sufis are noted.

....

BERRY: Perhaps I should start by asking you what Sufism is.

HAMID: The term "Sufism" normally refers to Islamic mysticism, but there are more esoteric definitions. One that I like defines Sufism as perfect purity. It's the state when God is in the seeker and the seeker is in God. They exist in Unity. From that point of view, Sufism is no longer an exclusively Muslim experience, but is available to people of all faiths, although it's commonly studied within the beauty of the Islamic religion. In light of all this, I'm sure you will understand when I say I would rather be called a student, a beginning student, of Sufism, not a Sufi.

BERRY: As I understand it, there are two main etymologies for the word "Sufi." Some scholars derive it from the Greek word for wisdom, *sophia*. Others derive it from the Arabic word *suf*, which means "wool." To my way of thinking, as a vegan who eschews wearing wool and other animal products, the derivation of the term "Sufi" from the Greek adjective *sophos* would seem to be more fitting for such a venerable mystical tradition. How do you feel about that?

HAMID: It depends on how you look at it. True wisdom is very important, of course, but according to scholars the "wool" derivation is a reference to the plain woolen garment many Sufis used to wear. This is akin to the simple habit worn by a monk. In Sufism you are not trying to become more, you're trying to become less, so there will be more room for God in your life.

BERRY: So wool is a more humble fabric?

HAMID: That plain garment is an expression of simplicity and humility. I think that most Sufis would find humility a more elevated quality than the wisdom that the world recognizes.

BERRY: Would it sound pretentious to say that "the term for my faith derives from wisdom"?

HAMID: Well, I think you'll find that people who have real wisdom don't go around saying so. I know that scholars love to debate the derivation of this word, but it's much more important to understand the state of being that it refers to.

BERRY: Isn't there another term sometimes used to describe Sufis — a dervish?

HAMID: Dervish is a word used, at least in my experience, much more commonly than "Sufi." It also refers to the seeker on the Sufi path. I was taught that the word also refers to the doorstep or threshold of a door, upon which everyone steps as he or she goes in or out. This was used as another example of the true humility that the dervish needs.

BERRY: The Sufi scholar, Idries Shah, in his book *The Sufis*, says that the Sufis as the curators of ancient Mediterranean spiritual culture were seeking protection under the aegis of a militant Islam; in other words, the Sufis as curators of ancient Mediterranean spiritual knowledge attached themselves to Islam, much as in the sixth century BC, the other Greek city states allied themselves with Athens — for protection against the threat of an invasion from Persia.

HAMID: It is difficult to imagine Sufis being afraid of anyone or anything other than God. If you are speaking of Islam as a political institution, it's ludicrous to think that it could be a protection for masters of wisdom. It's really the other way around. In all places and at all times the people who are repositories of inner knowledge are a manifestation of mercy for everyone else in society. They guard the fountainhead of truth that enlivens religion or faith. They protect the path to realization that exists within every religion, and that is in fact the reason for religion's existence. So it is not the organized religious structure of Islam that offers protection to the Sufis; it is the mystical truth within the religion, which the Sufis help to preserve, that is the real protecting and sustaining force.

BERRY: Muslims are supposed to eat only *halal* meat. Can you explain what *halal* meat is?

HAMID: *Halal* meat is meat that is obtained by lawful means from animals who are slaughtered in the name of God. They must be killed in a humane manner. One must show respect for the animal, killing it swiftly with a very sharp knife, and afterwards the blood must be removed, since it is considered spiritually harmful to eat. This is very close to Jewish kosher meat, and in fact many Muslims do eat Jewish kosher meat, considering it to be *halal*.

BERRY: Bawa Muhaiyaddeen, one of your Sufi teachers, has an even more exacting definition, doesn't he?

HAMID: Yes. Bawa Muhaiyaddeen taught that in addition to all the careful measures required by Islamic law to minimize the suffering of the animal, you must look in the animal's eyes as you slaughter it, and continue gazing into its eyes until the life has gone out of it.

BERRY: But isn't that an oblique way of prohibiting the slaughter of animals altogether? How many people are willing to look into the eyes of an animal, cut its throat, and keep looking into its eyes until the life goes out of it? There would be damn few meat-eaters if they had to do that every time they ate a cheeseburger.

HAMID: Careless, thoughtless, and unconscionable action is one of the things that causes so much suffering in our world, and conscious action would make a big difference. This is the way to slaughter an animal consciously. You can't look into that creature's eyes without understanding what you are doing, taking full responsibility for it.

BERRY: What about you? How did you become a vegetarian?

HAMID: I became one gradually, over the past twenty years. I didn't call myself a vegetarian, I just wasn't eating meat. It probably began when I was growing up. We didn't have much meat in the house for economic reasons, and I never much liked it anyway. I did notice, by eating it sometimes, that not eating meat made me feel lighter and more sensitive.

BERRY: Perhaps you were experiencing what Milan Kundera calls the "lightness of being." It's interesting that in his book *The*

Unbearable Lightness of Being, he says that Mankind's true moral test "consists of its attitude towards those who are at its mercy: the animals."

HAMID: Well, being "light and sensitive" is not always a good thing, unless you have a strong, stable foundation too. Luckily, about fifteen years ago I began my training in a traditional Sufi context. Sufism is a very comprehensive system that develops one's sensitivity and is "grounding" at the same time. It provides a touchstone with which to test the world. You start to learn what is real and what is not, what is important and what is not. That is true grounding. This carries over to everyday experiences when you realize that each moment provides a range of choices. Spiritual work is an attempt to disengage from the pull of one's own automatic or elemental urges. If you try to live with God's qualities such as Compassion, Patience and Faithfulness as your first reference, each moment's choices become different. Some are good for your life and some are not. That's where the sensitivity comes in. You have to use the touchstone.

Sufism teaches to regard all other lives as if they were our own; to feel the hunger and pain of other beings as our own suffering. We should feel this unity with all people, but also with every other being created by God. Gradually one becomes attuned to the experiences of all the other lives around us. Feeling this way about other creatures, it's more difficult to slaughter and eat them. When I began studying Sufism, that consciousness very slowly started to develop.

BERRY: Was that process helped along by the fact that one of your teachers, Bawa Muhaiyaddeen, was himself a vegetarian?

HAMID: I would say that by proximity to each of my spiritual teachers, I was able to experience the quality of God's true compassion. By gaining a taste of that, I was better able to recognize it and search for it within myself. This may result in one's becoming a vegetarian but it begins with the quality of compassion.

One of the things that is characteristic of the Sufis is that you can't easily characterize them. Sufism always presents its truth in a manner appropriate to each time, place and person. My first teacher, Shaikh Muzaffer Ozak Efendi, was an exemplary Sufi, but not a vegetarian. He did say, however, that it was better not to eat excessive amounts of meat, because it could interfere with our spiritual work. My second teacher, Shaikh M. R. Bawa Muhaiyaddeen, was a vegetarian, and recommended a vegetarian diet to many of his students; however, there were occasions when he actually prescribed meat for certain individuals.

BERRY: Sufi masters go by the title *shaikh*. What does the word mean exactly?

HAMID: We understand it to refer to a spiritual teacher or guide.

BERRY: In my interview with Steven Rosen, he made the point that the esoteric, mystical traditions of the Semitic-revelatory religions, such as Christianity, Judaism and Islam, tend to be vegetarian. For instance, it is the mystics in the Christian tradition who are vegetarians—St. Simeon Stylites, St. Theresa of Avila, St. John of the Cross, and others were vegetarians. Whereas the followers of the exoteric tradition tend to be non-vegetarian. He seemed to feel that this would also apply to Sufism. In other words, one would be apt to find more vegetarians among the Sufis because they are the esoteric, or mystical, branch of Islam. On the other hand, in the Eastern religions such as Buddhism, Hinduism, Taoism, Jainism, and so on, the followers of the exoteric tradition—the average layman—tend to be vegetarian. With this in mind, I'm wondering if the esoteric tradition of Islam—the Sufis—hasn't borne out this hypothesis? In other words, do the Sufis tend to be vegetarian?

HAMID: In Sufism, there is no real, clear-cut line between the esoteric and exoteric traditions. They are part of one continuum, and people travel this continuum in a myriad of ways. Everything that is taught in Sufism can be found within the traditional religion of Islam. It is quite possible for an "orthodox" Muslim to reach the highest mystical truth without ever having heard of Sufism, and many, many people on the Sufi path are extremely orthodox in their religious practices. One can make certain distinctions for the sake of academic discussion, but in practice these distinctions are much more blurred. So it is very difficult to answer your question. I could not say that people on the Sufi path tend to be vegetarian as a generalization. If in fact you find more vegetarians among Muslims with a predilection for mysticism, and I'm not sure that you do, I would

have to speculate about the reasons. The intense focus on the cultivation of inner qualities that we discussed before may lead to vegetarianism in some people, but you find this focus in orthodox Islam
as well as in Sufism. Many people strongly associate the religion of
Islam with the Arab culture and adopt things Arab with great zeal.
There is nothing inherently Muslim about wearing a long robe, for
instance, except that it is modest, and provides good protection
against the sun in hot climates. Some people may develop an attach-
ment to what they perceive as Arab cuisine, including meat, because
for them it is part of the flavor of Islam. Actually, Islam is a state of
purity that is not limited to any one time or place. It is possible that
people on the Sufi path would be less susceptible to these cultural
overlays, because they are always seeking the inner meaning of
something that is reflected in external form.

BERRY: I guess they're also more self-sufficient; more secure in
their beliefs?

HAMID: Well, no, orthodox people have very deep faith and
strong beliefs, too, but I think mysticism attracts people who have
questions. They feel compelled to penetrate through the outer
layer of anything. In fact it is an infinite process of continuing to
push through the veils until there is no one left to do the pushing.

BERRY: The four Eastern religions—Taoism, Jainism, Buddhism
and Hinduism—that urge a vegetarian diet, also propound a doctrine of reincarnation. The two—vegetarianism and reincarnationism—would seem to be complementary, because if a person believes
that the spirit of a departed friend or relative may inhabit the body
of an animal, then he would never acquire a taste for animal flesh;
since Sufism is the mystical branch of Islam, I'm wondering if there
isn't a latent doctrine of reincarnation within Sufism?

HAMID: I've heard Sufi teachers speak about reincarnation in
only the most oblique manner. What they usually stress is how
singular and rare a privilege it is to have a human birth, and how
one should not waste the opportunity it affords.

BERRY: So, it sounds as if there is a tacit belief in reincarnation
within Sufism.

HAMID: It varies from group to group. I've noticed that some groups discuss it more openly and specifically than others.

BERRY: There's a well-known story in the Sufi canon, which is supposedly true, in which the fifteenth century Egyptian Sultan al-Ashraf Qatbay was visited by the famous Sufi Shaikh al-Dashtuti. They fell into a heated argument in which the sultan poohpoohed the idea that Muhammad could have traveled to all seven heavens on his winged steed in a single night. The Sufi *shaikh* retorted by reaching over and grabbing the sultan by the scruff of his neck and plunging his head into a bowl of water for a minute. When the spluttering sultan raised his head from the bowl, he said that he had experienced several alternative lifetimes within a few seconds. That the sultan had experienced several lifetimes within the space of a minute, wouldn't this suggest an implicit belief in reincarnation within Sufism?

HAMID: Well, to me it would more suggest that time is a fleeting illusion—and so is all of this.

BERRY: So what do you make of it all?

HAMID: (*laughter*) I'll let you know when I'm at the end of the story. But to answer your original question about whether a belief in reincarnation has engendered vegetarianism among Sufis, I must say in all candor that I don't know anyone on the Sufi path who is a vegetarian for that reason.

BERRY: What is the reason then?

HAMID: I think everyone's path is unique, and of course each person's reasons will be different. For some it will have to do with the cultivation of inner qualities such as compassion, which we discussed before. For others it may have to do with following the teacher's example. This is an important concept in Sufism. The relationship between *shaikh* and disciple is a very special one. When you meet your *shaikh*, your heart is stricken with a love that is not emotional, but it is overwhelming. It is a love that goes beyond the personal.

BERRY: So, naturally, you want to imitate the *shaikh* and be as much like him or her as possible. If your *shaikh* is an ethical vegetarian like Bawa Muhaiyaddeen, then, naturally, you'd want to be one too.

HAMID: I would like to be as much like him as possible. I want to stress again, however, that a person's inner qualities are even more important than the outer form they adhere to. That is the part of Bawa Muhaiyaddeen I try to emulate. Some people are strict vegetarians but think nothing of chewing the flesh of their fellow human beings by slandering, and backbiting, or savaging them in some other way. Some people are so lacking in human qualities that if they eat meat, it is as Bawa Muhaiyaddeen puts it, "just one animal eating another." The main thing is not to "be" something just because of an idea, but to have one's actions emanate from an inner truth.

BERRY: Since the great Sufi thinker, Ibn-Arabi, had two female *shaikhs*, to whom he said he owed everything, isn't it worth noting that female *shaikhs* are not uncommon in Sufism?

HAMID: There have been and still are many female *shaikhs*. In the world of spiritual science there are no distinctions between male and female.

BERRY: When I was in the Sufi mosque taking part in the prayers this afternoon, I was struck by the sense of bonhomie and fellow feeling that came over the group, especially when we all embraced at the end of the prayers. The sense of tactile bonding is missing from the services in Western churches, where physical contact is discouraged.

HAMID: Yes, that's too bad, because I think that people would like it very much.

BERRY: Another thing that's missing from the Western churches is the communion meal that congregants share in the four Asian religions that advocate vegetarianism. The blood and wafer of the Eucharist is a poor substitute for the rich vegetarian meal that used to accompany the Mass prior to the end of the Middle Ages when the Mazdean ritual of blood and wafer were substituted for it.

HAMID: Although food is not a required element in most of our activities, there's a joke among us that where you find the Sufis gathered, you'll never go hungry. Food seems to flow abundantly when we gather together. The embracing after prayers and looking into each other's eyes; the sharing of food; these are all opportunities to put what we've been taught into action. It's also an honor to prepare and serve food for others. It's an irony of the spiritual path that the more you serve, the more you receive. The few times that I have truly attempted to serve, or have been permitted to serve, were the fullest, richest, most rewarding times of my life.

BERRY: You were saying earlier that the kitchen is a very important place in Sufism.

HAMID: Yes, in the traditional Sufi orders, you're not even permitted to enter the kitchen if you're a neophyte. It takes many years before you're considered qualified to perform even a menial task in the kitchen. To be permitted to cook and serve is considered an honor.

BERRY: That's fascinating, because when I posed a similar question to Philip Kapleau Roshi about the *tenzo*, or cook, in the Zen monastery kitchen in Japan, he said very much the same thing: to be a *tenzo* in the Zen kitchen is a very high honor. Kapleau Roshi himself was never allowed to be a *tenzo* because he hadn't yet reached the requisite level of spiritual attainment. It was thought that he might spoil the food by transmitting the wrong sort of psychic vibrations into it.

HAMID: Yes, in many groups it's preferred that a person of spiritual maturity prepare the food.

BERRY: Isn't that what's missing from Western religions, and Western culture generally? Our food has been so desacralized and deadened that people can't tell the difference between dead flesh and vegetables. On the other hand, in cultures that invest their food with spiritual value, more vegetarian food is consumed—perhaps it's because vegetarian food in those cultures is perceived as being fit for the gods.

HAMID: The Sufi gathering place is like an enormous kitchen in which we seek to feed the inner hunger of people's lives—spiritually as well as physically. Many Sufi communities make it a practice to serve food to the hungry on festival days, or after the congregational prayer on Fridays. Bawa Muhaiyaddeen used to feed hundreds of people at a time with food he had cooked with his own hands.

BERRY: Judging from his recipe book, *The Tasty Economical Cookbook*, he must have been a very talented cook.

HAMID: His food was wonderful. He fed us and comforted our hearts at the same time. A fully developed human being knows how to do many things just right—cooking, carpentry, doctoring, sewing, farming. With these talents he cared for us as both a mother and a father.

BERRY: That reminds me of the remark by Yamuna Devi, author of *Lord Krishna's Cuisine,* that the Vaishnava sect of Hinduism is often referred to as "the kitchen religion."

HAMID: (*laughter*) From what I've been taught, that would be a compliment.

BERRY: When Swami Prabhupada, the founder of the International Krishna Consciousness Movement, came to America from India in 1965, he attracted his earliest followers with his prowess as a chef.

HAMID: The wonderful aromas coming from the kitchen can be a great comfort to the spiritual seeker who is crossing the threshold. Everyone comes to the spiritual path because deep in their being they are longing for truth, but sometimes our mind is not quite in step with the rest of us. Our mind may tell us we are here because we're hungry and we want a meal, or we're lonely and want company; and for a time these things help to occupy and please the mind, until it starts to become aware of the greater sustenance that is being received.

BERRY: It's like that old adage that the way to a man's heart is through his stomach.

HAMID: Yes, and which of us doesn't live through his stomach?

BERRY: It's curious that Swami Prabhupada and Bawa Muhaiyaddeen both devoted themselves to preparing tasty vegetarian meals for their students.

HAMID: The true spiritual leader in a group is always a servant. You'll remember that in Herman Hesse's book *Journey to the East,* the servant was in fact the spiritual leader. A *shaikh* or *guru* will fuss and fret over his or her charges like a mother. Just like a mother, they will want to feed them with their own hands, or as Bawa Muhaiyaddeen puts it, from their own breast with the milk of compassion. Feeding is a natural extension of wanting to give their spiritual children every type of goodness so that they can grow into the finest human beings possible. They will give their last drop of blood and even their last breath to this end.

BERRY: Could you tell me about the famous cauldron in Ajmeer?

HAMID: Ajmeer is a town in Rajasthan in northern India where the tomb of a great Sufi saint Moinaddin Chisti is. It has become a place of pilgrimage for those seeking his blessing. They have a huge cauldron there the size of a room, out of which they serve food to multitudes of hungry people after the prayers on Fridays. Feeding the hungry is considered a sacred activity in Islam. There is a lot of blessing dispensed with the food, so it nourishes both body and soul. It's good to remember where our true sustenance comes from. It's not from the food that we eat; it is from God's constant outpouring of love and grace.

BERRY: The Sufis must feel singularly well-blessed and well-nourished. It's refreshing to see members of a religion who not only don't deny themselves the pleasures of the table, but positively revel in them. For the most part, I think Christians tend to feel that eating is a guilty pleasure; food is something that's to be enjoyed—if at all—surreptitiously. On the other hand, in view of the high flesh content of the diet of Christians in the West, perhaps there is good reason for Christians to feel ashamed of their eating habits. What about Muhammad? Was he a vegetarian?

HAMID: The only way to know for sure is to go and ask him.

BERRY: How? With mediums? Seers? Clairvoyants?

HAMID: No, I'm quite serious. There are people of spiritual station who have been able to meet the prophet Muhammad and the other prophets and saints. But if you should ever have the extraordinary good fortune to meet him, that would have to be your burning question. You could ask him if he was a vegetarian.

BERRY: What about your own *shaikh*, Bawa Muhaiyaddeen? Was he not a man of spiritual station?

HAMID: Yes.

BERRY: In reading Steve Rosen's interview with Bawa Muhaiyaddeen I got the impression that he believes the Prophet was a vegetarian. (Reads): "Steve Rosen: 'Would it be correct then to assume that the Prophet Muhammad, being the perfect Muslim, must have abstained from eating meat?'

Bawa Muhaiyaddeen: 'I have not seen him eating meat. I really do not know what he ate: perhaps two or three dates and a handful of rice. If he had a handful of rice, he would have kept it aside, and if someone came who was poor and hungry, he would give it to them. If no one came, then they would cook the rice along with whatever greens they might have, and again they would wait; if anyone came who was hungry, they would be served first. If no one came, only then would the Prophet eat a few dates and the food that had been cooked. No one has ever seen the feces or urine of the Prophet. No one has seen him defecating or doing any such thing—God only knows. Let us not be concerned whether he ate or not. One thing is for certain, he never had any thought of killing another being.'

"'Prophet Muhammad (Sal.) advised his son-in-law, Ali (Ral.), "O Ali, abstain from eating flesh for forty days consecutively. If you eat meat for forty days at a stretch, your heart will become as hard as stone; you will not have any compassion. Therefore, refrain from eating any flesh." He advised his son-in-law privately in many matters like this. He could not have advised everyone in this way, for they would not have listened.'

"Bawa Muhaiyaddeen went on to explain that because the Prophet could not forbid the killing of animals for food altogether, he greatly reduced the number killed by placing many restrictions and conditions on exactly how animals were to be slaughtered. For example, the person must look into the eyes of the animal he is about to kill. When he sees the tears in its eyes, he too will cry. He will realize that he doesn't want to do this anymore. 'The people had to understand this for themselves. They could not have been taught in any other way. Once the person reaches the right state he will give up these things.'"

HAMID: In Sufism, and Islam in general, the Prophet Muhammad is considered to be the ultimate example of beautiful and conscious behavior. An entire spiritual practice is built around emulating his behavior, called *adab*. There are people who scrupulously try to do everything the way they think he did it, from small things, like drinking a glass of water, to greater things, like the way he practiced charity, or the way he prayed. Emulating the outer actions does result in developing consciousness—the consciousness that very naturally results in beautiful behavior. Anyone would benefit from emulating the Prophet. Someone who sees all lives the way God does, with His eyes of Compassion, will feel those lives as his or her own. The Prophet's kindness to animals is an extension of this quality, which was also extended to all people, even those who came to attack him. People block out so much. They ignore other creatures, and even other fellow human beings; but people with consciousness cannot do this.

There is another classical Sufi analogy that comes to mind concerning the kitchen. In this kitchen—which is the Sufi school—the real thing that's being cooked is the *dervish* (student). The dervish has to be cooked like a chick-pea until it is soft and can be smashed and dissolved into the stew. Loud are the complaints of the chick-pea as it is boiling away in the pot. Heated conversation takes place between the chick-pea and the cook. There are many elaborate Sufi stories and poems on this theme.

BERRY: Isn't it painful being dissolved into the stew?

HAMID: Yes. (*laughter*) Not very vegetarian, is it? Once you are on the spiritual path and the honeymoon phase is over, there is a period of acute discomfort when you begin to be cooked, and all your unattractive qualities boil to the surface. My first *shaikh*, Muzaffer Efendi, said that in the beginning the spiritual path is very painful, but later on it gets easier. I think what he meant by that is in the beginning you think all of your attachments are so important, so it is painful to be separated from them. Later on, the remaining attachments you're only too glad to be rid of because they separate you from God. It may still hurt, but it's a relief too, and you're grateful for it.

BERRY: Your individuality dissolves.

HAMID: Losing your individuality doesn't mean you become an automaton. You don't lose your personality or uniqueness as a creation of God. You retain that beauty, but inside there is no busy-ness, no resistance, no insistence; only a beautiful open space where God is.

BERRY: And the *shaikh* is the cook?

HAMID: Yes, the *shaikh* acts as God's hands and stirs the stew.

BERRY: Harking back to what Kapleau Roshi said, it's the mature, fully developed human being who makes the best sort of cook.

HAMID: Yes, I think that type of human being does make the best sort of cook.

······································

PROTESTANT CHRISTIANITY

ALTHOUGH HUNDREDS OF Protestant denominations sprang up after Martin Luther had nailed his 95 Theses to the door of the church in Wittenberg, the only founder of a major Protestant denomination before the nineteenth century who was a quasi-vegetarian was John Wesley. He had vegetarian tendencies, but confided them only to his diary. To a man, all the other founders of Protestant denominations were carnivores; none more so than Luther himself, who was plagued by gout and constipation. He achieved his moment of deepest spiritual illumination while seated puffing and straining on the monastery privy[1]—doubtless brought on by the meat-rich monastery fare. However, in 1809 a Swedenborgian minister with the improbably bovine name of The Reverend William Cowherd started the first modern vegetarian church—the Bible Christian Church in Salford England. He had become a vegetarian after steeping himself in the mystical writings of Jacob Boehme and Emmanual Swedenborg, who asserted that eating flesh was an evil that had caused the fallen state of humankind. From his Swedenborgian pulpit, Reverend Cowherd preached

vegetarianism and harmlessness to animals. After his congregation balked at the vegetarian message, in 1809, Cowherd started
his own church—the Bible Christian Church, in the town of Salford, near Manchester. By coincidence, Cowherd had a son-in-law
with the no less improbable bovine name of the Reverend William
Metcalfe. In 1817, Cowherd charged his son-in-law with the mission
of transplanting a branch of the Bible Christians to American soil
with the object of converting the flesh-eating heathen of North
America to a civilized diet. So it was that with 41 other Cowherdites,
Metcalfe set sail that same year for Philadelphia, where he founded
the North American branch of the Bible Christian Church—the first
vegetarian church to be planted on American soil. (Despite the prophecies by its detractors of an early demise, the Church survived
into the early twentieth century.)

At first, the Cowherdites' reception in the Quaker city of broth-
erly love, Philadelphia, was decidedly chilly; other clergymen had
not yet perceived the connection between vegetarianism and pacifism, and the Cowherdites' message made them feel morally shab-
by—more like cannibals than Christians. They did their utmost to
persuade the Bible Christians to quit Philadelphia and go back to
England. But Metcalfe refused to budge; he continued to thunder
vegetarian homilies from the pulpit, and to write newspaper articles in which he argued vigorously for a principled vegetarianism.

For many years his efforts seemed to be unavailing, but in 1830 he
was successful in converting two prominent Americans to the vegetarian cause. The first was Dr. William Alcott, MD, cousin to Bronson Alcott (whom he converted), founder of Fruitlands, the first
vegetarian commune in North America, and father of the redoubtable Louisa May Alcott. Not long after hearing Metcalfe's sermons,
William Alcott gave up eating flesh and became the first practicing
vegetarian physician in North America. In his long medical career,
he wrote numerous books and treatises advocating a vegetarian diet.

Metcalfe's other illustrious convert was himself a Protestant minister, and no mean pulpit orator—the Reverend Sylvester Graham.
Although people tend to think of vegetarianism as a secular movement, the fact that Graham, a Presbyterian minister, launched the

modern health food reform movement in America and that his mentor Metcalfe initiated the first religious vegetarian society in America—the Bible Christian Church in 1817—is evidence of an underlying connection between diet and religion. (Reverend Metcalfe also instigated the founding of the first secular vegetarian society in America, the American Vegetarian Society, which was started in New York City in the year 1850.)

It is significant that Graham's reforms started with bread, which the commercial bakers were adulterating with stretchers, such as pipe-clay, alum and plaster of Paris. The result was a bread that was devitalized and devoid of nutrients. What did they do with the nutrients? With the bolting cloth, which because it rendered bread fiberless and nutritionally dead Graham predicted would be "the shroud of America," they filtered out the bran and other vital nutrients and sold them to the distillers who worked their wicked alchemy to convert them into grain alcohol—Graham's other *bête noire*. The religious symbolism of bread, particularly in the Western church where it has been transmuted into a symbol of Christ's body, need not be overstressed here. In a sense the bakers were defiling Christ's body; the distillers his blood; and the butchers in slaughtering the innocent, perhaps reenacting the Crucifixion. Perhaps that is why—in Boston, the scene of one of his most riotous speeches—Graham denounced the butchers and bakers as murderers and the doctors as vampires. He saw food reform as a holy crusade, as did another full-blown Protestant sect founded in this period—the Seventh-Day Adventists.

Inspired by Ellen White's health reform prophecy in 1863, the Seventh Day Adventists soon started to urge a vegetarian diet. It's no coincidence that the social historian Gerald Carson called his 1956 best-selling book about the Seventh-Day Adventists' invention of the cornflake, *The Cornflake Crusade*. Dr. John Harvey Kellogg, the protégé of Ellen White, was helping to fulfill her vision at Otsego (in which she divined that God had intended humans to be vegetarians) when he invented cornflakes. His other food inventions—peanut butter and ersatz meats made from wheat gluten, peanuts, and soy— were also designed to wean Americans from animal flesh as part of the Adventists' vegetarian crusade. Thus, such all-American food products as cornflakes and peanut butter, while seemingly secular, have their genesis in a religious movement.

Competing with cornflakes were other cereals of the period that were given such biblical-sounding names as "Elijah's Manna" (a cornflake counterfeit that was marketed by the C.W. Post Company and which later became Post Toasties); and let us not forget Quaker Oats, along with Quaker Puffed Oats and Quaker Puffed Rice. It's interesting that two quasi-religious food companies invented the cereal-flaking and the cereal-puffing process respectively—as though they were trying to transubstantiate a savior in a cereal bowl. Quakers, while not vegetarians, did boast some early vegetarian reformers like the abolitionist Benjamin Lay, but it's curious that it has taken the Quakers an unconscionably long time to perceive the connection between pacifism and vegetarianism. (Still only a small percentage of Quakers are vegetarians even now!)

Although the Adventists have since fallen away from their strict vegetarianism—it's reckoned that 50% of their congregation are now meat-eaters—strangely enough, they've kept their missionary zeal for promoting vegetarianism in foreign parts, with the result that many European and Asian cities boast Adventist vegetarian restaurants. Nonetheless, the Adventists are still something of an anomaly among Protestants.

More typically Protestant is the Anglican Episcopal Church of England, or The Episcopal Church as it is known in America and Canada. The Episcopal Church takes its name from the Greek word *episkopos* (bishop), because religious authority is invested in the bishops of the Church who claim that they are the spiritual successors to Christ's twelve apostles. Founded by that great trencherman Henry VIII, the Anglican Episcopal Church has spawned a number of brilliant but gourmandizing divines, as it were, in the image of their founder. One such was the Reverend Sidney Smith who liked to boast of his meat-eating: "Did I ever tell you my calculation. I found that between ten and seventy years of age, I had eaten and drunk over forty-four horse-wagon loads of meat and drunk more than would have preserved me in life and health...It occurred to me that I must by my voracity, have starved to death nearly a hundred persons."[2] Dietetically as well as ethically, the progress from the Reverend Sidney Smith to the Reverend Andrew Linzey is from the bathetic to the sublime. For years, in his books such as *Christianity and the Rights of Animals* and *Animal Theology* and in his teachings as the first animal-rights fellow at Oxford University, Andrew Linzey has been debunking the Aristotelian-Thomist view of animals that has perverted the attitude of the Church towards animals for a millennium and more.

Through the dark, distorted glass of scholastic theology the Church regards animals as having no purpose apart from their utilitarian value to humans. It is the Church's policy that animals are incapable of feeling pain and have no souls: this is why Pope Pius IX forbade the setting up of an animal protection office in the Vatican in the nineteenth century. On the contrary, Linzey believes that animals have "Theos-rights," since they were created by God as spirit-filled creatures at the same time that humans were created—on the sixth day. If animals have Theos-rights, then it follows that animals are God's creatures and humans have no right to meddle in their lives, much less to exploit them and to eat them. Moreover, the covenant that God made with Noah after the flood, Linzey argues, includes animals, so they enjoy its prerogatives and protections just like humans.

Like the Nazorean-Ebionites (Jewish Christians of the first to the fourth century CE who regarded Jesus as a vegetarian messiah), Linzey believes that Jesus was the savior for animals as well as for humans, but differs from the anti-sacrificial Ebionites in his belief that Jesus's death on the cross was the ultimate atoning sacrifice. Doubtless such modern Ebionites as The Reverend Dr. Carl Skriver and The Reverend Todd Ferrier would quarrel with Linzey's view that Christ's death was sacrificial, as they would find the whole notion of the atoning sacrifice to be barbaric and abhorrent. They would also fault Linzey's view that invertebrates and insects lack sentiency and that mammals are more deserving of Theos-rights than are other life-forms. (Unlike the Jains, Linzey is cautious about extending Theos-rights to insects, mollusks and other invertebrates.) And of course they would argue with Linzey's belief that Christ was a non-vegetarian who ate fish.[3] Nevertheless, Linzey's views are leagues ahead of other Protestant theologians', like Karl Barth (to name the most prominent), whose theology makes no provision for animals and who views vegetarianism as "a wanton anticipation of the new aeon for which we hope."[4]

In other words, it's hopelessly quixotic and impracticable. However, if Protestant thinkers such as the Reverend Dr. Andrew Linzey begin to exert their influence on the formation of Church doctrine, then they would go some way towards recovering the doctrine of *ahimsa* and nonviolence that was preached by the Jewish vegetarian on whom the faith was founded—Jesus Christ. Then "the new aeon for which we hope" might just become a reality. ✝

R.B.

・・・・・・・・・・・・

[1] Norman O. Brown, *Life Against Death* (Wesleyan: Wesleyan University Press, 1995), p. 109.

[2] Jane Grigson, *Food With the Famous* (New York: Atheneum, 1979), p. 112.

[3] Andrew Linzey, *Christianity and the Rights of Animals* (New York: Crossroad, 1991), p. 47.

[4] Cited in Linzey, *op. cit.*, p. 92.

Conversation/Protestant Christianity

....

REVEREND DR. ANDREW LINZEY

NDER THE INFLUENCE of Aristotelian-Thomist theology the Christian Church has long held that animals have no souls; that they were placed on earth for humans to do with as they pleased. With the exception of a few odd Church fathers such as Origen and Tertullian, saints such as St. Francis of Assisi and desert mystics such as St. Simeon Stylites and St. Anthony the Great, Christians  have been meat-eaters and exploiters of animals for almost 1,500 years. Hopeful signs that the Church may be re-thinking its doctrines and re-discovering its Pythagorean and Gnostic vegetarian roots, are starting to appear. One such harbinger: that as recently as last year, Anglican theologian Andrew Linzey, a specialist in the field of animal rights theology, was the first scholar to be awarded a fellowship in this subject at Mansfield College, Oxford University. This and other propitious happenings — (such as the increase in the number of clergymen becoming vegetarians) — promise well for the Church's adopting a more enlightened view towards animals in the new millennium. Not long after having taken his doctorate in theology from London University, Dr. Linzey wrote a pathbreaking book on the subject of animal theology called *Animal Rights: A Christian Assessment*. As

....

the first book to examine Christian theology from an animal rights perspective, it caused considerable comment in England. In the years since, a stream of other books have issued from his pen with titles that alone speak volumes—such as *Compassion for Animals*; *Christianity and the Rights of Animals*; and *The Status of Animals in Christian Religion*. His book *Animal Theology* is based on a series of lectures that he gave at Oxford. Its thesis is that justice requires a thoroughgoing revision of our treatment of animals, but also, quite specifically, that historical theology creatively expounded also requires this.

When the Reverend Professor Linzey invited me to interview him at his home in Oxford, I wasn't met at the door by a wizened old vicar (as one might have pictured him from the number and heft of the books he has written). On the contrary, although he's gone a touch gray at the temples, he's still an *enfant terrible* of Anglican theology and doubtless still will be when he's wizened and ninety-five. With his penetrating mind and his keen sense of humor, he's just the sort of person needed to breathe new moral life (and not a few gusts of laughter) into the old theology. He's also a compelling speaker, and as he talked into my tape recorder, I lost all sense of time and place. When we'd started, we could see the sun's reflected rays shimmering in the Cherwell River. By the time we'd finished, old *sol* was just beginning to set behind Oxford's dreaming spires.

•••••••••••

BERRY: What prompted you to become a vegetarian?

LINZEY: When I was young I used to keep all kinds of animals in cages. I can't say that I treated my captives very well. Ludicrously, I used to think that they enjoyed my enforced company. Of course, I ate meat and even went fishing for sport. During the time that I did all these things, I would have regarded myself as an animal lover. (One of the reason why I don't like being called an "animal lover" nowadays is that I know how despotic animal lovers can be towards their captives!) Looking back, one of the most significant things that moved me in the vegetarian direction was meeting two Oxford vegetarians—Margery and Arthur Jones—both inspiring people who introduced me to vegetarianism. I began to ask some radical questions about the ethics of our treatment of animals. And because I wanted to be ordained, I continued to ask these questions in a religious context.

BERRY: Did you become a vegetarian prior to your being ordained?

LINZEY: Yes, though the two things are not unrelated. When I was in my teens I had a series of intensely religious experiences. They deepened my sense of God as the Creator of all things. And they also deepened my sensitivity towards creation itself so that concern for God's creatures and animal rights followed from that. Some people think I'm an animal rights person who just happens, almost incidentally, to be religious. In fact, it's because I believe in God that I'm concerned about God's creatures. The religious impulse is primary.

BERRY: What exactly is your status in the Church?

LINZEY: I'm an ordained priest in the Church of England, known as the Episcopal Church in the States. I've been ordained for 20 years. My current job is teaching and researching the issue of theology and animals at Oxford.

BERRY: Are you considered a renegade within the Church of England for holding the views that you do?

LINZEY: I do receive hundreds of letters each year from individuals, many of them Christians, who are deeply concerned about the Church's indifference to animal welfare. Generally all churches are very backward on animals and the Church of England is no exception.

BERRY: Have you exerted any influence on the Church's position with respect to animal rights?

LINZEY: The Church of England is a very liberal, diverse community in which people have a wide range of views on a whole range of issues from sexuality to war. There are some signs of light. For example in 1992, forty-one bishops signed a pledge not to wear fur because of the cruelty inflicted on animals. I'm very proud of the bishops because of their moral stance. But there are also many signs of darkness. For example, I attended the General Synod debate in 1990 about hunting and factory farming on Church-owned land. I came away from the debate feeling deeply depressed—not only because the pro-animal motion was overwhelmingly rejected, but also because there was a lack of theological depth and seriousness with which the whole issue was treated. Anglicans, like most Christians, haven't really woken up to the moral issue of our exploitation of animals.

BERRY: Are there any vegetarian priests in the Church of England?

LINZEY: Some, perhaps a handful; but they tend to be vegetarians as a matter of health rather than on ethical grounds.

BERRY: Do you have anything in the Anglican Church that would correspond to the monastic orders in the Catholic Church?

LINZEY: Yes, we do have various religious communities, including Franciscan and Benedictine ones, but none of them to my knowledge practise vegetarianism, despite what St. Benedict said in his Rule about abstaining from flesh.

BERRY: I've interviewed Brother Ron Pickarski on this subject. He's a Franciscan monk, and he tells me that within the monastic orders of the Catholic Church, vegetarianism is virtually nonexistent. In fact, he was upbraided by members of his order for trying to put vegetarian main dishes on the menu when he was the monastery chef.

LINZEY: Of course, there is an ascetical tradition within Christianity. It is possible to make a strong argument for ethical asceticism in relation to animals, but, alas, most of the ascetical tradition in Christianity has been involved in a way of thinking that can only be called "world denying" rather than "world affirming." It's been concerned with denying creative pleasure—indeed, with denying pleasure itself as a means to some higher spiritual state.

Generally, I think asceticism is an entirely false trail in religion. What I mean by "asceticism" here is: asceticism *for itself*. There is a strong case for "ethical asceticism," that is: denying those things that harm others. But asceticism in itself, I think, is misconceived.

BERRY: But you yourself would probably be considered an ascetic for observing a vegetarian diet by the hearty, beef-eating, pubcrawling British churchgoer.

LINZEY: No one who seriously looks at my lifestyle as an occasional wine imbiber and a regular pipe smoker—not to mention someone who is married with four children—could possibly look at me and say, "Here is an ascetic!"

BERRY: But if they were to take solely your diet into account—they might consider you self-denying in that regard.

LINZEY: I'm reminded of those lines from Karl Barth that asceticism can be as much, if not more so, a vessel for moral evil in the world than sheer self-indulgence. He gives the example of someone who seemed to be a vegetarian, an anti-vivisectionist, a non-smoker, a teetotaler, and who was fastidious about his sexual habits, and, of course, his name is Adolf Hitler.

BERRY: Do you believe that Hitler was a vegetarian?

LINZEY: Roberta Kalechofsky [of Jews for Animal Rights] has re-educated me about the Nazis and their attitude to issues such as anti-vivisectionism in the Weimar Republic. I now think that the earlier claims that Hitler was a vegetarian were probably part of a subsequent propaganda effort to discredit the anti-vivisection movement.

BERRY: Yes. I wrote an article debunking Hitler's vegetarianism, which, I'm pleased to say, drew the approbation of Roberta Kalechofsky. In the article I cited a passage from a cookbook that had been written by a redoubtable European chef, Dione Lucas. On page 89 of *The Gourmet Cooking School Cookbook* (1964), Lucas, drawing on her pre-World War II stint as a hotel chef in Hamburg, remembered being called upon quite often to prepare for Mr. Hitler his favorite dish, which was not a vegetarian one: "I do not mean to spoil your appetite for stuffed squab (pigeon), but you might be interested to know that it was a great favorite with Mr. Hitler, who dined at the hotel often. Let us not hold that against a fine recipe though."

LINZEY: That's a splendid anecdote. It goes to confirm what Roberta told me. But being a vegetarian hardly makes me an ascetic nowadays. When I became a vegetarian 25 or more years ago, I suffered through deprivation simply because most eating establishments failed to cater to vegetarians. I think I ruined my health during my student days because of the poor quality of the food.

BERRY: Did you dine in the college refectory when you were an undergraduate?

LINZEY: Yes. I eked out my life as a vegetarian student with handfuls of nuts and fruit. Years later, it was my wife who with her superb cooking taught me how it was possible to be a gourmet vegetarian. Up until then I'd been a subsistence vegetarian; but she taught me how to enjoy food as one enjoys going to the cinema.

BERRY: In spite of all the textual corruptions and redactions that one finds in the Old Testament, the Genesis sagas have left the vegetarian world largely intact. The first chapters of Genesis really make it plain that God intended humans to be vegetarian. Could you comment on that?

LINZEY: At the heart of the Judeo-Christian tradition is the dream of peace. Many people refer to how humans are given "dominion" in Genesis 1, and that's true; but if you look at the whole saga, in verse 27, humans are made in the image of God; in verse 28, they're given dominion, and in verse 29, they're given a vegetarian diet. Herb-eating dominion is hardly a license for despotism. The original author was seeking to describe a relationship — not of egoistical exploitation — but of care for the earth. It's extraordinary that almost 2,000 years of biblical exegesis should so often have overlooked the radical vegetarian message in Genesis 1.

BERRY: But it's puzzling to me why the biblical editors and exegetes didn't tamper with the early chapters of Genesis, in which primordial man and woman are presented as strict vegetarians.

LINZEY: Yes, though of course it's not only in Genesis, it's in Isaiah as well. Also you had this harking back; now futuristically described as the state in which the lion will lie down with the lamb. So, it's not just in Genesis that you have this idea that peace between all creatures is God's will and that killing runs counter to that will.

BERRY: There's a similar primeval vegetarian world order that exists in Classical literature — in the works of Hesiod, Empedokles, Plato, Ovid, Virgil and Porphyry.

LINZEY: Yes, in Plato's *The Statesman*, it's when humans are given dominion over animals that the relationship degenerates into strife and violence.

BERRY: Plato envisaged the ideal state as being a vegetarian one

LINZEY: In your view, was Plato a vegetarian?

BERRY: Yes, as I point out in my book, *Famous Vegetarians*, Plato and Socrates were Pythagorean philosophers. By definition, Pythagorean philosophers were strict vegetarians.

LINZEY: I certainly regard Plato as one of the world's finest moral teachers. I'm inclined to agree with Whitehead that the whole of Western philosophy is but a footnote to Plato.

BERRY: I wonder if I could posit that ethical vegetarianism in the West is but a footnote to Pythagoras and his prize pupil Plato?

LINZEY: Do you believe that Pythagoras was an ethical vegetarian?

BERRY: I do, yes. If one believes what Ovid had to say about Pythagoras in the fifteenth book of his *Metamorphoses*, then Pythagoras was the *fons et origo* of ethical vegetarianism in the West. According to Ovid, the "Fall" of humans occurred when they began to sacrifice animals to the gods. Likewise, in the Old Testament, doesn't the "Fall" occur when Abel makes a blood sacrifice to Yahweh?

LINZEY: According to traditional Christian theology, the "Fall" happened when Adam and Eve ate of the forbidden fruit and were expelled from the Garden. I'm not sure that I believe in an historical Fall. I think the Genesis narratives reflect an ambivalence about the morality of killing in the sight of God. You need to remember that the Hebrew writers who wrote Genesis were not themselves vegetarians. What they were trying to do was to interpret the world in the light of their moral intuitions of what they thought God wanted, and who they thought God was. Genesis is their poetic narrative of how the world came to be such a desperate and violent place. Their view basically was that God's will was for peace and non-violence between all species, but that human wickedness threw the whole system into chaos—so much so, that God, for example in the saga of Noah, would rather us not exist at all if we must live and be violent.

BERRY: Is that why God destroys the world with a flood?

LINZEY: Yes, God looks at all the violence that humans have brought on the world and says (in Genesis 6:7): "I am sorry that

I have made them [humans]." It's a point of view for which — now and then — I have some sympathy.

BERRY: Besides man, are animals also the object of God's wrath? Do animals share in the expulsion from Paradise and the Fall?

LINZEY: The whole creation suffers as a consequence. Nowadays the Jewish tradition makes a very sharp distinction between humans and animals, but I don't see this sharp distinction in Genesis 9; after all, humans and land animals are created on the same sixth day of creation in Genesis 1. I would say that the surer biblical attitude is that humans and animals are inextricably linked by their creation so that when humans go wrong, the animal creation goes wrong too.

BERRY: Why should humans' Fall drag all the other creatures down with it?

LINZEY: Well, here I think you come to something very fundamental in the Judeo-Christian tradition: that's the idea that human beings are morally the center of the show.

BERRY: Do you believe in an anthropocentric universe?

LINZEY: I think there's a good humanocentrism and a bad humanocentrism. The bad humanocentrism holds that "man" is the measure and master of all things. The good humanocentrism sees humans as the servant species responsible for the divine-like work of looking after the whole earth.

I'm inclined to think that creation can never be set to rights so long as humans are so terribly violent. In that sense the colossal emphasis within the Judeo-Christian tradition on the salvation of human beings makes a lot of sense. My view is that the world of creation, and especially animals, will be redeemed as a matter of course; the only question is whether humans are going to be saved because they are often so faithless and violent.

BERRY: But the fate of animals is inextricably linked with that of humans, isn't it?

LINZEY: I am one of those people who believe that humans need to be saved for the sake of creation itself. We are — in the words that Noah might have uttered — "all in one boat together."

Let me take a practical example — hunting. Hunters often claim that they simply imitate the cruelties of nature. In fact, they frequently intensify whatever violent propensities there may be between animals. Terrier dogs are trained to mutilate other species. Hounds are taught to chase and kill; otherwise they themselves are killed. In many sports, including cock-fighting, bear-baiting, hare-coursing, deer, fox, otter and mink hunting, it is we humans who exacerbate whatever violent antipathies there may be in nature. Humans do not imitate the "cruelties" of nature; they create them.

BERRY: Are you saying that by upsetting the ecological balance, it is man who has made "Nature"—in Herbert Spencer's phrase— "red in tooth and claw"?

LINZEY: I'm open to the view that if human beings were to become less violent in the natural world, then new moral possibilities might be opened up to creation itself.

BERRY: Recently, there was a front-page article in *The Wall Street Journal* about the trend among vegetarians to convert their carnivorous pets to vegetarianism. There is also ample precedent for the larger carnivora, such as lions and bears, becoming vegetarians. The vegan panda, which feeds on bamboo shoots, is an example of a reformed carnivore. In his book *Little Tyke*, the animal trainer Georges Westbeau recounts the poignant, true story of a vegetarian lioness who disdained to eat meat from birth. In my previous book *Famous Vegetarians*, I cited the case of a 700-pound brown bear who could not be coaxed to eat meat. It seems to me that if present trends continue, with human and nonhuman carnivores coming over to vegetarianism, the prophecy set forth in Isaiah 11:1-9 may actually come to pass.

LINZEY: Some of that strikes me as a little fanciful, I'm afraid. But, on the other hand, we know so little about animals and creation. One of my pet peeves is hearing people pontificate about what animals are or are not capable of, because the truth is: we really don't know. All the stuff about animals not having language, not having rational souls, not having culture, not being persons—all these are human constructions; and I'm not sure how far any of these kind of things matter to God even if they *are* true. Part of me wants to ask how can we know that God does not fundamentally value some parts of creation, or regard them as much more intimate with Herself, than human beings? All uniqueness spotting on the part of humans is bound to be self-serving. Christians have been fiendishly good, of course, at drawing lines between humans and the rest of God's creatures.

I think that what we really need is a theocentric view. When we say to ourselves, "Oh, isn't that animal beautiful, or cuddly or lovable," or whatever, we need to appreciate that we are only expressing our own anthropomorphic preferences. In God's eyes, all creatures have value whether we find them cuddly, affectionate, beautiful or otherwise. Our own perspective, in a way, is neither here nor there. Theology, at its best, can help to liberate us from our own anthropocentric limitations.

BERRY: Are you prepared to go as far as the Jains, who hold insect life to be sacred and inviolate? For instance, they even have prohibitions against killing mosquitoes and houseflies.

LINZEY: Having said that we should be wary about making distinctions, I think I do make one, and that is sentience. Some beings have the ability to feel and to suffer. I think there is something terrible about the infliction of suffering on innocent creatures. After all, at the heart of the Christian faith is the Cross—which I take to be God's identification with innocent suffering.

BERRY: But how can you be certain that insects aren't capable of feeling? You said yourself that we know so little about the animal kingdom. The Jains have what one might call a hierarchy of sentience. They assign five senses to humans and other higher animals; higher insects are assigned four senses; lower insects, three senses; plants and crustaceans, two senses; and seemingly inanimate objects such as water beings, fire beings, air beings, and the microscopic beings that live in rocks are assigned one sense.

LINZEY: That's a fascinating schema. There's something to be said for that kind of schema, but part of me still wants to ask: "Who are we in creation to make these hard and fast distinctions about what is more or less valuable to God?" I wouldn't deny the possibility that insects are sentient, but in the case of mammals we can be almost certain (as certain as we are about anything) that they suffer like us only to a greater or lesser degree. That must mean that the killing of animals, that is, beings who indisputably possess self-consciousness and sentience, is of greater moral significance than those beings who are not.

But I don't want to be dogmatic here. We know so little. I'm open to the possibility that God's Spirit is alive and intimate in a whole range of beings in ways we cannot comprehend.

BERRY: At the same time, the Jain system also suggests that by virtue of our existing, we are ineluctably involved in the destruction of other life forms. Even when we are eating vegetables, we are, by the lights of Jainism, killing a two-sensed life form; it's not so barbarous as killing a five-sensed form; but it is destructive of life.

LINZEY: I don't think vegetables or stones are sentient. But I'm agnostic about insects. Without wishing to appear wholly eccentric, I must confess that I have spent hours watching ants; I do think they are incredibly interesting, complex, intelligent creatures—but *that*, of course, is only my anthropocentric view.

BERRY: The Jains were given to scattering breadcrumbs outside of ant heaps.

LINZEY: An admirable thing to do.

BERRY: Will that consciousness pervade the West someday?

LINZEY: Well, there is within Christianity the notion of Christ as the Logos, the Word, the creative principle of the universe that inheres in all things. It's there in early Christian reflection on the world, but I fear it hasn't been developed much in systematic theology to date. I'm open to the possibility that the Jains, and other world religions, are describing the same reality except in different language. It's orthodox doctrine that God is both transcendent and immanent within creation, though I have to say that I think God's Spirit is intimately present within sentient creatures—those beings with a developed capacity to feel and be harmed.

BERRY: What about the question of Christ's having been a vegetarian?

LINZEY: Interestingly, there is no recorded example of his eating meat, but, if the canonical Gospels are to be believed, he did eat fish.

BERRY: Are you familiar with the writings of The Reverend Todd Ferrier? As you may know, in 1903, Todd Ferrier founded the only exclusively vegetarian Christian Church—which is still flourishing—the Order of the Cross. In his writings, Todd Ferrier maintains that the references to fish in the Gospels are largely symbolic and shouldn't be taken literally.

LINZEY: Actually, the first vegetarian Christian Church was the Bible Christian Church founded by William Cowherd in 1809. He drew his inspiration from texts, such as Genesis 1:29, which command vegetarianism, and made vegetarianism compulsory among church members. Arguably, his Church, now sadly defunct, heralded the modern vegetarian movement in the West.

But to your main point: if the canonical Gospels are to be believed, Jesus was not a thoroughgoing vegetarian nor, it must be said, a feminist or a believer in Home Rule. We must beware of remaking the historical Jesus in our own image. I don't think that the contemporary Christian case for vegetarianism depends on Jesus himself being a vegetarian.

BERRY: But the canonical Gospels have been heavily edited and interpolated. They are hardly a pristine text.

LINZEY: That's true. All the canonical Gospels are editorialised compilations of the life of Jesus. Interestingly, there are apocryphal Gospels which do present Jesus in a rather different light with regard to animals. It is these—especially the *Gospel of the Holy Twelve* (of very recent invention)—which Todd Ferrier drew upon. But there are other sources. For example, there is a Coptic text—a fragment of which we have—which describes Jesus healing a donkey. Also, in the Acts of Philip, for example, Jesus's disciples, in obedience to his command, make peace with a leopard, and the leopard turns vegetarian. So there are a variety of apocryphal sources that present Jesus differently. I'm bound to say, however, that Christian tradition has never regarded these sources as authoritative, and has thought of them as legends or embellishments. One of my plans at Oxford is to write a book called *Jesus and Animals*, which will look at some of the alternative traditions about Jesus. It is, to say the least, rather unlikely that these traditions contain genuine historical reminiscence, but what is interesting is that Christians thought at some point that something *like that* must be true about him.

BERRY: Perhaps the apocryphal Gospels haven't been tampered with, as have the canonical Gospels, because the apocryphal Gospels have been marginalised.

LINZEY: Well, that presupposes a conspiracy theory about the composition of the canonical Gospels which I don't share. Among zoophiles, there is the well-known argument that Jesus was really an Essene.

However, if you're going along the Gnostic path, remember that the Essenes were largely Gnostic—the Gnostics, many of whom were vegetarians, were characterised by otherworldly perspectives. For example, they tended to regard all sexual behaviour as itself sinful. They were of course against drinking wine—doubtless they would have been against my pipe-smoking too! In short: the extreme asceticism of a lot of Gnosticism arguably undercuts one of the strongest Christian arguments for vegetarianism—namely a *this-worldly* concern for God's good earth and Her creatures within it. Much of the Gnostic religious motivation for vegetarianism is that materiality, including flesh and blood, is itself evil or impure; therefore one shouldn't have sex or eat dead flesh. But for me that wouldn't be a satisfactory theological or ethical basis for vegetarianism today. I can understand how it might inform an asceticism that leads to a kind of Christian vegetarianism, but I would say that the challenge to Christians is—after centuries in which they have reviled, hated, cursed and misrepresented the natural world—how they can develop a positive, this-worldly, theology of nature and especially one that teaches us how to love and revere God's creatures. Essene Gnosticism will not bring us to animal rights. Those zoophiles who want to press the case for Jesus being an Essene have not fully thought through the implications.

BERRY: However, there is a school of thought that says that the Essenes were Jewish Pythagoreans, and were closer to Pythagoreanism than they were to Gnosticism.

LINZEY: I think we have to ask what it would have meant for Jesus to have been a thoroughgoing vegetarian in first-century Palestine. It would probably have implied some association with Manicheism. (Manicheans were almost all vegetarians not on ethical but on ascetical grounds.) But Manicheism was inimical to the thrust of his teaching.

BERRY: But in the Hellenistic Age, and certainly in the early days of the Roman empire, there were many competing religions beside Manicheism that espoused vegetarianism: there was Buddhism, which had already permeated Mediterranean culture; there is some evidence that Vaishnavism and Jainism may also have permeated Mediterranean culture from India, and most important of all, there was Pythagoreanism and Orphism, which to borrow Nietzche's useful term, advocated an "Apollonian" vegetarianism — by which I mean that they practised vegetarianism because it was ethically sound, and that it was intellectually pure not to eat the carrion left over from animal sacrifices, which is what flesh-eating meant in those days: eating the leftovers from animal sacrifice.

LINZEY: Yes, but Manicheism was centrally significant theological-ly. After all, Christians confessed their belief in God who had become incarnate in flesh and blood — in the very materiality that the Manicheans thought impure. Even today one of the problems it seems to me is that Christian theology is still Manichean in a way, that is, too "other-worldly," too world-denying. I think it is a great mistake to oppose the flesh to the spirit. Christianity is about the enfleshment of God in the incarnation.

I like the Rabbinic saying that when we get to heaven we shall have to account for every legitimate pleasure that we didn't enjoy. For myself that provides a vast agenda in the present world, and I intend to take every advantage of it. (*laughter*)

BERRY: Isn't that rather sybaritic for a clergyman? They are sen-timents of which Marquis de Sade, or that old reprobate Alistair Crowley would not have been ashamed.

LINZEY: I see now that you are a Manichean — or at least a dual-ist — at heart! I believe that earthly pleasures are a foretaste of heaven. Pleasure is not to be despised. Pleasure that causes other beings pain should be despised, but pleasure in itself, delight in the world of the senses, in the contemplation of beauty and the ecstasies of human loving — these beautiful things are gifts of God to be savored. God became flesh so that the life of the flesh may be sanctified. What will we be doing in heaven — writing books? I would like to think that there's room for a little scholarship even in heaven, but I would say that the aim is to reach that point of utter ecstasy in the love of God—of which earthly pleasures are themselves an anticipation. Heaven is a place of perpetual pleasure. Indeed, at the end of the funeral service in the Church of England, there are now these amazing lines: "And in his sight, there is pleasure forevermore." Now, just think about that!

BERRY: So, in a sense, our mistreatment of animals, and our eating of their flesh, is an impediment to pleasure.

LINZEY: Absolutely! It's an impediment to spiritual pleasure. That's why I think vegetarianism is implicitly a theological act. It's not about saying "No" but about saying "Yes": about *enjoying* the lives of other creatures on this earth so much that even the thought of killing them is abhorrent. I think God rejoices in Her creatures, takes pleasure in their lives, and wants us to do so too. So much of our exploitation of animals stems from a kind of spiritual blindness: if we sensed and really felt the beauty and magnificence of the world, we would not exploit it as we do today.

BERRY: So your vision of what a vegetarian world would be like is unabashedly hedonistic?

LINZEY: One of the strongest metaphors for heaven in the Gospels is "the feast," or "the banquet," to which the elect are called. I don't think Jesus had in mind dinner at Mansfield College, Oxford—wonderful though that can be. Rather, I think, what Jesus had in mind was how creatures would satiate their full spiritual sensibility in the presence of God.

One of the wonderful things about being in Oxford is that I can close the door of my house and in five minutes be in a beautiful place like this. I can spend time meeting that deep spiritual hunger—a hunger that often shows itself in the desire for beauty—that is there within myself. I don't think I'm alone in that. Most people have that sense of wanting to be fulfilled at some deeper level, which is why people enjoy nature parks. They have the sense that somehow in the process they'll be reconnected and made whole with something deep within themselves.

Don't forget, Oxford is also my home town. It was here that I first had those religious experiences that led me to where I am now.

Spending time sitting on the banks of the Cherwell River in Oxford can provide the context for spiritual illumination.

As you know, in many of the lives of the saints, there are astonishing, even bizarre, tales of how the saints befriend animals, care for them, talk to them, even preach to them. And when one first starts reading all this stuff, one is struck by the idea that it might all be make-believe and fantasy. Indeed, many theologians have not been able to see any theological point in these stories at all. But there is a theological point and it is this: As one grows in love and unity with the Creator so one also comes to a greater sense of love and unity with all God's creatures. These apparently sentimental stories are actually the conveyors of a deep spiritual truth, but Christian theology is characterised by forgetting as well as remembering. The problem is that we've forgotten such a lot.

BERRY: To coin a phrase: We've forgotten everything and remembered nothing. In your *Christianity and the Rights of Animals*, you cite the various Christian ascetics and monks who befriend animals such as St. John Zedazneli and St. David Garesja. St. John befriends bears; St. David, deer and birds. Aren't these considered anomalies in the Christian tradition?

LINZEY: Well, yes and no. Something like two-thirds of the canonized saints of East and West befriended animals, and espoused the cause of animals. Now these are, after all, canonized saints. One cannot get away from it: They are supposed to be God-touched lives, inspired by the Holy Spirit. So, in fact, though the Christian tradition hasn't always taken much notice of them, they have always been in the background as examples of how holy people show their holiness by caring for animals.

BERRY: Doesn't this imply that in the Christian tradition, one has to be a "saint" to befriend and succor animals? Whereas in the Jain tradition, acts of befriending and rescuing animals are commonplace. In other words, one doesn't have to be superhuman to be compassionate to animals in the Eastern religious tradition—it's exoteric; whereas in the Christian, or Western tradition, it's still an esoteric doctrine.

LINZEY: Well, from my perspective, it's not inconceivable that Jainism in its care and respect for creation has more understood

the Christian doctrine of love than the Christians have themselves. I don't take the view that only Christians understand the
Gospel of Jesus. For me, Christ is not primarily a doctrine one
has to subscribe to; Christ is a way of selfless loving—a pattern of
self-sacrifice and moral generosity that is available to everyone in
the world. That reality is not just located by those who worship in
mosques, churches or temples; it is open to everyone who sits by
the riverbank and is open to spiritual illumination.

The great scandal of the Christian tradition is that those who
have claimed to follow Christ have often betrayed him. Churches
are often the least obvious expression of the living Christ. I do
make a sharp distinction between the Church and God. I would
describe my state as someone who believes more and more in God
but less and less in the Church of England, or any Church.

BERRY: What about the depiction of Yahweh in Genesis and in various other places in the Old Testament as delighting in the odor of
animal sacrifices? Unless one takes the Gnostic view that the world
is evil and that its creator, Yahweh, is really Satan, how does a vegetarian Christian or Jew rationalize it?

LINZEY: I'm not, of course, justifying the practice of animal sacrifice; but it's just conceivable that those who practised animal
sacrifice did not understand it as simply the gratuitous destruction
of God's creatures; it was in some ways thought of as the liberation and the returning to God of that life back to the very life-
source that caused everything to be. But, of course, there's no one
view of animal sacrifices even by those who practised it. And one
finds, for example in Isaiah, the contrary view—a rejection of sacrifice as cultically, if not morally, unacceptable to God.

From the Christian point of view, however, the important thing
theologically is that Jesus did not sacrifice animals.

BERRY: That marks a sharp divergence between the New Testament and the Old, doesn't it?

LINZEY: I think it does. Take for example the incident of Jesus
cleansing the Temple. The question to ask is: What did Jesus
cleanse the Temple of? People making money, yes, but they were
probably making money out of selling animals for sacrifice.

As Christians began to reflect upon the life of Jesus, they came to see that Jesus himself was the sacrifice that replaced the sacrifices of animals.

BERRY: Jesus was seen as the ultimate sacrifice?

LINZEY: It's all expressed in that incredible line: "The good shepherd lays down his life for the sheep." Now, if you think about it in context, the shepherd did not lay down his life for the sheep. The shepherd slaughtered the sheep. By saying that "the good shepherd lays down his life for the sheep," a whole new dimension of understanding is opened up. It is about how "the higher" should sacrifice itself for "the lower" and not the reverse.

BERRY: What about the communion ritual itself? Some anthropologists have described it as a barbaric ritual: They maintain that the drinking of Christ's blood and the eating of His flesh, however symbolic, smacks of anthropophagy.

LINZEY: Oh, on the contrary! It could be argued that Jesus jettisoned the traditional Passover meal, which would have been the sacrifice of the lamb, and took bread and wine—vegan elements—as substitutes for the whole tradition of animal sacrifice.

BERRY: What evidence is there for that?

LINZEY: Well, Christians continue to celebrate the Eucharist with bread and wine; it does not contain dead flesh. The Eucharist underlines—is expressive of—the very sacramentality of creation. When the Eucharist (thanksgiving) is offered to God, by the power of the Spirit, creation is renewed. Indeed, the Eucharist has been described as "the first fruits of the sanctification of all creation". And I think there is something in that—not just for humans, but also for animals.

I would go so far as to say that the Eucharist is the continuing expression of how Christ replaces the blood and flesh of animals. Christ becomes the true lamb. The theology is not "Oh, well, therefore we must go on sacrificing animals, because Jesus is the true sacrifice!" No! It's that Jesus has become The Sacrifice.

BERRY: Doesn't he become a scapegoat, lending color to the charge that some critics have made that Christianity is a scapegoat theology?

LINZEY: On the contrary: I see the Cross as God's act of radical identification with those innocents who suffer in the world. The Cross is the vindication of the oppressed and the vulnerable—including innocent animals.

BERRY: But doesn't this hark back to the ancient ritual of the *pharmakos* in which a specially selected animal was put to death in order to cleanse the community of its sins?

LINZEY: If I may say so: you've radically not got the message. The radical message is not about the goat should be "scaped." But how *we* should be sacrificed for the goats!

BERRY: That's a message that I think would be lost on the public at large without having someone so eloquent as you to explicate it for them.

LINZEY: Well, as I explained, theology is characterized by forgeting as well as remembering. For example, there's the little known sermon preached by John Henry Newman when he was Vicar of St. Mary's University Church in Oxford in 1842. Newman begins by taking up this biblical metaphor of Christ as the Lamb of God and points out how Christ is identified with the unprotected, defenseless and vulnerable. He goes on to argue that there is something "Satanic" in the infliction of suffering upon innocents and claims that the suffering inflicted upon innocent creatures is morally equivalent to the suffering inflicted upon Christ himself. He says: "Think then, my brethren, of the suffering inflicted upon brute animals and you will gain one sort of feeling which the history of Christ's Cross and Passion ought to excite within you." Very powerful words. I don't think that the scapegoating notion as normally understood does adequate justice to the idea of the atonement. It is rather that God so loves the creature that instead of allowing the creature to suffer and die, God, by an act of astonishing graciousness and love, becomes the creature itself.

BERRY: That's a beautiful disquisition, and I don't want to argue with it...

LINZEY: (*laughter*) Well, something that's beautiful might also be true...

BERRY: I would just put to you this question: how do Christians celebrate Easter? Ninety-eight percent of Christians throughout the world celebrate the resurrection of the Lamb of God by eating lamb! How did the message get so badly misconstrued that so many Christians eat lamb to celebrate the death and resurrection of the One who was himself identified with such a defenseless creature?

LINZEY: That question is as difficult to answer as it is to answer the question of how it is that the Gospel insight that in Christ there is neither Jew nor Greek, male nor female, should have been so neglected—so much so that even today in the largest Christian Church women are not allowed equal status as priests.

BERRY: Aren't women finally being ordained in the Church of England?

LINZEY: Yes, thank God, they are in the Church of England, but not in the largest Christian community, the Roman Catholic Church. It has taken the Christian Church 1,800 years to recognize the immorality of slavery; 1,900 years to recognize the oppression of women; it may not be until 2,000 or beyond that the Church finally comes to see that animal exploitation is inimical to the Gospel. If my faith depended on the institutional probity and sanctity of the Church, I would have given up believing years ago. I think the Church itself needs to be redeemed and saved because it's been so awful; I don't pretend that after years of indifference, thoughtlessness, cruelty and barbarism that the transformation of the Church in relation to animals is anything other than a daunting task.

BERRY: You have frequently referred to God as "She." What about the ideas advanced by feminists that matriarchal societies preceded patriarchal societies, and that matriarchal societies were inherently more compassionate and protective of animals than patriarchal ones?

LINZEY: It is orthodox doctrine that God has no gender: God is neither male nor female in the sense that we understand it. Therefore, to talk constantly (as most Christians do) of God only as "He" or "Him" mindlessly reinforces a masculinist-view of God. I more often than not refer to God as "She" simply to redress the balance.

I don't like the way some feminists seem to understand gender differences in terms of men having all the bad characteristics and women having all the good ones. I don't actually think that's true. I think the whole of humankind, male and female, is disordered, sinful, and confused. I would like to see the evidence for matriarchal societies being more compassionate to animals. The truth is much more likely to be that women, like men, are culturally and socially conditioned. Some are more sensitive, others less so. Gender, by itself, is an unreliable index of personal sensitivity.

BERRY: Perhaps male members of an oppressed minority would have equal sensitivity to the issue.

LINZEY: Don't misunderstand me: some women who have reflected upon their oppression *qua* women may have a unique insight into how we have exploited weaker species. I also happen to think that there are valuable feminist insights into animal rights. But I do question the view that either gender is more sensitive to animals generally.

BERRY: What do you think accounts for the truculence of animal rights groups? So many of their members are strict vegetarians with enlightened views about speciesism, yet they are often at daggers drawn with each other. Why?

LINZEY: One of the problems with the contemporary animal rights movement is that it's become too religious. It's taken to itself some of the worst features of fundamentalist religion—it has become highly moralistic, self-righteous and intolerant. In my book *Animal Theology*, I have frankly written of those who "enjoy a moral condemnation the way others enjoy a good dinner." I regard self-righteousness and fundamentalism as almost as morally objectionable as butchery or vivisection. Moralism is not enough; it needs to be filled out with a spiritual appreciation that we are all sinners.

In particular, I am deeply worried by the continued outbreaks of violence and lawlessness. I regard violence as incompatible with the peaceful philosophy of animal rights. I used to think that some limited forms of non-violent civil disobedience, after the style of Martin Luther King, Jr., might be justifiable, but now I have come to the sad conclusion that the movement is not spiritually or morally mature enough for that. Law-breaking has become indiscriminate, with activists threatening individuals with bombs and setting fire to shops. I believe it is absolutely imperative that all animal rights people oppose all violence and all illegality.

BERRY: Why is it that the Eastern religions have shown themselves to be more compassionate towards animals than the Western religions?

LINZEY: With the singular exception of the Jains in India, I'm not sure that any religion, East or West, has a very good record on animals.

BERRY: Well, there is the first precept in Buddhism and Jainism that prohibits harming or taking the life of an animal; it explicitly urges one to cherish all life. It's the first precept because it was held by Buddha and Mahavira to be the most important of the five precepts. It's not without significance that in Judaism and Christianity, the commandment against taking life is number six; (the first five commandments deal with such comparative bagatelles as keeping the Sabbath, not worshipping other gods, and not taking the Lord's name in vain): therefore, one might easily infer that cherishing life is not a priority in Western religions—a fact that is borne out in the bloodstained history of these religions, wouldn't you say?

LINZEY: Maybe, but the problem is that in practice many Buddhists have not behaved themselves any better than most Christians, in relation to animals, at least.

BERRY: But prior to the late nineteenth and twentieth centuries in China, Japan and parts of Southeast Asia, the great mass of the people were deeply religious Buddhists and devout vegetarians. With the advent of mass Westernization, however, many of them have adopted the barbaric eating habits of the West. In my interview with Zen Roshi Philip Kapleau, he pointed out that at the end of the nineteenth century, the Chinese were appalled at the sight of Westerners tearing and slashing at the flesh of sheep and bullocks with knives and prongs. The Japanese were equally dismayed by the spectacle of the Americans killing animals and eating them; unfortunately in their pell-mell haste to imitate the West, they broke faith with Buddhism and blotted their copybooks with animal blood.

LINZEY: That may well be; but as things stand now, it's not possible for me to say to other religious folk, "Look, in those areas of the world in which Buddhism is still a major force, here you will find a level of compassion—and a difference of practice significantly higher than that which you will find in other cultures"—that's my problem.

BERRY: Well, in India eighty-five percent of the population is vegetarian, and it's against the law to mistreat, or slaughter animals in nearly every Indian state. Isn't that a markedly higher level of compassion and practice?

LINZEY: But animal welfare legislation is no more advanced in India than it is in England or America, is it?

BERRY: I would say that there are ethical safeguards for the rights of animals within the doctrines of Hinduism, Jainism and Buddhism that obviate the necessity for animal welfare legislation. If there were ethical safeguards against the harming of animals within the Christian religion as there are within Buddhism or Jainism (with the first precept), then perhaps animal welfare legislation wouldn't be necessary in the West either.

LINZEY: Well, I don't think you can have it both ways. I don't think you can argue that there is a greater ethical consciousness in the East but there isn't the legislation; whereas in the West we have better legislation but not the ethical consciousness. The truth is that animal experimentation, trapping, caging—none of these things are outlawed in the East or the West.

However, don't misunderstand me, I'm delighted to find any ethically sensitive person for animals in any world religion of whatever kind. It's just that in general terms, I know how awful the Christian tradition has been; so I'm eager not to let any religious people off the hook in this regard. I know from firsthand experience how good religious people are at deluding themselves! Even within Buddhism, which is theoretically more advanced in this respect, it hasn't produced so strong an ethically concerned society for animals as one would have wished; however, that is not to say that in some respects it isn't better; I'm happy to acknowledge that it is.

BERRY: There are periods in Chinese and Japanese Buddhist history in which there has been concern for animals: During the Heiean period in Japan, for instance, people could earn Buddhist merit by being kind to animals, and abstaining from eating them.

LINZEY: Interesting. Yes, I wouldn't want to deny that religion can be a force for good—even nineteenth century England suddenly saw an outburst of humanitarian sentiment towards animals, almost all of it Christian-inspired—but in so many ways in the critical issues that face us today religions are so on the wrong side that it's almost a divine duty to be critical of all religions. I don't think that even good patches of history exonerate world religions of East or West from general indifference to animals.

BERRY: No less an historian than Arnold Toynbee derives the plundering of the planet from the concept of "dominion" as it is spelled out in Genesis 1. Is it wrong for ecologists and animal rights advocates to blame Christianity and Judaism for the rape of the planet and the "slaughter of the innocent" for thousands of years?

LINZEY: My answer is yes and no. On one hand, it's right for animal rights people to be critical and judgmental of the Christian tradition. It has been amazingly callous towards animals. Christian theologians have been neglectful and dismissive of the cause of animal suffering—and many still are. Christians and Jews have allowed their ancient texts, such as Genesis, to be read as licensing tyranny over animals, even though, as I have said, Genesis 1:29 commands vegetarianism. All this, and more, must be granted. I don't want to let Christians off the hook. On the other hand, animal rights people sometimes look on Christianity as though it was unambiguously "the enemy." I think it is wrong to write off Christianity in this way. All religious traditions have great resources for a very positive ethic in relation to animals. I would go further and say that, however awful the record of Christianity has been, Christian theology has some unique insights fundamental to valuing animal life.

From my perspective, without a sense of ultimate meaning and purpose, it is difficult, if not impossible, to justify any kind of moral endeavor. If Christian societies have been awful to animals, so also have atheistical ones. To my mind, it's not self-evident that one should live altruistically, or generously. The Judeo-Christian tradition and other world religions have the potential to give us a vision of ourselves in the world that we so desperately need. I'm one of those people who believe that morality really depends upon vision. Acting morally is to live in response to a vision of how we should be, and the truth is that the Judeo-Christian tradition, and the Buddhist tradition, and the Hindu tradition, and the Jain tradition do have visions of how the world could be at peace, indeed, of how we can and should make peace with other living creatures.

More fundamentally still, like all the great reforming movements, animal rights depends upon a certain perception—insight—in our case about the intrinsic worth of animals. I think reason and rational argument are important in defending this insight and showing its intellectual coherence, but the spiritual insight, I think, comes first. In other words, we are about trying to help people *see* animals differently. For me, animal rights is first and foremost a spiritual experience and spiritual struggle.

BERRY: Do you think we're tending towards the sort of Edenic existence that was envisaged in the Genesis sagas?

LINZEY: I don't think human volition alone, however well-intentioned, can ever bring about the kingdom of heaven on earth. That's one of the other reasons why I believe in God. I don't think we can become fully human without the grace of God. I like the line from Laurens van der Post: "Whatever we create, however truly it reflects our creation, is always invested with something more powerful than the selves which have produced it." And he continues: "The power and the glory is at our service, but never of our invention." This, I think, is not only true of the creative arts but also of all moral endeavor. At particular moments, almost against oneself, one finds the energy to do seemingly impossible things.

If you ask me if I am confident about human capacities alone, I must respond pessimistically. If you ask me if I believe that God's Spirit is beckoning us to a newer, more peaceful world, I can only respond in faith and hope.

Essay

··

THE ORDER OF THE CROSS

FOUNDED IN 1904 BY THE Reverend John Todd Ferrier, a former Christian minister who had grown disillusioned with the Congregationalist Church's ill-treatment of animals, the Order of the Cross gives promise of what the Christian Church may become in the new millennium if it is to adapt and survive in a more humane era. Just as Jesus may have fused together Judaism, Pythagorean philosophy and Buddhism to forge his anti-sacrificial (i.e., vegetarian) teachings, the Reverend John Todd Ferrier has fused Christianity with the humane doctrines of the Indic religions of Buddhism, Jainism and Hinduism that stress the idea of non-injury to all life forms. It is interesting to note that at about the time Todd Ferrier founded his fledgling vegetarian sect, Allan Bennett, the second Englishman to convert to Buddhism, began lecturing on the Buddhist concept of the interconnectedness of life—put simply: each time you kill or harm another life form, you incur a *karmic* debt that has to be paid for in full either now or in another lifetime. This is also the essence of Todd Ferrier's message—the interconnectedness of humans and "the creatures."

Indeed, the title of his book *On Behalf of the Creatures* could well serve as the Order's motto. As a condition of membership, the Order of the Cross requires that all members take a vegetarian vow and subscribe to the Order's teachings on reincarnation and compassion for animals.

It is characteristic of religions that promote a vegetarian diet that they also have a theory of reincarnation. The Order is no exception. Reincarnation is one of the fundamental tenets of the Order. Members believe that Jesus has been reincarnated forty-one times since his death in 49 CE. As with other "vegetarian" religions, the Order has a cyclic view of time. (On the other hand, in the "carnivorous" religions of the West time is viewed as being linear.) Members believe that there was a vegetarian Golden Age in which even the carnivora were frugivora, and that someday the Golden Age will return at which time the carnivora will again become frugivora. Lions will eat straw or strawberries, and wolves will lie down with lambs in a cyclical reprise of Genesis 1:29 in which "For all the living things of the earth, for all the fowl of the heavens, for all that crawls about upon the earth in which there is living being—all green plants [are] for eating."

The Order is located in a spacious town house at 10 DeVere Gardens in the Kensington section of London. Here members gather twice a week to sing hymns and listen to other members read from the writings of J. Todd Ferrier. They also give talks of their own in which they interpret the message of the Order, relating it to their own life experience. A lively question and answer period often follows. Afterwards, members share a vegetarian meal.

No cardinals, no popes, no archbishops, no turbulent priests are there in the Order. Like Mahavira, Todd Ferrier believed that priesthoods are the bane of existence, so he made it clear that there would be no priestcraft in the Order of the Cross. In theory, at least, every member is the equal of every other member.

Even though extensive selections from his works are read aloud during much of the service, it is unlikely that these readings could ever exhaust the supply. A prolific writer of books and articles, Todd Ferrier's works run to some forty thickish volumes. In books such as

The Master: His Life and Teachings and *The Logia* one can learn the inner meaning of the teachings of Jesus, whom Todd Ferrier calls "The Master," and who by Todd Ferrier's lights was a strict vegetarian.

It is striking how many points of similarity there are between Todd Ferrier's principles and those of the Jewish Christian Ebionites. Like the Ebionites, Todd Ferrier believes Jesus was a savior for animals as well as for humans. In the Ebionite Gospel, Jesus says "I have come to annul sacrifices [flesh-eating], and if you will not cease to sacrifice [eat animal flesh], the wrath will not turn from you."[1] Flesh, a luxury food in antiquity, was synonymous with animal sacrifice, since it was seldom consumed outside the sacrificial ceremony in the temples of the ancient world. According to Todd Ferrier, Jesus was born into one of the Jewish anti-sacrificial sects known as the Essenes, who were the forerunners of the Nazorean Ebionites. "The parents of the Master were living souls, they were alive to every pure and spiritual good. Between them and the Jewish priesthood, there was nothing in common. No part did they take in the Temple services though from the Gospel record it would seem as if they had done so. They were of the purest community of the Essenes. No creature was sacrificed to them in religious life, nor yet for food or clothing, for they knew that the only true sacrifice was spiritual, and that to eat any creature that had looked with conscious eye upon life was evil, a wrong done to the creature and to the soul."[2] "The sacrificial system of Jewry had to be repudiated in the most unreserved manner, and the barbarous habits and customs which it taught and embodied had to be put away forever."[3]

Also like the Jewish Christian Ebionites, Todd Ferrier deplores the Pauline influence on the gospels. "Perhaps the greatest contributory factor to this lamentable decline in the condition of things is to be found in the Epistolary Letters sent out in the name of Paul. For in some strange and unaccountable way, these epistles have exercised more influence than the Gospel stories upon the kingdom which grew up in the name of the Master. In the teaching of the reformed Churches, he even eclipses the Master. Yet Paul did not know the Master. His first knowledge of him was gathered from the oral tradition. He knew nothing of those profound teachings given to the inner group. He had not come under the influence of the life of the Master, and had no vision of its glorious purity and sweetness. Had he done so, he could never have said what he did concerning the eating of flesh and the taking of wine, nor would the personal element have found expression as it does in these letters."[4]

Again like the Ebionites, Todd Ferrier believes that the texts of both the New Testament and the Old Testament were falsified by meatatarian factions. So like the Ebionites he took it upon himself partly to restore the original Pentateuch. In books such as *The Message of Ezekiel* and *Isaiah: A Cosmic and Messianic Drama* he reinterprets stories from the Old Testament in the light of Divine Knowledge. In his book *The Logia,* he does the same for the New Testament. Using apocryphal and alternative gospels, he has pieced together what he considers to be the original, uncorrupted sayings of the Master.

Todd Ferrier doesn't take the Old Testament and the New Testament literally; rather, he treats the Old Testament and the New Testament texts as repositories of esoteric wisdom. He believes that stories in the Old Testament and the New Testament can be read as allegories and that many of its important messages have been written in code. "The Transcendent visions and Messages found in the Old Testament are the true Prophetic teachings. They are often cryptographic and frequently hieroglyphs are used to set them forth. For the innermost Mysteries conveyed in the messages had to be guarded from those who would have wrested them and put the knowledge to wrong uses with the danger of bringing disaster upon themselves and others, and even upon the Planet, as had been in other ages when great minds made wrong uses of the Planetary secrets, and caused great catastrophes to befall the elements, seas and outer planes.

"That is the reason why in the Prophetic Books the innermost mysteries were presented in the language of glyph, so that only the illumined could come into true knowledge of them."[5] And who were these people who might put the innermost mysteries to the wrong use? According to Todd Ferrier, they were none other than the priests and the scribes who deliberately misconstrued the various messages. Todd Ferrier sets himself the task of decoding these inner mysteries for the members of the Order. In his book *The Message of Ezekiel,* for instance, he says that the four-winged creatures with four faces in the book of Ezekiel are symbolic and prophetic of the four gospels of the New Testament.[6]

Here one must enter a small objection to what looks like an over-mystification of Biblical texts. To be sure, there are many incidents and episodes in the Old Testament and the New Testament that lend themselves to an esoteric reading, but often one feels that Todd Ferrier overdoes it. In *The Master,* for example, John the Baptist is interpreted by Todd Ferrier as being symbolic of the soul's progress to a higher state of awareness. He does the same thing with the shepherds and their "flocks upon the plains," who were really symbols of "little human children who were being tended by these devoted souls."[7] They too are symbols of the soul's progress. There's nothing inherently wrong with this; it's just that by over-interpreting characters and episodes in the Biblical literature Todd Ferrier weakens the force of his more cogent interpretations. As Freud himself once said, with self-deprecating humor, about the frantic symbol-hunting in Freudian psychoanalysis that sees a womb in every woman's purse and a phallic symbol in every cigar, "There are times when a cigar is just a cigar!"

Furthermore, since Todd Ferrier heaps so much scorn on the scribes who wrote the Old Testament and the New Testament and tampered with the original texts, how can he find uplifting symbols and allegories in texts that are manifestly corrupt? For instance, Biblical scholarship has shown that shepherds who attended Jesus's birth in a manger in Bethlehem were planted there by the writers of the New Testament in order to link Jesus with the house of David, which was associated with shepherds.[8] (David, it will be remembered, was called to the throne of Israel after having herded flocks for a living as a shepherd boy from Bethlehem.) Yet Todd Ferrier sees in these fake shepherds esoteric symbols of the soul's development. Ditto for the other *midrashic* stage props used by the writers of the New Testament to melodramatize the birth of Jesus and to bolster his Davidic pedigree[9]—such as the birth in the manger in Bethlehem, the swaddling clothes, the star in the firmament, the angelic messengers, the three wise men bearing gifts of myrrh, etc.[10]

This much having been said by way of animadversion, one must stand back and admire Todd Ferrier for being one of the first modern clergymen to champion the rights of animals. On almost every other page of his books he makes a plea on behalf of the creatures, and his criticism of the Church can be scathing. In one of his most unsparing essays on the Church's mistreatment of animals called *The Season of the Christ-mass*, he lambastes the modern celebration of Christmas, which makes a mockery of the emancipation of animals that the Master had tried to achieve. Here is a brief excerpt: "Whilst the Heavens are feasted on the bread and wine of great spiritual and Divine elements of which Eternal Life is constituted, and the real Shepherd on the plains listens to the joy and gladness expressed in the heavenly songs, the great cities, the towns, the villages, and even the outlying lonely places are filled with the cries of the creatures as these are slaughtered in order to provide piquant meals with which to satisfy the barbaric tastes of a still unredeemed humanity.

"When such a Christ-Mass is again realized by the Sons of God, and the Church, which should have been the Temple of the Holy One, is scourged unto purification, its tables of exchange overturned, and the gates of its shambles and abattoirs closed, then verily shall the creatures all share in the Divine Redemption, the Earth be delivered from her groaning, her pain and travail healed, her Edenic inheritance restored, and all her children walk in the golden streets of perfect Love even in their Human estate."[11]

Other members of the Order have taken up their pen to further the Message. The Reverend V. A. Holmes-Gore has written such books as *These We Have Not Loved*, *The Human Soul*, and *Christ or Paul?* that lend further scholarly support to views put forth by Todd Ferrier—that the early Church was Essene, that the apostle Paul was a traitor to the cause, that the theory of reincarnation is a tenable doctrine, and that Jesus was a vegetarian. In his book *The Human Soul*, Holmes-Gore ably defends the theory of reincarnation, which is one of the fundamental tenets of the Order. Like the Church Father, Origen, Holmes-Gore posits that the soul is pre-existent, that is to say that it reincarnates from animal-to-human, human-to-animal and into an infinitude of other permutations. "The belief in the pre-existence of the soul has however been put forward by enlightened ones in more recent days. It was also taught by Plato, Pythagoras and Buddha and has been held by many thinkers and poets."[12] Holmes-Gore goes on to cite Jerome, another Church Father, who like most of the thinkers of his age, believed in reincarnation. "When we turn to the days of early Christianity, we find that several of the Fathers believed in the pre-existence of the Soul. Thus Jerome could write: 'As to the origin of the soul: I could remember the question of the whole Church: whether it be fallen from heaven as Pythagoras, and the Platonists and Origen believe, or whether they are daily made by God and sent into bodies, or whether by traduction, as Tertullian and Apollinarius and the greater part of the Westerns believe, i.e., that as body from body so the soul is derived from the soul, subsisting by the same condition with animals.' "[13]

Next, Holmes-Gore poses the classic objections to the theory of reincarnation, then refutes them one by one. For example, to the objection that people cannot remember their past lives, Holmes-Gore answers that the reason that people in the West cannot remember their past lives is that the consumption of animal flesh beclouds the memory and hinders the recall of past lives. On the other hand, in the East where people refuse to pollute their bodies with animal flesh, they have no difficulty in recalling their past lives. To the objection that heredity argues against it, he answers that the sharply contrasting personalities that occur in members of the same family would suggest that there are other forces at work in shaping one's character and destiny than genetics alone — namely *karmic* forces. To the objection that *karma* and reincarnation are too unwieldy and fatalistic a system of rewards and punishments, he answers that on the contrary one lifetime may not provide enough scope for a person's deeds to be rewarded or punished; it may take several lifetimes before he or she may reap what they have sown. Did the Master believe in reincarnation? He not only believed in it, opines Holmes-Gore, but he actually taught it to his disciples.[14] This by itself would suggest that Jesus was a vegetarian, for as we've seen, people who believe that their soul may reincarnate in the body of an animal are much less inclined to eat them.

In his book *Christ or Paul?* Holmes-Gore echoes Todd Ferrier's belief that Paul was responsible for suppressing the ethical vegetarianism practiced by members of the early Christian Church. He sees irony in the fact that Paul considered adultery and fornication to be worse sins than the murder of creatures for food. As a Manichean who considered it only slightly better to marry than to burn, Paul held the seventh commandment ("Thou shalt not commit adultery") to be more important than the sixth ("Thou shalt not kill"). Holmes-Gore sees Paul as the father of puritanism, celibacy in the Church, and the denigration of the body in Western culture that led directly to such monstrosities as the 130 nuns who shuddered at the mention of bathing; the saint who prided himself on not having gazed upon a woman ("the doorway to hell") for 48 years; the saints who outdid each other in refusing to bathe; and the sixty year-old nun named Silvia who, though she was ill as a consequence, resolutely refused to wash any part of her body except her fingers.[15] He also blames Paul for popularizing the odious doctrine of vicarious atonement whereby Jesus is seen as the ultimate sacrifice whose flesh and blood redeem the world. Both Todd Ferrier and Holmes-Gore consider this to be a theology of human-sacrifice—a thing of the barbarians.

Another member of the Order who has written noteworthy books about the Order and its ideas is the Reverend Jasper Harold Kemmis. In his monograph entitled *The Church of the Future,* he delineates the four basic features that the ideal Church of the future should have, which, not surprisingly, are all possessed by the Order of the Cross. The first feature is a belief in the theory of reincarnation. He writes: "People today do not know how widely spread among the early Christians was the belief in this doctrine, and that it has never died out from certain groups within the Church, though it has been condemned by the orthodox...It

would be a great boon to mankind if this truth could again make
its way into the hearts and minds of Christians; for if the likelihood
of re-birth were recognized once more, people would no longer
fear death; they would realize that there is no death, but only
progress to other realms. If the truth of reincarnation were re-
captured, Christians would find the explanation of many of the
seeming injustices of life, and would find themselves at one with all
that is best in the great religions and philosophies of the world."

The second hallmark of the Church of the future—which may
well be the most controversial of the four—is a belief in the ability
of humans to commune with the spirits of the dead "beyond the
veil," as Kemmis phrases it. "I think that the Church of the future
will not deny the possibility of true communion with those who
have departed from this world, and also with the Angels who minister from the world above. The possibility of spirit communication
will be recognized in some circumstances where the spiritually
minded are ready for it, for it will be perceived that it is a natural
thing that the departed should be permitted to continue some
phase of their fellowship with their loved ones still on earth."[16]
Presumably these departed spirits would not yet have reincarnated, as it might be rather difficult to communicate with the soul of
the late lamented Aunt Agatha after it had transmigrated into the
body of a stallion, or a butterfly.

The third hallmark of the Church of the future would be its emphasis on pacifism. "I think the Church of the future will be truly pacifist
in its teaching. After all, one of the Beatitudes is 'Blessed are the Pacifists, for they shall be called the children of God,' though the Greek
text is not usually translated in that way. By pacifist I mean—entirely on the side of peace in all relationships of life. In the early centuries
it was not permissible for a Christian to be a soldier, for it was felt
that bloodshed was so utterly contrary to the spirit of the Gospel. In
the course of centuries the Church lost that ideal; and I feel it is utterly necessary that the Church should win it back, and teach that all
men should so act towards their neighbors, individual and national,
that the idea of settling disputes by force will be entirely ruled out."[17]

The fourth hallmark of the Church of the future is really the third (pacifism) extended to the creatures—ethical vegetarianism. Kemmis writes: "The Christian of the future will be a vegetarian, like the Essenes of old, and will take no life of his weaker brothers; for they are all the children of God in greater or lesser degree. I feel that the principle of pacifism towards all creatures is an integral part of Christianity, which has been forgotten and then denied. I know that the Scriptures seem to teach otherwise, but may it not be that the Scriptures have been altered to further the interests of the flesh-eaters?"[18]

Here again we meet with the same idea expressed by Philip Kapleau Roshi, Hans-Joachim Schoeps, Carl Skriver, *inter alios*, that the early texts of Buddhism and the early texts of Judaism and Christianity that call for humans to stop killing and eating their fellow creatures "have been altered to further the interest of the flesh-eaters." That is why the Churches of the West that are not based on Jesus's anti-sacrificial teachings are crumbling, and the gods whose food is the burning flesh of animal sacrifice are well and truly dead. ♁

R.B.

• • • • • • • • • • •

[1] "The Gospel of the Ebionites" in Ron Cameron, ed., *The Other Gospels: The Non-Canonical Gospel Texts* (Philadelphia: Westminster Press, 1982), p. 106.

[2] John Todd Ferrier, *The Master: His life and Teachings* (London: The Order of the Cross, 1980), p. 30.

[3] *ibid.*, p. 38.

[4] *ibid.*, p. 44.

[5] Ferrier, *The Message of Ezekiel: A Cosmic Drama* (London: The Order of the Cross, 1931), pp. 34-5.

[6] *ibid.*, p. 46.

[7] Ferrier, *The Master, op. cit.*, p. 115.

[8] John Shelby Spong, *Liberating the Gospels: Reading the Bible With Jewish Eyes* (New York: Harper Collins, 1996), p. 191.

[9] It is ironic that the authors of the New Testament should want to bolster

Jesus's Davidic pedigree because according to Jewish historian Hans-Joachim Schoeps, Jesus and the Nazorean Ebionite sect to which he belonged shunned any association with the house of David because as a warrior king, and a rather bellicose shepherd, David offended their vegetarian, pacifist sensibilities. *Vide* Hans-Joachim Schoeps, *Jewish Christianity: Factional Disputes in the Early Church*, trans., D. R. A. Hare (Philadelphia: Fortress Press, 1969) p. 87.

[10] Spong, *op. cit.*, pp. 185-189.

[11] Ferrier, *The Season of the Christ-Mass* (London: The Order of the Cross, 1977), pp. 8-13.

[12] The Rev. V. A. Holmes-Gore, *The Human Soul* (London: The Order of the Cross, 1989), p. 16.

[13] *ibid.*, pp. 19-20.

[14] *ibid.*, pp. 17-20.

[15] The Reverend V. A. Holmes-Gore, *Christ or Paul?* (London: The Order of the Cross, 1989), p. 30.

[16] The Rev. Jasper Harold Kemmis, *The Church of the Future* (London: The Order of the Cross, 1971), p. 4.

[17] *ibid.*, p. 5.

[18] *ibid.*

Conversation / The Order of the Cross

DR. CONRAD LATTO, M.D., F.R.C.S.

A RESPECTED SURGEON who publishes widely in British medical journals, Dr. Conrad Latto is the youngest of three physician brothers who have dedicated their lives to furthering the cause of vegetarianism and animal protection in Great Britain. Owing to a fateful encounter between Dr. Latto's father and the Reverend John Todd Ferrier, the founder of the Order of the Cross, Conrad and his

two older brothers, Gordon and Douglas, had the good fortune to be raised as vegetarians and to become members of the only church in the West that compels its members to take a vegetarian vow. I interviewed Dr. Latto in the sun-

dappled dining room of his rambling house in Caversham, Reading. The interview concluded, he served me lunch—a delicious vegan salad of his own devising. One of his favorite books, he told me between mouthfuls, was a book that a patient had given him, called *God's Acre*. It recounts a year in the life of all the creatures that live on the acre of ground surrounding a rural church. Because the church grounds were protected, the animals could live there without fear of human depredation. It occurred to me that if the other Christian churches were to imitate the Order of the Cross and require their members to take a vegetarian vow, then all the animals could live as free and untrammeled as the creatures on God's acre, and so—not incidentally—could we all.

∙∙∙∙∙∙∙∙∙∙∙∙

BERRY: The Order of the Cross would appear to be a singular sect; it's the only wholly vegetarian religious sect in the West since the (now defunct) Bible Christians in nineteenth-century England and America, and the Albigensians or Cathars in Southern France, who were exterminated by Simon de Monfort (at the behest of the Catholic Church) in the twelfth century CE.

DR. LATTO: I think that's probably correct. The Order of the Cross is the only Christian religious sect that makes it a condition of membership that you've got to be a vegetarian. Other churches have vegetarian sections like the Quakers and the Seventh Day Adventists. Amongst the Seventh Day Adventists, vegetarianism is optional but not required.

The Adventists are a unique group historically from a health point of view. None of them smoke; none of them drink; they all have the same spiritual outlook. So you have two groups—one who are vegetarians and the other who are meat-eaters. A study comparing the cancer and heart attack rates between these two groups revealed 40% fewer cancer victims and a 30% drop in heart attacks in the vegetarian group. A more recent, similar study in Oxford, comparing vegetarians and non-vegetarians, confirmed these figures. These are landmark studies.

BERRY: When was the Order of the Cross founded, and by whom?

DR. LATTO: The Order of the Cross was founded in 1904 by the Reverend John Todd Ferrier. He had been a Congregational Minister. He formed the Order of the Cross because he felt very strongly about the exploitation and slaughter of animals that the mainline Christian churches had condoned for centuries. So he gave up his ministry to form the Order whose aim was to link together those who believed in the rights of animals and the moral imperative to practice vegetarianism, and also to find those souls who could respond to the spiritual teachings of the message.

BERRY: So it's been going for almost a century. It must be the longest running vegetarian religious sect in the West since the Cathars.

DR. LATTO: Yes.

BERRY: Are you a life-long vegetarian?

DR. LATTO: I became a vegetarian at the tender age of three. When I was three years old my parents met the Reverend John Todd Ferrier. They were so impressed by him that they became instant vegetarian converts as well as members of the Order of the Cross.

BERRY: What are your worship services like?

DR. LATTO: At the Sunday worship services the ministrant reads from the writings of the Reverend John Todd Ferrier, which runs to forty volumes. They're very extensive writings. The purpose is to show the unity of all great spiritual aspiration and the relationship between Christianity and the teachings of the other great religions. During the service we sing some hymns, and the ministrant may give his or her personal interpretation of the message of the Order of the Cross relating it to their life's experience. During the services there are times of prayer and times of silence. It needs to be stressed that the Order's attitude toward the creature kingdom is one of compassion. We are not vegetarians for health reasons. Basically, the reason we are vegetarians as such is that we believe that the creatures have souls just as we have. They are sentient beings. To kill them for food or any other reason would be wrong. We feel that in the end the world will have to come around to this way of thinking. We firmly believe that Man will still fight fellow Man until he stops killing and eating the creatures.

BERRY: I understand there is a vegetarian meal after the service?

DR. LATTO: That's right; although an increasing number of our members are becoming vegan.

BERRY: There seem to be a lot of Hindu elements incorporated into the teachings—such as reincarnation, vegetarianism and even *ahimsa*.

DR. LATTO: Very much so! It's a marriage of East and West. It unites the wisdom of both Eastern and Western traditions. Reincarnation is very much a part of it. It is a fundamental tenet of the

Order of the Cross, as is pacifism.

The sad thing is that Christian teaching in the early days accepted reincarnation. It did so until the Second Council of Constantinople in 553 CE, when it was voted out on a democratic vote on a proportion of three to two. So what we firmly believe is that Eternal Truth was thrown out.

BERRY: You knew the Reverend Ferrier. I'm sure you formed an opinion of him?

DR. LATTO: Yes, he was a most exceptional person; most lovable and loving. The very soul of compassion and very humble. In my younger days as a doctor — I have been one for 58 years — I found some of Todd Ferrier's references to physiology and medicine rather unconvincing. But with the passage of time quite a number now have been shown to be correct. The appendix, for instance, we thought had no function. But Todd Ferrier described why it was there and what it did.

BERRY: What is its function?

DR. LATTO: It does a lot of things: it produces a mucous that helps to lubricate the bowel. It secretes various chemicals that assist bowel function and is part of the body's defense mechanism. It has been called "the abdominal tonsils." The tonsils, as you know, were at one time removed wholesale. Their true function was not understood. We now know that they sit at the gate of the alimentary tract and are a very important part of the body's defense mechanism.

BERRY: Supposing one has an inflamed appendix — appendicitis; then what?

DR. LATTO: There's no alternative: you must have it out. However, if you go to countries in Equatorial Africa where people's diets are high in fiber, there's very little appendicitis. In the early 1970s we compared the incidence of appendicitis at the Royal Berkshire Hospital, England where I was a surgeon with the Mulago Hospital in Kampala, Uganda — both serving the same number of people. In the Royal Berkshire there was one operation for appendicitis every twelve hours. In Kampala about one every six weeks — a striking contrast. As you know, vegetarians eat twice as much fiber as meat-eaters, and vegans four times as much. The incidence of appendicitis in these two groups is very small.

BERRY: Lord Soper once told me that the reason why his doctors took him off his vegetarian diet quite some years ago was that he had developed diverticulitis.

DR. LATTO: Well, that was quite extraordinary because I've personally been involved in the writing of various articles for the *Lancet* and the *British Medical Journal* on the importance of high fiber diet in relation to diverticular disease. Quite a few articles have been published showing that if people with diverticulitis are put on a high-fiber diet their symptoms are reduced by 85%. If Lord Soper were now to consult a modern gastroenterologist, I am sure he would get different advice.

BERRY: Does the Order of the Cross believe that Jesus was originally a vegetarian?

DR. LATTO: Yes, they think he was a Nazorean and had close relationships to the Essenes—a strict vegetarian group.

BERRY: I put the question to Lord Soper and to the Reverend Linzey and both said that there was no canonical evidence for Jesus's having been a vegetarian.

DR. LATTO: Now there is a very good book by a German scholar on that subject, Carl Anders Skriver, *The Forgotten Beginnings of Creation and Christianity*. He marshals an awful lot of evidence to show that Jesus was a vegetarian.

BERRY: Yes, I agree, but conventional Church dogma doesn't support it and very few clerics are willing to give their assent to it on the record, even if they may secretly believe it. The Order of the Cross is the only Christian Church that I know of that teaches that Christ was originally a vegetarian. What does the Order believe was Christ's *raison d'etre*?

DR. LATTO: We believe that there was a Fall; that there was a vegetarian Golden Age as it was depicted in the story of the Garden of Eden in Genesis. Originally there was a perfect world; then a catastrophe came over it. This catastrophe resulted in all sorts of things happening—the fixation of the elements; the deflection of the poles of the planet so that it didn't move in the proper plane and the generation of an atmospheric belt around the planet so that the angels could no longer get through to help the planet. So we were cut off. We believe that the Master, when he passed over in 49 CE, reincarnated forty times. During these incarnations he had a very special ministry, which was to purify the atmospheric belt (its heavens) around the planet so that the angels could approach and communicate with the world. We believe that this work, which we call the Oblation, was completed in 1914.

BERRY: Was Todd Ferrier himself an *avatar* of Christ?

DR. LATTO: Do you mean: was he the re-embodiment of the Christ soul? Yes, I think so, but this is what everyone must decide for himself. The point really is, as Todd Ferrier tells us in *The Message*, that this intermediary blockage has been removed and that angels are now approaching the planet—but before the final purification of the heavens—after most of the heavens had been cleansed—the remaining residual evil forces were cast down onto the surface of the planet and they are creating merry hell at the moment! But their days are numbered. The angels are back with us. The Message is now being fulfilled. All the presages that we read about in the Message, such as the liberation of women, the liberation of the black races, the liberation of the creatures, the spread of vegetarianism, the spread of the peace movement, the expansion of planetary consciousness, are coming to pass. This is the outcome of the fact that the heavens have been purified and the angels are coming back; and they're stirring it up; so many good things are happening.

BERRY: Todd Ferrier's notion of the forty reincarnations of the Christ soul would seem to owe something to the Hindu concept of the avatar; so Todd Ferrier must have been deeply influenced by Hindu philosophy.

DR. LATTO: It may have been so. Except, of course—there is the matter of the Fall: A lot of Indian religions don't accept a Fall; they accept a progress towards Nirvana.

BERRY: How would Todd Ferrier explain Darwin?

DR. LATTO: Like this: the world was once perfect. Eventually a catastrophe befell it, and it went down and down and down until all life was virtually extinguished. Then life reappeared, and it started to evolve. We would call this The Return: the soul is coming back to find a form in which it could function. Then the human form reappeared, and the soul entered the human form; thus the human form should be growing more and more towards perfection.

BERRY: Does the Order regard the human form as the ultimate form, the epitome of the evolutionary process?

DR. LATTO: Yes, the anthropomorphic form is considered the highest embodiment of the soul on this planet.

BERRY: So, the other animals are considered to be less than perfect embodiments of the soul?

DR. LATTO: In the teachings of Todd Ferrier, it says that the gentle creatures—not the ferocious creatures—are the evolutionary path through which the soul is learning lessons until eventually it incarnates in human form. It's a learning process.

BERRY: Doesn't Todd Ferrier also say that prior to the Fall, even the so-called carnivorous creatures were vegetarian.

DR. LATTO: Yes, prior to the Fall, there were no carnivorous creatures.

BERRY: The lion would have been herbivorous?

DR. LATTO: Yes, the lion and the other carnivores were originally herbivorous.

BERRY: Does the spread of vegetarianism that Todd Ferrier envisaged in his writings also apply to the carnivora? Will there come a time when the carnivora will be converted to a herbivorous or frugivorous diet?

DR. LATTO: Yes, when God's Law is re-established, all the manifestations of evil will vanish, and this will include the disappearance or redemption of the carnivorous animals.

BERRY: The classic question is, of course: "How could a benevolent God permit such a cataclysm to happen?"

DR. LATTO: Here we are face-to-face with the great mystery of free will and mistaken choices. When God's Law is willfully broken, then many tragic events must ensue. Through the clouds of evil that eventuate, the ministrations of a benevolent God are diverted or misrepresented. Reverend Todd Ferrier writes: "Divine Love and Wisdom do not make mistakes but the interception of them or opposition of them would lead to mistakes. It was in such a way there happened that which brought about the 'Fall' of the Planet—an event resulting in all the Earth's tragedies." However, the message of the Order of the Cross states that this is the age of the great return of the planet back to Eden, the healing of its mistakes and the restoration of harmony.

BERRY: In his writings, Todd Ferrier laments the influence of Paul on the Church, viewing him as having vitiated the message of Christ.

DR. LATTO: Very much so. When you look at the history of the New Testament, only two of the four gospels were written by his intimate disciples—that is Matthew and John. Mark and Luke were not of this group, and Paul, who was a great friend of Luke's, had never met the Master in person, but claimed he met him in a vision on the road to Damascus. We reckon that Paul managed to get access to some of the writings, and he tampered with them. He tended to lay stress upon the masculine to the detriment of the feminine. Women in his view were very much subordinate. And the other thing was his overweening egotism, which is reflected in his overuse of the pronoun "I."

BERRY: In his book *The Master*, Todd Ferrier states unequivocally that Christ came from an Essene family. Of Christ's parents, he writes: "The parents of the Master were living souls: they were alive to every pure and spiritual good. Between them and the Jewish priesthood there was nothing in common. No part did they take in the Temple services, though from the Gospel records it would appear as if they had done so. They were of the purest community of the Essenes. No creature was sacrificed by them in religious rite, nor yet for food or clothing; for they knew that the only true sacrifice was spiritual, and that to eat any creature who had looked with living conscious eye upon life, was evil, a great wrong done to the creature and the soul. The pure fruits of the Earth constituted their dietary." Is it your view that Paul tampered with the original portrayal of Christ as a vegetarian Essene and the son of Essenes when Paul recast the Gospels?

DR. LATTO: Certainly. That was Todd Ferrier's view. He believed that Paul had tampered with the Essene spirit of the Master's teachings, which caused the Church to deviate from the Master's message of compassion for the creatures. Of course, one can't lay 2,000 years of the Church's acquiescence in the exploitation of animals at Paul's door alone, but Todd Ferrier felt that the Pauline influence on institutionalized Christianity was deplorable.

BERRY: Todd Ferrier also takes Paul to task for treating Christ's death as a form of vicarious atonement, which he regards as a degrading doctrine.

DR. LATTO: The message of the Order of the Cross says that the Master didn't die on the cross at all, but that he swooned on the cross. He was taken down from the cross, was resuscitated and lived for another fifteen years. He was crucified when he was 33 years of age, but passed over when he was 49. It was during this fifteen-year period, after he had survived the crucifixion, that he taught his inner group of disciples.

BERRY: Some years ago, the Reverend Hugh Schonfield in his bestselling book *The Passover Plot* advanced a similar theory. He made a very convincing case for Christ's survival of the crucifixion.

DR. LATTO: At the Royal Society of Medicine of which I'm a member, there was a paper delivered recently called "Resurrection or Resuscitation?" It was a very interesting paper showing the evidence of Christ's having survived the crucifixion. I don't know whether you're familiar with the fine points of crucifixion, but when the average person was put up on the cross, it took him about three or four days to die. Now the Master was taken down in a matter of hours after he had been nailed to the cross because it was a Friday afternoon and they wanted to take down all the crosses because the next day was a special Jewish sabbath.

BERRY: But it was the Romans who had him crucified.

DR. LATTO: Yes. The Jews went to Pilate and said, "Can we take him down from the cross?" And they took him down and his followers revived him. Crucifixion is not an instantaneous death. It takes days to effectuate it. The cause of death wasn't loss of blood or exposure, but asphyxiation. The legs are broken, the body sags and you slowly become asphyxiated. It's a slow, gruesome process. Christ wasn't on the Cross long enough for any of this to have happened, and his legs were not broken. In the Gospel of Saint John it says that when the soldiers pierced his body "out came blood and water." Well, I can tell you as a surgeon that no blood comes out of a dead body.

BERRY: How does Todd Ferrier view the Old Testament God?

DR. LATTO: The God of the Old Testament is unrecognizable as a god of love. He's a god of tremendous ferocity.

BERRY: How does Todd Ferrier rationalize the cruelty and the animal sacrifice in the Old Testament?

DR. LATTO: He doesn't accept it at all. He says it's utterly wrong; but he does reinterpret many of the stories—the story of Moses and so forth—and elucidates their real meaning.

BERRY: So he circumvents the cruelty and the animal exploitation in the Old Testament by allegorizing it and reinterpreting it?

DR. LATTO: Yes, he reinterprets a tremendous amount of it, taking some wonderful gold out of the immense amount of dross, but it is all consistent.

BERRY: As Todd Ferrier reinterprets it, does the Old Testament become an ethical vegetarian document?

DR. LATTO: It's a spiritual document; it's a great call for us to become spiritually awake.

BERRY: How does the Order of the Cross envisage God—as a bearded patriarch or as an androgynous figure?

DR. LATTO: We refer to God as Father-Mother, as a duality. It combines aspects of male and female.

BERRY: In your view the Old Testament God would seem to have had an overdose of male hormones.

DR. LATTO: (*laughter*) That's a good summary of the situation! He's supermasculine! Whereas, the Order of the Cross views God as combining the best aspects of male and female.

BERRY: As we evolve into a more pacifistic, ethical vegetarian world, will the conventional Churches adopt the teachings of Todd Ferrier?

DR. LATTO: Well, I think so. Basically, I'm a tremendous optimist, because I see all these movements as evidence of the spread of the message of the Order of the Cross. The actual physical organization of a little Church is not important compared with the message of love and compassion—that's the thing that's going to change the world.

BERRY: What will happen to the Bible if the Western world becomes vegetarian? How will the vegetarian churchgoers be able to read these grotesque accounts of Noah offering animal sacrifices to God; and of God's delight in the odor of burnt offerings? How will they be able to read *Leviticus* and *Deuteronomy*, which are how-to manuals of animal sacrifice? Won't the Bible have to be re-edited, or scrapped altogether?

DR. LATTO: I take your point: it's like the story of the Prodigal Son! When the Prodigal Son returns, his father is so pleased to see him that he rewards him. But what of the other brother who stayed at home? Does he get a pat on the back for being a good boy? No, it's the one who was dissolute and comes back. He got this grand reception for which they killed the fatted calf. Someone was referring to the injustice visited on the good son, who stays behind and does his duty; but the one whom I was most sorry for was the fatted calf! Why should he have had to suffer? He's the true victim of the story.

BERRY: What about the search for the Holy Grail? Todd Ferrier lays a great deal of stress on that, does he not?

DR. LATTO: If someone asked me to sum up in one sentence the main teaching of the Order of the Cross, I would say that it would be "Live in the Consciousness of the Presence of God and Love." That would be the Holy Grail.

BERRY: The legend of the Grail in the medieval romances concerns itself with the search for the chalice or cup that Christ tossed off at the Last Supper. Does Todd Ferrier believe that the Last Supper was a Passover meal consisting of the paschal lamb?

DR. LATTO: No, certainly not! The Last Supper, according to the teachings of the Order of the Cross would have been in CE 49, when he was saying farewell to his disciples; that was when he left the earthly life to embark on his forty subsequent reincarnations.

BERRY: This was not the conventional Last Supper that preceded the crucifixion?

DR. LATTO: No, this was after the so-called crucifixion. Remember: according to the teachings of the Order of the Cross, Christ survived the crucifixion and lived for another fifteen years. At his final farewell supper, Christ told his disciples: "I go where I go, but I can't explain it to you; I go to do a great work; you spread the message while I am away, and I will return to you."

BERRY: So, then He's been reincarnated forty times in the form of great teachers?

DR. LATTO: Yes, forty times, but I couldn't vouch for the form he's taken during his forty reincarnations.

BERRY: One would presume that he had been reincarnated as a higher being—not as a brigand.

DR. LATTO: (*laughter*) No, I can be certain about that.

BERRY: Now the traditional Last Supper—before Christ was affixed to the cross—does the Order of the Cross believe that this was a typical Passover meal?

DR. LATTO: No, not in our teachings.

BERRY: Carl Skriver, for instance, believes that the so-called Last Supper was actually an Essene meal, and therefore a vegetarian one.

DR. LATTO: Yes, without a doubt. It's curious that the Church lays so much stress on the crucifixion—on the death of the master as if his dying were more important than his having lived.

BERRY: Yes, the rather ghastly display of his body. E.M. Cioran in his essay *New Gods* describes how shocked the ancient Romans were when they beheld the image of a corpse nailed to the cross as the symbol of the new religion. He says that they associated such images with diabolism and the infernal religions of the night and darkness. I'm wondering if the Order of the Cross makes a display of the Crucifix.

DR. LATTO: No, because our cross is the cross of the Resurrection—not the Crucifixion.

BERRY: How does your cross differ from the cross of the Crucifixion?

DR. LATTO: There's light radiating from it, and it's got three steps, which represent self-denial, self sacrifice and self abandonment. Then it's got the vertical, which represents Love and the horizontal, which represents Wisdom; and the circle, which represents Eternal Life.

BERRY: Todd Ferrier was primarily concerned with the welfare of the creatures.

DR. LATTO: Yes, very. That was his reason for founding the Order and the reason for its continued existence, but the prime purpose of Todd Ferrier's work was to restore to earth the Spiritual Teachings.

Recipes

....

Recipes

· · · · · · · · · · · · · · · ·

JAINISM

OF ALL THE AHIMSA-BASED religions in India, the Jains practice the most rigorous from of vegetarianism. They are so scrupulous—not to say finicky—in their eating habits that they will not eat after dark for fear that they might inadvertently swallow an insect, or that hapless insects may be fatally attracted to the candle flame lighting a Jain supper. Nor will they eat leftover food, (which must come as a shock to many Western families who virtually live on leftovers. The joke that goes, "In my family we ate leftovers so often that we could never trace the original dish," would provoke a disbelieving stare from an ortho-dox Jain). Food must be eaten the same day it is prepared lest it spoil and attract microorganisms. Jains are usually lacto-vegetarians. However, many American Jains—such as Saurabh Dalal, who furnished most of these recipes—having become aware of the cruelty involved in the dairy industry are taking the lead in trying to persuade Jains worldwide to become vegans. Some Jain *munis* or monks are already vegans because their religion prohibits them from eating foods that contain a surplus of microorganisms. So they forgo milk and yogurt because, like most fermented foods such as alcoholic beverages (which Jains

also eschew), milk products attract bacteria, and Jains try to minimize their consumption of even the most minute of life forms. For
instance, an orthodox Jain would not eat *kandmul* (root vegetables). The reasoning behind this practice is manifold and is based
on the belief that every life-form including a plant has a soul. Eating a root vegetable involves the killing of a significant part of the
plant if not the entire plant; whereas, the eating of, say, an apple
results in the dispersal of its seeds and thus assists in the propagation of the plant species. Root vegetables also contain an infinite number of microorganisms living in the root system. Moreover, Jains believe that an innumerable number of souls actually
live in the smallest portions of root vegetables. Since eating root
vegetables requires eradicating the root from its natural habitat,
and exposing the microorganisms to sunlight and other untoward
surface conditions, the microorganisms and the infinitesimal souls
will also die. Finally, the Jain belief in detachment from the material world is another reason for their abstention from root vegetables, which are held to be denser, less *sattvic* and more earthbound
than the aspiring fruits and vegetables that grow upwards, toward
the light.

In conclusion, it is appropriate that these recipes were collected
from the laity—a Jain family rather than from a priest—because
in Jainism, in keeping with the teachings of Lord Mahavira, the
laity act as their own priest.

············

MUNG BEANS FOR AYAMBIL

In the Fall, a special time of introspection, awareness and self-purifica-
tion called Paryusan is observed by the Jains. This period either lasts
eight days for Jains of the Shvetambara sect or ten days for the Digambara sect. Thoughts, words and deeds are more carefully monitored by
the Jain at this time. Paryusan allows the Jain a better opportunity to
understand the reality of the universe and the goal of spiritual progress.

Typically, during Paryusan, the Jain follows an even stricter diet. A *tapa* or dietary penance such as fasting or partial fasting is often observed during this time. The term for the type of diet observed during a Paryusan is "ayambil". For ayambil, the only spices acceptable are salt, black pepper, hing powder (asafoetida) and dry ginger powder. That means no oils, sugars, dairy products, other peppers, green vegetables, root vegetables, fruits, etc.; the only foods that it is permissible to eat are grains and beans.

Here is a typical dish that a Jain might eat during an ayambil. This may be eaten with roti (a wheaten, tortilla-like bread) or boiled rice prepared with the same precautions as stated above. **Serves 4.**

1 cup mung beans, rinsed	*1/3 tsp black pepper*
2 cups water	*1/4 tsp hing powder (asafoetida)*
3/4 tsp salt	*1/4 tsp dry ginger powder*

Pick over and wash the mung beans, then place them in a pan. Add two cups water and cook in a pressure cooker for five minutes. If cooking by conventional methods, double the volume of water and cook for one hour. Add spices fifteen minutes before the end of the process.

Note: Rawfoodists or livingfoodists may enjoy this dish by soaking split mung beans for twelve hours. Drain the water and set aside. Heat the spices. Turn off flame and add the soaked mung beans. Stir the spices into the mung beans and serve.

•••••••••••

JAIN STYLE CHOLE

2 tbs corn oil	*1/2 tsp red pepper*
1/3 tsp hing powder (asafoetida)	*1/3 tsp turmeric*
1/3 tsp cumin seeds	*1 tbs coriander-cumin powder (mix 8*
1/2 cup diced tomatoes	*parts coriander to 1 part cumin)*
2 cups cooked garbanzo beans	*1/2 tsp garam masala, or curry powder*
1/2 cup water	*juice from 1/2 lemon*
1/3 tsp salt	*1 tbs brown sugar*

Put 2 tablespoons of oil into a small frying pan; add hing, cumin seeds and diced tomatoes. Fry this mixture for five minutes and let cool. Into a larger pan put two cups of cooked garbanzo beans. Mash 10 of these garbanzo beans with a fork or spatula. Now add the cooled fried mixture and stir into the garbanzo beans. Combine remaining ingredients and mix thoroughly. Cook over medium flame until 1/3 of liquid remains. Serve with rice or roti. **Serves 2 to 3.**

Note: For a high enzyme version of this recipe, soak the garbanzos for 48 hours and add them to the heated spices. Do not cook the garbanzos.

· · · · · · · · · · ·

GREEN BEAN SABJI

10 oz green beans, cut into 1 inch lengths
1/2 cup water
2 tbs corn oil
1/2 tbs salt
1/2 tsp red pepper

1/3 tsp turmeric
1 tsp coriander-cumin powder
(mix 8 parts coriander to
1 part cumin)

Put the cut green beans into a saucepan, and cover with one cup of water. Add 2 tablespoons of corn oil and bring the water to a boil. Lower heat and add the remaining spices. Let simmer until the beans are tender. By then most of the water should have evaporated. Serve with roti (wheat tortilla-like bread) or boiled rice. **Serves 3.**

Note: For a high-enzyme version of this recipe, steam the green beans for four minutes instead of boiling them. Heat the spices in the oil. Turn off flame and add the green beans. Toss the beans in the heated spice mixture without further cooking, and serve.

· · · · · · · · · · ·

SPICED OKRA

1 lb okra
5 tbs oil
3 tsp coriander powder
1 tsp salt (or to taste)

1/4 tsp turmeric
1/2 tsp chili powder
1 tsp cumin seeds

Wash and dry each okra individually with a towel (you could also let it air dry, though it takes much longer.) Cut off the ends of the okra and cut the remaining okra into bite-size or 1/2 inch pieces. Heat oil in a heavy base pot. Add the cumin seeds. Once the seeds start to swell, remove pot from the heat for a few minutes. Add the okra. Then put in the remaining spices ie. coriander powder, salt, turmeric and chili powder. Hold the pot handle and toss its contents until the spices have been evenly spread. Avoid using a spoon. Cover the pot and place it on the burner at a low temperature. Cook for three minutes only; remove from flame and let sit in pot for five more minutes. The okra is ready once you see some of the oil reappearing at the bottom of the pot. **Serves 2.**

Note: For a high-enzyme version of this recipe, heat spices in oil. Turn off flame and add uncooked okra. Toss okra in heated spice mixture and serve.

• • • • • • • • • • • •

KHAMAN DOKLAS (A CAKE-LIKE SNACK)

1 lb besan or chick-pea flour   *1 tsp soda bicarb*
6 green chilies, dried   *3 tsp sugar*
1/2 tsp turmeric   *2 tsp salt to taste*
1/4 tsp hing (asafoetida)   *4 tbs corn oil*
2 tsp mustard seed   *coriander and coconut for garnish*

Place all ingredients in a large bowl and mix until they are homogeneous. Spread out evenly in portions about 1/2 inch high to fit into several *thalis* (flat metal plates with low rims). Heat each *thali* by placing it in a vegetable steamer, and steam until the portions are warmed through. Remove the *thalis* from the steamer, and cut the cake into two inch squares. Serve them warm. Garnish with chopped coriander and shredded coconut. **Serves 8.**

Note: My friend Saurabh Dalal who supplied this Jain treat points out that unlike most Jain desserts, this is strictly vegan.

"TO REDUCE THE AMOUNT of bloodshed in the world, one must start at the dinner table," was not one of the Buddha's aphorisms, but it very well might have been because the Buddha recognized the link between the killing and eating of animals for the table and the killing of humans on the battlefield. Buddha taught that humans and animals are spiritually interconnected. In Buddhism, as in Jainism and Hinduism, it is believed that by eating a living creature one runs the risk of being reincarnated as the very type of animal that one is eating for dinner. In fact, there is a favorite Buddhist tale in which an animal successfully pleads for its life by saying that he can foresee that the person who is about to kill him will himself be butchered for the table.

As a result of the Buddha's promulgating the first precept, it is believed by scholars such as David Kinsley and Christopher Key Chapple that Hinduism itself, which had practiced animal sacrifice and ritual flesh-eating, was induced to purge itself of these rites, (which, regrettably, are still practiced by Bengali Brahmins in Northeastern India who sacrifice goats to the goddess Kali). Furthermore, Buddhist cuisine, in the countries where Buddhism has taken root, not only reflects the ethical concerns of the Buddha's teachings, but it has also developed into a highly sophisticated and delectable cuisine—proving that *karma*-free food is also the tastiest food.

It has to be admitted, however that in the Theravada countries of Sri Lanka, Burma, Thailand and Singapore, etc., the Buddhists there often eat meat. They justify their meat-eating by using the sophistry that the Buddha permits people to eat flesh if the animal has not been killed expressly for them. On the other hand, in the Mahayana countries of Japan, Korea and China this spurious teaching has always been viewed with suspicion. In China for instance, it has never gained currency—probably because there is no tradition of mendicant monks who go on begging expeditions for their food, and don't inquire too closely into the often objectionable articles of food that are dropped into their begging bowls. Rather than imploring passersby for their food, as they do in Burma and Thailand, the Chinese Buddhists grow and prepare their own food in their monasteries. Therefore, it would be fatuous for them to pretend that they don't know where it comes from. As a result, all flesh foods, dairy products and alcohol are banned from Buddhist monasteries in China.

After studying Zen Buddhism for ten years in Japanese monasteries, Roshi Philip Kapleau founded the first vegetarian Zendo in America at the Rochester Zen Center. He is now semi-retired and is the abbot of a Zen center in Hollywood, Florida. He furnished me with two of his favorite recipes from the kitchen of the Zen center. The others I collected from former Zen monk Bill Shurtleff, from the family *shojin ryori* (pure vegetarian temple cuisine) recipes of Hideko Abe, the granddaughter of a Zen priest, and from the Po Lin Monastery on Lantau Island in China where I stayed for several days as a guest. The recipes are eclectic, but most of them bear the stamp of Buddhist cuisine in that many of them are made with tofu, miso, sesame seed paste, and sesame oil. Above all else, they are *karma*-free. Probably because they wanted to entice non-vegetarians to give up meat, Buddhist chefs excelled at creating mock meat dishes from soyfoods such as tofu and tempeh and from other ersatz meats such as wheat gluten or seitan. So skillful were these Buddhist chefs at making their mock meat dishes look convincing, that pious vegetarians had to be reassured they were not eating the real thing. Although it was first used by the Chinese Taoists, and may well have been invented by them, tofu has become a staple of Buddhism. When Buddhism traveled from China to Japan in the sixth century CE, the art of tofu-making went with it. And when Roshi Kapleau founded the first vegetarian Zen center in Rochester, he also set up one of the first American tofu shops, Northern Soy. Bill Shurtleff who trained as a Zen monk in Japan, helped introduce tofu and other soyfoods to the West, when he collaborated with his Japanese wife, Akiko Aoyagi, to write *The Book of Tofu*. He was partly alluding to his own spiritual journey when he recently told me that "many of the people who started pioneering soyfood companies in America are longtime practitioners of Asian spiritual paths."

············

CABBAGE WITH YUBA AND WATER CHESTNUTS

1 dried red chili, deseeded and chopped
1/2 Savoy cabbage, shredded
1/2 sweet red pepper, chopped
1/2 small onion, finely chopped
3 tbs sesame oil
2 cloves garlic, minced
1/2 inch fresh ginger, minced

8 oz yuba (tofu skin), chopped
10 water chestnuts, chopped
1 1/2 tbs soy sauce
1 tbs rice wine vinegar
1 tsp chinese five spice powder
1/2 tsp salt

Remove core from cabbage and shred the leaves. Soak the dried chili for half an hour. Drain and set aside.

Place the shredded cabbage into a large mixing bowl. Chop the hydrated red chili and add to the cabbage: then add the chopped onion and the chopped sweet red pepper. Next, add the onions, garlic, ginger, yuba and water chestnuts. Finally, add the seasonings and toss. Do not cook. Serve. **Serves 4.**

Note: This is a high-enzyme, uncooked *shojin* recipe.

1 lb okra, cut into thin, diagonal slices
3 tbs miso (sweet white)
4 scallions, chopped fine

2 tsp mirin (sweet rice wine)
1 tsp rice wine vinegar
1/2 tsp sesame seeds

In a *surabachi* (grinding bowl), grind the scallions to a fine consistency. Add three tablespoons of miso to the grinding bowl and stir until they are thoroughly blended. If the mixture is too thick add a bit of water or mirin and rice wine vinegar.

With a sharp cleaver or vegetable chopper, cut the okra into thin diagonal slices. Mix with the miso-scallion sauce. Do not cook. Let stand for two hours. Sprinkle with sesame seeds and serve. **Serves 4.**

Note: This is a high-enzyme, uncooked *shojin* recipe.

．．．．．．．．．．．．

CHILLED TOFU

6 to 8 oz tofu (regular or silken), chilled
1 1/2 to 2 tsp shoyu, or shoyu dipping sauces
sweet simmered miso, finger lickin' miso or regular miso

garnishes and condiments in order of popularity:
thinly sliced leeks or onions, thinly pressed
grated or slivered ginger root
crushed or minced garlic
7 spice chili powder
slivered yuzu peel
grated fresh wasabi or wasabi paste

wasabi pickled in saké
Less popular combinations:
ginger root and leeks
gingerr oot, leeks and 7-spice
*   chili powder*

Place the tofu on a small plate or in a shallow bowl. If desired, cut tofu into one-inch cubes. If using shoyu or a shoyu dipping sauce, sprinkle it over the tofu and top with your choice of garnishes and/or condiments. Or serve the shoyu separately on a separate dish and arrange the garnishes on a platter nearby. Invite each person to add garnishes to the shoyu to taste. If using miso or a miso topping, place a dab of the miso on top of the tofu and serve without garnishes. **Serves 2.**

Note: This recipe is from The *Book of Tofu*, by William Shurtleff and Akiko Aoyagi (New York: Ballantine Books). Reprinted by permission of the authors. For a high-enzyme version of this recipe use tofu made from sprouted uncooked soybeans.

BUDDHIST MANGO TOFU SALAD

Dressing

2 tbs sesame oil

1 tbs mirin (sweet rice wine)

2 tbs rice-wine vinegar

2 tbs tamari

2 tsp sugar (optional)

1 tsp fresh, minced ginger

1 tsp salt

Mango Tofu Salad

2 large ripe mangoes

2 one lb packets of tofu

1 red sweet pepper, cut into matchsticks

2 stalks celery, cut into matchsticks

1 container water chestnuts, sliced

oil for shallow frying

Combine the ingredients for the salad dressing; stir and set aside. Cut the tofu into 2 inch sticks, and cook for four minutes in boiling salted water. Remove with a slotted spoon. Drain on paper towels. As soon as the tofu sticks have dried, shallow fry them in the oil until they turn golden. Drain again on paper towels. Peel and chop the mangoes. Cut the celery and red pepper into matchsticks. Combine the mangoes, red pepper, celery and water chestnuts in a salad bowl. Add the dressing and toss. Finally, add the fried tofu sticks. Toss and let stand for five minutes. **Serves 4.**

Note: This is an adaptation of a dish I was served at the Po Lin Buddhist Monastery on Lantau Island near Hong Kong, where I spent several days as a guest. For a high-enzyme version of this recipe, use frozen tofu (*agé*) instead of fried tofu. Also, use tofu made from sprouted soybeans.

....

CAULIFLOWER IN MISO AND TAHINI

2 tbs sesame seeds

2 tbs miso

1 tbs mirin (sweet rice wine)

1 tbs rice wine vinegar

1/2 head cauliflower

Grind the sesame seeds in a *surabashi* or mortar and pestle. Stir in the miso, the tahini, the mirin and the rice wine vinegar and keep stirring until a sauce is formed. If sauce is too thick, add water.

Meanwhile, cut the cauliflower into bite-size pieces and steam for two minutes. Remove from steamer, and mix with sauce. Alternatively, cut it into smaller pieces. Leave it uncooked, and mix it with the sauce. **Serves 2.**

Note: This recipe for *shojin ryori* was furnished by my friend Hideko Abe, whose grandfather was a priest at the Soto Myogoni Temple in Nita County in Shimani, Japan.

EVEN THOUGH WESTERNIZ-
ation has caused many
Hindus to become casual
vegetarians, who are all-too-will-
ing to break the ancient taboo
against eating animal flesh over a
meat-stuffed paratha at a trendy
dinner party in Delhi or
Bombay, the great mass
of pious Hindus still
adhere to the vege-
tarian diet that is
enjoined on them
by the Code of
Manu (circa 300
BCE). Not unlike
the Jains, who
claim credit for inject-
ing the vegetarian ethos
into Hinduism and who believe
that every living being has a sentient essence, the Hindus believe
that every living creature contains
a little piece of Brahma, the creator God. Therefore to harm or to
eat an animal would be an inexpiable sin, akin to an act of cannibalism. According to the Code of
Manu all members of the twice-
born castes (those Hindus who
were human beings in a previous
incarnation) are required to be
vegetarian—that is, Brah-
mins (priests), Ksha-
triyas (warriors)
and Vaishyas
(merchants).
But as in Jain-
ism and Bud-
dhism, in Hin-
duism the doc-
trines of *karma* and
of reincarnation pro-
vide the most powerful
deterrent against meat-eating: for
in eating animal flesh one runs the
risk of eating the reincarnated
body parts of a deceased relative
or friend.

Yamuna Devi is an initiated

disciple of His Divine Grace A. C. Bhaktivedanta Swami (Shrila Prabhupada) the founder of the International Society for Krishna Consciousness, affectionately known as the Hare Krishnas. In addition to being a religious teacher, Shrila Prabhupada was a superb cook who trained Yamuna Devi to cook for him. He encouraged her to collect recipes from India's most talented Vaishnava cooks and to publish them in a cookbook that would make the exquisite temple dishes of India available to the average Westerner. The result was *Lord Krishna's Cuisine*, the first vegetarian cookbook to win the prestigious Seagrams Award. In her conversation with me, Yamuna acknowledged that in India, Vaishnavism is often called "the kitchen religion" because it is renowned for the delectable dishes that are turned out by the temple cooks and by the members of Vaishnava households—in India, every house is a small temple—in which all the family members regardless of gender learn how to cook. Shrila Prabhupada for instance was taught to cook by his mother alongside his sisters. (In India it isn't considered demeaning for a man to be a household cook, as it is in many Western countries.)

I interviewed Yamuna Devi after one of her cooking demonstrations in New York. She is by all accounts the premier interpreter of Indian cuisine to the West. By way of introducing some of her recipes, which she collected from the temples and private homes of India, I thought it would be appropriate to print some excerpts from that interview.

· · · · · · · · · · · ·

BERRY: There are probably as many different regional cuisines in India as there are regional dialects, which run into the hundreds. Which is the most sophisticated and refined of the regional vegetarian cuisines of India?

YAMUNA: I think the most refined of the regional cuisines are those of Gujarat and Maharashtra (western and central India); they are the most refined by our Western palate. However, each regional cuisine has its own beauty. Bengali cuisine is very robust and hearty, with big chunks of food. The cuisine of the south is completely different from that of the north. Northern cuisine was influenced by the Mughals, the Russians, the British, the Persians, the Greeks, etc.

BERRY: Could you say something about the tradition of temple cuisine?

YAMUNA: I had the great good fortune of being able to study with the best chefs in the temples. In the West, the best chefs work in restaurants, but in India, the best chefs work in places of worship. Of course, there are chefs in the tourist hotels. But the fact remains: the greatest chefs work in the temples where they have a generational program that has been going on for millennia. The edict for temple cuisine is quality, purity and cleanliness—external and internal. Standards of cleanliness are very strict—hands and feet must be clean before cooking, and during cooking no ingredients may be tasted or sampled. The Lord is the first one to taste the food.

BERRY: In the West, cooking as a profession has been regarded as being somewhat beneath one's dignity. Are the temple chefs responsible for raising it to the status of a high art form in India?

YAMUNA: Absolutely. It's a very expressive and necessary art, and it's one in which men as well as women are trained. But men were really the carriers of the flame in terms of temple cooking. Traditionally, women have never been temple chefs; it's more or less a male-dominated field.

BERRY: You say that men have been "the carriers of the flame." Were you speaking literally as well as figuratively? Is there an ever-burning flame in the temple kitchen?

YAMUNA: Yes, there's an eternal flame that burns in many temple kitchens; and embers of that flame will be kept alive for both the worship and the cooking: it's a symbol of eternal life, digestion and creativity.

BERRY: It's almost like the eternal hearth flame in the temples of ancient Greece and Rome, or, in this case, the Vedic fire god Agni.

YAMUNA: Yes, very much so.

BERRY: What was it like visiting all these temple kitchens with Shrila Prabhupada? Were you taking copious notes?

YAMUNA: That was a remarkable expedition, because I was one of the first women and certainly the first white-skinned woman to enter many of the temple kitchens. We traveled on foot from temple to temple for a few years, spending a few nights to a fortnight in one place, and then moving on to another. This is when I really learned about Vaishnava religion and cuisine. I visited hundreds of kitchens with an open notebook, speaking pidgin Hindi, Urdu, Sanskrit, Bengali, everything. It provided me with a culinary journal that I will continue to study because it's very rich, exciting, and edifying.

BERRY: Did the temple chefs willingly impart their secrets to you?

YAMUNA: Yes, there was such a rapport! The temple chefs were exceedingly generous with their time and information, although there was some difficulty with the language. In the particular regions we frequented, Hindi, Urdu, Marathi and Bengali were the predominant languages, but sometimes the temple chefs spoke any number of other dialects. Nonetheless, a great deal was conveyed through the universal kitchen language of close observation and sentences of one syllable illustrated with gestures galore.

BERRY: The temple chefs who prepare the *prasadam*—are they of a particular caste? Are they all Brahmins?

YAMUNA: That will depend on the temple itself. In some temples, the cooks are Brahmins; that is to say, they are the sons of other Brahmins and not actually qualified themselves. Shrila Prabhupada and his spiritual master, Shrila Bhaktisiddhanta, launched a vigorous attack against the caste system in the temples. Some temples still maintain this rigid brahminical caste chef status, while other temples employ the merit system whereby a Vaishnava, regardless of caste, can become a temple chef on his own merits. It is these latter temples that operate in the spirit of Shrila Prabhupada's teaching that "I am not this body; I am not this caste designation; I am not Hindu; I am not Muslim; I am not Christian—I am a servant of God."

BERRY: How many temple chefs would be working in a temple kitchen at any one time?

YAMUNA: It would depend on the size of the temple. For festival events some of the larger temples employ scores of chefs and servers.

BERRY: Rather like the cooks in a five-star French Hotel, each temple chef specializing in cooking a particular foodstuff. In fact, he might spend a lifetime preparing a particular dish over and over.

YAMUNA: That's right. They may be expert in one particular food category such as grain, wheat, rice, flour, fried sweets, boiled sweets, or baked sweets.

BERRY: Are there actually ovens in the temples?

YAMUNA: Not the sort of ovens that we would conceive of in the West. They are very primitive, open-hearth ovens. Sometimes breads can be baked in the lambent flames of the *tandoor*. The temples are equipped with huge frying pots called *karai*—they are big, bowl-shaped vessels that look something like a wok. They have high sloping sides and deep, rounded bottoms. You've seen stir-frying and deep-frying in a wok? The *karais* produce the same effect.

BERRY: A Taoist friend from China who was accustomed to partaking of temple cuisine after the religious service told me that he felt spiritually and physiologically famished after attending a Western church service. There is no tradition of temple cuisine in the Western churches—a state of affairs that he found incomprehensible.

YAMUNA: I guess the only ritual meal that Western churches observe that could be remotely compared to the temple cuisine of Eastern religions is of course the Eucharist.

BERRY: Yes. It strikes me that before the Western churches can begin to evolve an innocent (vegetarian) ritual meal or temple cuisine that they must first acknowledge the rights of animals, and recognize that animals are not food.

YAMUNA: Yes. In a Vaishnava kitchen it is sacred food that is being prepared, and I think that meat and the preparation of such food are mutually exclusive. How can something be offered to the Lord which involves the taking of a sentient creature's life?

BERRY: So the recipes that you've brought back to the West are the records of a sacred art.

YAMUNA: Yes, I would say that this cuisine is a hidden treasure that has never been seen by Western eyes. A culinary treasure as well as a spiritual treasure. When cooking is an act of devotion, as it is in so many Indian kitchens (whether home or temple), it becomes almost like a circle: You take something from the Lord; you offer it back to the Lord; then you take the remnants and use them to satisfy all aspects of your being. And this, in turn is of course pleasing to God.

BERRY: Wasn't Shrila Prabhupada hoping that you would bring these secrets to the West so that nutritionally benighted Westerners could taste these culinary treasures?

YAMUNA: Yes. But as I alluded to before, more important than giving Westerners the opportunity to taste these treasures, Prabhupada wanted to give Westerners the experience of spiritualizing the process of eating. This is food not primarily for the tastebuds — but for the soul, and that's what Prabhupada's intent was: to provide spiritual nourishment and not merely bodily nourishment.

CHICKPEA AND GINGER ROOT SALAD
Kabli Chana Adrak Kachamber

Whole chickpeas are soaked overnight, sometimes even slightly sprouted, before being used in this salad. Two types of rhizomes are suitable here: young camphor ginger or ginger-like mango ginger, (a member of the turmeric family). Their flesh should be virtually fiber-free, with a thin skin. Because they are only found sporadically, look for young or "green" fresh ginger at the corner produce store or supermarket.

This salad was a constant on my breakfast menus for Shrila Prabhupada. He taught it to me in 1967, and commented that ginger root for breakfast aided his digestion all day. Eight years later, when I forgot to soak the chickpeas one day, and had to omit the dish, he again reminded me how important this "digestive" breakfast salad was for his health. Later, another of his cooks, Palika Dasi, related that he also favored another variation using soaked mung dal instead of chickpeas—a variation he simply called chutney.

Try this dish with seasonal fresh fruits for a light breakfast, or include it in a "salad chutney" with lunch or dinner.

Dal soaking time: 8 hours or overnight
Preparation time after assembling ingredients: 10 minutes

1/3 cup whole chickpeas, sorted,
   soaked in 1 1/2 cups water
1 1/2 inch piece of fresh ginger root

1 1/2 tbs fresh lime or lemon juice
1/2 tsp chat masala (optional)
1/4 tsp freshly ground black pepper

Drain the chickpeas. Peel the ginger and slice into paper-thin rounds, then paper-thin julienne. Combine all the ingredients in a small bowl and toss well. Serve directly on the dinner plates in small rounds. **Serves 4-6.**

Note: The recipes in this section were furnished by Yamuna Devi from her cookbook *Lord Krishna's Cuisine*. I've adapted some of them slightly for the vegan table.

············

MELON BOWL SUPREME WITH MAPLE-LIME DRESSING
Carooj Mithai

This is a good dish for summer entertaining—a buffet showstopper, an appetizer at a party or a fruit dessert for a garden party. Watermelons are best at the height of the summer season. Vine-ripened sweet melons have a glossy thick skin with juicy scarlet or yellow flesh. Honeydew, casaba, Ogden, charentais and cantaloupe are excellent choices. The fruit is served in a melon bowl—hollowed-out with a zig-zag or ruffed cut edge. A three to four pound round watermelon will form the basis of a serving bowl; a 10 pound oblong melon can hold up to 20 servings.

Preparation time after assembling ingredients: 40 minutes
Chilling time: at least one hour

one 3-4 lb round watermelon
1 small cantaloupe or Ogden melon
1 small honeydew or charentais melon
1/3 cup maple syrup
1/4 cup lime juice
2 tbs orange juice
2 tbs lemon juice

1/4 tsp ground ginger or
1/2 tbs scraped, finely chopped
fresh ginger root
1/2 tsp cardamom seeds
2 tbs olive oil or almond oil
2 cups blueberries
a few sprigs of mint for garnishing

Using a large sharp knife, cut off the top third of the watermelon. Using a melon baller or a large spoon, scoop balls from the large section of the melon. Remove the seeds and refrigerate the balls. Spoon out the remaining melon flesh, leaving a melon shell. Cut a thin slice of rind from the base of the shell so it will stand without tipping. Cover with plastic wrap and refrigerate until required.

Halve the other melons and scoop out the flesh with a melon baller. Combine these balls in a bowl, mix, cover and refrigerate.

Combine the maple syrup, lime juice, orange juice, lemon juice, ginger, cardamom seeds and oil in a blender and process into a smooth sauce. Just before serving, drain the melon balls, mix well with the blueberries, and spoon into the watermelon bowl. Pour the sauce over the top and garnish with fresh mint. **Serves 4.**

• • • • • • • • • • • •

SWEET POTATO SALAD WITH MAPLE LEMON VINAIGRETTE
Sharkand Salaad

You can prepare this salad up to eight hours before serving. Though it is light and healthy, it is also substantial and filling, perfect as a fall or winter salad. The maple-lemon dressing is barely sweet, pleasantly warmed by candied ginger.

6 medium-sized sweet potatoes
(about 2 lbs), washed but not peeled

3 tbs orange or tangerine juice
3 tbs lemon or lime juice

4 tbs maple syrup
1/4 tsp freshly ground black pepper or
1/8 tsp cayenne pepper
1/2 cup olive oil, or 2 tbs almond oil
*   and 6 tbs sunflower oil*
2 tbs chopped, candied or stem ginger

1/4 tsp salt
1/3 cup finely chopped fresh
*   coriander or parsley*
3 medium-sized tomatoes, peeled,
*   seeded and cut into 1/2 inch cubes*

Peel the potatoes, cube them, steam them for four minutes, and let them cool. Combine the sweetener, juices, salt, cayenne or black pepper, oil, fresh herbs and ginger in a jar, cover and shake until emulsified. Pour the dressing over the potatoes, toss gently, cover and set aside, refrigerated for 1-8 hours. Before serving, add the tomatoes, gently toss and serve on a bed of mixed greens. (This recipe has been slightly adapted to make it as vegan and high-enzyme as possible.) **Serves 6.**

. . . .

SHREDDED RADISH, COCONUT AND CARROT SALAD
Mooli Naryal Kachamber

Try this dish when you have leftover fresh coconut on hand, or if you have frozen, shredded coconut. In large cities, frozen shredded coconut is sold in 1 pound bags at many Cuban and Spanish grocery stores, and, for occasional use, it is a convenient alternative. Use any fresh radish — little round pinks as a vivid color contrast to the carrots, for example.

Preparation time after assembling ingredients: 6 minutes

1/2 cup shredded radishes
1/3 cup shredded fresh coconut
1/3 cup shredded, scraped carrots
1/4 tsp salt
1/4 tsp paprika or cayenne pepper

2 tbs chopped fresh coriander or parsley
1 1/2 tbs avocado oil
1/4 tsp ajwain seeds or celery seeds
1/4 tsp fennel seeds
1/4 tsp cumin seeds

Combine the radishes, coconut and carrots in a strainer and press out the excess liquid. Place them in a bowl and add the salt, paprika or cayenne and fresh herbs. Heat the oil in a saucepan over moderate heat. When it is hot but not smoking, add the ajwain, fennel and cumin seeds and fry until they darken a few shades. Pour the seasoning into the salad and toss well. **Serves 6.**

You can try this dish with a date sugar-citrus juice topping or with an apple juice-apricot purée. Both are excellent contrasts to the banana halves. This quick, natural dessert should be assembled just before serving, for it takes only a few minutes to prepare. To make the apricot purée, place 8 peeled apricot halves and 2 tablespoons apple juice in a blender and reduce to a purée.

Preparation and cooking time after assembling ingredients: 15 minutes

1 tbs fresh lemon juice
1/4 cup strained fresh orange juice
1/4 tsp freshly ground nutmeg
1/4 tsp ground cardamom
2 tbs peanut oil

4 firm bananas
1/4 cup date sugar or maple sugar
  granules
2 tbs blanched sliced almonds

Combine the lime juice, orange juice, nutmeg and cardamom in a small dish. Preheat the grill. Brush a film of peanut oil on a small cookie sheet. Peel the bananas, split them lengthwise in half, and lay them cut side up on the cookie sheet. Spoon the juice over the banana halves, drizzle with the remaining oil, then evenly sprinkle with the sugar. Grill the bananas for 3-4 minutes or until the surface is bubbly and lightly browned. Remove from the grill, sprinkle the almonds evenly over the banana halves, and grill again until the almonds are toasted and golden brown. Serve piping hot. **Serves 4.**

Note: In this recipe, I've substituted peanut oil for ghee.

Recipes

· · · · · · · · · · · · · ·

TAOISM

LTHOUGH IT IS DAIRYLESS, fleshless, totally vegetarian and wholly delectable (like Buddhist temple cuisine), Taoist temple cuisine is unique in that it uses herbs and seasonings that are selected to promote health and longevity. It is worth quoting the redoubtable Chinese chef, Florence Lin, who in her *Chinese Vegetarian Cookbook*, credits the Taoists with having invented Chinese vegetarian cooking: "Lao Tzu, a contemporary of Confucius and another philosopher and great teacher, taught Chinese Taoism—leading a natural life of peace, harmony and happiness. Taoists believe in simplicity, meditation and tranquility. They also believe in eating good natural foods from the earth. Good foods and good health always have been closely associated. The Taoists believed that plants, seeds, and nuts, which are life-giving foods for animals, were good for human beings as well...Taoists in their return to nature discovered many edible vegetables, spices and herbs. These discoveries, occurring in the early stages of Chinese history, helped create the basis of Chinese vegetarian cooking." It is a tribute to the tonic and life-enhancing properties of a strict vegetarian diet that the Taoists—physical immortalists who have been seeking the elixir of immortality—have been practicing a vegetarian diet for thousands of years. Obviously, experience has taught them that such a diet has rejuvenative powers.

It's important to emphasize that unlike Buddhist vegetarianism, Taoist vegetarianism has its basis in the Taoist hypochondria that rejected any foodstuff that threatened to subvert their quest for physical perfection and immortality. The Taoists avoided eating animal flesh because they believed that it was enervating and life-shortening. They also avoided it for apotropaic reasons—so as not to attract evil spirits. Maspero mentions in his study of Taoism that the early Taoists believed that when humans ate flesh they scared away the beneficial spirits. Although Taoism may have originated in a cult of physical perfection and immortality, it evolved into a highly principled vegetarianism. With their strict ban on animal foods of any kind, Taoist monasteries for centuries have been a bastion of ethical vegetarianism.

One of the differences between Taoist cuisine and Indian cuisine for instance is that the vegetables in Taoist cooking are barely cooked or flash cooked so as to preserve their freshness (and, not incidentally, to promote longevity in the diner); in Indian cooking, on the other hand, vegetables are often slightly overcooked and even double cooked in highly spiced sauces to strengthen their flavor.

··············

DRIED FRUITS AND NUTS

1 bowl of dried dates
1 bowl mixed nuts (filberts,
  pine nuts, cashews, almonds)

1 bowl of raisins
1 bowl mixed dried fruits (figs, dates,
  apricots, dried pears and dried apples)

"Dried and candied fruit has a special meaning in the Taoist temple and monastic tradition. Since dried fruit keeps almost indefinitely, it is used as a symbol of longevity, good health and life after death."

From Dr. Michael Saso, *A Taoist Cookbook*, (Rutland: Charles E. Tuttle) p. 83. The other recipes in this section were furnished by Dr. Maoshing Ni from his books: *The Tao of Nutrition* (Santa Monica: Seven Star Communications) and *101 Vegetarian Delights* by Lily Chuang and Cathy McNeese. Lily Chuang is Dr. Ni's mother.

· · · · · · · · · · · ·

Lo Han (Monk's Fare)

When traveling in China, vegetarian food is sometimes difficult to order. This is what you want to ask for to get some variation of a dish fit for a monk.

2 carrots diagonally sliced
10 Chinese mushrooms soaked, sliced
  (save the soaking water for cooking)
1 burdock root (gobo), diagonally sliced
1 ear black fungus, soaked, sliced
2 pieces tofu cake or gluten, cubed

2-4 other seasonal vegetables,
  cut or cubed such as squash,
  cabbage, bell pepper, broccoli, etc.
1 tbs (or more) salted black beans
toasted sesame oil (season to taste)
cilantro for garnish

Cook the mushrooms, carrots, burdock, black fungus and any other slowcooking vegetables in a little mushroom soak water. You may need to add more soak water as it dries out. When these vegetables are almost soft, add the wakame, tofu, salted black beans, and faster-cooking vegetables (i.e., squash, broccoli, cabbage, etc.). When these are done, stir in the sesame oil. Turn off flame and garnish with cilantro. **Serves 4-6.**

· · · · · · · · · · · ·

Curried Tofu Stir Fry with Tender Seaweed

1 lb plain tofu, cut into bite-sized cubes
small amount wakame seaweed
  (or any tender kind), soaked, chopped
1 small tomato, cut into bite-sized cubes

1/3 cup green peas
1 tbs curry
1 tbs thickener (cornstarch,
  arrowroot, etc.)

Stir fry the tofu and curry over low flame for five minutes. Then add seaweed and tomato for a few minutes. Stir in thickening (dissolved in a little water) and stir well. Add peas. Turn off heat, mix in oil and stir well. **Serves 4.**

1 lb plain tofu

Seasoning

1 sheet nori, torn into little pieces · 1. *cilantro/grated ginger*
sesame oil or other oil · 2. *basil/grated ginger*
soy sauce · 3. *mint/grated ginger*
one of the following finely chopped · 4. *celery/grated ginger*
  herb combinations:

Cook whole squares of tofu in boiling water for two minutes (or steam). Then put on a plate and press out some of the water. Use a chopstick to make several holes through top of tofu (top to bottom). Mix together well one of the herb combinations, soy sauce and oil, then pour over the tofu. Spread pieces of Nori on top. **Serves 2-4.**

....

SESAME CARROTS WITH NORI

2 carrots sliced · *2 scallions, chopped finely*
1 sheet nori, torn in small pieces · *1 sprig basil, chopped finely*
4 oz thin noodles, cooked, drained · *cilantro for garnish*

Sauté carrots in a little sesame oil, or Chinese mushrom soak water (for about two minutes). When almost soft, add scallions, nori and basil and cook for about a minute. Stir in the cooked noodles and sesame seeds. Season to taste with a little soy sauce or Bragg's Liquid Aminos. If you did not cook in oil, add a few drops of toasted sesame oil before serving. Garnish with cilantro. **Serves 2.**

....

BASIC VEGETABLE STIR FRY

Use a variety of vegetables, diced or sliced. Stir fry in a small amount of water or broth, covered, the slower-cooking vegetables first (i.e. carrots, green beans, cauliflower, etc.). When the last vegetables go in, you can add tofu or gluten pieces also. Presoaked seaweeds can be added near the beginning. When everything is done, season to taste with oil, soy sauce (or Bragg's Liquid Aminos, or herb salt) or your favorite cooking herbs. Basil and cilantro are particularly good with vegetables. **Serves 4.**

Variations:

1. Add steamed peanuts or vegetables.
2. Add 1 clove of garlic at the beginning.
3. Add finely grated ginger toward the end of the cooking.
4. Add green onions at the end.
5. Add Chinese mushrooms (presoaked) at the beginning.

············

ALMOND STIR FRY

1 small yam
1 small head cauliflower
1 leek or onion

2 summer squash
1 handful green beans
1/4 lb white mushrooms

Chop vegetables into small pieces. Put in skillet in about 1/4 inch water. Cover and steam until vegetables are tender. Pour out any remaining water into a bowl. Add 1 tbs arrowroot or cornstarch and stir until dissolved; pour back into vegetables and heat briefly until liquid thickens. Stir in 1/2-3/4 cup crushed almonds and 1/2 tsp toasted sesame seed oil. **Serves 2-4.**

Recipes

·················

JUDAISM

A S WE HAVE NOTED, PRO-
fessor Robert Kole is a
Jewish vegan rawfood-
ist; consequently the recipes in
this section call for unfired ingredients. A blender or food processor, a refrigerator, a knife and
cutting board and spoon are
just about the only
utensils that a raw-
foodist needs to
prepare his food.
What is specifi-
cally Jewish a-
bout this diet,
one may well
ask? Well, kosher,
they certainly are:
there's no mingling of
dairy with meat; and the food in
its raw or near-raw state is
evocative of the early chapters of
Genesis in which the earliest
progenitors of the race, Adam
and Eve, ate their food just as

nature serves it up raw.

Professor Kole agrees with
Rabbi Abraham Isaac Kook that
the Messianic Age can be has-
tened by practicing a vegetarian
diet. In the Messianic Age, says
Kole, there will be no warfare, no
carnivorism, no strife, and
love will prevail. The
last days before the
Messianic age
will resemble
the first, and as
we know from
Genesis the first
days were fruit-
arian. "I have giv-
en you every herb-
bearing seed, which is
upon the face of all the earth and
every tree in which is the fruit of
a tree yielding seed, it shall be for
you as food." (1:29) Many mod-
ern-day fruitarians take this to be
a specific mandate to eat an

············
357

almost exclusively raw fruit diet. The apostle of the modern fruitarian movement is T. C. Fry, (a curious name for a rawfood-ist). Fry's definition of fruit, which encompasses more than just oranges and apples is: "everything that ripens and bears seeds." This includes many fruits that are conventionally held to be veg-etables such as tomatoes, avocados, peppers, eggplants, and squash. The author of *The Curse of Cooked Food*, Fry believes that we are the symbiants to fruit-bearing vines and trees. In return for nourishing us with their fruit, we spread their seeds and assist in their propagation. By eating animal flesh, and cooked foods, we are violating the symbiotic compact, and we pay the price for it in shortened life spans and diminished quality of life.

In addition to Professor Kole's favorite rawfood dishes, I've col-lected some rawfood recipes from "Wildman" Steve Brill, a botanist and horticulturist who conducts foraging tours of Central and Prospect Parks as well as in other parks in New York City. His book *Identifying and Harvesting Edible and Medicinal Plants* has become a Baedeker for wildfood foragers. Jewish rawfoodist Dafne Mordechai has also contributed a rawfood recipe to this section (Tropical Fruit Pie). Why so many Jewish rawfoodists? Is there a preponderance of Jews among rawfood practitioners? If Jews are disproportionately represented among rawfoodists, it may be a reaction to the heavy carnivorism that was practiced by generations of their forebears. In keeping with the tendency of Northern cultures to consume more animal products than South-ern cultures, by and large, in the old world, the Ashkenazim (the Jews of Poland, Russia and Eastern Europe) ate more meat than fruit and vegetables, and the Sephardim (the Jews who were dri-ven out of Spain and Portugal as well as the Jews of African and Middle Eastern countries such as Yemen and Morocco) ate more vegetables and fruit than meat. But even the Sephardim—whose diet more closely resembles the Mediterranean diet that is touted by doctors for its healthfulness—have been regular meat-eaters. Nonetheless most of the raw fruit and vegetable recipes in this section are taken from the cuisine of the Sephardim. The Friday night meal in Sephardic religious households started with a range of appetizers that usually consisted of raw vegetables — crudités — and cold salads. And at least on one day a week — on Saturdays, when eating cooked food was forbidden — they enjoyed a day of eating the most delectable unfired vegetable and fruit dishes.

I've tried to relate these dishes to the Jewish calendar, e.g., "Wildman" Steve Brill's Mortar recipe for Passover, and his recipe "Wildman's Marzipan" for Purim. (Steve insisted that I attach his sobriquet to the recipes.) That they should be called "Wildman's Marzipan" and "Wildman's Mortar" is also rather fitting for another reason: it's worth remembering that it's the wild men in the culture who are often the bearers of occult wisdom. In ancient India it was the *rishis* and the *sadhus* who were the custodians of sacred knowledge of the pre-Aryan religion that was soaked in *ahimsa* or non-violence. The same was true of Taoism. The forest sages of Taoism were the wisemen who were the custodians of the ancient Chinese religion of vegetarianism and non-violence. One suspects that wildmen of ancient Israel were also the curators of this sacred knowledge of plant lore and non-violent eating that one finds exemplified in the life of "Wildman" Steve Brill. In fact, my conjecture was confirmed by the Jewish historian Hans-Joachim Schoeps who in his book *Jewish Christianity* informs us that the anti-sacrificial sects of Judaism such as the Nazoreans, and the Ebionites took to the wilderness to protest the sacrificial cult in Jerusalem and that they considered the wilderness to be a state of grace.

Do rawfoodists enjoy better health? They claim to enjoy a higher energy level because so little of the body's energy is expended on digesting foods — fruits are the easiest food for the body to digest and assimilate — that there is a surplus of vital energy for the body to draw upon.

If there's a plethora of desserts among the rawfood dishes, it's because as one frugivore puts it: "As a fruitarian, I eat dessert at every meal." Just so. Why shouldn't the fruit of a Paradisal diet be a voluptuous delight at every meal?

"WILDMAN'S" MARZIPAN

Almond paste or marzipan is an indispensable ingredient in the confectionery and pastry making of Sephardic Jews. It is a festal food that is served at births, weddings, and bar mitzvahs. It is also a tasty treat that is served at Passover and Purim. **Serves 4.**

1 lb raw blanched almonds
almond oil
dash vanilla extract

barley malt, or natural glycerin
carob powder

Grind almonds in a blender with a dash of almond oil. Keep adding almond oil gradually until the blade goes around in a circle without stopping. Add a dash of vanilla extract and the barley malt. Remove the almond paste from the blender and form the almond paste into balls. Roll the balls in carob powder and serve.

•••••••••••

"WILDMAN" STEVE BRILL'S MORTAR FOR PASSOVER

Mortar, or Haroset, is meant to evoke the texture of the clay that was used by the Jews when they were in captivity in Egypt. Tradition has it that the clay was used by the Jewish slaves to help build Pharaoh's cities. Mortar is customarily put on the Passover Seder plate.

4 apples (mix Rome, Granny Smith,
* Macintosh, etc.)*
1/2 cup organic grape juice or wine
dash lemon juice

1/4 cup walnuts
1/2 tsp powdered cinnamon
pinch nutmeg
1/2 tsp grated ginger

Grate apples in hand grater or food processor. Moisten with wine or grape juice. Add dash of lemon juice. Add enough walnuts to make it crunchy. Add powdered cinnamon (or sassafras), nutmeg and ginger (or wild ginger) to taste. **Serves 4.**

•••••••••••

TABBOULEH WITH PARSLEY AND TOMATOES

This is a Sephardic recipe for an uncooked dish that is typical of the cracked wheat salads that were made a hundred years ago in Aleppo and Damascus by Sephardic Jews before they emigrated to Egypt and the Americas. It contains a greater proportion of wheat to greens than the tabboulehs to be found in Lebanese restaurants today. **Serves 4.**

1 cup (175 g) fine bulgar (cracked wheat)	*juice of one or more lemons to taste*
1 lb (500 g) firm, ripe tomatoes,	*1/4 cup fresh mint, finely chopped*
cut into small pieces	*6 tbs extra virgin olive oil*
1 cup flat-leafed parsley or	*lettuce or radicchio leaves*
Chinese parsley, chopped fine	

Soak the cracked wheat in two cups of water for 15 minutes. Rinse and drain in a sieve, then place the cracked wheat in a bowl with the tomatoes. Allow the cracked wheat to absorb the tomato juices for 30 minutes. Then add the remaining ingredients and toss. Use the lettuce or radicchio leaves to scoop up the tabbouleh.

This recipe was adapted from Claudia Roden's *The Book of Jewish Food: An Odyssey from Samarkand to New York* (New York: Alfred Knopf).

. . . .

ORANGE SALAD WITH OLIVES

This Moroccan salad is a favorite of Moroccan Jews and Jews throughout the Near East. For best results, use oranges that are slightly sour or bitter, but sweet oranges like California navels will work as well. The Jews of Essaoiura traditionally use the rare argan oil to give it a distinctive flavor. **Serves 4.**

4 oranges	*1/2 cup black, herbed olives*
juice of 1/2 lemon or	*1 tsp cumin powder*
2-3 tbs wine vinegar	*1/2 tsp paprika*
3 tbs light or extra virgin olive oil	*a dash of cayenne pepper or a*
3 garlic cloves, minced	*small red chili, minced*
sea salt	

Peel and section the oranges; then cut the sections crosswise into pieces. Make a dressing of lemon juice, oil, garlic and salt; pour dressing on the oranges, and add the olives. Sprinkle with cumin powder, paprika and cayenne pepper.

This recipe was adapted from *The Book of Jewish Food: An Odyssey from Samarkand to New York* by Claudia Roden (New York: Alfred Knopf).

DAFNE MORDECHAI'S TROPICAL FRUIT PIE

Dafne Mordechai is a Jewish rawfoodist who was raised by her parents to eat uncooked food from a tender age. Her parents were students of natural hygienists T.C. Fry and Herbert Shelton. Her Tropical Fruit Pie is suitable for serving at a Passover seder. **Serves 4.**

For the crust:
2 cups walnut
3/4 cup pecans
2 cups pitted dates

For the filling:
6 bananas
4 mangoes
9 kiwis
1 pint strawberries

Process nuts in a food processor with an "S" blade until finely chopped. Add dates through feeder until a ball is formed. Mold mixture into an 8 x 12 inch pyrex dish. Line the dish with the crust. Peel two bananas and cut lengthwise into thin slices. Spread the banana slices evenly over the crust to make the first layer. Next, peel 1 1/2 mangoes and cut them lengthwise into thin slices. Use them to make the second layer. Then peel and cut three kiwis into thin slices and make the third layer. Cut 1/3 of the strawberries into thin slices and make the fourth layer. Repeat the layers in that order twice more.

Recipes

....

CHRISTIANITY

THESE RECIPES ARE FOR the sort of dishes that Brother Ron would make for his fellow friars, if he were in charge of drawing up the monastery menus today—a job that despite his separation from his order he said he would resume with alacrity. Not since the days of the early Church, before the influence of the vegetarian Jewish Christian sects (the Essenes, the Nazoreans, the Ebionites) had waned, have Christians been able to dine so spaciously on vegetarian cuisine as they do at Brother Ron's table. In the early days of the Church the Eucharist was celebrated in the form of a substantial vegetarian meal that took place after the public services were over. It was a feast of thanksgiving, hence the Greek name *Eucharist,* which means "thanksgiving." Later on, in the thirteenth century, Pope Innocent III changed the Eucharist into what some scholars consider to be a ritual of cannibalism, by decreeing that it was the actual blood and body of Christ that was consumed in the wafer and chalice of the communion mass. Happily Brother Ron's dishes hark back to the earlier days of the Church when the *agapē* or love feast consisted of a sumptuous vegetarian meal. One could easily picture such vegetarian Church fathers as Clement of

....

Alexandria, his pupil Origen, and Tertullian eating Brother Ron's food with relish. Rather than thinking of Brother Ron as having invented a Christian vegetarian cuisine, it would be more to the point to think of him as having revived the early Christian vegetarian cuisine via the influence of the four *ahimsa*-based religions of Asia—Jainism, Buddhism, Hinduism and Taoism.

Indeed, it's worth noting that many of Brother Ron's recipes call for ingredients such as hijiki, arame, tofu, tamari, ginger, seitan, etc., which are staples in the Chinese Buddhist and Taoist kitchen. A recipe such as "Hijiki with Green Beans," "Miami Delight" with its marriage of tofu and mangoes, or "Sautéed Arame with Vegetables," or even his "Seitan Pesto Sandwich" (seitan or wheat gluten has been used to make mock meat in Taoist and Buddhist cuisine for centuries) combine elements of Eastern and Western cuisine. It's not too farfetched to suggest that these recipes are emblematic of the growing influence of Eastern "vegetarian" religions on Western cuisine and Western belief systems. Do they not also lend color to Brother Ron's belief that someday Christianity will incorporate aspects of the Indian "Nirvana religions" such as the doctrines of *karma*, transmigration of souls, reincarnation and ethical vegetarianism?

· · · · · · · · · · · ·

MONASTIC SALAD[1]

This salad is truly monastic, simple, pure and wonderful. —*Brother Ron*

Dressing

6 tbs extra virgin olive oil	*1 tsp Sucanat*
6 tbs apple cider vinegar	*1/4 tsp black pepper*
6 tbs water	*3 medium tomatoes, thinly sliced*
9 cloves minced garlic	*1/2 lb fresh mushrooms, halved*
1 1/2 tbs chopped parsley	*1 1/2 cups sauerkraut*
1 1/2 tsp basil	*1/2 cup diagonally sliced scallions*
1 1/2 tsp oregano	*green lettuce leaves and black olives*
1 1/2 tsp sea salt	*for garnish*

In a large mixing bowl, combine the dressing ingredients and mix well. Add the tomato slices and mushrooms. Rinse the sauerkraut, lightly squeeze dry and add with the scallions to the dressing. Cover bowl and refrigerate overnight to marinate the vegetables and develop the flavors. Serve cold on leaves of green lettuce and garnish with black olives. **Serves 2** (as main course salad).

....

MIAMI DELIGHT

A dinner served by Father Jim Murphy of St. Patrick's Catholic Parish in Miami Beach inspired this dish. It is an elegant and sophisticated presentation of tofu and the fruits of Florida. —*Brother Ron*

8 plum tomatoes, rubbed with olive oil
6 garlic cloves, peeled, rubbed with olive oil
3 cups peeled, seeded, diced mango
2 cups peeled, seeded, diced avocado
4 halved, seeded, diced plum tomatoes
2 tbs chopped fresh cilantro
2 tbs peeled, minced fresh ginger

1 tsp sea salt
1/4 cup lime juice
1/4 cup mirin (sweet rice wine)
2 tbs white miso
2 tbs cashew butter
1 lb tofu, cut into 8 triangles

Preheat oven to 300 degrees F. Place the 8 plum tomatoes and the garlic cloves on a baking sheet and roast them for 20 to 30 minutes. Meanwhile, combine the diced mango, avocado and tomatoes in a bowl, then set aside. Remove the roasted vegetables from the oven, and increase temperature to 350 degrees F. In a blender, combine the roasted vegetables and blend until smooth. In a large mixing bowl, pour mixture from blender and add the diced mangoes, avocados, tomatoes, cilantro, ginger, and salt, then mix everything well. In a small bowl, blend the lime juice, mirin, miso and cashew butter into a glaze. Spread the glaze evenly over the 8 tofu triangles, place in a covered baking pan and bake them for 8 to 10 minutes or until heated through. Remove pan from oven. Pour 1/2 cup of the mango-avocado sauce on each plate. Drizzle the remaining sauce over tofu pieces. **Serves 4.**

Note: For a high enzyme version of this recipe, instead of roasting the tomatoes, soak 12 sun-dried tomatoes in 1/2 cup water for one hour. Then blend the tomatoes and the soak in a food processor, and add them to the mango-avocado mixture.

....

SALAD ARGENTEUIL

This salad follows the classic French salad and has a surprising array of flavors and textures. Combined with a sandwich, it makes a great summer salad.

12 asparagus tips, 2 inches long
1/4 cup Easy French dressing (see below)
2 cups peeled, finely diced potatoes
1/2 cup peeled, finely diced carrots
1/2 cup fresh or frozen peas
1/3 cup soy mayonnaise

1/4 tsp sea salt
1/8 tsp black pepper
6 cups shredded romaine or
  other crisp lettuce
1/2 cup crumbled, firm tofu

In a vegetable steamer, steam asparagus tips for five minutes or until tender-crisp. In a shallow bowl, combine asparagus and Easy French Dressing and let marinate for one hour. Steam the potatoes and carrots together for 15 minutes, then add the peas and cook until tender-crisp. In a mixing bowl, combine the potatoes, carrots, peas, and soy mayonnaise, and toss lightly. Add the salt and pepper and adjust to taste. Arrange vegetables in a mound on a serving dish. Top the mound with marinated asparagus tips. Surround vegetables with the shredded lettuce and crumbled tofu. Refrigerate for one hour or until chilled. **Yields 6 servings.**

············

EASY FRENCH DRESSING

Serve with Italian Mixed Green Salad, Potato Salad, Whole Wheat Orzo with Cilantro, or any green leafy salad.

1 cup apple cider vinegar
1 cup canola oil
1/4 cup maple syrup
1 medium tomato, peeled, seeded, minced
2 tbs chopped fresh parsley

2 tbs chopped fresh basil
2 tbs Dijon mustard
2 cloves minced garlic
1/2 tsp sea salt

In a mixing bowl, combine all the ingredients and whisk until well blended. Transfer to a covered container and refrigerate for one hour. Serve cold.

Note: For a high-enzyme version of this recipe, reduce steaming times for carrots and potatoes to four minutes, and leave peas uncooked.

2/3 cup dry arame soaked, drained
2 cups water
1 tbs sesame oil
2 cups peeled, julienned carrots
2 cups thinly sliced fresh leeks
  (use lower 1/3 of stem only)

2 cups thinly sliced fresh fennel
1 tsp ginger powder
1 tsp fennel powder
1/2 tsp sea salt
2 tbs mirin or sweet sherry

In a one-quart saucepan, combine the arame and water and cook on medium heat for about 7 to 10 minutes. Remove from heat, drain and set aside. In a 10-inch skillet, heat the oil and sauté the carrots on medium heat for four minutes. Add fennel, leeks, ginger, fennel powder and salt, and sauté for 7 minutes. Add arame and mirin, then continue cooking another one to two minutes or until mixture is heated thoroughly. Serve hot.

Note: For a high enzyme version of this recipe, reduce cooking time to three minutes, and do not cook the arame.

....

HIJIKI WITH GREEN BEANS

1/2 cup dried hijiki
1 tbs tamari
1/2 cup halved, sliced onions
1 tbs finely chopped garlic
2 tbs canola oil

1/2 tsp salt
2 cups fresh green beans
2 tbs grated ginger
  (or 1 tbs ginger juice or
  1 1/2 tsp ginger powder)

Soak the hijiki in 3 cups of water for about 1 hour. Then wash it carefully to remove any sand, and place it in a saucepan with tamari and a few cups of water. Cook at medium heat until the water has nearly evaporated.

Meanwhile, sauté the onions and garlic in oil along with the salt for about 4 minutes. Cut the tips from the green beans and add them to the sautéed onions. Cook until the beans are tender-crisp. Then add the hijiki and ginger and mix well. Continue cooking for another minute or so, and serve immediately. **Yields 4 servings.**

Note: For a high enzyme version of this recipe, don't cook the hijiki. Soak it and add it to the partially cooked green beans.

[1]Monastic Salad and all other recipes in this section are taken from *Eco-Cuisine* and *Friendly Foods*, published by Ten Speed Press. Reprinted by permission of Brother Ron Pickarski.

ISLAM

THE RECIPES IN THIS section are from the cuisine of an Islamic country whose people are mainly vegetarian — Hunza, a remote mountain kingdom in the Himalayas that was recently annexed by Pakistan. Lean, long-legged, fair-complexioned, and bursting with vitality, the Hunzakuts look strikingly different from their neighbors to the south (Pakistan) and east (China). Legend has it that the country was founded by three Greek soldiers and their Persian wives, who had deserted from Alexander the Great's Army (which had occupied Persia in the fourth century BCE). And certainly the Hunzakuts' rather Classical cast of features gives color to this theory. Noted for their longevity, and their boundless energy, the Hunzakuts have been studied by teams of gerontologists, ophthalmologists, dentists, doctors and anthropologists who have been trying to find out why it is that the Hunzakuts are almost without exception disease-free, even to the point of not having dental cavities. Ophthalmologists found 20-20 vision in people up to a hundred years of age, and coronary specialists have been unable to find any trace of high cholesterol or coronary disease in men ranging in age from 90 to a hundred. It is not uncommon for male Hunzakuts into their nineties and beyond to father children—that is, when they're not tearing around on horses, playing the national sport, polo. Hunzakuts usually die of natural causes, often when they are well past the century mark, or else they die by misadventure—in a fall from a cliff or in a spill from a polo pony. Because of the treacherous footing on steep mountain trails, Hunzakuts frequently sustain broken bones; but their recuperative powers are remarkable. Three weeks in a cast is usually all the time it takes to mend a broken arm or leg. What is the secret of the Hunzakuts' longevity and their fabled vitality? Obviously the Hunza valley itself is a salutary place. Its clear, unpolluted mountain air is bracing; its soil is fertile, and yields nutrient-rich fruits and vegetables that are organically cultivated and bacteria-free; its mineral-laden, glacier-fed streams provide a tonic drinking water. But their fleshless diet is clearly an important factor in their good health. Owing to the scarcity of arable land, which makes it almost impossible to raise livestock, the Hunzakuts are near vegans who consume dairy products sparingly. Because of the lack of firewood and fuel they eat much of their food in its uncooked state. Seventy percent of their vegetables are consumed raw. When they do cook their food, it's usually only for a few brief minutes. Like other Muslims in the Near East and Northern India, they eat wheat puddings, vegetable curries and lots of dishes that feature nuts and dried fruits. Apricots are a staple in their diet and the Hunzakuts usually eat either fresh or dried apricots at every meal. Indeed a family often counts its wealth in apricot trees. They press apricot oil from the apricot pits and use it both as a cooking medium and as a flavoring agent. Here are some recipes for typical Hunza dishes that I've adapted for the vegan table.

HUNZA BREAKFAST CEREAL

This recipe contains ingredients that are native to Hunza, and which the first settlers probably brought with them to the lush valley of the Hunza—ingredients such as apples, apricots, wheat, almonds and walnuts, which grow there in profusion, but are not indigenous to the region. This is a typical Hunza breakfast dish that I've adapted slightly.

1 cup cracked wheat, barley, or millet	*1 tbs chopped almonds*
2 cups apple juice	*1 tbs maple syrup*
1 cup chopped apricots	*1 tsp caraway seeds*
1 tbs chopped walnuts	

Soak the cracked wheat in apple juice for 3 1/2 hours. When the wheat has doubled in size, add the remaining ingredients and serve. **Serves 2.**

· · · · · · · · · · · ·

HUNZA FRUIT AND NUT SNACK

1 cup dried apricots	*1 tbs chopped almonds*
1 cup other dried fruit, or	*1 tbs maple syrup*
a combination of several	*1 tsp caraway seeds*

Soak the dried fruit in a small amount of filtered water until the fruit softens. Put the fruit through a food mill and add the nut meats. Form portions of the fruit and nut mixture into patties. Serve wrapped in lettuce leaves. The Hunzas wrap these patties in birch leaves and call them "Travelers' Food."

· · · · · · · · · · · ·

HUNZA RAW APPLESAUCE

3 apples	*1/4 tsp cinnamon*
1/4 cup maple syrup	*pistachio nuts for garnish*
1 tbs lemon juice	

Peel and core the apples. Then quarter them and put them into a food processor or blender. Add the remaining ingredients and purée. Serve garnished with chopped pistachios. **Serves 2.**

In the spring and summer Hunzakuts eat their vegetables raw. This soup consists entirely of uncooked ingredients.

1 cup raw almonds, soaked overnight
3 cups filtered water
1 tsp apricot oil
2 spring onions, chopped
(including green tops)
3 ears tender corn, dekerneled
1 large cucumber, diced
4 large mushrooms, chopped
1 cup fresh peas
1 large tomato, chopped
1 cup fresh asparagus tips, chopped

1/2 large sweet red pepper, seeded,
chopped
1 cup fresh spinach or watercress,
finely chopped
2 tsp fresh or dried mint leaves,
finely chopped
1 tsp chili powder
1/4 tsp cayenne pepper
1 clove garlic, minced
salt to taste
1/2 cup raw almonds, chopped

Soak the almonds overnight to loosen their skins; or, plunge the almonds into a pot of boiling water for ten seconds; with a slotted spoon, remove and cool them in cold water. Squeeze the almonds between thumb and index finger and they will pop out of their skins. Put the almonds into a blender with three cups of filtered water, and blend on high speed until it yields four cups of thick almond milk. Pour the almond milk into a large bowl, and add the remaining ingredients. Stir and refrigerate for two hours. Serve garnished with chopped almonds and mint leaves. **Serves 4.**

Note: This is a classic summer soup among the Hunzakuts. I've substituted almond milk for yogurt in order to veganize it.

· · · · · · · · · · ·

APRICOT FRUIT SALAD

This salad combines the staple of the Hunza diet, the apricot, with apples and peaches, which are among their favorite fruits. It is garnished with pistachios for which the Hunzakuts have a particular passion. **Serves 4.**

1 cup dried apricots, soaked
1/2 cup raisins, soaked
1 large apple, chopped
1 stalk celery

2 peaches
1/2 cup pistachio nuts,
or chopped walnuts
4 large cabbage leaves

Soak the apricots and raisins in separate containers for eight hours. Peel, chop and mash the peaches and place them in a salad bowl. Peel and chop the apples; chop the celery; then add them to the salad bowl. Remove the soaked apricots from the soak water, dice them and add them to the salad bowl. Remove raisins from soak water, and add them to the salad bowl. Toss the fruits in the salad bowl. Arrange each cabbage leaf in the shape of a small plate. Spoon the salad onto each leaf. Sprinkle with pistachio nuts and serve.

Note: I've adapted several of the recipes in this section from Thelma White and Sally DeVore's fascinating chapter on the Hunzakuts in their anthropological cookbook, *The Appetites of Man* (New York: Anchor Books).

About the Author

······················

RYNN BERRY

YNN BERRY IS THE HISTORICAL adviser to the NAVS (North American Vegetarian Society). In his lectures, articles, and books, he has specialized in the study of vegetarianism from an historical perspective. His first book, *The New Vegetarians*, was a collection of biographical sketches and interviews of famous contemporary vegetarians. His second book, *Famous Vegetarians and Their Favorite Recipes* is a biographical history of vegetarianism that ranges from Pythagoras and the Buddha to Nobel laureate Isaac Bashevis Singer and the Beatles. In *Food for the Gods*, Rynn has written

essays on vegetarianism in each of the world's religions: Jainism, Buddhism, Hinduism, Taoism, Judaism, Christianity and Islam. He has also included interviews with prominent vegetarian thinkers from each of these religions. In the back of the book *Food For The Gods* brings together at least five vegetarian recipes from each religious tradition (most of which are for living food dishes). At the University of Pennsylvania and Columbia, where Rynn did his graduate and undergraduate work, he specialized in ancient history and comparative religion. A popular lecturer in New York, where he lives, Rynn teaches a college course on the history of vegetarianism. His hobbies include book collecting, listening to classical music, translating ancient Greek texts, and theater-going; his favorite pastimes include running, swimming, tennis and cycling.

Notes

....

Notes

....

BOOKS BY RYNN BERRY

FAMOUS VEGETARIANS
and their favorite recipes

Lives and Lore from Buddha to the Beatles

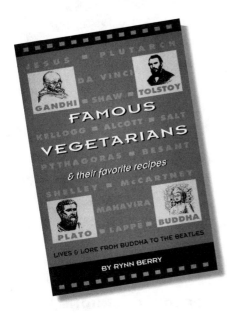

"Berry writes beautifully, with a genuine gustatory relish for words and savory asides. The recipes are delightful...many researched and translated for the first time." —*The Boston Book Review*

"Scholarship at the end of a fork—and for writing it Berry deserves an 'A'."
—*Vegetarian Times*

"Entertaining and educational..."
—*Vegetarian Voice*

"Impeccably researched and written."
—*The Animals' Agenda*

"The 70 recipes are not only fascinating, but have been kitchen-tested by the author for savoriness..." —*Yoga Journal*

292 pages   ***$15.95** paperback*

Copy this form to order books. Other books by Rynn Berry on reverse side.

✂ --

PYTHAGOREAN PUBLISHERS / P.O. Box 8174 / New York, NY 10116

—— copies *Famous Vegetarians & Their Favorite Recipes* @ $15.95 $ ——
—— copies *The New Vegetarians* @ $10.95 $ ——
—— copies *Food for the Gods* @ $19.95 $ ——

Add postage: $3.00 for one book, $1.00 for each additional book $ ——

TOTAL ENCLOSED $ ——

NAME _____

ADDRESS _____

CITY _____ STATE/ZIP_____ PHONE_____

BOOKS BY RYNN BERRY

THE NEW VEGETARIANS

Fourteen famous men and women tell why they have joined over 10,000,000 Americans who have turned to vegetarianism.

"Well-written and fascinating..."
—*M.F.K. Fisher*

"Recommended." —*Library Journal*

"If you"re still eating at occasional hamburger, this fascinating account of 14 famous vegetarians may just turn the tide for you." —*Pacific Sun*

192 pages **$10.95** *paperback*

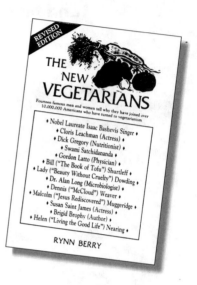

FOOD FOR THE GODS

VEGETARIANISM & THE WORLD'S RELIGIONS

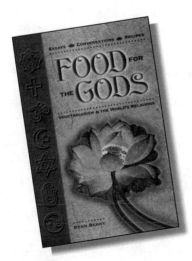

"Rynn Berry's widely read book *Famous Vegetarians and Their Favorite Recipes* presented the teachings of the great humanitarians and furnished readers with the means of reproducing their preferred dishes. Two thirds of those chosen belonged to the past. His current study deals exclusively with contemporaries, although with roots in the past. Their 'recipes' have a more spiritualized connotation, as they are not human fare but divine ambrosia. Rynn Berry's present offering is truly Food for the Gods."
—**Clay Lancaster**, *author of The Incredible World's Parliament of Religions.*

374 pages **$19.95** *paperback*